THE CAMBRIDGE
COMPANION TO

HAROLD PINTER

Second Edition

EDITED BY

PETER RABY

Homerton College, Cambridge

CAMBRIDGE
UNIVERSITY PRESS

CAMBRIDGE UNIVERSITY PRESS
Cambridge, New York, Melbourne, Madrid, Cape Town, Singapore, São Paulo, Delhi

Cambridge University Press
The Edinburgh Building, Cambridge CB2 8RU, UK

Published in the United States of America by Cambridge University Press, New York

www.cambridge.org
Information on this title: www.cambridge.org/9780521713733

First published 2001
Second edition 2009

Printed in the United Kingdom at the University Press, Cambridge

A catalogue record for this publication is available from the British Library

Library of Congress Cataloguing in Publication data
The Cambridge companion to Harold Pinter / edited by Peter Raby. – 2nd ed.
p.   cm.
ISBN 978-0-521-88609-3
1. Pinter, Harold, 1930– Criticism and interpretation – Handbooks, manuals, etc.
I. Raby, Peter.   II. Title.
PR6066.I53Z6255   2009
822'.914–dc22
2008048863

ISBN 978-0-521-88609-3 hardback
ISBN 978-0-521-71373-3 paperback

Harold Pinter was one of the world's leading and most controversial writers, and his impact and influence continues to grow. This *Companion* examines the wide ra [...] his writing [...] theatre, radio, television and screen, and also has highly successful work as a director and actor. Substantially updated and revised, this second edition covers the many developments in Pinter's career since the publication of the first edition, including his Nobel Prize for Literature win in 2005, his appearance in Samuel Beckett's play *Krapp's Last Tape* and recent productions of his plays. Containing essays written by both academics and also leading practitioners, the volume places Pinter's writing within the critical and theatrical context of his time and considers its reception worldwide. Including three new essays, new production photographs, five updated and revised chapters and an extended chronology, the *Companion* provides fresh perspectives on Pinter's work.

A complete list of books in the series is at the back of this book.

CONTENTS

ILLUSTRATIONS

NOTES ON CONTRIBUTORS

MIREIA ARAGAY is a Senior Lecturer in English Literature at the University of Barcelona. She has written on contemporary English and Irish drama, and on film adaptation. She is editor of *Books in Motion: Adaptations, Intertextuality, Authorship* (2005) and co-editor of *British Theatre of the 1990s: Interviews with Directors, Playwrights, Critics and Academics* (2007). In 1996, her Spanish translation of *One for the Road*, *La última copa*, was awarded the 10th National Translation Prize by the Asociación Española de Estudios Anglonorteamericanos.

RICHARD ALLEN CAVE is Professor of Drama and Theatre Arts at Royal Holloway in the University of London. He has written extensively on Renaissance, nineteenth-century and modern theatre, and in particular on Anglo-Irish drama. His most recent publication is *W. B. Yeats: 'The King of the Great Clock Tower' and 'A Full Moon in March': Manuscript Materials* (2007). As a director he has staged productions of plays by Lady Gregory, Yeats and Brian Friel, and is joint artistic director of Border Crossings Theatre Company.

FRANCESCA COPPA is Associate Professor of English and Director of Film Studies at Muhlenberg College, where she specialises in British drama and cultural studies. She has edited and written critical introductions for three volumes of Joe Orton's work, and is the editor of *Joe Orton: A Casebook* (2003).

HARRY DERBYSHIRE is Programme Leader for English at the University of Greenwich. Recent articles include 'Stamping Ground: London as Disputed Territory in the Plays of Harold Pinter' in *Literary London* and 'Roy Williams: Representing Multicultural Britain in Fallout' in *Modern Drama*. As company writer with the theatre company sob, he has scripted several shows at Battersea Arts Centre.

CHARLES EVANS is a retired naval officer, and lecturer at the Service colleges, with an honorary doctorate from Moscow University. He has held research fellowships from the British Academy and the Leverhulme Trust, and has travelled widely in Russia. In 2005 he was awarded a

Hawthornden Fellowship. He continues to write on Russian life and culture, and is also a playwright and poet.

JOHN FOWLES'S novels include *The Collector* (1963), *The Magus* (1966) and *Daniel Martin* (1977). *The French Lieutenant's Woman* (1969) was filmed in a screenplay by Pinter in 1981. He was in addition a very keen natural historian, and interested in all aspects of local history.

STEVEN H. GALE holds the University Endowed Chair of the Humanities at Kentucky State University. He was the founding President of the Harold Pinter Society, the founding co-editor of *The Harold Pinter Review: Annual Essays* and the author or editor of a number of studies of Pinter, including *Butter's Going Up: An Analysis of Harold Pinter's Work*, and, most recently, *Sharp Cut: Harold Pinter's Screenplays and the Artistic Process* (2003).

SIR PETER HALL formerly the Artistic Director of the Royal National Theatre and the Royal Shakespeare Company, has directed many of Pinter's plays, and drew on this first-hand knowledge in his discussion of Pinter in his Clark Lectures of 2000, later published as *Exposed by the Mask*. His most recent Pinter production was *Old Times* (2007).

RONALD KNOWLES is a former Senior Lecturer in English Literature at Reading University. He is associate editor of *The Harold Pinter Review*, and the author of two books and many articles on Pinter. His most recent publication, as editor, is *Henry VI, Part II* (The Arden Shakespeare, 1999).

MARY LUCKHURST is Professor of Modern Drama and the co-founder of the new Department of Theatre, Film and Television at the University of York. Her books include *Dramaturgy: A Revolution in Theatre* (2006) and the Blackwell's *Companion to Modern British and Irish Drama*. In 2006 she was made a Fellow of the Higher Education Academy.

DREW MILNE is the Judith E. Wilson Fellow in Drama and Poetry in the English Faculty at the University of Cambridge, and a Fellow of Trinity Hall. He co-edited *Marxist Literary Theory: A Reader* (1996) with Terry Eagleton, and edits the journal *Parataxis: Modernism and Modern Writing*. Among his recent books of poetry are *Mars Disarmed* (2002) and *Go Figure* (2003). His publications in 2008 are *Reading Marxist Literary Theory* and a collection of essays, *Agoraphobic Poetics*.

MICHAEL PENNINGTON has been a leading actor for thirty years, with the Royal Shakespeare Company, the Royal National Theatre, on tour with his own English Shakespeare Company and in London's West End. His publications include *The Story of the Wars of the Roses*, User's Guides to *Hamlet* (1996) and *Twelfth Night* (2000), and *Chekhov in Mind* (2001).

AUSTIN QUIGLEY is the Brander Matthews Professor of Dramatic Literature at Columbia University, where he has also been serving as

Dean of Columbia College since 1995. He is the author of *The Pinter Problem* (1975), *The Modern Stage and Other Worlds* (1985), *Theoretical Inquiry: Language, Linguistics and Literature* (2004). He has served on the editorial boards of *New Literary History*, *Modern Drama* and *The Harold Pinter Review*, and is currently working on a book on Postmodernism and the Drama.

PETER RABY is Vice-Principal of Homerton College, University of Cambridge. He edited the *Cambridge Companion to Oscar Wilde* (1997). Among his other books are *Bright Paradise* (1996), a study of Victorian scientific travellers, and a biography, *Alfred Russel Wallace* (2001). He is the book-writer of the musical *The Three Musketeers* (Chicago Shakespeare Theatre, 2007).

ANTHONY ROCHE is Associate Professor in the School of English, Drama and Film at University College, Dublin. He has written extensively on Irish theatre of the twentieth and twenty-first centuries. He contributed the chapter 'Contemporary Irish Drama: 1940–2000' to the *Cambridge History of Irish Literature* (2006) and edited the *Cambridge Companion to Brian Friel* (2006). A revised edition of *Contemporary Irish Drama* will be published in 2008.

JOHN STOKES is Professor in the Department of English at King's College London. His most recent publications include *The French Actress and her English Audience* (2005) and, co-edited with Maggie Gale, *The Cambridge Companion to the Actress* (2007). He reviews theatre regularly for *The Times Literary Supplement*.

STEVE WATERS is a playwright whose plays include *World Music*, *The Unthinkable*, and *Fast Labour* (Hampstead Theatre, 2008), all published by Nick Hern Books Ltd. He is the convenor of the M.Phil(B) in Playwriting Studies at the University of Birmingham.

YAEL ZARHY-LEVO is a senior lecturer in the Department of Literature at Tel Aviv University. She is the author of *The Theatrical Critic as Cultural Agent: Constructing Pinter, Orton and Stoppard as Absurdist Playwrights* (2001), and her most recent book is *The Making of Theatrical Reputations: Studies from the Modern London Theatre* (2008).

CHRONOLOGY

1930 (10 October) Harold Pinter born at 19 Thistlewaite Road in Hackney, north London, the son of Jack and Frances Pinter.

1939 Evacuated to Caerhays, near Mevagissey, Cornwall, the first of a number of wartime stays outside London.

1944 Gains a place at Hackney Downs Grammar School, where he is particularly influenced by an excellent English teacher, Joe Brearley.

1947 Plays Macbeth in a school production, reviewed in the *News Chronicle*.

1948 (Autumn) Enters Royal Academy of Dramatic Art.
      (October) Called up for National Service, registers as a conscientious objector.

1949 Brought before a military tribunal. Is twice arrested and fined. Drops out of RADA. Lives at home, writing and reading, and applying for acting jobs.

1950 Two poems appear in August number of *Poetry London*. Small roles on BBC Radio.
      (19 September) First professional performance, *Focus on Football Pools*.

1951 (January to July) Spends two terms at Central School of Speech and Drama.
      (August) Is engaged by Anew McMaster for a six-month tour playing Shakespeare and other classic drama in Ireland.

1952 In McMaster's company, with Pauline Flanagan and Barry Foster. Continues to write poetry. Discovers Beckett.

1953 Joins Donald Wolfit's company. Works on his novel *The Dwarfs*.

1954 Changes stage name to David Baron. Joins Huddersfield Repertory company for the winter.

1955 Acting at Colchester Rep.

1956 Acting in Bournemouth, with Vivien Merchant.

(14 September) Marries Vivien Merchant. After a honeymoon in Cornwall, they join the repertory company in Torquay.

1957 Acting in Torquay, Birmingham, Palmer's Green, Worthing.

(15 May) *The Room*, produced at Bristol University Drama Department.

(December) New production of *The Room* entered for *Sunday Times* student drama competition, praised by Harold Hobson.

1958 (28 April) *The Birthday Party*, Arts Theatre, Cambridge, and later (19 May) at Lyric Theatre, Hammersmith.

Writes *The Hothouse*.

1959 (January) Directs *The Birthday Party* at Birmingham.

(15 July) *The Black and White, Trouble in the Works*, in the Revue *One to Another*, Lyric Theatre, Hammersmith.

(18 July) *The Dumb Waiter* produced in German, at Frankfurt Municipal Theatre.

(29 July) *A Slight Ache*, radio (BBC Third Programme).

(23 September) 'Last to Go', 'Request Stop' and 'Special Offer' in the Revue *Pieces of Eight*, Apollo Theatre.

1960 (21 January) *The Room* and *The Dumb Waiter*, Hampstead Theatre Club, both transferred to the Royal Court.

(1 March) *A Night Out*, radio (BBC Third Programme) (with Pinter as Seeley).

(22 March) *The Birthday Party*, television (Associated Rediffusion).

(24 April) *A Night Out*, television (ABC).

(27 April) *The Caretaker*, Arts Theatre Club, London.

(30 May) *The Caretaker*, Duchess Theatre (with Pinter, later in the run, playing Mick) (1960 *Evening Standard* Drama Award).

(21 July) *Night School*, television (Associated Rediffusion).

(27 July) *The Birthday Party* opens at the Actors' Workshop, San Francisco – the first Pinter professional production in the United States.

(19 September) Last acting appearance as David Baron.

(2 December) *The Dwarfs*, radio (BBC Third Programme).

1961 (18 January) *A Slight Ache*, Arts Theatre Club, London.

(11 May) *The Collection*, television (Associated Rediffusion).

(17 September) *A Night Out*, Gate Theatre, Dublin.

(4 October) *The Caretaker* opens at the Lyceum Theatre, New York – first Broadway production for Pinter.

1962 (18 June) Directs with Peter Hall *The Collection*, Aldwych Theatre.

1963 (28 March) *The Lover*, television (Associated Rediffusion) (awarded the Prix Italia for Television Drama).

(18 September) Directs *The Lover* and *The Dwarfs*, Arts Theatre Club, London.

The Caretaker, film, directed by Clive Donner (Berlin Film Festival Silver Bear) (released, 1964, in the United States as *The Guest*).

The Servant, film, directed by Joseph Losey.

1964 (April/May) *That's Your Trouble, That's All, Applicant, Interview* and *Dialogue for Three*, radio (BBC Third Programme).

The Pumpkin Eater, film, directed by Jack Clayton.

Plays Garcin in *In Camera*, by Jean-Paul Sartre.

1965 (25 March) *Tea Party*, television (BBC).

(3 June) *The Homecoming*, Royal Shakespeare Company, Aldwych Theatre.

1966 Created Commander of the Order of the British Empire.

(25 September) *Night School*, radio (BBC Third Programme).

The Quiller Memorandum, film, directed by Michael Anderson.

1967 (3 January) *The Homecoming*, Music Box, New York.

(20 February) *The Basement*, television (BBC), with Pinter as Stott.

Accident, film, directed by Joseph Losey.

The Homecoming receives New York Drama Critics Award.

1968 (25 April) *Landscape*, radio, BBC, after Pinter refuses to amend the text at the Lord Chamberlain's request.

(10 October) *The Basement*, and *Tea Party*, Eastside Playhouse, New York.

The Birthday Party, film, directed by William Friedkin.

1969 (2 July) *Silence* and *Landscape*, Royal Shakespeare Company, Aldwych Theatre.

(9 April) *Night* in Revue *Mixed Doubles*, Comedy Theatre.

Plays Lenny in *The Homecoming*, Watford.

1970 (18 January) *The Birthday Party* (BBC radio).

(17 September) *Tea Party* and *The Basement*, Duchess Theatre, with Pinter as Stott.

Directs *Exiles*, by James Joyce, Mermaid Theatre.

Awarded the German Shakespeare Prize.

Filming *The Go-Between*, film, directed by Joseph Losey.

1971 (May) *The Go-Between* awarded the Palme d'Or at Cannes Film Festival.

(1 June) *Old Times*, Royal Shakespeare Company, Aldwych Theatre.

Directs *Butley*, by Simon Gray, Criterion Theatre.

1972 Works on *The Proust Screenplay*.

1973 (13 April) *Monologue*, television (BBC).

Directs *Butley*, by Simon Gray, television (BBC).

The Homecoming, American Film Theatre, directed by Peter Hall.

1974 *The Last Tycoon*, film, directed by Elia Kazan.

Directs *Next of Kin*, by John Hopkins, Royal National Theatre.

1975 (23 April) *No Man's Land*, Royal National Theatre at the Old Vic Theatre, transfers (15 July) to Wyndham's Theatre.

(22 October) *Old Times*, television (BBC).

Directs *Otherwise Engaged*, by Simon Gray, Queen's Theatre, and later in New York.

Directs *Blithe Spirit*, by Noel Coward, Royal National Theatre.

(3 December) Acts in *Monologue*, radio (BBC).

1976 *The Homecoming* (film), released in UK.

1977 Directs *The Innocents*, by William Archibald (New York).

The Last Tycoon, film, directed by Elia Kazan.

1978 Directs *The Rear Column*, by Simon Gray, Globe Theatre.

(20 September) *Langrishe, Go Down*, television version of screenplay (BBC), directed by David Jones.

(3 October) *No Man's Land*, television (Granada).

(15 November) *Betrayal*, Royal National Theatre.

Directs *The Rear Column*, by Simon Gray, Globe Theatre.

Publishes *The Proust Screenplay*.

1979 Directs *Close of Play*, by Simon Gray, Royal National Theatre.

1980 (24 April) Directs *The Hothouse*, Hampstead Theatre Club, Ambassador Theatre.

Directs *The Rear Column*, by Simon Gray, television (BBC).

Marries Antonia Fraser.

1981 (13 February) *Family Voices*, Royal National Theatre, and (22 January) radio (BBC Radio 3).

The French Lieutenant's Woman, film, directed by Karel Reisz.

Directs *Quartermaine's Terms*, by Simon Gray, Queen's Theatre, London.

Directs *Incident at Tulse Hill*, by Robert East, Hampstead Theatre.

1982 (27 March) Directs *The Hothouse*, television (BBC).

(14 October) *Other Places* (*Family Voices*, *A Kind of Alaska*, *Victoria Station*), Royal National Theatre.

Betrayal, film, directed by David Jones.

1983 Directs *The Trojan War Will Not Take Place*, by Jean Giraudoux, Royal National Theatre.

(18 December) Directs *Precisely*, in *The Big One* (anti-nuclear performance), Apollo Victoria Theatre.

1984   Directs *The Common Pursuit*, by Simon Gray, Lyric Theatre, Hammersmith.

      (March) Directs *One for the Road*, Lyric Theatre, Hammersmith.

      (16 December) *A Kind of Alaska*, television (Central).

1985   (7 March) *One for the Road* with *A Kind of Alaska* and *Victoria Station*, Duchess Theatre.

      (25 July) *One for the Road*, television (BBC).

      Turtle Diary, film, directed by John Irvin.

      (July) Directs *Sweet Bird of Youth*, Tennessee Williams, Theatre Royal, Haymarket.

      Plays Deeley in *Old Times*, St Louis and Los Angeles.

      (23 July) *The Dumb Waiter*, television (BBC).

1986   (6 March) *Victoria Station* (BBC radio).

      Directs *Circe and Bravo*, by Donald Freed, Hampstead Theatre Club, Wyndham's Theatre.

1987   (28 June) *The Birthday Party*, television (BBC).

1988   (20 October) Directs *Mountain Language*, Royal National Theatre.

      (11 December) Directs *Mountain Language*, television (BBC).

1989   *Reunion*, film, directed by Jerry Schatzberg.

      The Heat of the Day, film, directed by Christopher Morahan.

1990   Directs *Vanilla*, by Jane Stanton Hitchcock, Lyric Theatre, Hammersmith.

      Publishes *The Dwarfs*, novel.

      The Comfort of Strangers, film, directed by Paul Schrader.

      The Handmaid's Tale, film, directed by Volker Schlondorff.

1991   (20 June) Directs *The Caretaker*, Comedy Theatre.

      (19 July) Directs *The New World Order*, Royal Court Theatre Upstairs.

      (31 October) Directs *Party Time*, Almeida Theatre, in a double bill with *Mountain Language*.

      (26 October) *Old Times*, television (BBC).

      Publishes *Poems and Prose*, collected anthology.

1992   Plays Hirst in *No Man's Land*, Almeida Theatre, Comedy Theatre.

      (17 November) Directs *Party Time*, television (BBC).

1993   (7 September) *Moonlight*, Almeida Theatre, Comedy Theatre.

      The Trial, film, directed by David Jones.

      Directs *Oleanna*, by David Mamet, Royal Court Theatre (later at Duke of York's).

1994   *The Birthday Party*, Royal National Theatre.

First Pinter Festival, Gate Theatre, Dublin (*Betrayal*, *The Dumb Waiter*, *Old Times*, *One for the Road*, *Moonlight* and *Landscape*).

Directs *Landscape*, transferred to Royal National Theatre.

1995 (3 July) Directs *Taking Sides*, by Ronald Harwood, Chichester Festival and Criterion Theatre.

Plays Roote in *The Hothouse*, Chichester Festival and Comedy Theatre.

(21 October) Directs *Landscape*, television (BBC).

Awarded David Cohen British Literature Prize, for lifetime's achievement in literature.

(31 December) *The Proust Screenplay* (BBC Radio 3).

1996 Directs *Twelve Angry Men*, by Reginald Rose, Bristol Old Vic and Comedy Theatre.

(12 September) Directs *Ashes to Ashes*, Royal Court Theatre at the Ambassadors Theatre, later seen in Palermo and Paris.

Receives Laurence Olivier award for lifetime's achievement in theatre.

1997 (23 January) *The Homecoming*, Royal National Theatre.

Second Pinter Festival, Gate Theatre, Dublin (*The Collection*, *Ashes to Ashes*, *A Kind of Alaska*, *No Man's Land* – plays Harry in *The Collection*, directs *Ashes to Ashes*).

Plays John Smith in *Breaking the Code*, by Hugh Whitemore, television (BBC).

Directs *Life Support*, by Simon Gray, Aldwych Theatre.

1998 (13 May) *3 by Harold Pinter*, Donmar Warehouse (*A Kind of Alaska*, *The Collection* and *The Lover*).

The Collection, with Pinter as Harry, and *The Lover* subsequently tour to Theatre Royal, Bath and Richmond Theatre.

Plays Sam Ross in *Mojo*, by Jez Butterworth (BBC films).

Publishes *Various Voices: Prose, Poetry, Politics 1948–1998*.

1999 Directs *The Late Middle Classes*, by Simon Gray, Palace Theatre, Watford.

2000 (16 March) Directs *The Room* and *Celebration*, Almeida Theatre.

Plays Sir Thomas Bertram in *Mansfield Park*, film.

(8 October) *Moonlight* (BBC Radio 3) with Pinter as Andy.

(13 October) *A Slight Ache* (BBC Radio 3) with Pinter as Edward.

(15 November) *The Caretaker*, Comedy Theatre.

(23 November) *Remembrance of Things Past* (adapted by Di Trevis from Pinter's screenplay), Royal National Theatre.

2001 Receives S. T. Dupont Golden Pen Award for a Lifetime's Distinguished Service to Literature.

(26 June) *Mountain Language* and *Ashes to Ashes* (Royal Court).

(3 July) Plays Nicolas in *One for the Road* (New Ambassadors).

(30 September) *The Homecoming* (Comedy Theatre).

(6 December) Directs *No Man's Land* (Lyttleton, Royal National Theatre).

2002 (14 January) *Monologue* (Cottesloe, Royal National Theatre).

(8 February) Performs in premiere of *Press Conference*, Royal National Theatre.

(8 February) 'Sketches I' – *The Black and White, Tess, That's Your Trouble, Trouble in the Works* (Lyttelton, Royal National Theatre).

(11 February) 'Sketches II' – *Last to Go, Special Offer, That's All* (Lyttelton, Royal National Theatre).

Made Companion of Honour for services to literature.

2003 (23 April) New adaptation of *The Dwarfs*, by Kerry Lee Crabbe, Tricycle Theatre.

War (collection of war poems) published.

(8 October) *Betrayal* (Duchess Theatre).

2004 (16 June) Receives D.Litt, University College, Dublin.

(1 July) Directs *The Old Masters*, by Simon Gray.

(7 July) *Old Times* (Donmar Warehouse).

Awarded the Wilfred Owen Poetry Prize.

2005 (10 October) *Voices* (BBC Radio 3).

Third Pinter Festival at the Gate Theatre, Dublin (*Old Times*; *Betrayal*; readings of *Family Voices* and *Celebration*; and *The Pinter Landscape*, a reading of poetry, prose, and extracts from the plays).

(13 October) Awarded the Nobel Prize for Literature.

(1 December) *Celebration* (staged reading) (Albery Theatre, presented by the Gate Theatre, Dublin).

(7 December) Delivers his Nobel laureate lecture by satellite link.

2006 (27 March) *A Kind of Alaska* and *A Slight Ache* (The Gate, Notting Hill).

(11 May) Performs in *Apart From That*, sketch, Inner Temple, London. Awarded the European Theatre Prize.

(15 October) Plays Krapp in Beckett's *Krapp's Last Tape* (Royal Court).

2007 (30 January) *Pinter's People* (sketches and monologues) Theatre Royal, Haymarket.

(2 February) *The Dumb Waiter* (Trafalgar Studios).

(18 March) Plays Max in *The Homecoming* (BBC Radio 3).

(April) *Old Times* (Theatre Royal, Bath).

(5 June) *Betrayal* (Donmar Warehouse).

(18 July) *The Hothouse* (Lyttelton, Royal National Theatre).

Awarded Légion d'honneur.

Sleuth (screenplay).

2008   (29 January) *The Lover and The Collection* (Comedy Theatre).

(14 February) *Being Harold Printer* (Belarus Free Theatre) (Soho Theatre).

(25 July) *A Slight Ache* (Lyttelton, Royal National Theatre).

(21 August) *No Man's Land* (Gate Theatre, Dublin).

(8 September) Discusses post-war British theatre, British Library.

(13 September) *A Slight Ache and Landscape* (Lyttelton, Royal National Theatre).

(7 October) *No Man's Land* (Duke of York's Theatre, Gate Theatre Production).

(24 December) Harold Pinter dies in London.

(31 December) Funeral, Kensal Green Cemetery, London.

NOTE ON THE TEXT

The references to Harold Pinter's plays within the text vary, with respect to edition, from chapter to chapter. Full details of editions used are given in the notes to each chapter.

Within the quotations from Pinter's plays, three dots (...) is a Pinter convention, and four dots (... .) indicates an omission

PETER RABY

Introduction

Putting together a collection of essays about a living writer carries a special sense of excitement, even danger. Harold Pinter, at the age of seventy, is still extremely active, and prominent, as a playwright, as the double bill of *The Room*, his first play, and *Celebration*, his latest, at the Almeida Theatre in spring 2000, demonstrated: he also directed both plays. His acting career continues, for example with his role of Sir Thomas Bertram in *Mansfield Park*. Later in the year, *Remembrance of Things Past*, a stage version of *The Proust Screenplay*, was produced at the Royal National Theatre. Meanwhile, there is a steady stream of productions of earlier plays, written over a period of more than forty years, both in English and in translation, which ensures a continuing refreshment and reappraisal of the whole range of Pinter's work. Pinter the dramatist is protean: his writing moulds itself apparently effortlessly to the forms of radio and television, as well as to the stage, and several plays have been successful in all three media. Major plays – major, in terms of length – have been successfully adapted for film, and Pinter has had an additional career as an outstanding screenwriter, perhaps most notably in conjunction with Joseph Losey. He was a poet before he became a playwright, and has written a novel and a substantial number of essays. His career as a professional actor began in 1951, and as a director in 1959. The problem he poses is both where to begin, and where to end.

Pinter is, by purely statistical reckoning, one of the most widely performed and best-known dramatists in the contemporary world. He has also become an academic subject. There is an active Pinter Society in the United States, producing an annual *Pinter Record*. There are Pinter conferences, and an increasingly formidable body of Pinter studies. British playwrights have become more used to being part of the canon, a literary phenomenon of the later twentieth century. In the 1960s, a search for the individually published plays of Pinter and Stoppard in the main catalogue of Cambridge University Library would draw a blank; they could be tracked down to the handwritten supplementary catalogue: the clear assumption was that individual plays were ephemeral, and certainly not material for serious enquiry. Now that drama and theatre have become recognised and valued areas of study, in spite of occasional disparaging comments about 'soft' subjects by the relentlessly philistine, Pinter is unequivocally a focus for a wide range of critical approaches. Pinter's presence on the syllabus of, for example, Advanced Level Theatre Studies has meant that generations of English sixth-formers have been introduced to his distinctive voice; and his plays are frequently and widely performed in schools and universities, ensuring that he is very far from being simply the province of older theatre-going generations. In Sir Peter Hall's recent Clark Lectures at Cambridge, on the idea of the mask, he concluded by discussing the plays of Beckett and Pinter, in a series of reference points that stretched, in terms of dramatic writing, from Aeschylus to Shakespeare and Mozart. There seemed no incongruity, only continuity.

If Pinter was embraced warmly, and relatively early by academia, he has been treated a little more erratically by theatre critics. *The Birthday Party* foxed them in 1958, with the striking exception of Harold Hobson, who had had the benefit of seeing *The Room* in Bristol. *The Birthday Party* was a new kind of theatrical writing, posing challenges for director, actors and audiences; though audiences at Cambridge and Oxford, uninfluenced by any critical lead, responded positively. Over the years, the reviewers' response has adjusted, both to 'early' Pinter, and to successive shifts and developments in his work. Even some of Pinter's most fervent admirers have been wrong-footed by specific later plays, which for different reasons have seemed uncharacteristic, or out of key. Michael Billington, for example, examines, in *The Life and Work of Harold Pinter*, why he himself was so hostile initially to *Betrayal*, and suggests that he failed to realise at a first viewing that the play is about, in Peter Hall's phrase, self-betrayal. Pinter's plays share the nature of innovative work in not necessarily revealing themselves at first sight: a dangerous trait in the ephemeral world of theatre, where first impressions often dictate success or rapid failure. Critics, reviewers and academics constructed a vocabulary to help us deal with the elusive quality in Pinter: Pinteresque, the Pinter pause, comedy of menace. Pinter went on evolving, ignoring the categories. If *Betrayal* seemed a sharp swerve of direction, the overtly political plays such as *One for the Road* and *Mountain Language* threw down another kind of gauntlet; then there is the different mode of *A Kind of Alaska*, and the shift apparent in *Ashes to Ashes*; while *Celebration* seemed to provoke bafflement in certain quarters by being so blatantly comic. Pinter is a playwright who constantly reinvents himself. That he remains so open to new forms, and voices, in theatre was demonstrated by his unequivocal support, together with Edward Bond, for Sarah Kane, when her first play *Blasted* was viciously dismissed by the London critics.

Audiences, readers, theatre critics, academics – overlapping categories – have particular reasons for responding to and appreciating Pinter's work, and the man who writes, directs and performs it. There is no doubting the recognition that Pinter attracts: international awards and honorary degrees form part of that recognition; and you only need to be present at a Pinter reading, for example at the second Pinter Festival in Dublin in 1997, to be aware of the immediacy of response for a young audience. But Pinter also seems to exist, in England at any rate, as a separate phenomenon, a special construct labelled 'Pinter'. This may be just a particular example of English anti-intellectualism, in which journalists practise the time-honoured sport of putting the boot in to anyone who is too successful, but especially anyone who is successful in the 'high' arts of the theatre, or literature. This practice is far less prevalent in the United States, or the rest of Europe. It may also reflect another English trait, a distrust of anyone who is not a politician or a political commentator yet who takes politics seriously, and is prepared to shoot from the hip. Pinter has never shrunk from taking up causes, and from acting, and speaking, publicly for what he believes to be right. His unequivocal stance in recent years has ensured not just a high profile, but intermittent sniper fire.

This collection of essays does not attempt to be exhaustive. A much larger book would be necessary. A number of considerations informed the choice of topics and authors. It centres on Pinter's writing for the theatre, the most enduring and accessible form of his writing, and also, by its nature, the most open to reinterpretation. There are some inevitable gaps, for example in Pinter's writing specifically for radio or television, and this is partly deliberate, since the performance aspect of those events is difficult to recapture, unlike the relative accessibility of film. The writers include both academics and theatre professionals (in any event not mutually exclusive categories), and in many of the essays there is a strong explicit or implicit sense of the performance dimension. The collection acknowledges the worldwide interest in Pinter, with chapters on Pinter in specifically Russian and Irish contexts, and by the inclusion of authors from the United States, Spain and Israel, as well as from Ireland and the United Kingdom. Some of the essayists have been writing on Pinter for many years, and attended the first productions of the early plays; some have come to respond to his work comparatively recently. We share a common enthusiasm, but not, I hope, an undiscriminating one. One factor struck me, as editor: even where topics were quite tightly defined, the writers tended to move, at some point, towards an overview, suggesting that Pinter's dramatic writing has, collectively, a strong coherence, a sense of continuity and evolution, and forms a body of work that invites constant re-evaluation. This collection seeks to offer one such set of perspectives.

Note on the second edition

For this revised second edition of the *Companion*, three new chapters have been added, by Mary Luckhurst, John Stokes and Steve Waters, each of which responds in different ways to the writer, to his work, to his influence and to his own powerful presence on both theatre and public stages. Other chapters have been extended, most notably those by Charles Evans on 'Pinter in Russia', Anthony Roche on 'Pinter and Ireland' and Harry Derbyshire on 'Pinter as Celebrity'. The public perception of Pinter has shifted significantly in the last seven years, in response to his illness and to his winning of the Nobel Prize for Literature, the most conspicuous of a steady stream of national and international awards and distinctions. His contributions as actor, film-writer and poet have been extensively recognised and celebrated, as the citation for the Nobel Prize demonstrated. There have been radio and television programmes devoted to him, and many new productions of his plays, including striking revisitings of much of his early work. The integrity, prescience and fierce consistency of his political statements seem all the more striking in the context of the twenty-first century than they did at the close of the twentieth. Pinter's voices are various, entirely distinctive and compelling.

The contributions to this volume were all completed before Harold Pinter's death on Christmas Eve, 2008, and it was thought best to leave them unaltered. The immediate tributes, showing an unusual degree of unanimity, acknowledged Pinter's stature as Britain's greatest living dramatist, and the extent of his significance in the context of British and world culture. They also provided moving evidence of his loyalty and generosity. 'Allow the love of the good ghost. They possess all that emotion trapped.' (*No Man's Land*)

I
Text and Context

I

AUSTIN QUIGLEY

Pinter, politics and postmodernism (1)

Pinter's plays have fascinated many people over the years for many reasons, not the least of which is their capacity to resist large-scale generalisation. The emphasis in the plays on complex and diverse local detail makes it very difficult to argue that the plays as a group exemplify the large general truths of any existing theory about the nature of society, personality, culture, spirituality, anthropology, history or anything else of similar scope. This is not to say that insights into the plays cannot be derived from all these sources. Indeed they can, as several astute Pinter critics have demonstrated. The trouble is that these various perspectives serve best as ways into the texture of the plays rather than as summations of the implications of that texture, and if excessively relied upon, they begin to obscure what they seek to clarify.

Stoppard uses an illuminating phrase to characterise the baffling experiences of the leading characters in *Rosencrantz and Guildenstern are Dead* when he describes them as constantly being intrigued without ever quite being enlightened.[1] That sense of being fascinated by something we do not fully understand is, as Van Laan has argued, an irreducible aspect of the experience of Pinter's plays, and we have, I think, over the years come to recognise that the role of the critic is to increase the sense of enlightenment without diminishing the sense of intrigue.[2] To insist on defending the intrigue against any enlightenment is, of course, to reduce all experience of a play to the first experience, to insist on each play's inviolable particularity and thus effectively to abandon the task of criticism. To insist upon full enlightenment is to erase the sense of intrigue, to allow the critical perspective to supplant the play, and thus effectively to undermine the play's capacity to function as a Pinter play. What we appear to need from criticism is the kind of enlightenment that clarifies and enhances the subtlety of the intrigue rather than the kind that, in explaining the nature of the intrigue, explains it away.

These issues are not without their significance for the work of any playwright, but there is something about Pinter plays that makes the balance between intrigue and enlightenment particularly difficult for criticism to get right. And Pinter's intermittent forays into the realm of political commentary have served to make it even more difficult.[3] Should we adopt the political guidance he sometimes offers us and announce that we have finally found the enlightening larger picture of which all the plays' complexities are simply constituent parts, or should we be defending his early plays against their author's belated desire to convert them into illustrations of political oppression and abuse of authority?

Before we surrender to the urge to reinvent phrases like 'the personal is the political', we should remember that response to such slogans in the past has included lengthy arguments about the meaning of the terms 'personal' and 'political'. But just as important is the often overlooked issue of the meaning of the word 'is'. Do we mean it in the sense that 2 + 2 *is* 4, a sense of total equivalence, or do we mean it in the sense of Pinter *is* tall, i.e. he is *among other things* tall? Is all of the personal political, most of it, or just some of it? As far as Pinter's plays are concerned, it is important to note that even as he begins to argue in the 1980s that many of his earlier plays were, indeed, political, he exempts from this claim *Landscape*, *Silence*, *Old Times* and *Betrayal*.[4] And if whole plays can be exempted from the claim that the personal is the political, it would follow that whatever the political component of the other plays, they are not necessarily only or even centrally political.

Leaving to one side Pinter's comments on these matters, it is well to remind ourselves of the way in which literary theory, in one of its rare enlightened phases, used to draw attention to the dangers of excessive explanatory claims. One discipline or mode of enquiry after another was able to make foundational claims on the basis of the argument that its material and concerns had a bearing on almost every aspect of our lives. Thus it could be claimed that everything is a matter of history, or that everything is a matter of economics, or that everything is a matter of psychology, or that everything is a matter of language and so on. The recognition that these claims can be made with equal conviction and justification by a variety of equally convinced groups should temper the enthusiasm for currently competing claims that everything is a matter of politics, or of power, or of gender, or of race, or of culture, or of the postmodern era, or of any other factor that helps constitute the multifaceted complexity of our lives.

Though such enthusiasm should be tempered, it should not, of course, be eradicated because all of these frameworks have something to contribute – but preferably if developed in the context of what the other ones might also, in varying degrees, have to offer. Pinter's 1980s enthusiasm for the politics of art should likewise be neither overvalued nor undervalued. It simply asks to be put in the appropriate perspective, along with his 1960s efforts to distance each from the other.[5] The trajectory of Pinter's avowed interest in political issues seems to have become one of oscillation between undervaluing and overvaluing the political, an oscillation fortunately by no means as visible in the plays themselves, for reasons that can be abstracted from his political comments.

Pinter's initial hostility towards politics was largely a hostility towards institutional politics and politicians because of their tendency to indulge in reductive social analysis.[6] Built into institutional politics, he felt, was the need to establish positions and programmes that could earn widespread support among large numbers of very different people. Such procedures require simplification and a search for common denominators. Politicians consequently tend to display a readiness to settle for what is currently possible rather than to register a sustained determination to deal with all the imponderables of the actual or to confront the intractability of the necessary. Pinter's early refusal to get involved in political matters was thus born not of indifference to social problems but of serious doubt that political channels, political arguments and political action could serve to ameliorate social problems rather than exacerbate them. When he warned us in 1962 to 'Beware of the writer who puts forward his concern for you to embrace, who leaves you in no doubt of his worthiness, his usefulness, his altruism, who declares that his heart is in the right place, and ensures that it can be seen in full view, a pulsating mass where his characters ought to be', he is not just indicating how to avoid writing bad plays but also suggesting how to avoid promoting the kind of inadequate social analysis characteristic, he feels, of politicians in general.[7] 'To be a politician,' he argued, 'you have to be able to present a simple picture even if you don't see things that way.'[8] To be a successful dramatist, by implication, you have to be free to explore complex pictures that clarify without necessarily reducing the complexity of social experience.

Pinter's early dramatic technique is less one of moving from the local community context to the larger political context than of scrutinising the local context so closely that it becomes difficult to abstract simple generalisations about individual responsibility, community convictions or collective goals. His preoccupation with confined spaces, with small rooms, with constraining circumstances and brief events provides a context for exploring the complexities of local pictures, the instability and indispensability of verbal interaction, the shifting status of social realities, the precariousness of attempts to establish general agreement and the riskiness of anyone's efforts to function as leader or spokesperson for a social group. For the Pinter of these plays, the local picture in all its simplicity and complexity precedes and succeeds any large one, and national political action, if it were to make sense at all, would have to be an extension of, and not a substitute for, the daily activity of people coping with self and others in the local spaces his characters inhabit. One of the most prominent of Pinter's early statements was the remark: 'Before you manage to adjust yourself to living alone in your room, you're not really terribly fit and equipped to go out to fight battles.'[9] It is not yet clear that Pinter's dramatic technique has changed in this respect, in spite of his intermittent readiness to make large political statements both about his plays and about global social issues. But what he has effectively done is to transfer to the realm of political situation the exploration of complex local social interaction that is characteristic of his plays as a whole.

Rather than showing that the personal is the political by dissolving the personal into the political, Pinter has, effectively, dramatised the converse: that the political is, among other things, the personal. As such, it is as complex and dangerous and as worthy of our scrupulous attention as any other sphere of social interaction; and Pinter demonstrates this in spite of the limited development of individual character in the more overtly political plays. It is, in fact, the procedures by which political imperatives can produce attempts to reduce individuality to mere enmity that a play like *One for the Road* so carefully depicts. And in the resistance of individuality to such reduction, the personal is not so much equated with the political as reinstated as a form of resistance to it. But Pinter's refusal to situate plays like *One for the Road* and *Mountain Language* in specific historical locales has led to criticism that without such specificity we do not know what to be for or against that we were not for or against before. To try to persuade a theatre audience that it should in general be against physical torture, murder and rape seems somewhat gratuitous in spite of the prevalence of all three in the modern world. What interests Pinter, however, is exploring the modes of presupposition and self-justification that enable such things to be done in the name of or on behalf of citizens and governments who might publicly and even sincerely condemn them. What is dramatised is not the physical torture, murder and rape so frequently referred to in critical discussion, but the processes of self-justification they promote and the differing consequences for the oppressors and the oppressed of their limited persuasiveness.

In *One for the Road*, Nicolas, the interrogator, derives some of his sense of legitimacy and authority from his conviction that he speaks for a national consensus. Citing his country's leader, he portrays himself as one acting on behalf of a unified group against a lone dissenter, and the existence of that larger unity suffices to convert the dissenter into a traitor: 'We are all patriots, we are as one, we all share a common heritage. Except you, apparently. *Pause.* I feel a link, you see, a bond. I share a commonwealth of interest. I am not alone. I am not alone!'[10] The repeated phrase 'I am not alone' mobilises the claims to legitimacy of the voice and of the actions it endorses.

The social 'bond' of fellowship that strengthens Nicolas's convictions that what he is doing is justified is the same bond that excludes Victor not only from that society but also from the civil rights its members might otherwise enjoy. The voice of exclusion seeks to derive its legitimacy from the voice of inclusion.

In such a context, the 'I' in the repeated phrase 'I am not alone' is not the 'I' of bourgeois individualism, nor the 'I' that functions merely as the spokesperson for an unreflecting 'we', nor the 'I' that is the involuntary voice of a cultural or linguistic code. This is an 'I' that justifies itself in a variety of ways, but – most important – is its evident need to do so. Like the old woman who is unwilling or unable to speak in *Mountain Language*[11] Nicolas exists outside the codes he uses to construct, exhibit, and justify himself. Like so many Pinter characters he can be illuminated by, but not exhaustively summarised by, any description of inherited cultural codes or ideological commitments. Here at the edge of the civilised world, inhuman acts are justified by individuals who invoke general social bonds as a justification for abandoning them in the case of dissenting individuals. Indeed, part of the torture to which the victims are subjected consists of turning the psychological and emotional bonds of a family group into weapons to be used against each of them. The rape of the wife and the murder of the son invoke, even as they break, some of the strongest bonds that hold civilised human beings together. The personal and the political are, indeed, intertwined, but we will make little sense of these plays if we simply equate the one with the other.

Though the context in which we encounter them prevents the characters in *One for the Road* and *Mountain Language* from being developed in great detail, Pinter conveys enough of the personal in social and political contexts to make these scenes continuous with scenes in his other plays in which we feel we are encountering individual characters with, among other things, familiar social histories, rather than abstract characters representing narrow social and political agendas, or, to put it another way, individual characters whose representativeness follows upon and includes their individuality, rather than preceding and supplanting it.

These points are made at some length for two reasons. First, neither in Pinter's so-called political plays nor elsewhere do we encounter characters with an explicit ideological position to exemplify and defend. Second, after a time when literary theories of various kinds became obsessed with the death of the subject, Pinter is continuing to create characters whose irreducible idiosyncrasy makes a significant contribution to our conviction that the plays themselves retain an irreducible singularity, no matter which modes of explanation we adopt to convert intrigue into enlightenment. And it is in this context of irreducible singularity and strategic avoidance of ideological debate that we should make the link between Pinter, politics and postmodernism.

It seems to me quite true, as Chin has argued, that 'postmodern' has become 'one of those terms, like "existential" for an earlier generation, which everyone tosses around like a beanbag, while aiming at different targets'.[12] I find myself much persuaded by Lyotard's argument that we would benefit by thinking of postmodernism as one of the recurring phases of modernism rather than as something posterior to and opposed to modernism.[13] Indeed, if we are to make sense of the modernism/postmodernism relationship we would do well not only to acknowledge that modernism has always been many things anyway, but also to put that recognition to work in our attempts to distinguish its various kinds. I would thus be inclined to follow and extend Hassan's argument on this issue by conceiving not just of three major kinds, but of three major voices, of modernism: avant-garde modernism, high modernism and postmodernism.[14] All three voices are liable to occur in the work of any one writer or any single decade, but proportional representation of those voices has changed gradually (though not uniformly) over the decades from the prominence of avant-garde modernism, through the prominence of high modernism, to the prominence of postmodernism.

In terms of the characteristics critical commentary usually associates with these concepts,[15] the avant-garde modernist voice would be the one rejecting the *status quo* and demanding that it be totally replaced. This is the voice insisting on a sense of crisis, of generational conflict, of the complicity of art with the existing order and of the need for radical artistic and social reform.

The high modern voice would be the one more concerned with providing the new than with rejecting the old. This is the modernism associated with establishing the aesthetic domain as the alternative to the religious and political domains, whether or not it can claim equivalent scope.[16] It is the modernism of art as aesthetic object, as cultural artefact, as difficult, abstract, reflexive, ironic, distanced, autonomous, an art for the elite and for the initiated, and strongly opposed to the popular, the easily accommodated or the easily reproduced.

The postmodern voice would then be the one that pursues the new without the avant-garde gesture of radical opposition or the high modern gesture of radical affirmation. It is a voice of eclectic mingling, including the mingling of art with everything else, a voice refusing to claim legitimacy on the basis of radical change, cheerfully mixing high art and pop art, the interests of elite culture and those of mass culture, a voice questioning exclusionary canons and insisting upon the value of diversity, otherness, difference and discontinuity, a voice that opposes less than the avant-garde modernist and affirms less than the high modernist, a voice that is content to explore variety rather than indulge in premature judgments of its novelty, nature and value.[17]

Instead of the avant-garde modernist's concern with opposing something monolithic, instead of high modernist concern with affirming something of monolithic value if not quite monolithic scope, like the redemption of social life through the restructuring of culture, the postmodern concern is with the local and with the irreducible multiplicity of things local. And just as important is the re-emergence, in these concerns for the local, of that most local of elements of social analysis, the individual, who is not readily dismissible as a pawn in an ideological system, nor susceptible to being dismantled into a variety of social codes, but an agent who functions at the site at which different forms of cultural and multicultural conflicts converge and require accommodation. In these terms, postmodernism deals as much with emergent as with residual forms of social and cultural practice and renews concern for personal responsibility, individual creativity and social engagement, but it does so primarily in local social contexts. A key challenge that is thus constantly latent in postmodernism's focus upon the local and heterogeneous is how to make of the local something large enough, so that an acceptance of irreducible multiplicity does not degenerate into the passive acquiescence of radical relativism. The need is for something larger that can establish and sustain social bonds without aspiring to attain universality or threatening to become intolerant, exclusionary or oppressive.

These are, of course, schematic contrasts drawn from much of the literature on these issues, but their pertinence to our understanding of Pinter and even of politics will probably already be clear. We can hear alternately in his public utterances the voice of Pinter the avant-garde modernist railing against the political *status quo*, and the voice of Pinter the aesthetic high modernist insisting that his plays do not have to be about anything, for anything, or against anything outside themselves. But it is in his plays that we encounter most strongly the voice of Pinter the postmodernist depicting characters struggling to come to terms with social complexity and striving not so much to eliminate it as to manoeuvre to advantage their future relationship to it. Unwilling or unable to attribute their individual problems to large abstract forces of social, psychological, political or economic origin and unwilling or unable to pursue solutions on a similar scale, they play out the local hand that has been dealt, and they play with differing degrees of imagination, enthusiasm, determination and flair. Their collective recognition of irreducible difference does not precipitate a resigned indifference[18] but a commitment to making something work in some way for a while. Even Spooner, in *No Man's Land*, who announces with pride his rejection of expectation, deploys the announcement strategically to promote hopes he is prepared to acknowledge neither to himself nor to others.[19]

In this respect Pinter's plays lean towards Lyotard rather than Habermas in one of the key debates about postmodernism. For Habermas, as Lyotard reads him, the continuing goal of a democratic society is the Enlightenment pursuit of social and political consensus; for Lyotard, the great danger of the pursuit of consensus is that if too many people agree on too many things, disagreement becomes a sign of social abnormality, dissent becomes unpatriotic and difference becomes intolerable[20] – precisely the scenario implied by Nicolas's attempt to invoke social consensus in *One for the Road*. But if the pursuit of consensus and shared values is not to be the goal of our social interaction or the basis for our social bonds, what is? Lyotard's alternative is a revision of the notion of social contract, once so dear to political thinkers of the eighteenth century.[21] But such social contracts in a postmodern world of irreducible multiplicity are themselves multiple rather than single, local rather than global and often implicit rather than explicit. Emerging from social interaction they guide rather than govern social interaction and are constantly open to reconsideration, renegotiation, extension or rejection. And it is in this reconfiguration of the nature of social contracts that the commitment to the local, so often encountered in discussion of postmodernism and Pinter, can make contact with something larger, including larger political contexts.

Pinter's early insistence that he found most political thinking and terminology suspect and deficient, that he disliked didactic and moralistic plays, and that he wrote not only without religious or political commitments but also without any consciousness that his work had any general social function at all was an insistence that led to charges that his plays had no implications beyond their own particularity and idiosyncrasy, that they could appeal only to aesthetes, and that they were socially and politically irrelevant.[22] When an argument like this was put directly to Pinter in the 1960s, he acknowledged that he had no political arguments to make but that there was a distinction to be drawn between the political and the social.

> If I write something in which two people are facing each other over a table ... I'm talking about two people living socially, and if what takes place between them is a meaningful and accurate examination of them, then it's going to be relevant to you and to society. This relationship will be an image of other relationships, of social living, of living together ... [23]

To think of the plays providing images of social living is to recognise the way in which the local can achieve a degree of largeness without becoming symptomatic of a preceding or succeeding form of ideological consensus. As images of social living, the plays acquire a generality of implication that follows from rather than precedes their local complexity. And it is in this sense that we can think of Pinter's work and Pinter's politics in postmodern terms.

Like modernism in general, postmodernism is, of course, constituted by its own variants, variants which we can heuristically characterise but not exclusively define. What is at issue here is not whether Pinter to be postmodern must invoke pop art and deploy multi-media nor whether he is prepared to abandon the dramatic text in favour of a performance art of scenic imagery and ritualistic gesture, but the contribution he might make to our understanding of postmodernism and of the kind of political play that could be consistent with it. In Pinter's plays the political, when it becomes overt, is always one component of situations of larger social complexity, and as the political problems emerge from no clearly defined institutional base, their resolution or evasion depends upon no particular political programme. Political thinking for Pinter audiences involves not so much questions about occupying the right or left on the political spectrum or commitments to one political party or another, but a requirement to explore the complexities of local social exchange in terms of local social contracts, both those invoked by the characters and those emerging from their interaction.

It is noteworthy, in this respect, to see how often the relationship between characters becomes explicitly contractual, as personal, family and professional concerns so often intermingle and collide. Sarah, in *The Lover*, resists Richard's attempts to introduce afternoon games into their evening life by insisting, unsuccessfully, upon their formal status: 'You've no right to question me. ... It was our arrangement. No questions of this kind.'[24] Disson's psychological equilibrium, in *Tea Party*, is disrupted in spite of his attempts to relate separately to Wendy with a secretarial contract, to Willy with a partnership contract and to Diana with a marriage contract, because each fails to control the evolving complexities of the interacting relationships. Ruth, in *The Homecoming*, adjusting to the challenges of her proffered role with Teddy's family, likewise demands that 'All aspects of the agreement and conditions of employment would have to be clarified to our mutual satisfaction before we finalized the contract' – a contract which would, of course, require 'signatures in the presence of witnesses'.[25] Len, in *The Dwarfs*, describes in contractual terms his relationship with the dwarfs: 'They don't stop work until the job in hand is finished, one way or another. They never run out on a job. Oh no. They're true professionals. Real professionals.'[26] The whole action of *A Dumb Waiter* is about the personal interaction of two characters who are contracted to kill the next person coming in through the door; the decline of Edward's relationship with his wife in *A Slight Ache* culminates in his being given the Matchseller's tray and the job that goes with it; Max, in *The Homecoming*, tries to defend his status in the family on the basis of his professional expertise as trainer and butcher; and the personal interaction between Duff and Beth in *Landscape* is one much affected by its occurring in the home of the man who hired them as housekeeper and chauffeur: as Duff puts it, 'Mr Sykes took to us from the very first interview, didn't he? *Pause*. He said I've got the feeling you'll make a very good team. Do you remember? And that's what we proved to be. No question.'[27]

In similar terms the relationship between Aston, Davies and Mick in *The Caretaker* focuses upon Davies's rights and responsibilities as caretaker, Aston's as decorator and Mick and Aston's both as brothers and as putative owners, while Davies repeatedly tries to shore up his position with appeals to official papers left in Sidcup and to employees' rights asserted in conversations with previous employers: 'I got my rights. ... I might have been on the road but nobody's got more rights than I have. Let's have a bit of fair play.'[28] This appeal for fair play invokes, however, a level of contractual generality that subsumes all business contracts and social commitments and consequently rings immediately hollow. But the recurring links in this and other plays between personal and occupational rights and responsibilities serve to highlight both the contractual basis of social concerns and the constantly re-emerging conflict between the limited status of such contracts and the character's less limited needs, hopes and expectations. Similar enabling and constraining contractual concerns emerge in other plays, whether it is the blind intruder reminding Rose of former responsibilities in a former home in *The Room*; Spooner, in *No Man's Land*, trying to convert his invitation to Hirst's home into a long-term working arrangement; Emma, Jerry, and Robert, in *Betrayal*, trying to evaluate their rights and responsibilities in the context of competing bonds as spouses, friends, colleagues and lovers; and, illuminatingly for this line of enquiry, James, in *The Collection*, trying to clarify his spousal claims on Stella in the light of Bill's strategic invocation of a stereotype that implies that there is more to her than any contract could ever regulate or encompass: 'Every woman is bound to have an outburst of ... wild sensuality at one time or another. That's the way I look at it, anyway. It's part of their nature.'[29] And all of this helps us understand Pinter's retroactive political claim that Petey's 'don't let them tell you what to do [Stan]' in *The Birthday Party* is one of the most important lines he has ever written.[30] In a world of local and contingent social contracts persisting negotiation takes precedence over presumed authority, every contract that emerges from social interaction involves rights as well as responsibilities that may or may not hold for the duration of the contract and even those not directly involved in the negotiation have a stake, as Petey does, in the principles and procedures that emerge in the process.

As social contracts emerge from social interaction they are, unlike business contracts, rarely explicit or exhaustive and consequently require frequent checking and renegotiation. And what Pinter's plays depict is that process in action, with *The Lover* exemplifying it in intricate detail.[31] Overall the plays deal not with the comparative simplicities of larger social governance that lead directly to political policies but with the proliferating complexities of local community organisation and reorganisation. What is at issue is what binds us together in micro-contexts not what we establish at the level of the macro-context to determine the abstract relationship between the governing and the governed. The source of appeal against the behaviour of brutal government agents in plays like *One for the Road*, *Mountain Language* and *Party Time* is not to one ideology or another, to one brand of political conviction or another, but to the local relationships that individuals contract with each other, particularly in small social and family contexts, and to the rights and responsibilities thereby invoked.[32] It is here that the personal becomes the source of appeal against anything political that loses touch with the personal.

The issue is not, of course, that personal bonds or family bonds are of a single kind or of exemplary status. The strength of family bonds in *A Slight Ache*, *The Homecoming*, *Tea Party* and *The Lover*, and the strength of personal bonds in *The Collection*, *The Basement*, *Betrayal* and *No Man's Land* are not such that they exemplify the kind from which anyone would confidently seek to build a lasting civilisation. But the expectations, hopes and needs encountered in these local forms of interaction, whether satisfied or not, provide the model for understanding similar expectations, hopes and needs that shape social interaction in a political context or any other context. And if the larger political exchange is not a motivated extrapolation from the local social exchange, then a dangerous discontinuity is added at a larger scale to the social discontinuities that have to be constantly mediated at a smaller scale. And what is at issue in these implicitly regulative local contexts is not how we achieve consensus but how we accommodate competing claims for our allegiances. Pinter's characters in this respect are an unlovely lot, often self-serving, unreliable, exploitative and defensive. But we have understood little of the nature of their interaction until we have understood why, when asked about the meaning of *The Homecoming*, that apparently most vicious of family plays, Pinter replied that it was about love, and, in effect, about our search for it, our need of it, our expectation that we will find it and our hope that we can give it.[33]

Love in this sense can be as romantic as the fantasies that Beth indulges in in her memories of her lover on the beach in *Landscape*, as qualified as Jerry's 'I don't think we don't love each other' in *Betrayal*, or as minimal as Petey's 'don't let them tell you what to do' to Stanley in *The Birthday Party*.[34] It can also be as challenging and bewildering and as conventional and creative as that depicted in the ever-evolving relationship between Richard and Sarah in *The Lover*.

In a world of competing values and irreducible individual differences what is at issue in *The Lover* and elsewhere is not the model of making two people into one, that sadly misleading goal for a successful marriage, but the making of a functioning group out of an aggregate of different individuals with differing allegiances and differing goals. That the group is always unstable and functions successfully only for a while is the measure not of the characters' fickleness but of the conflicting demands different individuals make upon the same group and of the conflicting demands different groups make upon each other. The love that Pinter's characters express for each other is that they try to accommodate the differences for as long as they can, that they manage at times, as Sarah and Richard do in *The Lover*, even to celebrate them. But in the world of postmodern contractual expectations they do not, by and large, seek the eradication of difference, the achievement of complete agreement or the conviction that there is some one right, best and enduring way of living or judging. And when characters do register such extensive hopes and expectations, they flounder helplessly, as do James in *The Collection* and Deeley in *Old Times*, or they sustain their hopes only through an intermittently indulged nostalgia for a former way of life, like Hirst, in *No Man's Land*, who first invokes it in his album and then dismisses it with: 'We can't be expected to live like that.'[35] But the danger of some postmodern perspectives, that an acceptance of unlimited forms of difference leads ultimately to indifference, is never a danger in Pinter plays in which the demands that characters make upon each other seem not to disappear no matter how often expectations are disappointed. And it is this continuing expectation that the local might yet prove larger, more satisfying, and more durable that promotes both the social bonds that link individuals to each other and the sense of violation that indicts political programmes and initiatives that fail to accommodate it.

But the expectations themselves are situated on a continuum of variable strength and scale as the characters struggle to reconcile competing local claims on their personal allegiances. The continuum extends from Beth's entranced 'Oh my true love I said' in *Landscape* at one end to Spooner's dismissal of all expectations in *No Man's Land* at the other, with Ruth's memories of her modelling days in *The Homecoming*, the mother's recollections of her son's childhood in *Family Voices*, and Bridget's posthumous sense of responsibility for her parents in *Moonlight*, situated somewhere in between.[36] But even Beth's commitment to a moment of putative transcendence is situated in the selectively contemplated past and tempered by her continuing, more minimal, commitment to Duff in the present. The challenge for character and audience alike is to calibrate carefully the value of competing commitments which, in characteristic postmodern style, are local in origin, scale and scope, but which, in seeking to become larger and more durable, inevitably encounter conflict with other allegiances, with the consequence that the local can only become larger as complex social circumstances and unpredictable individual convictions permit.

The incipient conflict between personal values and political values thus becomes symptomatic of the recurring clash in the plays between competing allegiances of various kinds on various scales which require of the characters constant and complex adjustment. And the recurring pursuit of greater largeness from local relationships provides the structural manifestation in Pinter's plays of the competing voices of high modernism and postmodernism. When Len, in *The Dwarfs*, exclaims, in the midst of conflict over divided loyalties between himself, Mark and Pete, that 'There must be somewhere else',[37] the appeal is explicitly for another place, and implicitly for another kind of place, and perhaps a more inclusive place. But whatever the urgency of the need or hope for radical social transformation, neither in explicit expectation nor in the course of subsequent events does the world of the dwarfs (whose very name signals the scale of potential gains) promise to be maximally inclusive, satisfying and liberating. This uncertainty about the scale of encountered problems, of required solutions and of appropriate expectations provides the characters with persisting difficulties in unstable and unstabilisable social situations, but it also provides Pinter, as a playwright, with important challenges and opportunities. For Pinter is not content to allow the role of a drama preoccupied with the postmodern local and saturated with the socially particular to limit its own exploration to the merely local. In this recurring conflict for the characters between the currently local and the potentially larger Pinter situates a drama in which current actuality, future aspiration and nostalgic recollection register the competing scales of coexisting postmodern and high modern voices. And in his later plays, the effort to extend the local to implicate expanding domains of largeness becomes increasingly sustained and increasingly intense.[38]

In the early plays, the people and pressures offstage alluded to by the characters and exemplified in their behaviour onstage seem quite continuous in scale and scope with the local experience of the characters onstage. In spite of Pinter's retroactive references to the Gestapo,[39] Monty in *The Birthday Party* who, like Wilson in *The Dumb Waiter*, never appears onstage, holds out no more promise for providing access to something radically discontinuous or potentially transcendent than the Matchseller or Riley or Max who do show up in *A Slight Ache*, *The Room* and *The Lover*, or than the variety of intruders who disrupt the flow and extend somewhat the range of established experience in a number of rooms and relationships. But in Pinter's more recent plays, the effort to implicate disparate experience offstage, with which characters will somehow have to come to terms onstage, is much more extensive, involving issues even more remote and even less readily accessible than Stella's putative encounters with Bill in Leeds or Davies's with unrecoverable papers in Sidcup. Though the difference is one of degree, the later plays seek more often to normalise the initially abnormal than to make increasingly mysterious the less radical discontinuities confronted in the earlier plays. Whatever is offstage in terms of political forces in *One for the Road*, *Mountain Language* and *Party Time*, it is invoked as larger, more homogenous and more radically indifferent to individual suffering than the forces invoked offstage in most of the earlier plays. Indeed, the strength of what is offstage in the early plays seems to grow in inverse proportion to the weaknesses of the characters onstage, whereas the relationship between the strengths of victors and victims in the later plays is not so symmetrically proportioned. But what makes Pinter's plays less reducible to the truisms, political and otherwise, of the 1990s, is that he is less prepared to reduce relationships to mere battles for power and more prepared to explore the variety of ways in which competing claims can be made upon the characters' allegiances and interests, as their efforts to link the irremediably local to something larger reach across more and more challenging terrain.

If the claims upon Disson in *Tea Party* can justly be summarised in the competing allegiances he feels to his parents, his wife, his sons, his friends and his employees, the scale of continuity of these discontinuous claims is rarely challenged in the play by some other scale, although the aesthetic claims of floodlit basins and bidets register most strongly the possibility of another scale of consideration for not fully circumscribed aspirations in search of an appropriate object or ally.[40] But Deborah's twenty-nine years of almost inaccessible experience in *A Kind of Alaska* provide a radically extended dimension of dramatised discontinuity. Along with the peculiarly situated speaking voice of the dead father in *Family Voices*, the depiction of the dead sister Bridget moving and speaking onstage in *Moonlight* and the domestic invocations of genocide in *Ashes to Ashes*, these explorations of discontinuous experience collectively register an increasingly ambitious effort to reach not only beyond the boundaries of the local but also beyond the boundaries, however variously defined, of everyday human experience.[41] And the recurring effort is to link apparently normative human experience to what would initially be perceived as lying outside that normative range. In effect, Pinter moves beyond the challenge for politics and politicians of linking persuasively the socially local to the nationally and internationally large by challenging himself as a dramatist to link persuasively the socially local to even larger contexts – those that reach beyond the normative boundaries of human experience itself. For Pinter's remarkably inventive reconciliation of the large scope of high modernism's concerns with the smaller scale of post-modernism's particularity manages to extend radically the scope of postmodernist exploration even while writing plays whose scale of presentation remains determinedly local. Whatever the success of the attempt in *Ashes to Ashes* to link, in a short play, two characters' domestic experience of love, hatred and violence in a middle-class marriage with the catastrophic experience, for millions of global victims of genocide, of related emotions and actions, the combination of small scale and large scope is the recurring theatrical strategy of the later Pinter. His various claims, at different points in his career, that his local situations are to be only locally interpreted, that his theatrical creations are not of larger than theatrical consequence, that the local relationship may serve as an emblem of other social relationships, that many of his plays are not only of local and personal consequence but also of social and political consequence, are claims none of which do full justice to the range of his efforts to reconcile a local scale of presentation with an ever increasing scope of implication.

But we would have missed everything of importance about this means of expanding the implicative scope of the small-scale presentation if we viewed the reaching for further scope in terms of avant-garde modernism or high modernism's aspirations of extensive inclusiveness. The scope is extended not by seeking the synthesising perspective, the 'new world order' so ironically invoked in his play of that title, but by imaginatively orchestrating the interaction of competing local perspectives, contrasting local values and complex local claims upon character allegiances. The experiential divisions that are bridged in these plays nevertheless remain divisions, as Bridget's evocative name and *Moonlight*'s split staging so clearly confirm. Pinter is pursuing not a renewed notion of worldwide human solidarity, but, as in *Family Voices*, *A Kind of Alaska* and *Ashes to Ashes*, a complex means of connecting the disparate dimensions of human experience that will help us recognise and understand collective human strengths and weaknesses. For characters and audience alike the plays raise troubling questions, not susceptible to single or final resolution, of the priority of competing personal, family, social, professional, political and otherwise human claims that we make on each other and that others make on us. These claims rarely line up in a single direction, their spheres of influence overlap without being coextensive and, within the scope of their competing appeals and pressures, the larger aspirations and fears of the characters engage with their local exhilarations, satisfactions, disappointments and disasters.

As I have argued elsewhere, the insistence on these competing demands gives Pinter plots a multilinear rather than a linear structure, with elements of progress, regress and circularity constantly leading towards and beyond moments of insight, agreement, harmony and union, that, no matter how fondly anticipated or remembered, refuse to stay firmly in place.[42] Though limited in scale or duration, these moments provide the basis for expectations that keep many of the characters together no matter how disappointing and abrasive the forms of interaction that threaten constantly to drive them apart. Pinter's use of multi-linear plots provides a structural basis for his depiction of irreducibly different characters with competing goals, needs, wishes, aspirations and expectations. These individual requirements emerge from and are negotiated within contractually oriented social interaction, and Pinter's interwoven narratives are consequently able to offer disconcerting models of the complex nature of social exchange in realms of varying scope and complexity. The multi-linear plots of the various plays serve not simply to reinforce the image of the characters' multi-linear experiences but to give them in different cases different shapes, shapes that characterise the unexpected possibilities and unusual dimensions of emergent social contracts. Because they are emergent, these social contracts are often surprising, but because they emerge from what we can readily recognise, they also provide apt and disturbing frameworks for considering the processes by which human beings form and break bonds, adopt and reject responsibilities and receive, test and transmit values.

Whenever Pinter's work is challenged for its lack of ideological fervour, it is helpful to remember Ionesco's rejoinder to Kenneth Tynan, who challenged his work on the same assumption: that social engagement can only be achieved through political and ideological advocacy, rather than through complex local exploration.

> I beg of you, Mr Tynan, do not attempt, by means of art or any other means, to improve the lot of mankind. Please do not do it. We have had enough of civil wars already, enough of blood and tears and trials that are a mockery, enough of 'righteous' executioners and 'ignoble' martyrs, of disappointed hopes and penal servitude. Do not improve the lot of mankind, if you really wish it well ...
>
> It is in our solitude that we can all be reunited. And that is why true society transcends our social machinery.[43]

And that is also, of course, why Ionesco argues that 'Ideology is not the source of art. A work of art is the source and the raw material of ideologies to come.'[44] Tynan was certainly right to reply that art and ideology should be seen as siblings and not vie for the roles of parent and child,[45] but for Pinter, as for Ionesco, the concern for the locally emergent is as important as concern for the politically received.

In taking on a characteristic postmodern challenge of making the local into something larger and more durable Pinter helps us reconsider what we mean when we use the terms love, loyalty and commitment in the context of the conflicting allegiances that provide inescapable elements of community formation and self-construction. In doing so he also helps us reconsider what we might mean by deploying the terms personal, political and postmodern. To know something of what holds a society together, what makes a small community out of disparate individuals and a larger society out of small communities, we need to look not just at society's institutions, public forums and public debates, but at the modes of social interaction that give these institutions, forums and debates their social legitimacy and social function.

To speak in a Pinter play, to engage or refuse to engage in that most hazardous of forms of interaction, is not just to participate in a community but to engage in a process of community reinforcement, community contestation and community reorganisation in which the precarious status of the self is constantly mediated through its precarious and conflicting allegiances to others. Speaking is a means of consolidating the *status quo*, exploring the *status quo* and altering the *status quo* and it involves attempts to exert control that always put the speaker at risk of being controlled. But the local site of social exchange is the one at which the claims of the individual in a small community context can most powerfully challenge or sustain the claims, however formulated or presented, of a larger collective life.

In his own life, the early Pinter as a public figure recognised the risk of moving beyond local artistic contexts to larger public forums and judged the potential losses to be greater than the potential gains. The later Pinter, determinedly addressing public forums, reverses that judgment without losing sight of the risks involved. Whether he is justified in taking such risks remains to be seen, but both early and later Pinter share the same recognition of what is at stake in speaking out directly, speaking indirectly or refusing to speak: 'You and I, the characters which grow on a page, most of the time we're inexpressive, giving little away, unreliable, elusive, evasive, obstructive, unwilling. But it's out of these attributes that a language arises.'[46] And it is through such languages that differences are mediated, contractual commitments are reconciled, individual convictions arise, communities emerge and complex societies seek politically and otherwise both to stabilise and to reconstitute themselves.[47]

NOTES

Earlier versions of different parts of this chapter were included in presentations made at the American Repertory Theatre for its 1991 production of *The Homecoming*, at the 1991 International Pinter Festival at Ohio State University honouring Pinter on reaching the age of sixty, at the American Repertory Theatre for its 1993 production of *The Caretaker* and at the 1997 International Pinter Symposium at Trinity College, Dublin.

1. Tom Stoppard, *Rosencrantz and Guildenstern are Dead* (New York: Grove Press, 1967), p. 41.
2. Thomas F. Van Laan, '*The Dumb Waiter*: Pinter's Play with the Audience', *Modern Drama*, 24 (December 1981), 494–502. See also my brief response in 'The Temporality of Structure in Pinter's Plays', *The Pinter Review*, 1 (1987), 18–19.
3. Susan Hollis Merritt traces the changes in Pinter's political positioning in 'Pinter and Politics', in *Harold Pinter: A Casebook*, ed. Lois Gordon (New York and London: Garland, 1990), pp. 129–60.
4. Harold Pinter in *Conversations with Pinter*, ed. Mel Gussow (New York: Grove Press, 1994), p. 82.
5. See, for example, his remark in 1961: 'I'm not committed as a writer, in the usual sense of the term, either religiously or politically. And I'm not conscious of any particular social function. I write because I want to write.' 'Writing for Myself', *Complete Works: Two* (New York: Grove Press, 1977), p. 12.
6. See, for example, Pinter's remarks in his interview with Nicholas Hern: 'I came to view politicians and political structures and political acts with something I can best describe as detached contempt. To engage in politics seemed to me futile.' 'A Play and Its Politics', *One for the Road* (New York: Grove Press, 1986), p. 12.
7. Harold Pinter, 'Writing for the Theatre', *Complete Works: One* (New York: Grove Press, 1977), p. 13.
8. Harold Pinter, interview with L. M. Bensky, 'The Art of the Theatre, iii', *Paris Review*, 10 (Fall 1996), 27.
9. Harold Pinter, '"Funny and Moving and Frightening": Pinter' (interview with Kathleen Halton), *Vogue*, 150 (1 October 1967), 236.
10. Harold Pinter, *One for the Road*, pp. 50–1.
11. Harold Pinter, *Mountain Language* (New York: Grove Press, 1988), pp. 43–7.
12. Daryl Chin, 'Interculturalism, Postmodernism, Pluralism', *Performing Arts Journal*, 33/34 (1989), 163–75.
13. Jean-François Lyotard, *The Postmodern Condition: A Report on Knowledge*, trans. Geoff Bennington and Brian Massumi (Minneapolis, MI: University of Minnesota Press, 1984), pp. 79–82.
14. Ihab Hassan, *The Dismemberment of Orpheus: Towards a Postmodern Literature* (Madison, WI: University of Wisconsin Press, 1982), p. 264: 'We are all, I suspect, a little Victorian, Modern, and Postmodern at once. And an author may ... easily write both a modernist and postmodernist work.' For Hassan, the avant-garde, the modern and postmodern are 'three modes of artistic change', p. 266.
15. Besides the works cited by Lyotard, Hassan and Chin, other useful commentaries include Fredric Jameson's essay 'Postmodernism and Consumer Society', in *Postmodernism and Its Discontents*, ed. E. Ann Kaplan (London and New York: Verso, 1988), pp. 13–29; Andreas Huyssen, *After the Great Divide* (Bloomington, IN: Indiana University Press, 1986); Linda Hutcheon, *The Politics of Postmodernism* (London and New York: Routledge, 1989); Christopher Norris, *What's Wrong with Postmodernism: Critical Theory and the Ends of Philosophy* (Baltimore, MD: Johns Hopkins University Press, 1990); David Harvey, *The Condition of Postmodernity* (Oxford and Cambridge, MA: Blackwell, 1989).

These arguments are not, however, all of a piece, and there is significant and continuing disagreement over the nature of and relationship among the avant-garde, modernism and postmodernism, not the least of which is whether postmodernism should be considered a genre category or a period category.

16. Harvey deals illuminatingly with the tension in high modernism between the ephemeral and the eternal, *The Condition of Postmodernity*, pp. 10–38.

17. A writer as prolific and as inventive as Artaud regularly moves from one voice to the others and back again. See, in particular, his *The Theatre and Its Double*, trans. Mary Caroline Richards (New York: Grove Press, 1958).

18. This concern is strongly voiced in intercultural terms by Chin, 'Interculturalism, Postmodernism, Pluralism', pp. 165–6.

19. Harold Pinter, *No Man's Land, Complete Works: Four* (New York: Grove Press, 1981), p. 80. This tension between assertion and aspiration is central to the play and to the moments of arrested motion that recur within it. For further development of this argument see my essay 'Time for Change in *No Man's Land*', in *Harold Pinter: A Casebook*, ed. Gordon, pp. 33–59. See also the use Michael Billington makes of this argument in his book, *The Life and Work of Harold Pinter* (London: Faber, 1996), pp. 242–50.

20. Lyotard is responding to Jürgen Habermas's *Legitimization Crisis*, trans. Thomas McCarthy (Minneapolis, MI: University of Minnesota Press, 1975).

21. Lyotard, *The Postmodern Condition*, pp. 10 and 66.

22. See, for example, Bernard Levin's review of the 1977 revival of *The Caretaker*:

> The truth remains that Mr Pinter has nothing whatever to say, and that a drum makes a noise when you hit it because it is empty … [From *The Caretaker*] nothing emerges. There is no sense of a view, however oblique, of these characters, no disclosure of a general truth based on particular conclusions, no comment, wise or otherwise, on anything. We come out exactly the same people as we were when we entered; we have been entertained, we have admired the author's ability, we have not been bored. But we have advanced our understanding and our humanity not a whit, and every experience we have had has been of an entirely superficial nature.
>
> 'The Hollow Art of Harold Pinter', *The Sunday Times*,
> 30 October 1977, 38

23. Harold Pinter, quoted by Arlene Sykes, *Harold Pinter* (New York: Humanities Press, 1970), p. 101.

24. Harold Pinter, *The Lover, Complete Works: Two*, p. 193.

25. Harold Pinter, *The Homecoming, Complete Works: Three* (New York: Grove Press, 1978), p. 93.

26. Harold Pinter, *The Dwarfs, Complete Works: Two*, p. 102.

27. Harold Pinter, *Landscape, Complete Works: Three*, p. 188.

28. Harold Pinter, *The Caretaker, Complete Works: Two*, p. 19.

29. Harold Pinter, *The Collection, Complete Works: Two*, p. 151.

30. Harold Pinter, in *Conversations with Pinter*, ed. Gussow, p. 71. The reference is to *The Birthday Party, Complete Works: One*, p. 96.

31. For further discussion, see my essay 'Design and Discovery in Pinter's *The Lover*', in *Harold Pinter: Critical Approaches*, ed. Steven H. Gale (London and Toronto: Associated University Presses, 1986), pp. 82–101.

32. As Pinter uncertainly put it in 1989,

   I'm only concerned at the moment with accurate and precise images of what
   is the case. I can no longer write a play about a family and what happens to
   it, except that in *One for the Road*, I remind you, the man, woman and child
   are actually husband, wife and he's their child. Therefore, in a rather odd
   way, that play is about what happens to a family.
                           Conversations with Pinter, ed. Gussow, p. 92.

   At this point, of course, *Moonlight* was still some years ahead.

33. 'It's about love and lack of love … There's no question that the family does behave
   very calculatingly and pretty horribly to each other and to the returning son. But
   they do it out of the texture of their lives and for other reasons which are not evil
   but slightly desperate.' Harold Pinter, quoted by Henry Hewes, 'Probing Pinter's
   Play', *Saturday Review* (8 April 1967), 56.

34. Harold Pinter, *Landscape*, pp. 197–8; *Betrayal, Complete Works: Four*, p. 197;
   The Birthday Party, p. 96.

35. Harold Pinter, *No Man's Land*, p. 108.

36. Harold Pinter, *Landscape*, p. 198; *No Man's Land*, p. 80; Harold Pinter, *The
   Homecoming*, pp. 73–4; *Family Voices*, in *Other Places* (New York: Grove Press,
   1983), p. 76; *Moonlight* (New York: Grove Press, 1993), p. 1.

37. Harold Pinter, *The Dwarfs*, p. 107.

38. 'I was always termed, what is the word, "minimalist". Maybe I am. Who knows?
   But I hope that to be minimalist is to be precise and focused. I feel that what I've
   illuminated is quite broad – and deep – shadows stretching away.' Harold Pinter,
   in *Conversations with Pinter*, ed. Gussow, p. 75.

39. 'I thought, what would happen if two people knocked on [Stanley's] door? … The
   idea of the knock came from my knowledge of the Gestapo … The war had only
   been over less than ten years.' Harold Pinter, in *Conversations with Pinter*, ed.
   Gussow, p. 71.

40. Harold Pinter, *Tea Party, Complete Works: Three*, p. 103.

41. The use of the title 'Other Places' both for a combined performance of *Family
   Voices*, *Victoria Station* and *A Kind of Alaska* and for their collective publication
   signals a continuing interest in Len's 'There must be somewhere else' (*The Dwarfs*,
   p. 107) along with a sustained further extension of the realm of exploration.

42. 'The Temporality of Structure in Pinter's Plays', pp. 7–21. See also Pinter's
   comment: 'I still feel there is a role somewhere for a kind of work which is not
   in strict terms pursuing the normal narrative procedures of drama. It's to be
   found, and I'm trying to find it.' *Conversations with Pinter*, ed. Gussow, p. 92.

43. Eugène Ionesco, *Notes and Counter Notes: Writings on the Theatre*, trans.
   Donald Watson (New York: Grove Press, 1964), pp. 106–8.

44. *Ibid.*, p. 93.

45. Kenneth Tynan, quoted in Ionesco, *Notes and Counter Notes*, p. 95.

46. Harold Pinter, 'Between the Lines', *The Sunday Times*, 4 March 1962, mag.
   sec. 25.

47. For further discussion of the modern/postmodern context of Pinter's work, see
   Austin Quigley, 'Ibsen's Ghosts and Pinter's Heirs: Tracing the Trajectories of
   Modernism' in *One Hundred Year Commemoration of the Life of Henrik Ibsen*,
   ed. G. O. Mazur, Semenenko Foundation, New York, 2007, pp. 49–80.

2

JOHN STOKES

Pinter and the 1950s

What did the actor David Baron prefer to read when he came off the stage at the Palace Court Theatre, Bournemouth, in 1956 after an evening playing Mr Rochester in an adaptation of *Jane Eyre?* Where did he turn for intellectual stimulus during that long season at the Pavilion Theatre, Torquay, in the same year when he played, among some thirteen roles in all, minor characters in Coward and Colette? What confirmed, what disturbed, his view of the state of English drama when, two years later, at the Intimate Theatre, Palmers Green, he coupled routine detective roles with Cliff in *Look Back in Anger?*[1]

Allowing that nothing could be as pressing as the cricket scores, we do know that he turned to Kafka, Yeats and Beckett because their presence is palpable in the subsequent plays of his *alter ego*, Harold Pinter. We might assume that, as a professional, Pinter/Baron would have turned to the trade journals, probably to *The Stage*, and it is a reasonable guess that, as an intellectual, he would have read *Encore*, founded in 1954, the foremost radical theatre journal of the time. Even if he had already determined to go his own way, showing the lack of interest, sometimes active distaste, for theatre criticism that has characterised his later career, the contributors to *Encore* themselves certainly studied his plays as soon as they arrived on the scene and, through a series of developing aesthetic assumptions, made powerful sense of them.

It is, of course, entirely possible that these *Encore* critics found in the plays significances of which Pinter himself was completely unaware. Their responses remain important. Current reception theory makes much of the interpretative structures, the habits and the preconceptions, that shape the meanings that are given to texts, arguing that these invariably override any authorial intention.[2] Interpretation has less to do with the passive business of recognising influences than with the interactive expectations that any member of an audience brings to each new theatrical experience.

There certainly were shared assumptions at work in *Encore*, of which the most important, by far, was the conviction that theatre is in essence a social art. From *The Birthday Party* (1958) to *The Homecoming* (1965), Pinter's plays were subjected to long and serious criticism on that basis, and it was the Encore Publishing Company that produced, in 1959, the first edition of *The Birthday Party*, which it advertised as 'not only pungently funny and disquietingly macabre, but rich with concern about the state of our society'. This enthusiasm challenges the myth of baffled incomprehension that has surrounded Pinter's emergence. It was by no means only Harold Hobson, politically conservative and religious, who recognised something new and important; a more radical wing did too.[3]

Although *Encore* saw its main function as championing new drama and challenging the *status quo*, it drew heavily on the ideas of the 'New Left', the collective name for those young intellectuals who, in the wake of Suez and the Hungarian revolution, both of 1956, were inspired by Richard Hoggart, Raymond Williams and E.P. Thompson to advance new ways of understanding the relationship of culture to society.[4] So, for instance, the major talking point in *Encore* in 1957 and 1958 was Lindsay Anderson's radical polemic, 'Vital Theatre', in which he maintained that '*Encore* should not be expressing *every* point of view, but the *right* one.'[5] This provoked more reaction than any other single item, with correspondence both supporting and questioning Anderson's belief that the value of ideas ultimately lay in their political effectiveness and, at other times, insisting on the need to distinguish between ideological correctness and intellectual authoritarianism.

Inevitably, *Encore* contributors displayed a burgeoning interest in Brecht, not that this precluded space being given to Ionesco and Sartre and, among local heroes, to Joan Littlewood and Sean O'Casey. Among the up and coming directors Peter Brook, George Devine, Charles Marowitz, Stephen Joseph, all offered their opinions, so did Tyrone Guthrie; among practising playwrights Bernard Kops, Ted Willis and John Whiting joined in discussions; among established critics Eric Bentley and Kenneth Tynan, who orchestrated symposia. The magazine reached out beyond the theatre to the 'Angry Young Men' of the popular newspapers, to Colin Wilson, and even to Kingsley Amis, who, unhelpfully, told its readers, 'I think I am like many people of my age and upbringing in that I know almost nothing about the theatre, and more or less make a point of not finding anything out.'[6] A few unbroken spirits of an older generation were welcome. Priestley sent attacks on 'bardolatry'; O'Casey savaged *Waiting for Godot*:

> That Beckett is a clever writer, and that he has written a rotting and remarkable play, there is no doubt; but his philosophy isn't my philosophy, for within him there is no hazard of hope; no desire for it; nothing in it but a lust for despair, and a crying of woe, not in a wilderness, but in a garden.[7]

O'Casey's fighting talk was founded on a traditional Marxist, materialist, dislike of all forms of pessimism, but there are plenty of signs elsewhere in *Encore* of another, more up to date, political context within which the work of new playwrights, Pinter among them, would be received. It was largely derived from French existentialism.

Sifting through the early issues of *Encore* now,[8] the special interest in all things French is immediately noticeable. This was, in some ways, a development out of the francophilia of the 1940s, which had embraced French culture as part of the post-war attempt to return to 'civilised values'. In 1945 and 1946 A. J. Ayer contributed pieces on Sartre and Camus to Cyril Connolly's *Horizon*, setting a precedent which carried over into, for instance, Iris Murdoch's first book: a study of Sartre published in 1953.[9] By the mid 1950s, though, the emphasis had shifted from pure philosophy to existentialism's attempt to cut through the rhetoric of the Cold War.[10]

The keyword was 'commitment'. Anderson ended his 'Vital Theatre' piece with the war cry, 'You see – the question of commitment raises its obstinate, contemporary head. You can't get away from it',[11] but in its original Sartrian sense the word had less to do with loyalty to a single '*right*' point of view than with, almost the opposite, the ability to remain open to political circumstance and to respect what that might mean for the writer. Sartre himself had put it this way in 'The Case for Responsible Literature' (*La littérature engagée*), parts of which were published in *Horizon* in 1945:

> We write for our contemporaries, we do not wish to view our world with eyes of the future – for that would be the surest method of destroying it – but with our fleshly eyes, with our real, mortal eyes. We do not wish to win our case by appeal, and we have no use for a posthumous rehabilitation: it is here and in our lifetimes that cases are won and lost.[12]

A 'committed style', then, was one that strove above all else to grasp the present. This ideal had important implications for the drama. As Raymond Williams explained in *Encore* in 1959: the Left had for so long in the past been associated with particular kinds of drama – initially realism, later expressionism and its offshoots – that it was hard to realise that these equations 'have been partly the result of a crude Marxist theory of culture; partly of national and historical circumstances'. Speaking for himself, Williams asserted that he was now interested in any claim for the progressiveness of a particular theatrical form, and that he would remain open to multiple possibilities as long as they gave evidence of having grown out of 'a real common consciousness'.[13] In the writings of the *Encore* critics, as well as those by members of the New Left, often Williams-inspired, we find, again and again, this stress on communal experience.

Although Williams always insisted that drama must exist in relation to a community, he was aware that, in the modern world, communities could overlap and interact. Indeed, most people belonged to several. The working class, in particular, was part of a universal network of mass communications at the same time as daily lives remained rooted in local customs – which now rarely included theatre-going, if indeed they ever had done.

'Community' and 'commitment' were therefore closely related ideas. The young radicals writing for *Encore* were able to respond positively to new forms because 'commitment' was a concept broad enough to embrace many different kinds of creativity and they could relate them to notions of social community (despite the traditional associations of 'social drama') because the concept itself was changing. As Williams had gone on to explain, realist conventions involved 'both gain and loss: a gain for reality as against outworn theatrical artifices; a loss in being limited, by the criterion of probable behaviour and probable conversation, to a single dramatic dimension: the loss in intensity of language being the most serious'.[14] *Encore* critics would be able to show that Pinter's dramatic milieus, where the language could be exceptionally intense, were permeated with secret threats precisely because of the willed blindness, the Sartrian 'bad faith', of social life.

Irving Wardle's celebrated essay on Pinter, 'Comedy of Menace', published in *Encore* in 1958, follows this line by drawing attention to Pinter's handling of 'destiny': 'not as an austere exercise in classicism, but as an incurable disease which one forgets about most of the time and whose lethal reminders may take the form of a joke'. Destiny as disease is 'an apt dramatic motif for an age of conditioned behaviour in which orthodox man is a willing collaborator in his own destruction'.[15]

The nature of dramatic speech was at issue here. While Pinter's language was obviously not transparently realistic in the manner of Ted Willis or even Arnold Wesker, neither did it derive from symbolism like the lapidary style of Beckett. The *Encore* view in general was that Pinter mimicked a social discourse degraded and deformed by environmental pressure, and that he was politically apposite for just that reason – though the critics could nevertheless recognise the comic and expressive qualities of demotic idioms when they contested the supposed impersonality of modern life.

And so, at the same time as Pinter himself was pronouncing that there were 'two things', men and society, 'both exist and the one makes the other',[16] Tom Milne was writing about *The Dumb Waiter* and *The Room* that not only were they 'wildly funny, macabre, studded with moments of startling theatrical excitement', but they 'lift themselves out of the rut of the fashionable genre by their relevance to the problems aroused by our particular society, and our relationship with that society'.[17] Milne looked forward to a 'second full-length play' which he understood 'was on its way'. This, when it arrived in 1965, turned out to be *The Homecoming*, described in *Encore* by the sociologist Stuart Hall very much on his own terms. It was, wrote Hall,

> Pinter's contribution to the growing literature about, and interest in, the so-called close ties which exist in the extended-kinship family. It is a sort of bizarre footnote to *Family and Kinship in East London*. It is a sort of sketch for a thesis at the Institute of Community Studies. Its roots lie in the fantasies, rather than the social relationships, which seem to Pinter to underpin these families. His purpose is to expose the machinery of fantasy. In this limited aim he is brilliantly successful – his grip on the reality behind the rituals finding, in his use of language, a near-perfect stylised expression.[18]

The repeated move from community to language and back again, initially sanctioned by Williams, allowed critics to pay attention to the distinctive qualities of Pinter's dialogue without questioning the reality of the social experience that produced it. Hall's term, 'fantasy', refers not to the delusory dreams of the playwright but to the closely observed behaviour of his characters, which again displays something like Sartrian 'bad faith': unawareness, self-deception, a passive and disabling response to apparently deterministic processes and an acceptance of institutional oppression.

The enthusiasm of the *Encore* critics reveals the political dimension of Pinter's work; his abiding perception that political reality invariably lies buried beneath official language, was grasped from the start. The famous interrogation scene in *The Birthday Party*; the Director's Christmas Day speech to 'the staff, the under-staff and the patients' in *The Hothouse*, Churchillian in its self-regard, quite regal in its banal cosiness; the horror of coercive psychiatry – ECT in *The Caretaker*, therapy as torture in *The Hothouse* – are only the most obvious vindication of their claims.

Pinter's early visions of local totalitarianism spoke directly to a constituency that, like himself, was steeped in Orwell and Kafka and the anti-fascist plays of Sartre and John Whiting. Indeed, *Encore*'s recognition that Pinter's skill lay in political uncovering has been ratified further by his work for Amnesty, his demands for human freedom and his hatred of imperialist foreign policies because they all tell lies, co-opting the language of human rights while secretly supporting despotism. The young man who refused to do National Service, not because he was uncompromisingly pacifist on all occasions but because he could not see the point of the Cold War, has matured into a political activist who consistently attempts to judge situations in their authenticity by dispelling the miasma of ideological rhetoric.

It would be wrong, though, to see the *Encore* critics (or any other school) as having the final say. There were gaps in their approach which the passage of history has subsequently revealed – just as our current blind spots will no doubt be exposed in their turn. The current orthodoxy which insists that what we call 'identity' is exclusively determined neither by social nor by biological pressures (nor even by a combination of both), but is actively constructed out of ideas – of class, of race, of gender, and of sexuality in particular – has led to a concern with the power of language that has made us at the millennium even more sensitive to the ways in which political power operates, at every level and in every sphere. The contexts have changed and the political priorities of *Encore* are no longer quite in place.

It is instructive to note, for example, that although Raymond Williams in 1959 was happy to concede that Errol John's *Moon on a Rainbow Shawl*, which is set very precisely in post-war Trinidad, was 'interesting because it brings in a new way of life', he should have been even more concerned to place it within the context of 'the traditional liberal revolt – the break-out of the frustrated individual'.[19] Today we might well wish to reverse those comments by stressing the importance of John's play in the history of modern Caribbean drama. In a similar way, the presumption that 'community' is the prerogative of a white working class obscures the existence of other sectors. When Pinter turned to middle-class milieus in the 1970s it was too easy to condemn him as a traitor, a victim of intellectual *embourgeoisement* and to forgo intelligent critical analysis of the plays. And while *Encore*'s account of his dramatic speech as the 'fantasy' born of social deprivation steered a useful middle course between the claims of 'pure poetry' on the one hand and the absurdist view of language as a net over a void on the other, it underestimated the power of those subcultural codes, those private languages, in which Pinter obviously specialised and which more recent commentators have come to appreciate for their own sake.

Above all, the political aspect of the sexual behaviour portrayed not just by Pinter but by all the new (and less new) dramatists of the fifties and early sixties, was seriously underestimated, in radical magazines as much as in the public prints. In many critical accounts of Pinter the relationships between and among men and women are passed over without comment, with the result that his seemingly ritualised view of sexuality is taken for granted. His depiction of female experience goes unquestioned, and there is an unwillingness to acknowledge the same-sex relationships which range from sibling loyalty in *The Homecoming*, to male bonding in *The Dumb Waiter*, to something close to gay marriage in *The Collection*.

II

If to be 'committed' is to be alert to the times in which one lives, and to one's own position in relation to events, then in matters of class, race, gender and sexuality Pinter's early work undoubtedly showed 'commitment'. This was not so much by overt political argument, 'propaganda', as by formal innovation, by interventions and disruptions, the ways in which the plays continually turn the object of social disquiet into a matter of subjective concern. Pinter brought new perspectives to a London that was cut across by barriers of class, a city that was racially divided, sexually violent and generally exploitative. The urban grid is revealed as the squared board of some mysterious power-playing game.

When Irving Wardle in 1958 described Pinter as 'the poet of London transport',[20] he recognised him, rightly, as someone on the move. But the routes are not equally available (getting to Sidcup takes a good deal of thought and preparation) and there are barriers to be crossed. Pinter's London is zoned and it is only permeable for those who have the right qualifications. To move around with ease and confidence requires documents, intellectual or academic credibility, cash. Not until Teddy in *The Homecoming* is there much in the way of upward mobility – and little good it does him. Yet, like the indifferent sound of London traffic that can be heard in the background throughout the TV production of *The Collection*, the city is always there. From the early *The Black and White* monologue, where even crossing Waterloo Bridge is an adventure, to *Old Times*, where cultural London is a landscape of memory, the city is a place of journeys to be measured not by distance but by difficulty, by territorial hurdles and unexpected invitations.

Pinter's 1950s London, then, is very different from the capital of immediately post-war sentiment – the undifferentiated city of Hubert Gregg's 'Maybe it's because I'm a Londoner' or Coward's 'London Pride', though these versions were still on offer. Joan Littlewood was not immune to the rough charms of Cockneydom and in 1957 the playwright Wolf Mankowitz could still pronounce (in, ironically enough, *Encore*) that so far as he was concerned the true English hero was 'the veteran cockney, old, out-moded, old-fashioned, an infantryman who sweats, and stinks, and is stewed to the eyebrows, and who has no place at all and who is not wanted, can contribute nothing, yet embodies – for me – much more fundamental qualities than the outsiders, the insiders, and the backsiders'.[21]

Mankowitz, though he shared Pinter's Jewish background, was in almost every other respect his opposite as a writer. The film of his *A Kid for Two Farthings* (1955) begins with a god-like view of London that follows the flight of a pigeon from the dome of St Paul's down to a bustling Petticoat Lane as if freedom of movement were as easy and uncomplicated for human beings as it is for birds. And unlike his other contemporary, Lionel Bart, Pinter has never had much interest in the schmaltz that eases pain; overripe sentiment is more often a weapon in the interpersonal armoury. Pinter's London is the place where a good time is categorically not had by all. There's nothing jovial or communal about Harry's 'slum slug' speech in *The Collection*:

> Bill's a slum boy, you see, he's got a slum sense of humour. That's why I never take him along with me to parties. Because he's got a slum mind. I have nothing against slum minds *per se*, you understand, nothing at all. There's a certain kind of slum mind which is perfectly all right in a slum, but when this kind of slum mind gets out of the slum it sometimes persists, you see, it rots everything. That's what Bill is. There's something faintly putrid about him, don't you find? Like a slug. There's nothing wrong with slum slugs in their place, but this one won't keep his place – he crawls all over the walls of nice houses, leaving slime, don't you, boy? [22]

Even now this shocks as much by its vindictive determination to keep the spatial hierarchies of the city firmly in place as by its reversion to a Darwinistic language of urban degeneration last heard in, say, Jack London.

Pinter's most famous travelling man is Davies, the tramp in *The Caretaker*. Apparently inspired by at least one real individual,[23] Davies is someone with a strong sense of where he wants to go, though uncertain about where he belongs. He is, for a start, Welsh, not a born Londoner. He's neither a minimalist philosopher nor a free spirit. Though Pinter's admiration for Beckett is self-confessed, Davies is as far a cry from Didi and Gogo as he is from a Chaplin waif or from Bud Flanagan's stoical dossers. He does have a social identity, though: his refusal to concede to others the right to relocation that he demands for himself makes him, if not the first, then certainly the most authentic, portrait of a contemporary racist in modern British drama.

In 1948 when the famous 450 Jamaicans on the *Emperor Windrush* disembarked at Tilbury they were greeted with curiosity, and even charity, along with the inevitable signs of 'race prejudice' – but it was not long before they, and the other Caribbean immigrants who soon followed them, provoked deeper and more single-minded attitudes. This ugly potential is signalled in an ironical moment at the end of Basil Dearden's 1950 film *Pool of London*: a West Indian sailor (Earl Cameron) returns home after a brief but brutal stay in London where he has been tricked, betrayed by a white friend and prevented by neighbourhood hostility from developing his relationship with a white girl. The final shot shows him standing on deck looking back on the city that has rejected him as his ship returns to sea. In reality, most of the West Indian immigrants stayed on to face a groundswell of opinion epitomised in Davies's pathetic resentment, and to endure a grim social climate whose most famous symptom was the Notting Hill riots of 1958.

Although the authorities were eager to explain them away as the work of a handful of Teddy-boy extremists, the riots had complex and, to a degree, local causes. If they reflected endemic racism throughout the country, that was mainly because they 'were as much about the feelings of exclusion and deprivation experienced by a wide swathe of the English population as they were about the presence of black migrants'.[24] Liberal white playwrights, those who tried to appreciate the truth of this situation, responded with dramas based on the assumption that the appropriate response to what was called, offensively, 'the colour problem' could only be 'problem drama'. A pioneering TV play, A Man from the Sun (1956), follows the picaresque journey of a Caribbean immigrant through the largely prejudiced and totally uncomprehending white world.[25] In Ted Willis's Hot Summer Night (1958) a senior white trades unionist is made to face the fact that his reactionary antagonism to black immigrants runs counter to radical tradition, though once again the issue hangs equally on fears of a sexual relationship between his daughter and a black man. In these kinds of realist drama the risk is always that black people will become the honourable victims of white complexity and, to that extent, be reduced to ciphers. While purporting to be about blacks, the plays are really about whites.

Although Pinter was alert to the political situation, his way of working was different. None of his allusions to race respect the realist rule that an unquestioning focus on a previously identified – and prejudged – situation is the only starting point. For Pinter racism is a tactical premise, a subjective position, rather than an objective 'problem', despite the fact of it being so widespread. He neither explains nor excuses, but shows racism in action as a state of mind, as an incidental phenomenon not to be understood in isolation. This is even true of the looming presence of Riley the mysterious 'blind Negro' in The Room, Pinter's first play. While the housewife, Rose, merely worries about 'foreigners', her husband Bert, with a cry of 'Lice', assaults him violently. In many ways Riley has the appearance of being a symbolic figure owing something perhaps to Yeats or to those prophetic figures who feature in the dramas of the thirties and forties – the Inspector in Priestley's An Inspector Calls or Sir Henry Harcourt-Reilly in Eliot's The Cocktail Party. Pinter would probably concur with this placing. 'I've always seen Riley', he once said, 'as a messenger, a potential saviour who is trying to release Rose from the imprisonment of the room and the restrictions of her life with Bert. He's inviting her to come back to her spiritual home; which is why he gets beaten up when Bert returns. But, to me, Riley has always been a redemptive figure ...'[26]

If The Room casts the black man in the role of a representative redeemer, The Caretaker puts black people collectively offstage. Davies's racist outbursts recoil against himself; they are indiscriminate ('Poles, Greeks, Blacks, the lot of them, all of them aliens'[27]) and they are paranoid ('them Blacks making noises, coming up through the walls'[28]). In the fragmented awareness of a racist society aliens are always simultaneously there and not there, provoking violence and fear by their absent presence. The nasty fantasies of Davies, the self-dispossessed hobo, make that point with unmistakable force.

Sexual imaginings, by virtue of their private nature, have, in contrast, to be drawn out by processes of attribution – often, paradoxically, by the very forces that would seek to hide them away. The 1950s are a supposedly dull period in the history of sexual mores and it is true that many of Pinter's would-be genteel characters (Meg in *The Birthday Party*, for instance) have perfected a curiously respectable double-speak which enables them to hint at sexual longings without actually naming them. In fact, the decade witnessed an obsessive interest in the subject in which, in classic Foucauldian fashion, political and medical attempts to control sexual behaviour through surveillance did more than simply mask, they actively expressed, the elusive play of desire.[29] Once again the works of Pinter, no less than any of his contemporaries, belong in this context. Sex for Pinter is invariably a double bind, a power struggle and a mind-game in which there is no certain victor and no end in sight.

The ways in which processes of liberalisation and surveillance can intertwine were epitomised by the enquiry conducted by Sir John Wolfenden into the laws on prostitution and on homosexuality in the middle of the decade which culminated in his famous report published in 1957, the Street Offences Act of 1959 and the changes in the laws governing homosexual behaviour that were eventually enacted in 1967. The coupling of issues, linked through legislation alone, is revealing and, in both cases, it can be said that Wolfenden's recommendations led, at least at first, to increased persecution as new offenders were hunted down and brought into the courts to face even more intrusive questioning. The drive against prostitution in the form of increased penalties for public solicitation was motivated by worries about the public displays of immorality that all too obviously gave the game away about 'the British way of life'. (According to some reports, the Wolfenden enquiry had originally been prompted by Parliamentary embarrassment at the spectacle of sexual opportunities that the West End offered to foreign tourists visiting London for the Coronation in 1953.[30]) Homosexual 'reform', while liberal in intent, was equally punitive in practice.

The prevalence of prostitution in early Pinter is unmissable, socially evident while socially taboo – as it was on the streets of London until, probably as the unforeseen result of Wolfenden, there was a switch from 'street-walkers' to 'call-girls' with an accompanying increase in the power of the pimps. That process may well remind us of the chosen lifestyle of Ruth in *The Homecoming* as well as of the anonymous, would-be genteel, woman in *A Night Out* (1960) who 'entertains a few gentlemen', and who displays a photograph of herself as a little girl pretending that it is her own daughter now away at boarding school. It is also true, of course, that prostitution was a common theme in influential dramas from abroad: Tennessee Williams's *A Streetcar Named Desire*, for instance, or Sartre's *The Respectable Prostitute*, both of which represent the woman's plight in bleak but sympathetic terms. In Vivien Merchant's extraordinary performance for the television version of *A Night Out* enforced solitude begets fragile fortitude, as if Blanche DuBois had somehow been transplanted to East London. As so often in Pinter survival in the city brings with it thoughts of oblivion, 'sometimes I wish the night would never end' – alongside dreams of leaving – 'Yes, you can see the station from here. All the trains go out, right through the night.'[31]

The popular 1950s view that, in the end, prostitution is merely picturesque (compare *Irma la Douce*, *Can-Can*, or *Fings Ain't Wot They Used T'Be*) has little place here, though *The Lover* (1963), which ends with the husband calling his wife 'you lovely whore', does suggest that sex becomes more interesting when it is transgressive and that bought favours can be an enlivening counterpoint to conventional monogamy. Not surprisingly, a key and often passionate debate about *The Homecoming*, prompted by the developing feminism of the late 1960s and 1970s, has centred on the question of whether by offering herself for prostitution Ruth is regressing to a passive role within the patriarchal structure or rather, by acknowledging her worth and making others respect and pay for it (including her violent pimps), she might not be seen to empower herself through erotic means. Whatever a critic or director finally decides on this issue, the situation is obviously as distant from the jolly pimps and cheeky tarts of Soho musicals as it is from the tear-stained victims of modern melodrama.

In later Pinter the figure of the prostitute will become less significant and from *Old Times* to *Betrayal* to *No Man's Land* to *Moonlight* issues of adultery, of sexual fidelity and of sexual rivalry will dominate in their own right, without reference to the sex industry. This is a mature, and largely middle-class, world of sexual relationships not without its own pain, a sophisticated post-sixties climate where the lifting of public inhibitions only discloses a welter of psychological conflict.

'Are you *virgo intacta*? Have you always been *virgo intacta*?' runs a taunting enquiry in *The Hothouse*, more threatening in 1958 when the play was written than it would have been in 1980 when it was eventually produced on stage. Set in the context of changing sexual mores Pinter's concern with verification becomes more than just an interest in philosophical riddles; it can be recognised as a recurring feature of sexual behaviour that nevertheless varies according to context. In *The Collection*, Pinter takes the clichés of homosexual life and underlines them with broad emphases so that almost any line begins to resonate with a possible *double entendre*: 'You're supposed to be able to use your hands', 'a wow at parties', 'an opera fan', 'a man's man'. Phallic competitiveness (brawling with cheese-knives) is matched by tropes of deceptive, dangerous female attraction (white kittens lovingly stroked) which raise the level of erotic intensity to the point where it topples over into comedy and the game becomes too obvious for words. *The Hothouse*, in particular, presents the sexual life as one in which style counts for everything, 'masculine' and 'feminine' are fashion accessories, aspects of the personality to be over- or underplayed according to the needs of the moment and the demands of other people. Social uncertainty replaces shame and guilt.

Correspondingly, the innate deceptiveness of gender characteristics is frequently expressed through the instability of signification. There is a jump cut in the television production of *A Night Out* which switches from the mother of the hero, Albert Stokes, enjoining him to 'look like a gentleman' to the 'GENTLEMEN' notice on a public toilet, an unfortunate metonymic chain that is extended later on when Albert is accused of 'making a convenience' out of the family house they share. One recalls the unfortunate nickname of an old friend of the Director in *The Hothouse*: 'Boghouse' Peters. There is usually something precarious and messy about masculinity. According to Albert's mum, having sex is 'mucking about with girls', not having sex is 'living a clean life'.

Such theatrical blatancy, the superfluity of sexual imagery, the endless potential for sly double meanings puts sexuality undeniably on display. Instead of hiding sex behind realism, or teasing us with obviously gay goings-on as in the camply elegant but evasive manner of Coward or Rattigan, Pinter draws upon the darker *guignol* of the English thriller tradition – Emlyn Williams's *Night Must Fall*, say, with its sinister 'mother's boy', or Patrick Hamilton's *Rope*, that still popular drama of sado-masochism in which a pair of thrill-seeking killers taunt their elders with good manners and ghoulish acts.[32] At the same time he adds the 'funny voices' of 'intimate revue', strains of Beryl Reid and Sheila Hancock. Though prepared to admit in a letter to the *Sunday Times* in 1960 that he had laughed himself when writing *The Caretaker*, Pinter insisted that the play was only funny 'up to a point': 'Beyond that point it ceases to be funny, and it was because of that point that I wrote it.'[33] The effect is both disorientating and familiar; skimming all geniality from the surface of English comedy.

Throughout early Pinter West End deadpan is faced with steely moments of indecision. Endings are unresolved; events are uncertain, behaviour is unpredictable. Yet in every area of modern urban life – whether the crux is class, race, gender or sexuality – Pinter allows a slim margin of freedom, or potential freedom. 'Stan, don't let them tell you what to do!', as Petey shouts at the end of *The Birthday Party*. To lose the power of choice, to have that taken from you, is to lose the freedom that counts. And this, at heart, is why Pinter himself has always disclaimed prior or privileged knowledge of his characters and why his imagination has consistently delivered works that may be puzzling, but which are never simply 'absurd'.

III

A fundamental truth about Pinter and his relation to historical context was glimpsed in 1960 by the playwright John McGrath in an admittedly digressive article in *Encore* entitled 'Some Other Mechanism'. McGrath was then aged twenty-five, his own early plays lay ahead, but the importance of dramatic freedom was already quite clear to him. Convinced by the failure of Marxism to adapt to present realities, the inability of economic determinism to foresee the future, McGrath looked for other principles upon which to base plays. Having initially divided the theatre of the 1950s into two: 'poetic' plays and 'dramatic' plays, he eventually discovered these in existentialism. The writer of 'poetic' plays takes on the role of God, manipulating his or her characters according to intellectual ends which might be utopian or totalitarian. McGrath is able to cite a string of celebrated 1950s plays of this kind, including Arthur Miller's *The Crucible*, John Arden's *Serjeant Musgrave's Dance*, Nigel Dennis's satire on religion, *The Making of Moo*, Jean Genet's *The Balcony*, and works by Jean Giraudoux and T. S. Eliot. 'Dramatic' plays, on the other hand, replace the demands of the playwright with those of the character. The examples are O'Neill, Chekhov, Ibsen, Chayefsky, Wesker and Sartre.

In order to underline the point that characters and meaning emerge only with the act of writing, McGrath quotes a famous passage in which Sartre criticised the novelist, François Mauriac.

> If I suspect that the hero's future actions are determined in advance by heredity, social influence, *or some other mechanism* [McGrath's italics], my own time ebbs back into me, there remains only myself, reading and persisting, confronting a static book. Do you want your characters to live? See to it that they are free.[34]

McGrath picks up on this by maintaining that the ideal writer should be 'in a position to *explore* the human condition further, deeper, and more intimately, because he is thinking through the condition of the characters he has created, rather than in the abstract'.[35] This allows him to put forward the idea, which has also been consistently maintained over the years by Harold Pinter, that it is an essential paradox of imaginative creation that characters should remain independent of authorial design.

Pinter's own disinclination to attribute an unambiguous motivation to his characters is at one then with the existentialist's refusal to reduce a lifetime of decision-making to a predetermined pattern set in motion by origin or attribute alone. This is not to say that the concepts of identity based on race, on class, on gender, on sexuality, which are now so heavily stressed by critics, are illusory or unimportant, but that their power depends upon the fact that they are continually shifting, lightening, deepening, realigning. It is this that makes them so persistent. Culturally sanctioned identities are capable of frightening reversals, as Pinter famously shows when members of oppressed groups – McCann and Goldberg in *The Birthday Party* – become, seemingly, the oppressors themselves;[36] when, in *The Dumb Waiter*, the hunters become the hunted; when, in *The Hothouse*, the Director ends up at the mercy of his own staff; when, in *The Caretaker*, the tramp gains the upper hand (doesn't he?); when, in *The Homecoming*, the woman is the victor (isn't she?).

Critics have often said that the process of alienation in Pinter's theatre depends on the ways in which the familiar interacts with the unfamiliar.[37] But to be familiar is, by definition, to be historical, to exist in the collective consciousness, to be part of context, and therefore to be susceptible to change. In certain lights, the familiar is unfamiliar too. In which case, the 'real common consciousness', Raymond Williams's phrase, does not exist outside the theatre, clearly visible via a stage representation, so much as inside, where it is made up of the multiple interpretative faculties brought to bear. It is here, within the auditorium, if anywhere, that the playwright belongs himself. He is no longer represented on stage – the modern writer has no spokesman – he observes like any other spectator, watches, wonders and judges. He retains the most important of all freedoms.

This was the existential ideal, and no writer of the fifties came closer to matching it than Harold Pinter. Always in Pinter the terror only culminates, the menace is only confirmed, when observation is banned, when Stanley's spectacles are broken, when he is blindfolded, when he loses sight of context. As for the playwright, his fifties accolade must be, in a sentence he composed himself, where the word 'attended' bears the dual weight of both 'cared for' and 'concentrated upon': 'He attended to the particular but rarely lost sight of the context in which it took place.'[38] That was written about another great games-player of the time, the cricketer Len Hutton, but it describes Pinter's own art precisely.

NOTES

1. David T. Thompson, *Pinter: The Player's Playwright* (Basingstoke: Macmillan, 1985), describes and comments upon Pinter's early career as an actor. Also see Michael Billington, *The Life and Work of Harold Pinter* (London: Faber, 1996).

2. See Susan Hollis Merritt, *Pinter in Play: Critical Strategies and the Plays of Harold Pinter* (Durham, NC, and London: Duke University Press, 1990), and Susan Bennett, *Theatre Audiences: A Theory of Production and Reception* (London: Routledge, 1990).

3. As did an older guard: Clemence Dane paid tribute to Pinter in her English Association lecture, *Approaches to Drama*, of 1961 and Noel Coward admired *The Caretaker* (see Philip Hoare, *Noel Coward: A Biography* (London: Sinclair-Stevenson, 1995), pp. 457–8).

4. See Dan Rebellato, *1956 And All That: The Making of Modern Drama* (London and New York: Routledge), pp. 18–25, and Alan Sinfield, *Literature, Politics and Culture in Postwar Britain* (London and Atlantic Highlands, NJ: Athlone, 1997), chapter 6.

5. Reprinted in a useful selection published in 1965 and reissued in 1981: Charles Marowitz, Tom Milne, Owen Hale (eds.), *New Theatre Voices of the Fifties and Sixties* (London: Eyre Methuen, 1981), pp. 41–51, p. 47.

6. *Encore*, 9 (June–July 1957), 10.

7. *Encore*, 6 (Easter 1956), 7.

8. Easier said than done as the British Library possesses nothing before 1956.

9. Iris Murdoch, *Sartre, Romantic Rationalist* (London: Bowes and Bowes, 1953).

10. There is evidence that Pinter himself was aware of the basic texts. *The Dwarfs* considers suicide as philosophical topic in a way that is ironically reminiscent of Camus's *Myth of Sisyphus*; suicide is also mentioned in a letter about *The Birthday Party* written in 1958. This same letter defines Stanley's dilemma in an existentialist way: 'Stanley cannot perceive his only valid justification – which is he is what he is – therefore he certainly can never be articulate about it', and goes on to rail against 'the shit-stained strictures of centuries of "tradition"' (Billington, *The Life and Work of Harold Pinter*, pp. 77–8). In *The Homecoming*, Pinter appears to have Lenny send up Sartre: 'all this business of being and not-being' (*Plays Three* (London: Faber, 1997)). He has repeatedly referred to writing itself as an act of freedom and the 'nausea' a writer can feel when confronted with the dead weight of stale language ('Writing for the Theatre', *Plays One* (London: Faber, 1996), pp. xi–xii). And it seems more than a coincidence that, in 1964, by now famous, Pinter chose to play Garcin, the epitome of bad faith, in a television production of *Huis Clos*. Sartre's vision of stasis, a permanent state of powerless remembering, might make us think of similar pairs and trios in the plays of Pinter himself.

11. *New Theatre Voices*, p. 47.

12. *Horizon*, 11, 65 (May 1945), 311–12.

13. Raymond Williams, 'Drama and the Left', *Encore*, 5, 2, 19 (March–April 1959), 6–12, p. 6.

14. *Ibid.*

15. Irving Wardle, 'Comedy of Menace', *Encore*, 15, 5, 3 (September–October, 1958), 28–33, p. 33 and *New Theatre Voices*, pp. 86–91, p. 91.

16. Billington, *The Life and Work of Harold Pinter*, pp. 89–90.

17. Tom Milne, 'Double Pinter', *Encore*, 24, 7, 2 (March–April 1960), 38–40, p. 40.

18. Stuart Hall, 'Home, Sweet Home', *Encore*, 56, 12, 4 (July–August 1965), 30–4, p. 34.

19. Williams, 'Drama and the Left', 6.

20. Wardle, 'Comedy of Menace', 33.

21. *Encore*, 9 (June–July, 1957), p. 35.
22. *Plays Two* (London: Faber, 1996), pp. 142–3.
23. Billington, *The Life and Work of Harold Pinter*, pp. 114–16.
24. Mike Philips and Trevor Phillips, *Windrush: The Irresistible Rise of Multi-Racial Britain* (London: HarperCollins, 1999), pp. 169–70.
25. See Jim Pines (ed.), *Black and White in Colour* (London: BFI Publishing, 1992).
26. Billington, *The Life and Work of Harold Pinter*, p. 60. Pinter directed the play himself in 1960, first at Hampstead and then at the Royal Court, 'with a fine black actor called Thomas Baptiste'. The relative absence of black characters has in Pinter had no correlation with the lack of black actors. There were many available – and black writers were achieving higher visibility. See Stuart Hall, 'New World Voices', *Encore*, 5, 3 (September–October 1958), 33–6, and Philip Riley, 'Negro Theatre', *Encore*, 28, 7, 6 (November–December 1960), 11–15.
27. *The Caretaker*, Plays Two, p. 6.
28. *Ibid.*, p. 21.
29. Foucault's ideas underpin Rebellato's account of theatre and sexuality in *1956 And All That*.
30. Paul Ferris, *Sex and the British* (London: Michael Joseph, 1993), p. 157. Wolfenden is discussed in Chapter 8.
31. *Plays One* (London: Faber, 1986), p. 368.
32. 'David Baron' had appeared in the play in Ireland: Billington, *The Life and Work of Harold Pinter*, p. 43. For a discussion of this tradition see my 'Body Parts: the Success of the Thriller' in *Inter-War Theatres*, ed. Maggie Gale and Clive Barker (Cambridge University Press, 2000), pp. 38–62.
33. The *Sunday Times*, 14 August 1960, p. 21.
34. John McGrath, 'Some Other Mechanism: "Poetic" and "Dramatic" Structure in some plays', *Encore*, 7, 4, 26 (July–August 1960), 20–6.
35. *Ibid.*, p. 23.
36. Unless, of course, the pair are answerable to some anonymous, offstage control as was suggested in Sam Mendes's brilliantly period Royal National Theatre production in 1994 – though that, perhaps, only intensifies the insecurity.
37. Merritt, *Pinter in Play*, p. 81.
38. *Collected Poems and Prose* (London: Faber, 1991), p. 95.

3

FRANCESCA COPPA

The sacred joke: comedy and politics in Pinter's early plays

In *Jokes and Their Relation to the Unconscious*, Freud explains that three people are required for the successful telling of a tendentious or purposeful joke. '[In] addition to the one who makes the joke, there must be a second who is taken as the object of the hostile or sexual aggressiveness, and a third in whom the joke's aim of producing pleasure is fulfilled.'[1] In other words, jokes are constructed like theatrical events, and are verbalised for the purpose of pleasing or impressing an audience. If this were not the case, there would be no point in saying the joke aloud: the joke-maker could simply think his amusing thoughts for his own pleasure. The fact that the joke-maker goes to the effort of actually *telling* the joke shows that he is not the primary receiver of pleasure, that the joke is being told for the purpose of creating a relationship with someone else.

Thus the public telling of a joke creates recognisable positions: the aggressor, the victim and the audience. Furthermore, the act of telling a joke forces everyone within earshot to become a part of the event: there is no neutral position. To be within earshot is to be involved: merely to listen to a joke is to declare oneself one way or the other, to be *compromised*. The third party, the audience, is forced to take sides in the conflict between the joke-teller and the victim: to laugh is to ally oneself with the aggressor, to refuse to laugh is to ally oneself with the victim. Comedy thus functions as a sort of litmus test for the audience. Will they laugh or not laugh? With whom will they side?

Freud's joke-theory provides a useful key to Harold Pinter's early plays, which were labelled comedies of menace by the theatre critic Irving Wardle. The early plays are in fact structured like Freud's tendentious jokes. Pinter's plays tend to feature triangulated relationships: as Christopher Innes notes, Pinter's typical cast is three, 'the smallest unstable relationship in which changing alliances can be formed and individuals isolated'.[2] Innes further notes that Pinter's plays are 'variations on the subjects of dominance, control, exploitation, subjugation and victimisation. They are models of power structures.'[3] So, too, do tendentious jokes model power structures; so, too, do jokes illustrate dominance and subjugation. Jokes, like Pinter's plays, create moments of theatrical and dramatic crisis which reveal previously invisible alliances and antagonisms.

It is therefore unsurprising that Pinter's work has been most easily understood by comic playwrights and *farceurs*. Writers such as Noel Coward, Joe Orton and Simon Gray understood Pinter's dramatic project most immediately and instinctively. Similarly, critics have tended to group Pinter with comic playwrights – witness Kenneth Tynan's famous assessment that the playwrights of his time fell into two categories: 'the hairy men – heated, embattled, socially committed playwrights, like John Osborne, John Arden, and Arnold Wesker' and 'the smooth men – cool, apolitical stylists, like Harold Pinter, the late Joe Orton, Christopher Hampton, Alan Ayckbourn, Simon Gray, and [Tom] Stoppard'.[4]

Certainly Pinter's high-level comedic technique puts him on a par with any of the great comic writers. The early plays are often deliberately funny; many of the exchanges within them are structured with the strutting rhythm of polished comedy routines. Consider the opening of *The Dumb Waiter*:

BEN: Kaw!
> *He picks up the paper.*

What about this? Listen to this!
> *He refers to the paper.*

A man of eighty-seven wanted to cross the road. But there was a lot of traffic, see? He couldn't see how he was going to squeeze through. So he crawled under a lorry.

GUS: He what?

BEN: He crawled under a lorry. A stationary lorry.

GUS: No!

BEN: The lorry started and ran over him.

GUS: Go on!

BEN: That's what it says here.

GUS: Get away!

BEN: It's enough to make you want to puke, isn't it?

GUS: Who advised him to do a thing like that?

BEN: A man of eighty-seven crawling under a lorry!

GUS: It's unbelievable.

BEN: It's down here in black and white.

GUS: Incredible.[5]

The timing of this section makes the story a blackly humorous tall tale, and the 'man of eighty-seven' recalls both the 'man who walks into a bar' and 'the chicken that crosses the road'. Pinter invokes that notorious comedic chicken more overtly in the interrogation scene in *The Birthday Party*: 'Why did the chicken cross the road?' is one of the unanswerable questions Goldberg and McCann pose to the beleaguered Stanley Webber. Pinter also skilfully uses comic devices such as repetition (Meg's repeated use of the word 'nice' in *The Birthday Party*'s opening scene), repartee (Mr and Mrs Sands's comic argument over whether or not she saw a star in *The Room*), and physical farce (Gus and Ben's frantic interactions with the dumb waiter in that play), just to name a few.

But Pinter's skilful use of comedy is not incidental or merely pleasurable but rather crucial: the comedy routines in the early plays are maps to the themes and meanings of the plays as a whole. In an early book on George Bernard Shaw, G. K. Chesterton noted that 'amid the blinding jewelry of a million jokes' one could generally 'discover the grave, solemn and sacred joke for which the play was written'.[6] Pinter's works also tend to have identifiable 'sacred jokes' which reproduce the larger play in microcosm: Pinter uses the tendentious joke structure on the micro level as well as the macro. We may not, in the final event, find the larger work *funny*, but that does not mean that the play is not constructed like a joke. Rather, our failure to laugh may be an indication that we, the audience, have come to side (or have been *taught* to side) with the victim over the victimiser.

Consider, again, the opening joke of *The Dumb Waiter* as quoted above. Gus and Ben are hitmen, waiting for their targeted victim to appear. Throughout the play, Ben passes the time by reading stories out of the newspaper. In his essay, 'Mindless Men', Robert Gordon claims that Ben's choice of stories is random, revealing the randomness of Pinter's universe: 'His [Ben's] eyes passed over the page, probably, and happened to stop where they did – perhaps because a bit of dust, swept up when Gus walked in, dropped under Ben's eyelid.'[7] Gordon argues that there had to have been more 'notable' stories in that day's paper than the ones Ben quotes to Gus; hence Ben is reading from the newspaper at random.

But the stories Ben chooses to tell are not random. In the first instance, Ben is deliberately reading the stories *aloud*; like Freud's joke-teller, he is making the effort to announce something he could well keep to himself, since people do generally read newspapers silently. The fact that Ben is taking on the work of reading aloud indicates that he is desiring a particular kind of reaction from Gus, and selecting articles that will produce such a reaction.

Secondly, the stories Ben chooses to tell all follow a very similar pattern. Ben picks out stories which illustrate the stupidity or cruelty of his fellow human beings. An eighty-seven-year-old man wants to cross the street, crawls under a lorry and is killed. The correct response to the story is, 'What an idiot!' In other words, the joke is certainly on him, the little old man. Freud's joke-roles quickly fall into place: Ben, by telling the story, becomes the joke-teller; the old man is the object of the joke; Gus is the third party, the audience member who is supposed to appreciate the story. And Gus makes an effort to appreciate the tale, reacting with encouragement ('He what?') and excited disbelief ('Go on!').

The creation of an alliance between the joke-teller and the audience is the point of the exercise. 'We' are supposed to be laughing at 'them'. Ben, the joke-maker, tells the joke at the expense of the old man, for the purpose of bonding with Gus, whose role is to laugh. Their shared laughter over the story is also a confirmation of their shared ideology. After all, the subtext of Ben's story is 'Stupid people deserve what they get!': this is presumably a comforting ideology for a hitman. You might need to believe that if you are going to kill effectively: yours is not to question why. Someone else has selected your victim, and presumably for good reason. People are stupid and cruel: they deserve whatever comes to them.

But right from the beginning of *The Dumb Waiter*, Gus is not properly filling his appointed role. After his first, correct, expressions of eagerness and interest, Gus then replies: 'Who advised him to do a thing like that?' This is very much the wrong response. By presuming that someone has improperly *advised* the old man, Gus shifts responsibility away from him, placing it instead on the shoulders of the hypothetical adviser whom Gus pictures lurking menacingly in the story's shadows. The world is suddenly more complicated: perhaps the old man did not deserve to die, perhaps the old man was a victim to be pitied. Gus's question begins to undermine the legitimacy of their entire enterprise as hitmen; presumably one cannot kill effectively if one thinks like this. The key problem of the play, the eventual split between Ben and Gus, is foreshadowed in the very first joke.

Pinter repeats the joke a moment later with the newspaper story of the girl who kills a cat. By this point in the play, Gus is even less able to share in Ben's world view:

BEN: A child of eight killed a cat!
GUS: Get away.
BEN: It's a fact. What about that, eh? A child of eight killing a cat!
GUS: How did he do it?
BEN: It was a girl.
GUS: How did she do it?
BEN: She –
      He picks up the paper and studies it.
     It doesn't say.
GUS: Why not?[8]

This time, Gus is even less encouraging; he doesn't just prompt Ben, he questions the story. How did she do it? Why doesn't the article say?

Moreover, Gus actually goes so far as to argue the girl's innocence, suggesting instead that she was framed by her eleven-year-old brother.

Ben is forced to agree with Gus's theory, but almost instantly shifts targets, providing, as he does so, the punchline for the joke: 'A kid of eleven killing a cat and blaming it on his little sister of eight!' Someone must be to blame, someone must be responsible or require punishment, and Ben adds disgustedly, 'It's enough to –' Enough to what? Ben never finishes his sentence. Enough to make you sick? Enough to make you lose your faith in people? Enough to make you want to kill them? What is enough?

But Gus refuses to just laugh along with Ben, to play his role in the joke work. In fact, Gus's questions even manage to shake Ben's faith in the tale he's telling, and in his own aggressive position. But Ben's need to attack soon reasserts itself, and he manages to cap the exchange with a successful punchline.

By the end of the play, Pinter has trained us to see that the content of the joke-exchange is meaningless: what is important is the structure, and the alliances and antagonisms it reveals. Just before the end of the play, he trots out the joke one last time, this time utterly devoid of substance.

BEN: Kaw!
     He picks up the paper and looks at it.
     Listen to this!
     Pause.
     Kaw! What about that, eh?
     Pause.
     Have you ever heard such a thing?
GUS: (*dully*) Go on.
BEN: It's true.
GUS: Get away.
BEN: It's down here in black and white.
GUS: (*very low*) Is that a fact?
BEN: Can you imagine it.
GUS: It's unbelievable.
BEN: It's enough to make you want to puke, isn't it?
GUS: (*almost inaudible*) Incredible.[9]

Ben's position as the aggressive joke-teller is illustrated by the stage action that immediately follows: '*BEN shakes his head. He puts the paper down and rises. He fixes the revolver in his holster.*' Ben tells his story and literally reaches for his gun; as Joe Orton, a fervent admirer of Pinter's, once noted: 'Laughter is a serious business and comedy a weapon more dangerous than tragedy.'[10] Here the weapon-like nature of comedy is made manifest in the stage picture: a connection is made between the joke-maker's verbal violence and his potential for physical violence.

But Gus is now overtly failing to fill his appointed role in his relationship with Ben. Gus has stopped laughing; he has already allied himself with the wrong side in the aggressor–victim conflict. He has failed the litmus test that the joke-structure creates; he is failing to bond with Ben at the expense of another. From the very first joke in *The Dumb Waiter*, Gus has been on the wrong side of the 'us', of the 'we who laugh'; we should not be surprised that by the end of the play Gus literally finds himself on the wrong end of Ben's gun.

Other early Pinter plays follow a similar pattern. *A Slight Ache* also contains a 'sacred joke' which illustrates the play's themes in microcosm. At the beginning of the play, Edward and his wife Flora deal with the small matter of a wasp buzzing around their breakfast table, which produces the following, meticulously timed, comic exchange:

EDWARD: Cover the marmalade.
FLORA: What?
EDWARD: Cover the pot. There's a wasp.
      He puts the paper down on the table.
      Don't move. Keep still. What are you doing?
FLORA: Covering the pot.
EDWARD: Don't move. Leave it. Keep still.
      Pause.
      Give me the 'Telegraph'.
FLORA: Don't hit it. It'll bite.
EDWARD: Bite? What do you mean, bite? Keep still.
      Pause
      It's landing.
FLORA: It's going in the pot.
EDWARD: Give me the lid.
FLORA: It's in.
EDWARD: Give me the lid.
FLORA: I'll do it.
EDWARD: Give it to me! Now … Slowly …
FLORA: What are you doing?
EDWARD: Be quiet. Slowly … carefully … on … the … pot! Ha-ha-ha. Very good.
      He sits on a chair to the right of the table.
FLORA: Now he's in the marmalade.
EDWARD: Precisely.[11]

The joke rebounds on Edward, who, in taking control of the situation, ends up doing the exact opposite of what he first intended, however much he bluffs to the contrary. He has trapped the wasp in the marmalade when his voiced intention was to shoo it away; he has locked in the thing he wanted to expel. This, again, is the play in microcosm. Edward will later identify another intrusive presence: the Matchseller who has been ominously standing by their gate. Again, Edward will bluff and bluster, but he will ultimately invite the Matchseller into his study for a chat. Again, the joke will be on Edward: the end of the play finds the Matchseller welcomed into Flora's home, and Edward himself expelled.

The dynamics of the smaller joke help to illustrate the larger one, the play *A Slight Ache* itself. In the early routine about the wasp, Edward reveals himself to be the arrogant, hyper-masculine husband of comedy: the man who thinks he is in control when he is not, who insists on not getting directions when he gets lost, who insists on tackling home-improvement projects beyond his skill. He goes forth in his aggression against the Matchseller confident in his abilities and in his wife's support, only to learn that his confidence in both is ill-founded. Edward is a man who knows the map, but not the territory – and who has never learned that the map is not the territory. Edward fails to recognise the flowers in his own garden; Edward fails to protect the marmalade. Edward fails, too, to understand and protect his relationship with his wife, the aptly named 'Flora' – and he loses her too as she chooses, instead, to ally herself with the Matchseller at the play's conclusion. Edward thinks he is the joke-maker, but Flora is not amused; like Gus, she has stopped laughing, like Gus, her allegiance instead goes to the victim.

Both *A Slight Ache* and *The Dumb Waiter* end with one character isolated. Gus finds himself staring down Ben's gun; Edward finds himself on the other end of the Matchseller's tray, expelled from his own home. Both endings depict stunning reversals for these characters, in the technical, theatrical sense. The power structures abruptly shift; those who might have expected to find themselves 'on top' are suddenly stripped of their status and brought low. Pinter stretches his sacred joke until it snaps; the conflict that was funny in microcosm becomes unsettling or even horrifying when magnified and examined, when the brutality of the Freudian positions are revealed. What was comedy has now become menace; and lo and behold, they are precisely the same thing.

It is certainly tempting to read Pinter's early plays bleakly, as narratives of sudden, hostile isolation. After all, Pinter's background as a British Jew, growing up in the 1940s under the spectre of Fascism and Nazism, certainly encourages such a reading. Despite Tynan's assessment of Pinter as an apolitical playwright, there is certainly a politics at work here. Perhaps it is the small-'p' 'politics' of power structures (or of tendentious jokes – jokes with a distinct *investment* or *interest*), rather than the large-'p' 'Politics' which deals with specific causes and parties, but it is a politics nonetheless. The largest, summarisable plot of *The Birthday Party*, 'two men arrive unexpectedly and take a third man away', is hardly 'abstract' or 'absurd' or 'mysterious' – except, of course, to the extent to which such an event might seem so to the man's friends and neighbours. The plotline of *The Birthday Party* was being played out as the most utter realism throughout Europe during Pinter's childhood and teens.

But Pinter's plays are not solely about unexpected moments of isolation; they are equally about unexpected moments of *alliance*. Again, Freud's joke triangle produces a two against one result. In the successful joke, the swing vote, the audience, allies with the aggressor; in the failed joke, the third party allies with the victim. The dramatic tension is in the moment of uncertainty; in the moment after the joke and before the reaction.

In Pinter's works, the alliances are perhaps even more surprising than the alienations. In *A Slight Ache*, Flora allies herself with the Matchseller and not with her husband, as one might expect. Gus allies himself with the unseen third character in *The Dumb Waiter*: the victim for whom the hitmen are supposedly waiting. In Pinter's first play, *The Room*, the final scene dramatically illustrates a strange alliance: that of Rose and Riley, the blind Negro. Rose has been fearing a threat from the outside world for the entire play. Finally, Riley appears, and they have a strange confrontation. She calls him names ('creep', 'nut'); he then calls her by the name of Sal, and tells her that her father wants her to come home. He touches her. She touches him: '*his eyes, the back of his head, and his temples*'. When Rose's husband Bert arrives home a few moments later, he kicks the Negro into unconsciousness or death, and Rose suddenly declares that she is blind. In the last beat of the play, Bert walks away, and Rose '*stands, clutching her eyes*' and says, 'Can't see. I can't see. I can't see.'[12] The dialogue and stage picture illustrate the connection between Rose and the blind man; we might not know exactly what the connection *is* between them (familial? occupational? sexual?) but we are shown that it exists.

By declaring herself blind, Rose declares that she is, on some level, *like* the Negro, connected to the person who previously represented everything that she seemed to fear. We are startled into silence by the revelation of that alliance, that Rose is somehow more tied to the blind Negro than to her brutish husband, who simply '*walks away*'. While there are many overt comic exchanges in *The Room*, this last scene gives us not a joke but the raw, aggressive impulse behind it. Bert attacks Riley, but there is no laugh here, because Rose does not show any pleasure or joy at this attack, though she might be expected to do so. Instead, by her actions, she allies herself with Riley, the victim.

All of these surprising alliances leave us with more questions than answers: how exactly has Gus come to be Ben's next victim, why exactly is Flora attracted to the Matchseller, what exactly does Rose have in common with

Riley? Pinter rarely provides these sorts of answers; he seems to be more interested in the *fact* of these alliances than the *reasons* for them. Pinter does not seem to be interested in detailing the particular reasons why his characters act as they do – instead, he seems content to confront us with their unknowability, with the fact that we, the audience, cannot assume from just a brief encounter with them what side the characters are on, with whom they will align themselves or what they will find funny. Instead, he suggests that human beings have depths that can only become evident in moments of dramatic or comedic crisis.

While Pinter refuses to specify the reasons why his characters take the sides they do, other writers influenced by Pinter have been more than happy to fill in the gaps. Pinter's comedy of menace can be seen to have inspired a generation of black comedy written by playwrights who were willing to provide the explanations Pinter omits. Black comedy can be seen as a kind of antithesis to the comedy of menace. Menace depends on ignorance; the terror of it stems from the vagueness of the threat. We do not know what is happening or why, and the lack of information leads us to fear the worst: that the threat is somehow beyond articulation – literally unspeakable. Black comedy, on the other hand, treats serious themes comedically, without the 'respect' they deserve; it says *too much*, it says what *should not* be said.

Joe Orton is the most obvious example of a post-Pinterian playwright, though many other writers have built their careers filling in Pinterian silences. Ironically, the black comedies inspired by Pinter simply *overflow* with talk. Orton's characters exchange epigrams at rapier speed. David Mamet's characters chatter nervously to each other, entangling themselves and others into terrifying, linguistic complicity; in Mamet's world, merely *listening* to such talk makes you an 'accessory before the fact'.[13] Stoppard's characters engage in verbal fireworks and displays of intellectual bravado as they try to remember the first thing that they remember, or sift through the detritus of what is apparent, looking for what is real.

But Orton's plays are closest to Pinter's in terms of structure: Orton deliberately rewrote a number of Pinterian triangles, supplying the missing plot and character motivations. The first work Orton ever sold, the radio play *The Ruffian on the Stair*, is a rewrite of *The Room*. In both plays a woman who is trapped in a room fears a threat from the outside world: in both cases that threat is embodied in a male character who is not her husband. Pinter's Rose, Bert and Riley become Orton's Joyce, Mike and Wilson (the eponymous threatening ruffian). The haunting subtexts in Pinter's work become shocking certainties in Orton's: Mike is a hitman who drives a van, Joyce an ex-prostitute who has been known by many 'professional' names. In Orton's play, Mike's van is at the heart of the matter. Mike has killed Wilson's brother by running him down with the van. It turns out that Wilson and his brother were lovers, and Wilson, who is grief-stricken, has been terrorising Joyce with the specific purpose of provoking Mike into killing him. Wilson wants to commit suicide, and wants Mike to be exposed as the killer he is. Mike finally shoots Wilson dead, but unlike Rose, Joyce throws her lot in with the killer. Joyce will lie to the police by claiming that Wilson was about to rape her, and thus Mike will get away with murder once again.

Like *The Room*, *The Ruffian on the Stair* is full of surprising alliances. Not the least of them is the relationship between Wilson and his dead brother, a relationship that manages to be both homosexual and incestuous. Mike is drawn to Wilson even though he has been terrorising Joyce. Joyce allies herself with Mike even after he has murdered Wilson. But Orton gives us specific explanations for these alliances. The odd relationships between the men are the result of homosexual desire, which, Orton coyly explains, is as common as snow is in Lapland.[14] Joyce's alliance with Mike is ultimately practical – she is a woman who is concerned, above all else, with achieving social conformity. She is not in fact married to Mike, although she pretends to be: her life with Mike gives her some sort of social status in her own mind.

For Orton, the surprising alliances revealed by the triangular joke-structure are a way of examining what lies hidden behind the veneer of social conformity. Like Rose and Bert in *The Room*, Orton's Joyce and Mike might appear to an outsider to be a completely normal married couple. But Orton wants to tell the stories that appearances might conceal: for Orton, heterosexual marriage is figured as the union between hitman and whore, a literal marriage of violent masculinity and sexually manipulative femininity. Moreover, Joyce and Mike's socially approved relationship survives only at the expense of Wilson's life: for Mike and Joyce to continue their lives comfortably, the homosexual outsider at their door must be silenced and eliminated. Wilson is ultimately not the terroriser but the victim of this allied couple, and *that* is the punchline of Orton's black joke.

Orton's play *Entertaining Mr Sloane* is another Pinterian rewrite. This time, Orton borrows the initial situation of *The Birthday Party*. Pinter's play features Meg, Petey and their lodger Stanley; Orton gives us the brother and sister Kath and Ed, and their lodger Mr Sloane. *The Birthday Party* features a tense maternal/sexual flirtation between Meg and Stanley. Orton makes the implied situation explicit in his version: Kath orchestrates an outrageous and hilarious seduction of Sloane, all the while insisting that her affection is purely maternal. Sloane gives in finally and becomes Kath's lover, eventually making her pregnant. But it turns out that Kath's brother Ed desires Mr Sloane as well, and both siblings want Sloane so much that they are prepared to ignore the fact that he has murdered their father. The triangle of Kath, Ed and Sloane works out in an unexpected way, with Kath and Ed suddenly joining forces to blackmail Sloane into sexual servitude. They will each have him as a lover for six months of the year; if he balks, they will turn him over to the police for murder. Orton concludes the play with Ed's punch-line, 'Well, it's been a pleasant morning',[15] – 'pleasant' being an odd way to describe a morning which has included murder and blackmail.

Orton's work is all about speaking the unspeakable: his characters make their strange alliances (and strange bedfellows, literally) because of character-istics that are simply not visible on the surface. Sometimes, the unseen element is corruption; in Orton's play *Loot*, the police detective ultimately allies himself with the criminals, and not with the 'honest' members of society, as the naive might expect. The bank-robbing trio of Hal, Dennis and Fay ultimately buy Inspector Truscott's silence and assistance with a share of their 'loot', and blithely conclude that 'It's comforting to know that the police can still be relied upon when we're in trouble.'[16] Sometimes Orton's char-acters are invisibly connected by a blood tie. In *What The Butler Saw*, the working-class characters Nick and Geraldine turn out to be the illegitimate children of psychiatrist Dr Prentice and his wife Mrs Prentice. Since Dr Prentice has been sexually pursuing Geraldine over the course of the play, and Nick has already slept with Mrs Prentice, the concluding revelation of a familial relationship between the characters means that there has been not one but *two* cases of incest in the plot.[17] Incest, rather hilariously, explains the events of the play not only in terms of the pop-psychology which is the object of the play's satire, but also in terms of dramatic history; the incest plot connects Orton's farce to its highbrow classical and Shakespearean ancestors – although, Orton wryly implies, his play might itself be something of a bastard child. Whether literal or theatrical, the revelation of illegitimate parentage makes the invisible tie visible, speaks the unspeakable, tells what had been secret.

But generally, what is invisible and unspeakable in Orton's plays is sexual desire. For Orton, desire brings together people of varying ages, classes and genders. It allies those who would in normal social terms be defined as oppo-sites. In particular, Orton saw homosexuality as a force which destabilised social categories and defied easy labels. In his book, *Literature, Politics, and Culture in Postwar Britain*, Alan Sinfield claims that post-war literary culture has been constructed according to a series of opposing binaries – masculine/ feminine, working class/leisure class, the state/the personal. Homosexuality was the unspoken element which subverted the model because 'homosexuals often chose their partners across it (as Oscar Wilde had done), producing connections where the model envisages oppositions. The "effeminate", leisured literary intellectual sought relationships – either personal or (equally provocatively) impersonal – with masculinity and the working class.'[18] Homosexuality can threaten precisely because it unites unexpected people and blurs the binaries that make us comfortable, that define the parameters of our world. Two apparently dissimilar people can be suddenly revealed as alike, unified, joined literally or figuratively.

Orton's ability to explain unexpected alliances by way of sexual desire was enabled by Pinter's repeated depiction of unexpected alliances in his early plays. Pinter presented the theatre with complex dramatic situations which inspired explanations: his use of *subtext* paved the way for other writers to broaden the themes of actual *text*. Black comedy writers like Orton would provide explanations for apparently menacing or unconventional behaviour by bringing formerly unspeakable ideas on to the stage in their plays.

In both the comedy of menace and the black comedy it subsequently inspired, the important jokes are generally the ones which make the audience *stop* laughing, which make the audiences question their own alliance with the aggressive joke-tellers. The simple 'us' versus 'them' positions of the joke-triangle became complicated as theatrical characterisation became more complicated, as previously unspeakable personal realities were expressed on stage, as previously hidden alliances were brought into view.

In short, Pinter's manipulation of the Freudian joke triangle in his early plays might not have seemed 'political' in a theatrical context where 'political' plays focused on the Suez crisis, or nuclear disarmament, or Stalin's Russia. Ultimately, however, Pinter's sacred jokes, skilfully stretched to the point where easy assumptions were questioned, where the lines of certainty about character blurred and comedy itself disintegrated, were the foundation for two generations' worth of important small-'p' 'political' comedy – black comedy about the power of the individual in society, and about the complex personal identifications and motivations that questioned traditional comedy's easy divisions and easy laughter.

NOTES

1. Sigmund Freud, *Jokes and Their Relation to the Unconscious* (New York: W. W. Norton, 1960), p. 100.
2. Christopher Innes, *Modern British Drama 1890–1990* (Cambridge: Cambridge University Press, 1992), p. 281.
3. *Ibid.*, p. 281.
4. Kenneth Tynan, 'Tom Stoppard', *Profiles* (New York: HarperPerennial, 1989), p. 296.
5. Harold Pinter, *The Dumb Waiter, Complete Works: One* (New York: Grove Press, 1976), pp. 129–30.
6. G. K. Chesterton, 'A 1909 View of *Major Barbara*', in Bernard Shaw, *Bernard Shaw's Plays* (New York: W. W. Norton, 1970), p. 357.

7. Robert Gordon, 'Mind-less Men: Pinter's Dumb Waiters', in *Harold Pinter: A Casebook*, ed. Lois Gordon (New York and London: Garland, 1990), pp. 203–4.
8. *The Dumb Waiter*, pp. 131–2.
9. *Ibid.*, p. 163.
10. John Lahr, *Prick Up Your Ears* (New York: Vintage, 1987), p. 160.
11. Harold Pinter, *A Slight Ache, Complete Works: One*, p. 171.
12. All quotes from *The Room, Complete Works: One*, pp. 123–6.
13. David Mamet, *Glengarry Glen Ross* (New York: Grove Press, 1982), p. 45.
14. Joe Orton, *The Ruffian on the Stair, The Complete Plays* (New York: Grove Weidenfeld, 1976), p. 50.
15. Joe Orton, *Entertaining Mr Sloane, The Complete Plays*, p. 149.
16. Joe Orton, *Loot, The Complete Plays*, p. 275.
17. Note that Orton thus gives us two interlocking incestuous triangles: mother–father–daughter and mother–father–son. In both cases we have surprising alliances: the son turns out to be related to his lover's husband; the daughter turns out to be related to her seducer's wife.
18. Alan Sinfield, 'Queers, Treachery, and the Literary Establishment', *Literature, Politics and Culture in Postwar Britain* (Berkeley: University of California Press, 1989), p. 66.

4

PETER RABY

Tales of the city: some places and voices in Pinter's plays

The double bill of *The Room* and *Celebration* at the Almeida Theatre in March 2000[1] provided a unique occasion on which to attempt to obtain some view or perspective on Pinter. Here were his first and his latest play, forty-three years between them, directed by the author, with an excellent cast, many of them experienced Pinter actors, four of them playing in both plays: *The Room* given an evocatively detailed 'period' setting, drab, utilitarian, a murky refuge warmed by a flickering gas-fire and filled with the depressing lodging-house furniture of the 1950s; *Celebration* took place in a smart, postmodern restaurant, all curved banquettes and ostentatious table linen, a glance, according to some of the first-night critics, at 'The Ivy', but replicated in many of the smarter establishments in the streets outside the theatre. Private and public, domestic and social: nice weak tea and bacon and eggs in *The Room*, duck, osso bucco and Frascati for the ladies in *Celebration*. Even the names resonate differently: ordinary or formal in *The Room*: Bert and Rose, Mr Kidd, Riley; and a less specific, apparently classless fluidity in *Celebration*'s Lambert, Prue, Suki, Richard. This was London, and Islington, then and now.

Pinter's plays have always challenged the critics, from the initial bewilderment over *The Birthday Party*, to their responses to later shifts of tone and mode such as those deployed in *One for the Road*, or *Ashes to Ashes*.[2] Understandably, the juxtaposition of *The Room* and *Celebration* seemed like a challenge, and few resisted. Bizarrely, some even reviewed the audience – 'gales of sycophantic laughter' (Charles Spencer, *Daily Telegraph*);[3] 'cyclonic gales of snobby laughter' (Roger Foss in *What's On*, who went on to source some of them).[4] The laughter reviewed was in reaction to *Celebration*, which formed the second part of the bill; and other reviews commented on the unexpectedly relentless comic nature of the play, 'certainly his funniest and also perhaps his most accessible script for many years', according to Sheridan Morley.[5] Was there a sense that Pinter, who has always used comedy in the most uncomfortable contexts, should not be making an audience laugh quite

1 Lindsay Duncan and Steven Pacey in *The Room*, directed by Harold Pinter,
The Almeida Theatre Company, 2000

so much, or so easily? Certainly, the direction and acting were brilliant –
almost all the critics agreed about that. So was it the wrong sort of laughter, or
the wrong target? Was Pinter being trivial, or satirising the trivial?

At one level, the comedy begins in a relatively straightforward manner.
There are two tables of diners, two celebrations. At one, a pair of brothers
married to a pair of sisters, celebrating a wedding anniversary: they are brash,
vulgar, aggressive. The men are 'strategy consultants', peaceful ones – they do
not carry guns; the women do charities. At the other, a banker celebrates his
recent promotion with his wife, who teaches infants. The jokes come fast:
'Well I know Osso was Italian but I know bugger all about Bucco.' 'I didn't
know arsehole was Italian.' 'Yes, but on the other hand what's the Italian for
arsehole?'[6] Not brilliant on the page, perhaps, but effective in the theatre –
gales of laughter, possibly. But the payoff to the opening sequence is Prue's
toast: 'Julie, Lambert. Happy anniversary.' The celebration is under way, and
as in previous Pinter plays, special occasions – birthday parties, homecomings –
are not quite what they seem. At the other table, Russell begins, 'They believe
in me.'[7] When Suki replies a little later, 'Listen. I believe you. Honestly. I do.
No really, honestly,' we know almost all we need to know about Russell's
lack of integrity; and when she completes her defining speech, 'I want you to
be rich so that you can buy me houses and panties and I'll know that you

2 Keith Allen, Lia Williams, Lindsay Duncan, Andy de la Tour, Susan Wooldridge and Steven
Pacey in *Celebration*, directed by Harold Pinter, The Almeida Theatre Company, 2000

really love me,' she has laid bare a whole world of compromises and hypoc-
risies, while the one word 'panties' points to Russell's infidelity. 'Listen', he
counters, 'she was just a secretary', only for Suki to take the cue, 'Like me.'[8]
The implication lies on the table like a hand grenade, until Lambert recognises
her as a girl from his past. Two worlds, two registers. One apparently crass,
predatory, wealth scarcely concealing the successful struggle for power,
men and women behaving badly in public; the other controlled, suave,
on-message, but equally lethal. The worlds, registers, rhythms, play alternately, but with increasingly matching themes. Betrayals, mistrust, lightly
buried phobias, rise to the surface.

A third group is introduced: the staff – urbane restaurateur Richard,
efficient *maîtresse d'hôtel* Sonia and a young waiter who specialises in inap-
propriate interjections. Again, the comedy operates at different levels within
these 'customer' exchanges: the routine professional banality – 'Been to the
theatre?'; the subversion of the code – 'She said she could cook better than
that with one hand stuffed between her legs'; the insincere compliment –
'Everyone is so happy in your restaurant.' But just as the two groups of diners
coalesce, so the motifs that emerge in the apparently superficial encounters
between clientele and staff begin to link them. Sonia, asked by the banker
about her upbringing, rather than her background, replies, 'Well, I was born

in Bethnal Green. My mother was a chiropodist. I had no father.' Richard
volunteers, 'I was brought up in a little village myself.' The waiter's interjections are based on the people he claims his grandfather knew. United through
the patterns of reference to the past, the characters inhabit an increasingly
arid present, as the play moves to a collective finale with a magnum of
champagne, a cuddle for Richard and Sonia, £50 notes for the staff, a final
coarse thigh-slapping burst of vulgarity from Lambert and Matt, and a fading
chorus of 'see you soons' and 'lovely to see yous' as they drift away. Only the
waiter remains. Pinter gives this character a stunning coda to the play,
through the waiter's memories of standing with his grandfather on the edge
of the cliffs. The images reach the audience as though in a poem, translucent,
self-contained, like a series of pebbles dropped into the silence. 'The sea
glistened.' The comic mode has gone, wiped clean by the sequence, so that a
sentence such as 'My grandfather introduced me to the mystery of life and I'm
still in the middle of it',[9] spoken straight out to the audience, offers a critique
on everything that has gone before, on the whole satirical, edgy, entertaining
ritual of state-of-the-art urban civilisation. The waiter emerges from the
kitchen quarters into the foreground a little like Riley, the figure from the
basement in *The Room*. *Celebration* may be disarmingly set in a minor key,
but Pinter's power to disturb and question, and to strip away layers of veneer
from the brave new world of contemporary Britain, is undiminished.

One of Pinter's most powerful effects is his ability to introduce other places
and times, and other voices, into the dramatic world he has created, and to do
this economically, unexpectedly, often poignantly. The most noticeable way,
perhaps, is through memory, through the stories the characters tell, or imply,
or invent. Lambert, the chief celebrant, shifts the raucous mood by a confessional memory, in a statement that follows, significantly as always in Pinter, a
'*Silence*':

> LAMBERT: But as I was about to say, you won't believe this, I fell in love
> once and this girl I fell in love with loved me back. I know she did.
> > *Pause.*
> JULIE: Wasn't that me, darling?[10]

It wasn't. It was a girl Lambert used to take for walks along the river. 'That's
funny,' comments Lambert's brother, Matt, 'I never knew anything about
that. And I knew you quite well, didn't I?' In return, in revenge, the glossy
sisters, Julie and Prue, create a scenario that deliberately excludes the men.
Julie recalls that Lambert fell in love with her on the top of a bus. 'It was a
short journey. Fulham Broadway to Shepherd's Bush, but it was enough.'
Prue corroborates: 'I was there when you came home. I remember what you
said. You came into my room. You sat down on my bed.'[11] The bond between

the sisters seems suddenly stronger than any other, the potential for hostility between the brothers alarmingly overt: honeyed words, and naked aggression. Any commentary must also take into account the impact of the comedy, triggered by, for example, 'Wasn't that me, darling?' or the banal precision and recognition factor of 'Fulham Broadway to Shepherd's Bush', which clearly adds an ironic dimension to the sense of complexity. Through sequences such as this, the occasion and its media-chic setting are transformed, and the broad parallel with *The Room* emphasised. The upmarket restaurant becomes a kind of confessional for the twenty-first century, an urban monument to success and pleasure that seems to function like the setting of Sartre's *Huis Clos*, though in *Celebration* the exit-door is always open for the guests to depart, while the audience is left trapped in the company of the waiter.

Presenting *Celebration* with *The Room* allowed the plays to reverberate with each other, and the use of experienced actors of Pinter such as Lindsay Duncan, Keith Allen and Lia Williams helped to define echoes of other intervening plays. When Keith Allen as Lambert said to Richard, 'Let me give you a cuddle', the verbal parallel with Teddy and Max in *The Homecoming* (Royal National Theatre, 1997, Keith Allen as Teddy) struck that much more sharply; or Russell to Suki, 'You're a whore', recalling Richard to Sarah in *The Lover*, 'You lovely whore' (Donmar Warehouse, 1998, Lia Williams as Sarah). *Celebration* does seem unobtrusively, perhaps inevitably, self-referential: sometimes it is a structural element – the waiter's last speech, for example, is reminiscent of Jimmy's at the close of *Party Time*; the waiter's earlier interjections are not unlike Deeley's reminiscences, or ironic parodies, in *Old Times*. But more striking than the sense of unity achieved by these echoes and correspondences, is the realisation of the range of Pinter's work, of the varied ways in which he can create a milieu, a specific place and time, with economy and precision. Between the claustrophobic, pinched atmosphere of *The Room*, with its evocation of unknown terrors pressing in on Rose – from the basement, from prospective lodgers, from the icy, empty streets of north London – and the barbed, lavish, raucous rituals of *Celebration*, stretches a distillation of life in the metropolis in the second half of the twentieth century. Pinter is, among other things, the dramatist of the city, and specifically of London.

Pinter's realisations of London, London as the social and cultural network that both represents and allows access to an idea of England, have some affinities with those of T. S. Eliot. *No Man's Land*, especially, contains explicit and implicit references to Eliot, set in Hampstead, one of Eliot's 'gloomy hills of London'.[12] Spooner's early half-quotation from 'Little Gidding', 'now and in England and in Hampstead and for all eternity', invites the association, and the figure of Spooner himself might seem drawn from Eliot's 'The first-met stranger in the waning dusk', a familiar compound ghost, who offers himself to Hirst, both consciously and ironically, as the boatman who will ferry him across the black waters. Spooner, decrepit minor poet and literary odd-job man, might credibly have half-lines of Eliot conveniently to hand, just as he incorporates phrases of Yeats, but the patterned repetitions of 'I have known this before' reinforce the allusion to Prufrock;[13] and the London of *No Man's Land*, apparently quite specific and localised – Hampstead Heath, 'Jack Straw's Castle', 'The Bull's Head', Bolsover Street – becomes universalised, just as the unreal city of Eliot's *The Waste Land* cracks and reforms into Jerusalem, Athens, Alexandria, Vienna.

This widening of the frame is partly achieved by the shifts and twists of the dialogue, by the references – the Hungarian émigré lately retired from Paris, the café in Amsterdam, Foster's Siamese girls, the Australian desert – and partly by the ironic construction of Englishness, something heralded from the beginning with the characters' names: 'I'm Mr Foster. Old English stock.'[14] 'All we have left is the English language,' comments Spooner in his early probings of the situation. *No Man's Land* presents a parodic exploration of Englishness. Spooner and Hirst share 'A memory of the bucolic life'. A cottage, tea on the lawn, a village church, its beams hung with garlands, are conjured up, mocking shadows to set against the icy silence of no man's land. These evocations can be pastoral, half-teasing, but gentle; or wildly and robustly parodic, as in Hirst's and Spooner's competitive sexual pursuits of Stella Winstanley and Arabella Hinscott; or sharp and elegiac, as in Hirst's comment on the gullies of the English countryside: 'Under the twigs, under the dead leaves, you'll find tennis balls, blackened.'[15]

In the arid no man's land of the well-furnished book-lined Hampstead room, where minds are fuelled by too many glasses of the great malt which wounds, the world is defined by what is absent. There are no children. Youth exists only in the photograph album. The most powerful images are conveyed by memories of dreams, of a body drowning in a lake.

The setting of *No Man's Land* does not mention Hampstead, just 'A large room in a house in North West London', which seems to fit with the metaphorical everywhere and nowhere suggested by the title. The programme for the 1997 Royal National Theatre production of *The Homecoming* reproduced a page of the London A–Z, making the laconic, apparently non-committal description, 'An old house in North London', more specific. Whatever the intention behind the inclusion of the map, it placed the play in an identifiable district of the city. Michael Billington quotes Pinter on the filming of *The Homecoming*, and the particular Victorian house in Hackney which was used for an external shot of Teddy and Ruth arriving in a taxi: '*The Homecoming* did not take place in that house. Nor was there any one source. There was the image of the old man and of the street itself if you look at the shot in the film, that's how I see it. That's where it takes place. In that district. After all, the play was embedded in the East End.'[16]

The idea that *The Homecoming* is embedded in the East End does not necessarily contradict the sense that Pinter's plays take place anywhere, or everywhere, in no man's land and especially in rooms: 'A room in a large house' – *The Room*; 'The living room of a house in a seaside town' – *The Birthday Party*; 'A basement room' – *The Dumb Waiter*; 'A room' – *The Caretaker*. Locations in the television plays, unsurprisingly, are more precise: 'Harry's house in Belgravia – James's flat in Chelsea' (*The Collection*, 1961); 'A detached house near Windsor' (*The Lover*, 1963). Pinter's plays, city-centred, reach out to embrace the suburbs, the home counties, even the accessible seaside towns. Their power to have resonance for other places and cultures stems from Pinter's skills in constructing a particular urban landscape, a topography which has as much to do with attitudes of mind as with factual detail.

Just as Wilde mapped the power structure of England in his social comedies ('Time: the Present – Place: London'), pinning it and framing it with deadly accuracy, so Pinter's plays construct not just a sense of reality, of recognisable settings and environments, but an idea of place and time, defined as much by what it is not as by what it is. In *The Birthday Party* – in the unspecified seaside town which sprang from an experience in Eastbourne[17] but which might be Worthing, Margate, Brighton – the first place names introduced are the venues for Stanley's imaginary world tour. He tells Meg that he is considering a job in a nightclub in Berlin – 'playing the piano. A fabulous salary. And all found.'

MEG:	How long for?
STANLEY:	We don't stay in Berlin. Then we go to Athens.
MEG:	How long for?
STANLEY:	Yes. Then we pay a flying visit to … er … whatsisname …
MEG:	Where?
STANLEY:	Constantinople. Zagreb. Vladivostock. It's a round the world tour.[18]

Out of this wild litany comes the personal truth, the memory which defines Stanley:

STANLEY:	Played the piano? I've played the piano all over the world. All over the country. (*Pause*) I once gave a concert.
MEG:	A concert?
STANLEY:	(*reflectively*)
	Yes. It was a good one, too. They were all there that night. Every single one of them. It was a great success. Yes. A concert. At Lower Edmonton.[19]

Without the established world context, from Berlin to Vladivostock, this revelation would not have so much of a comic dimension – or, when Stanley repeats it, the power to move. 'My father nearly came down to hear me. Well, I dropped him a card anyway. But I don't think he could make it. No, I – I lost the address, that was it. (*Pause*) Yes. Lower Edmonton.'[20] (This is where, so Billington tells us, Pinter unexpectedly won the 220 yards race, and broke the school record, when he was sixteen.[21])

Stanley's fulfilment, his moment of creativity and independence, happened, perhaps in his imagination, at a specific place. 'And then,' Meg reinvents the story for Goldberg, 'And then he got a fast train and he came down here.'[22]

You 'come down' from London. The seaside, and the seaside boarding-house, are where you escape to from London (in life, as in a theatrical seaside farce; where, too, you lose a parent, or a baby, or steal a weekend with a lover). The pier, with the sea surrounding it, provides the Londoner with the illusion of freshness, of temporary freedom, of a voyage undertaken without the necessity of leaving land: 'A concert party on the pier'. Goldberg was also taken to the seaside by his uncle Barney – Brighton, Canvey Island, Rottingdean – all refuges from the city; and now Goldberg brings McCann down to the seaside for a few days.

London contains the controlling images in *The Birthday Party*. The characters invoke other places. Stanley claims Maidenhead as his ominous-sounding birthplace – 'A quiet, thriving community. I was born and brought up there. I lived well away from the main road.'[23] He constructs, desperately, the suburban, genteel calm of Fuller's teashop and Boots library, unlikely as these are to appeal to McCann. A few minutes later, Maidenhead is transformed alarmingly into Basingstoke, a name of comedy, already used as a theatrical device by W. S. Gilbert, but also, less comfortably, the town where Goldberg's Uncle Barney bought a house. McCann recollects the sun falling behind the town hall in Carrikmacross. But it is Goldberg's evocation of his childhood that strikes the sharpest – going for a walk down the canal with a girl who lived down his road. 'I can see it like yesterday. The sun falling behind the dog stadium.'[24] (Echoes for an audience, perhaps, of some of Eliot's images in the London passages of *The Waste Land*.) As Petey, who sees more of what happens than anyone else in the play, comments – 'Yes, we all remember our childhood.'[25]

These images and references precede the verbally violent cross-examination of Stanley. The nature of the interrogation changes sharply at the moment when McCann snatches Stanley's glasses – and Stanley stands, bent over the chair which McCann has moved 'downstage centre':

GOLDBERG: Webber, you're a fake, When did you last wash up a cup?
STANLEY: The Christmas before last.

GOLDBERG:	Where?
STANLEY:	Lyons Corner House.
GOLDBERG:	Which one?
STANLEY:	Marble Arch.[26]

The sequence is given added power by taking the same form as Meg's questions about the world tour. Fuller's teashop, Maidenhead – Lyon's Corner House, Marble Arch. The two sets of references seem to stand for different orders of truth. At the birthday party which follows the interrogation, the audience is reminded of the contrast when Goldberg constructs his fictional benevolent persona: 'I believe in a good laugh, a day's fishing, a bit of gardening ... A little Austin, tea in Fuller's, a library book from Boots, and I'm satisfied.'[27] So when Goldberg recalls his lecture at the Ethical Hall, Bayswater, it also brings to mind, in its parodic pattern, Stanley's moment of glory at Lower Edmonton.

One of the themes unobtrusively suggested by the pattern of reference is the anonymity of the city, of urban life. Although the play is structured around what happens to Stanley, every character seems to be implicated within a more or less conscious loss of innocence. For all of them, the landscape which has replaced the Garden of Eden – Ireland, Maidenhead, even the temporary respite of a deckchair on a crowded beach – is urban. The world of work is reached by commuter train, and so Goldberg and McCann seek to reassure the motionless, sightless, speechless Stanley on the morning after his party – 'We'll renew your season ticket', 'We'll give you a discount on all inflammable goods.'[28] He will have a prospect, once he has been taken for special treatment to Monty. The party, the games, the old morality, are all over. Lulu laments – 'He was my first love, Eddie was. And whatever happened, it was pure. With him. He didn't come into my room at night with a briefcase', to which Goldberg replies, 'Who opened the briefcase, me or you?'[29] Goldberg, who brought the briefcase down from London, is the city's mouthpiece, and Stanley, clean-shaven if sightless, in a dark well-cut suit and a white collar, is destined for the city, by now an image of bureaucracy, organisation, routine, conformity – a constructed environment where only faint traces of family life, childhood, religious belief, linger in the memory and in the phrases quoted from another era.

Goldberg, the briefcase bearer, speaks all the languages of the city. Like some chameleon master of ceremonies, he parodies different orders of geniality and moral values, through his excessive courtesy. 'What a carriage', 'Like a Countess, nothing less,' he flatters Meg; 'Madam, now turn about and promenade to the kitchen. What a deportment!'[30] 'Lift your glasses, ladies and gentlemen'; 'What's happened to the love, the bonhomie, the unashamed expression of the day before yesterday, that our mums taught us in the nursery?'[31] Finally, as he begins to crack after the night's events – 'Play up, play up, and play the game. Honour thy father and thy mother. All along the line.'[32] These are the hollow values of the urban state, unsustaining, ridiculous slogans, but retaining nevertheless a faint residue of their former power even as they are desperately voiced: tokens, uttered to fill the silence, charms to ward off the anonymous void.

In *The Caretaker*, Pinter creates the idea of the city in a different way. The action takes place in a house in west London, and both the city's geography, and its inhabitants, are called to the audience's mind. Davies is brought into the room, and Aston gives him a chair. 'Ten minutes off for a tea-break in the middle of the night in that place and I couldn't find a seat, not one. All them Greeks had it, Poles, Greeks, Blacks, the lot of them, all them aliens had it.'[33] This city is made up of all the nationalities of the world, most of them, in Davies's mouth, prefixed by a disparaging or racist adjective – Scotch, Irish, Indians, or simply Blacks. This sequence is parodied and extended by Mick in Act Two, in his story about his uncle's brother – 'I think there was a bit of the Red Indian in him'; 'Married a Chinaman and went to Jamaica.'[34] Then there is Davies's elusive identity, constructed partly through a series of located incidents: the tin of tobacco which was knocked off on the Great West Road, the sole of his shoe which came off on the North Circular just past Hendon, and, famously, Sidcup, where he left his papers. Again, the 'Welsh' Davies/Jenkins's painful mapping of his life is savagely echoed by Mick's lyrical variations, based on his imagined resemblance to 'a bloke I once knew in Shoreditch':

> Actually he lived in Aldgate. I was staying with a cousin in Camden Town. This chap, he used to have a pitch in Finsbury Park, just by the bus depot. When I got to know him I found out he was brought up in Putney. That didn't make any difference to me. I know quite a few people who were born in Putney. Even if they weren't born in Putney they were born in Fulham. The only trouble was, he wasn't born in Putney, he was only brought up in Putney. It turned out he was born in the Caledonian Road, just before you get to the Nag's Head.

He continues with a diversion into the bus routes to Dalston Junction, and concludes: 'Yes, it was a curious affair. Dead spit of you he was. Bit bigger round the nose but there was nothing in it. *Pause*. Did you sleep here last night?'[35] The personal inquisition emerges from the recital of places, which creates a set of fiercely protected territorial rights, a passport. The itinerant Mac Davies/Jenkins is disconcerted: 'Shifting, about to rise'; 'banging on floor'; 'groaning'. The big question follows:

MICK: You a foreigner?
DAVIES: No.

MICK:	Born and bred in the British Isles?
DAVIES:	I was!
MICK:	What did they teach you?[36]

Davies, cornered, grabs his trousers and announces his intention to go to Sidcup. In the city, in the city of jobs and rooms and your own permanent bed, you need credentials, references, papers. Like Goldberg, Mick employs his command of language, his mastery of the apparently redundant but empowering knowledge of localities and bus routes, to intimidate the outsider, the rootless Davies. Significantly, at the end of the play, Davies cannot even articulate the one word which might define him: 'Would you … if I got down … and got my …'[37] Sidcup, from being a predominantly comic trigger, with its suggestions of suburban respectability and dullness, has become unutterable: a tragi-comic Eldorado.

In *The Homecoming* the urban landscape is filled in with a detail which matches the carefully designated sense of interior history explored within the play. Pinter sets out a series of locations and districts which vividly convey the idea of the city. There are the routes Sam follows as a chauffeur in the Humber Super Snipe, which might take in the Savoy, the Caprice, Eaton Square and finally Heathrow. There is Max's territory, territory largely of his past: up the West End with MacGregor, down to the paddock at Epsom racecourse, behind the slab in the butcher's shop. Joey moves between the demolition site and the gym. Lenny has a more versatile, varied and alarming series of habitats: snow-clearing with the Borough Council, under an arch down by the docks, in the Ritz bar, or Greek Street, or up near the Scrubs with Joey on their violent little survey of North Paddington.

What has Teddy to offer that can match this litany? 'It's a great life, at the University … you know … it's a very good life. We've got a lovely house … we've got all … we've got everything we want. It's a very stimulating environment.'[38] The place seems nothing: it has no names to define it. The only specific statement Teddy makes at this point, which prompts a reaction, is 'We've got three boys, you know' – something that does match the family pattern.

In contrast Ruth, also a north Londoner – 'I was born quite near here' – provides a crisply defined picture of America, not in terms of lovely house and swimming pool, but of the physical landscape: 'It's all rock. And sand. It stretches … so far … everywhere you look. And there's lots of insects there. *Pause.* And there's lots of insects there.'[39] When Ruth first arrives at the house, she expresses her ease and confidence by going for a stroll, for a breath of air. She takes the key to the house with her. She has come home to the city.

Teddy and Ruth contest their territories in terms of 'clean' and 'dirty':

TEDDY: The boys'll be at the pool ... now ... swimming. Think of it.
              Morning over there. Sun. We'll go anyway, mmmn? It's so clean there.
RUTH: Clean.
TEDDY: Yes.
RUTH: Is it dirty here?[40]

For Teddy, there is nowhere to bathe in London, except the swimming-bath down the road, which is like a 'filthy urinal'. As a last resort, he even invokes Venice. Then, when Teddy has left to pack, Ruth closes her eyes – and opens them to find in his place Lenny, to whom she recounts her memory of the house with a lake, where she once did her photographic modelling for the body. This is an image securely connected to her London life, an urban vision of the country. Pointedly, she recalls that she – alone, not with Teddy – went down there just before 'we' went to America: 'I walked from the station to the gate and then I walked up the drive. There were lights on ... I stood in the drive ... the house was very light.'[41] This lyrical evocation of Ruth's independence, a moment of peace and pleasure which is a kind of farewell to her former life, is also her invitation to Lenny, a sign that she is free – the verbal equivalent to the glass of water. The recollection introduces the shocking sequence of the slow dance and the kiss, which itself leads to her carefully calculated demands for a flat with three rooms and a bathroom. Ruth's cool dismissal of Teddy – 'Don't become a stranger'[42] – is a warning to someone whose vaguely expressed picture of campus life cannot compete with the familiar territory of the city.

One of the attributes of the city dweller is verbal confidence. In the city, you move from context to context: the languages of class, race, social occupation are available for inspection, analysis, imitation. Here is a potential mobility which gives power to those who can exploit it. Lenny destroys Teddy, who has eaten his cheese roll, by his parody of 'American' values – 'tons of iced water, all the comfort of those Bermuda shorts and all that, on the old campus, no time of the day or night you can't get a cup of coffee or a Dutch gin ...'[43] Teddy is despatched back to the land of rock, sand and insects, to the less real, campus life of the soft intellectual. The city reclaims Ruth.

Pinter's plays are international. A London audience will react in particular ways to the local references, but other cities will have their equivalents: their West End, Soho, airport, docks, racecourses, and their worlds of modelling, boxing, chauffeurs, pimps and butchers, their entertainment and tourist industries. Most urban cultures, too, contain that uneasy element of suspicion or hostility towards 'abroad' which Lenny voices so fluently.

The urban world of *The Homecoming* is, initially, overpoweringly, un-naturally, male. Jessie is the unseen presence within the play; and her shifting, ambivalent roles are given shape for us partly through the actions of Max and Sam; until she and Ruth, also a mother of three sons, are fused in the play's final tableau. For all the shock that Ruth's decision to stay arouses, the final sequence of the play offers a positive image: an image which at least recognises need, even suggests healing. Against the violence of the preceding language and action, expressed by Sam's body lying at their feet, the closing tableau contains a sense of peace, as well as stillness. There has been movement from the jaunty, edgy challenge of Max to Teddy, 'What about a nice cuddle and kiss, eh?' to his plain statement to Ruth in the last words of the play, 'Kiss me.'[44]

In *The Homecoming*, Pinter shapes a particularly urban myth. Out of the hard city culture of control and exploitation, where everything has its price, and where everything is expressed in terms of consumption – cheese rolls, whiskey on the rocks, discounts on sex from Pan-American, the world of going the whole hog, getting the gravy, and the butcher's trade of the chopper and the slab – emerges a realignment, or at least a resting place which momentarily stills the relentless struggle for survival. In terms of sexual politics, Ruth's actions are as shocking as Nora Helmer's when she closed the door on her husband and children. Pinter makes Ruth's decision to stay seem normal.

Another controversial play, first produced, like *The Homecoming*, in 1965, also closes with an enigmatic tableau. In Edward Bond's *Saved*, four characters sit silently: doing the football pools, staring into space, reading the *Radio Times*, pondering how to mend a chair. Bond argued forcefully for the play's inherent optimism: at least Len, the carpenter, stays. The two playwrights' dramatic worlds and methods contrast sharply, but *The Homecoming* and *Saved* together present two extraordinary sets of images of the city, far removed from popular constructions of the decade. This is a city which has been created by a particular society, in which people survive, intact or largely intact, with considerable difficulty: people living close to the edge.

The Homecoming also shares with *Saved* an often alarming comic energy. Urban societies, perhaps, need a resilient sense of comedy to survive, and the sheer business of living as part of a great mass of people sharpens the sense of difference. There is a wider range of material to work on, more varieties of language to hear – on the bus, in the café or the Ritz bar; a constantly evolving set of registers to be reworked, elaborated, parodied, exploited. When you meet so often as strangers, it becomes crucial to place people from the way they speak.

In *Old Times*, a play set in a converted farmhouse but taking place, through memory, largely in London, Deeley monitors Anna's speech. When she observes, 'I would not want to go far, I would be afraid of going far, lest when I returned the house would be gone,' he pounces on the word 'lest' – 'Haven't heard it for a long time.'[45] A little later, when he asks her, with increased hostility, 'Don't you find England damp, returning', he seizes on her reply, repeating it: 'Rather beguilingly so? What the hell does she mean by that?'[46] Anna uses English in a different, and, to Deeley, threatening way, a way which is old-fashioned, pretentious, or the speech of someone who has learned it – or, rather, the speech of someone who now speaks Italian every day, and is revisiting the English she used all those years ago: an English of the art-loving young in the pubs and bedsits of 'lovely London'. In this play of memory, Pinter both evokes London, and somehow disposes of it, as though it has lost its validity. Anna reminisces, seeking a response from Kate: 'Don't tell me you've forgotten our days at the Tate? and how we explored London and all the old churches and all the old buildings, I mean those that were left from the bombing, in the City and south of the river in Lambeth and Greenwich? Oh my goodness. Oh yes.'[47] While Anna's enthusiastic litany is both an exercise in nostalgia, and a kind of burial ceremony, Kate's commentary, more muted, more measured, is a lament, and an image of the loneliness of the city: 'The only nice thing about a big city is that when it rains it blurs everything ...'[48] The death that took place is made to seem more desolate by the way Pinter places it within a global frame of reference, as Deeley, representative of the 'arts business', peppers his speeches with glances at Rome, Sicily, 'a slim-bellied Côte d'Azur thing'.[49] The play becomes an epitaph for the city of a certain period, and for its inhabitants, the Edgware Road gang, the Maida Vale group, Big Eric and little Tony who lived somewhere near Paddington Library; and for Deeley, whom Kate remembers as dead.

Pinter explores the voices of the city, the languages of the capital. He deconstructs and reconstructs them. English is a language of pauses and hesitations, of polite evasions, of incompleteness, of what is implied but often left unspoken. It can also be a language of clipped precision, which can give the impression of certainty and clarity, but which also simultaneously contrives to obscure, and to threaten. In *One for the Road*, many elements are present that seem uncomfortably familiar – an interrogator, a glass of whisky, the silence of the man being interrogated, the vulnerability of eyes – but it is the language used by the interrogator, Nicolas, which most disturbs. His language is, initially, civilised, the language of the English ruling class, or official class, a language that asserts power and authority, and which is interlaced with cliché, often a cliché with an uncomfortable connotation:

Hello! Good morning. How are you? Let's not beat about the bush. Anything but that. *D'accord?* You're a civilised man. So am I. Sit down.[50]

The next part of the speech is accompanied by Nicolas's gesture with his fingers, big and little, and immediately we are reminded of *King Lear*, of Gloucester bound to a chair, of the vulnerability of eyes, and, with the comment 'The soul shines through them', of Macbeth's greeting to the murderers, 'Your spirits shine through you'. The play's dramatic method is brutal in its compression. There is an absence of context. We don't know precisely where we are, what the political situation is, what Victor has said or done, or not said or done. But we are undoubtedly in England, and most probably in London.

> You probably think that I'm part of a predictable, long-established pattern, i.e. I chat away, friendly, insouciant, I open the batting, as it were, in a light-hearted, even carefree manner, while another waits in the wings, silent, introspective, coiled like a puma.[51]

Nicolas seems to parody the interrogation mode of fiction, or of television drama – itself based on reality – and Pinter thereby establishes a new level of reality, where everything is less predictable, more ruthless, less capable of a just outcome. Even the comic flourish, 'coiled like a puma', intensifies rather than releases. What is apparent throughout this short play is its extraordinary compression. There is no process of theatrical seduction, no transition from the known to the unknown. Pinter does not lead us across a frontier, either in terms of narrative or shifts of language: he plunges us straight in; and no doubt he does this entirely intentionally, because this is the world that we live in. It is here and now, in England.

> I have never been more moved, in the whole of my life, as when – only the other day, last Friday, I believe – the man who runs this country announced to the country: We are all patriots, we are as one, we all share a common heritage. Except you, apparently.
> *Pause*
> I feel a link, you see, a bond. I share a commonwealth of interest. I am not alone. I am not alone![52]

This is not quite normal language, though all the words are normal. It contains too much information. The idea is over-expressed. The repetition draws attention to the sense of strain which overlays the simplicity – and emphasises that the simplicity is that of cliché. It is a false language, not unlike John le Carré's imitation of the language of officialdom, especially the mandarin of the foreign office and the forces of control, in novels such as *The Constant Gardener*. At the same time, the rhetoric is entirely familiar. The man is both mad, and might pass for sane. Later in the play, as the series of interrogations proceeds with Victor's son Nicky, and his wife Gila, the hollow note of patriotism is repeated: 'They are your country's soldiers';[53] 'Your father was a wonderful man. His country is proud of him.'; 'He would die, he would die, he would die, for his country, for his God.'[54] We hear echoes of Rupert Brooke, and then, with a gratuitous, hijacked cultural note of approval, Shakespeare once more, Hamlet to the Ghost of his murdered father, 'Oh, poor, perturbed spirit'.[55]

The house where the action takes place, like other Pinter houses, including *The Hothouse*, has many rooms. It may be a 'safe' house, as in a Le Carré novel, or a more public, but still anonymous, building. But it is an institutional building, as opposed to the house where the family lived, or the room where Gila first met Victor. Pinter brings the public and the private into the starkest conflict, and ranges language against silence; excessive rhetoric against spareness; lies against truth; power against apparent weakness; the state against family.

In his urban plays, Pinter explores and exposes an extraordinarily wide range of Englishness and English speech, cataloguing the voices of the city as accurately as he has indicated the topography. What Wilde did for the early 1890s, in terms of 'high' or 'aristocratic' society, Pinter achieved for the London-centred English society of the second half of the twentieth century. It is not a particularly comforting experience, in spite of, or perhaps because of, the comic manner which is never far away.

> NICOLAS: When did you meet your husband?
> GILA: When I was eighteen.
> NICOLAS: Why?[56]

Such exchanges bear the form of comedy, like a shadow, and yet are bleak and mirthless, as in the plays of Webster or Middleton. Nicolas, like the chattering characters of *Party Time*, has appropriated a range of language, which asserts a sense of dominance. But against the flow of places and voices, the unerring dissection of verbal nuance and evasion, falls a series of images that accuse the noise and fluency by their quietness, their clarity, and simplicity: Ruth's 'The house was very light', Hirst's 'But I hear sounds of birds', Kate's 'Sometimes I walk to the sea'; Dusty's 'Does anyone know what's happened to my brother Jimmy?'. The city does not easily contain or endorse those moments, just as it does not seem to guarantee the presence of children. Julie in *Celebration* comments, 'It's funny our children aren't here.' Perhaps the most poignant line in these plays that dramatise London, and England, is the blind Negro Riley's thrice repeated message to Rose from her father at the close of *The Room*: 'Come home, Sal.'[57]

NOTES

A section of this chapter formed part of a lecture at the Pinter Symposium at the Samuel Beckett Centre, Trinity College, Dublin, in 1997.

1. *The Room* and *Celebration* were first presented as a double bill at the Almeida Theatre, London, on 16 March 2000. *The Room* was first produced at Bristol University Drama Department on 15 May 1957.
2. *The Birthday Party*'s London opening (19 May 1959) had a largely hostile, or uncomprehending, reception by the critics (after success at venues such as Cambridge and Oxford). See Michael Billington, *The Life and Work of Harold Pinter* (London: Faber, 1996), pp. 84–6, and, for responses to different phases of Pinter's work, the chapters (and notes) by Yael Zarhy-Levo and Harry Derbyshire in this volume.
3. Charles Spencer, *Daily Telegraph*, 24 March 2000.
4. Roger Foss, *What's On*, 29 March 2000.
5. Sheridan Morley, *Spectator*, 1 April 2000.
6. Harold Pinter, *Celebration & The Room* (London: Faber, 2000), p. 5.
7. *Ibid.*, p. 6.
8. *Ibid.*, p. 7.
9. *Ibid.*, p. 72.
10. *Ibid.*, p. 34.
11. *Ibid.*, p. 36.
12. The list of 'the gloomy hills of London' comes in section III of 'Burnt Norton' in *Four Quartets*. In places *No Man's Land* seems almost like a meditation on some of the themes of the poem. See also Billington, *The Life and Work of Harold Pinter*, p. 242, and Ronald Knowles's chapter in this volume.
13. Spooner's phrase seems to echo the speaker in 'The Love Song of J. Alfred Prufrock', and his repetitions of 'I have known them all already.'
14. Harold Pinter, *No Man's Land*, *Plays Three* (London: Faber, 1997), p. 342.
15. *Ibid.*, p. 385.
16. Billington, *The Life and Work of Harold Pinter*, p. 163.
17. *Ibid.*, pp. 75–6.
18. Harold Pinter, *The Birthday Party*, *Plays One* (London: Faber, 1996), p. 16.
19. *Ibid.*
20. *Ibid.*, pp. 16–17.
21. Billington, *The Life and Work of Harold Pinter*, p. 82.
22. Pinter, *The Birthday Party*, p. 26.
23. *Ibid.*, p. 33.
24. *Ibid.*, p. 37.
25. *Ibid.*
26. *Ibid.*, p. 43.
27. *Ibid.*, p. 50.
28. *Ibid.*, p. 76.
29. *Ibid.*, pp. 73–4.
30. *Ibid.*, p. 48.
31. *Ibid.*, p. 50.
32. *Ibid.*, p. 71.
33. Harold Pinter, *The Caretaker*, *Plays Two* (London: Faber, 1996), p. 6.

34. *Ibid.*, p. 29.
35. *Ibid.*, p. 30.
36. *Ibid.*, p. 31.
37. *Ibid.*, p. 76.
38. Harold Pinter, *The Homecoming*, *Plays Three* (London: Faber, 1997), p. 58.
39. *Ibid.*, p. 61.
40. *Ibid.*, p. 62.
41. *Ibid.*, p. 66.
42. *Ibid.*, p. 88.
43. *Ibid.*, p. 72.
44. *Ibid.*, pp. 51, 90.
45. Harold Pinter, *Old Times*, *Plays Three*, p. 257.
46. *Ibid.*, p. 279.
47. *Ibid.*, p. 276.
48. *Ibid.*, p. 297.
49. *Ibid.*, p. 305.
50. Harold Pinter, *One for the Road*, *Plays Four* (London: Faber, 1998), p. 223.
51. *Ibid.*, pp. 224–55.
52. *Ibid.*, p. 232.
53. *Ibid.*, p. 236.
54. *Ibid.*, p. 240.
55. *Ibid.*
56. *Ibid.*, p. 237.
57. Harold Pinter, *The Room*, *Plays One*, p. 108.

5

RONALD KNOWLES

Pinter and twentieth-century drama

In 1956 Harold Pinter trod the boards in Bournemouth and Torquay in over thirty thrillers and comedies, the standard repertory company staple of the pre- and post-war periods,[1] while J. B. Priestley, Noel Coward and Terence Rattigan dominated the West End theatre with comforting spiritualism, stylish comedy of manners and sentimentalised social problem play, all designed to reassure the self-applauding middle-class patrons, through laughter or tears. Alternatively, by the early 1950s, the plays of Arthur Miller and Tennessee Williams with their contrasting realistic modes of incidental expressionism (*Death of a Salesman*, 1949) and passionate naturalism (*A Streetcar Named Desire*, 1947) were quite free from the all-constrictive self-censorship of the British class system dominated by virtual terror of the vulgar and lower class. Along with changing post-war social conditions the seeming freedom signalled by the Americans provided an impetus for the rise of the Angry Young Men (pre-eminently John Osborne, Arnold Wesker and John Arden) at the Royal Court Theatre, from the *annus mirabilis* of 1956. Of equal importance, but less sensational in immediate impact was the translation of French absurdism, most famously Samuel Beckett and Eugène Ionesco, to London productions at the Arts Theatre (respectively, *Waiting for Godot*, 1955; *The New Tenant*, 1956).

With his outstanding success by the early 1960s, Pinter was frequently associated with the social realism of the Angry Young Men and with the absurdism of Beckett and Ionesco. Furthermore, it is probably safe to say that there is not a single dramatist of the twentieth century with whom Pinter has not been compared or contrasted, from Ibsen to David Mamet. Beginning with the question of 1950s realism, this chapter then looks at Ionesco and Beckett and selects various dramatists with whom Pinter's plays have been associated – namely Chekhov, Strindberg, Pirandello, Eliot, Joyce – and, as far as space allows, assesses Pinter's debts, affinities or differences, to gain thereby a sharper recognition of his individual contribution to twentieth-century theatre.

Plays like Osborne's *Look Back in Anger* (1956), Wesker's *Chicken Soup with Barley* (1958) and Arden's *Live Like Pigs* (1958) displaced the middle-class drawing room with the lower-class *mise-en-scène* of 'kitchen sink' realism and without condescension faithfully represented ordinary lives. Each had an implicit left-wing agenda deriving from contempt for the dominant middle-class values of past and present conservatism. Plays like Pinter's *The Room, The Birthday Party* and *The Caretaker*[2] with their realistic sets and hyper-real demotic dialogue seemed part of this movement, but only at first glance: 'I'd say that what goes on in my plays is realistic, but what I'm doing is not realism',[3] Pinter recorded. In comparison with the realists Pinter did not speak from a recognisable political platform. In contrast, he deconstructs social realism by divorcing the identification of character and environment, defamiliarising the pedestrian and destabilising the audience with ultimately self-recriminating laughter. For the realists the accurate presentation of the material conditions of persons in society was a didactic end in itself.

An exception in Pinter's work was *A Night Out*, which he contributed to Sydney Newman's 'Armchair Theatre' series for ABC television of the late 1950s, early 1960s. Newman, a Canadian, had been deeply influenced by the social realism of American television drama. *A Night Out* presents the social entrapment of Albert, an office clerk: intimidated by his mother, bullied by an office superior, blamed for a misdemeanour at an office party, he takes out all his resentments and frustrations on a genteel prostitute before returning to the confinement of home. The often-made comparison with *The Birthday Party* brings out the essential difference. Practically everything in *A Night Out* is explicit. Character and motivation are generally unambiguous, the circular plot supplying if not the satisfying resolution of the well-made play, a significance which is clear. Quite the opposite to the numbing circularity of *The Birthday Party* which leaves us aghast, asking where? how? when? why? 'If I'm being explicit I'm failing',[4] Pinter said. *A Night Out* was highly successful, but its adherence to 'kitchen sink' realism meant that it lacked that 'core of our living ... this ambiguity'[5] which Pinter saw as his main dramatic concern.

Alternatively, the ambiguity of such plays as *The Birthday Party* and *The Caretaker* prompted comparison with the absurdists. Ionesco founded his anarchic, surrealist drama on a premise: the 'Absurd is that which is devoid of purpose ... Cut off from his religious, metaphysical, and transcendental roots, man is lost; all his actions become senseless, absurd, useless.'[6] Consequently the tragic is mixed with the comic, which ultimately liberates through recognition of the confining morality of society. Ionesco's basic technique was a radical estrangement by literalising the metaphorical in concrete stage objects, and by defamiliarisation and deformation of language.

The origin of *The Bald Prima Donna* (1950) derived from Ionesco's discovery of an English phrase book which reduced all life to the social repetition of banal, indicative propositions. His parody of this led to comparison of *The Birthday Party* to the 'inconsequential gabble ... of Ionesco'.[7] However, the realism of *The Caretaker* prompted another reviewer to claim that it was free from the 'fantastic Ionesco-like world of nightmare' found in *The Room* and *The Dumb Waiter*.[8] A significant distinction was made in another review, comparing *The Caretaker* to Ionesco's *The Chairs*: 'nowhere does Mr Pinter treat non-communications as an extraneous, rather banal "point" to be made'.[9] The major contrast was made in the most perceptive of all early reviews of *The Birthday Party*, 'Mr Pinter's world is one of fantasy; not however of the Ionesco school with its formalism of swelling corpses, piling furniture and gathering chairs',[10] referring to the externalised stage symbols of, respectively, *Amédée or How to Get Rid of It* (1953), *The New Tenant* (1953) and *The Chairs* (1951). The implicit allegory of Ionesco's theatre appeared most overtly in *Rhinoceros* (1960).

In this play, all but one in a small provincial town turn into a rhinoceros. The allegory of conformist fascism is very clear, heavily so in places: 'Good men make good rhinoceroses, unfortunately. It's because they are so good that they get taken in.'[11] At one point a character turns into a rhinoceros before our eyes. The visual power is stunning but reflection shows that the originality of theatre is incommensurate with the orthodoxy of thought. Compare *The Birthday Party* – to what extent is Goldberg and McCann's abduction of Stanley analogous to fascist atrocity? Pinter's multi-levelled theatricality thwarts a simple allegorical reading.

Pinter denied the influence of Ionesco, claiming that he had never heard of him until after his early plays. Yet in 1959 he acknowledged seeing *The New Tenant*[12] (which had been produced with *The Bald Prima Donna* in London in 1956) and there does seem to be a likeness between the garrulous concierge and Rose in *The Room*. Moreover, Ionesco's theatre provided a public debate in 1958.[13] With the realism of *The Caretaker* Pinter moved on from the absurdism of the 1950s, but his name was still to be associated with that of Beckett.

In 1970 Pinter declared Beckett to be 'the greatest writer of our time'.[14] A forceful indication of his respect survives in a brief letter of 1954: 'I don't want philosophies, tracts, dogmas, creeds, way outs, truths, answers, *nothing from the bargain basement*. [Beckett] is the most courageous, remorseless writer going.'[15] At this point, just before the first London production of *Godot*, Pinter is responding to the artistic integrity of Beckett's fiction. 'I didn't read a play of Beckett's for a long time' Pinter recorded in 1963.[16] Michael Billington gives an account of Pinter's discovery of *Godot*. In Ireland during 1955, Pinter learned of Peter Hall's forthcoming production, obtained a copy of *Godot* in French which he worked through, translating with friends, and then saw the play in London.[17] In another interview Pinter mentioned hearing Beckett's *All That Fall* (1957), which demonstrated 'a certain uniqueness about radio',[18] namely a complete imaginative absorption not possible in the theatre. We may assume that, correspondingly, this is what Pinter hoped to achieve in the original radio production of *A Slight Ache*, some of the dialogue of which L. A. C. Dobrez acutely compares to the prose reveries of Beckett's *Watt*.[19]

Reviewers of *The Birthday Party* occasionally linked Beckett and Ionesco's names, but Beckett's name was regularly invoked with *The Caretaker* – for praise or blame. Mac Davies, the prevaricating tramp, along with the procrastinating Aston, immediately prompted comparison with Estragon and Vladimir of *Godot*. At an unsympathetic extreme it was suggested that 'this is the way in which all original visions are reduced by inadequate imitation into conventional realism'.[20] Robert Brustein made an analytic distinction: though Pinter may have borrowed some Beckettian techniques, 'the comparison is more misleading than illuminating … In *Waiting for Godot* the action is metaphorical and universal; in *The Caretaker* it is denotative and specific.'[21] My own view is that Beckett and Pinter use theatricality to quite opposite ends: *Godot* dismantles religion and philosophy to reveal the emptiness of teleological truth, whereas *The Caretaker* ultimately transcends theatricality by realising arguably the only truth we have, existence itself.

Still further indebtedness was claimed with the production of *Landscape* and *Silence* in comparison with Beckett's *Play* (1964). Beckett's work had three figures buried in notorious urns speaking in cross-cut monologues, alternately illuminated by a spotlight. To some extent this minimalist immobility is reflected in Pinter's plays as, indeed, is the content of failed love. *Silence*, it may be conceded, is the most Beckettian of all of Pinter's plays particularly in its use of past and present voices in relation to the fragmentary arbitrariness of memory, as can be found in such plays as *Krapp's Last Tape* (1958) and *Embers* (1959). And yet it possibly anticipates *That Time* (1976). Let a reviewer of 1960 have the last word here: *The Caretaker* 'stands up with full stature to the comparison' with *Godot*, 'it savours of Chekhov, Beckett and Ionesco but, still more, of life itself'.[22]

Life for Pinter's great predecessor, Anton Chekhov, was pedestrian: 'life … as it really is', that is, not life 'on stilts' of nineteenth-century melodrama.[23] Pinter said something similar in considering 'Life with a capital L, which is held up to be very different to life with a small l, I mean the life we in fact live.'[24] The two dramatists have been compared many times and, indeed, there are several common factors in their work.

Chekhov and Pinter wrote for a proscenium arch theatre; strong curtain lines are found in both. Chekhov favoured the exposition of the well-made play, which Pinter abhorred as false. However, Chekhov replaced the catastrophe–denouement with the long drawn out coda of the last act. In spite of Stanislavsky's emphasis on the realism and tragedy, Chekhov insisted that the comedy of his plays should be stressed. Conversely, while Pinter is always enjoyed in the theatre as a distinguished writer of comedy, it is very rare for any criticism to take this into account. Each uses comedy to preempt the audience from slipping into a consolatory emotional response of pathos and sentiment. Realism is thereby compromised by theatricality of speech, situation and character. In Chekhov some characters hide their pain behind a comic mask, whereas Pinter uses laughter to induce a retroactive guilt as audience insecurity parallels that of his characters.

Stanislavsky defined the Chekhovian subtext as 'the manifest, the inwardly felt expression of a human being in a part, which flows uninterruptedly beneath the words of a text, giving them life and a basis for existing'.[25] Comparably, Pinter writes '[t]here] are two silences. One when no word is spoken. The other when perhaps a torrent of language is being employed. This speech is speaking of a language locked beneath it. That is its continual reference. The speech we hear is an indication of that which we don't hear.'[26] Typical of Chekhov's dialogue is the way that characters will occasionally talk across each other, as if encapsulated in private worlds. In contrast, evasion of communication characterises Pinter's dialogue. As John Russell Brown points out, one of the striking features of Chekhov's and Pinter's plays is the way in which the most profound expression of feeling is through silence, as at the close of *Uncle Vanya* and *The Caretaker*, for example.[27] Chekhov is famous for his 'orchestration' of detail as if his dialogue were composed like a musical score. Again, his promotion of ensemble acting, as opposed to the somewhat operatic star system, often drew comparisons with chamber music. Comparably, a reviewer of *The Caretaker* praised Donald McWhinnie for directing 'with melodic perfection'[28] and the interweaving allusions to 'shoes', 'Sidcup' and 'papers', 'shed', 'saws' and 'roof' indeed suggest the contrapuntal augmentation of musical composition. But such likenesses should not blind us to the differences, which some examples will bring out.

The last words of Toozenbach to Irena, in *The Three Sisters*, before going off to possible death in a duel, are 'I didn't have any coffee this morning. Will you tell them to get some ready for me?'[29] In Act One of *The Caretaker*, having been told by Aston that the gas stove does not work, Davies asks 'What do you do for a cup of tea?'[30]

Because of the crucial situation Toozenbach's celebrated lines, in spite of their banality, give expression to the subtextual emotional impasse that has just been admitted – he is passionately in love with Irena who has agreed to marry him, although she does not love him. Therefore Toozenbach cannot make a certain kind of romantic appeal because he knows it cannot truly be reciprocated. The psychological truth is recognisable, but so is Chekhov's anti-conventional agenda. As an ironic consequence the lines cannot escape melodrama, albeit of an inverted kind.

Davies's question could be taken literally and the lines simply accepted as an incidental example of Pinter's superb ear for colloquial accuracy. But the inflexible self-interest created by a tramp's way of life suggests that Davies, once more the hard-done-by victim, is indirectly protesting 'Ain't I even going to get a cup of tea?' The first of a number of references to the stove is made here, which subsequently show that Davies just cannot get it into his head that the appliance is unconnected. Thus the question can be taken in terms of Davies's fears of leaking gas as one more example of a malevolent world: 'I don't believe that stove's not working [since you must make a cup of tea].' Alternatively, the question can be read as revealing the basic imperative of a way of life which keeps complete deprivation one symbolic cup of tea away, with the added irony that all that it represents – sustenance, warmth, society – have already been precluded by Davies's habitual repugnance. With Toozenbach's words we know exactly where we are: with examples like that of Davies, which are characteristic of Pinter on the whole, we are drawn into the endless permutations of possibility.

In comparing Chekhov's and Pinter's plays generally, consider the conventional pattern of arrival–disruption–departure as it is found in *Uncle Vanya* and *The Homecoming*. In the Chekhov, individual psychology and emotion are coordinated and conditioned by class structure. Thus Yeliena and Serebriakov start a chain reaction of cause and effect on the other characters according to status, age and position within a determining social microcosm. In *The Homecoming* all cultural values are deconstructed by the visceral, atavistic animality revealed by the reaction to Ruth. Thus for Chekhov existence is always measured against the domestic sphere of social reality, but here Pinter's almost anthropological insight reveals a reality beneath the social.

Chekhov, Ibsen and Strindberg are commonly regarded as the founding fathers of twentieth-century drama. Though Pinter is infrequently compared to Ibsen, a general and a highly specific case for influence can be made. Thomas Postlewait sees Ibsen as bequeathing the conventional characterisation of women in terms of sexual identity, desire and power in the male-dominated home, and builds a fascinating comparison between Hedda, of *Hedda Gabler*, and Nora, of *A Doll's House*, with Ruth, in *The Homecoming*.[31] The specific case is an unusual one, as I shall show below in arguing that the direct influence of Ibsen in James Joyce's *Exiles* reappears in Pinter's *Betrayal*.

August Strindberg's restless dramatic experimentalism anticipates the major developments of the twentieth century. Pinter's plays are occasionally compared with Strindberg, particularly *The Collection*, which featured in a double bill with Strindberg's *Playing With Fire* (1892), directed by Peter Hall in 1962. In one way this was a curiously prescient choice since its concern with a husband abetting his own adulterous betrayal by a friend anticipates Pinter's *Betrayal*. Recently Michael Billington paired *The Lover* with Strindberg's *The Stranger* (1889), a monologue in which a wife addresses her husband's former lover. In his review Adrian Noble called Pinter 'Strindberg's natural heir'.[32] Looking at Strindberg's realist period, in plays like *The Father* (1887) and *The Creditors* (1888), it is possible to identify the power struggles of sexual politics, outright misogyny and the fixation with the male's impotent defeat by the female, with those in such plays as *The Lover*, *The Collection* and *The Homecoming*.

More specific influence is difficult to argue, but it can be said that Pinter is the heir to some of Strindberg's theoretical innovations, namely his pause/silence technique, and his concept of dialogue in relation to the exploration of musical form. 'Silence cannot hide anything – which is more than you can say for words'[33] says Hummel just before the 'ghost supper' of *The Ghost Sonata* (1907) which is, indeed, structured around pauses, silences and long silences. Probably by way of Beckett, Pinter became notorious for this technique, which Strindberg developed before Chekhov. Eventually, Pinter structured a whole play by the feature that was to provide its title, *Silence*. In the preface to *Miss Julie* (1888) Strindberg stressed the irregular, haphazard nature of his realistic dialogue in contrast to the mechanistic symmetries of French drama. Strindberg's aleatory dialogue 'is worked over, picked up again, repeated, expounded, and built up like the theme in a musical composition',[34] which sounds exactly like a description of Pinter's dialogue in *The Caretaker*, that Irving Wardle characterised as like a 'sonata movement', 'undergoing development and combination'.[35] Another influential experimentalist and theorist was Luigi Pirandello.

In 1980, when Pinter received the 'Premio Pirandello' in Palermo, he remarked that he was surprised as he felt that his plays were 'at the other end of the telescope' from those of Pirandello himself.[36] Pinter probably had in mind the metadrama of a philosophy of life and art as found in *Six Characters in Search of an Author* (1921) and *Henry IV* (1922). None of Pinter's plays are self-reflexive or cerebral in the same way, but Pirandello's mixture of the comic and tragic, his dislike of symbolism and abstraction, and above all his destabilisation of the audience, are all common to Pinter's drama. One of the principal modes of promoting audience instability in both is to frustrate the need for verification. In this respect Pirandello's *Right You Are (If You Think So)* (1917), is usually compared with *The Collection*.

Both plays are concerned with the problem of verification where two conflicting versions of a situation are given and a third party has to decide on which may be true. Pirandello is seemingly concerned with revealing the social snobbery of the bourgeoisie in a comedy of manners, but the existential twist at the close raises the psychological and philosophical question of the relativity of the truth and the alienation of identity. In *The Collection* James pursues the truth of apparent adultery in the conflicting stories of his wife and Bill, who use fictions to reposition themselves in the power struggles of domestic relationships. But it emerges that James is possibly as much in flight from the truth of his own situation, from heterosexual rejection and homosexuality. Elsewhere, among several interesting allusions to Pirandello, L. A. C. Dobrez compares the Matchseller of *A Slight Ache* as object of Edward's and Flora's fantasies to the veiled figure at the end of *Right You Are*, who declares 'I am the one you believe me to be.'[37]

Pirandello paradoxically entitled his collected plays 'naked masks'. Comparably, a major aspect of Pinter's drama is to disclose the verbal 'stratagem to cover nakedness'.[38] A significant difference, however, is that for Pirandello identity is deeply subjective and incommunicable – the 'private world' of the Father in *Six Characters*, the 'impenetrable world' of *Henry IV*[39] – whereas Pinter's characters evade communication to resist 'being known'.[40] As a consequence, for each dramatist to discover a character is to encounter an autonomous otherness rather than each creating a fiction out of omniscient imagination. In his famous preface to *Six Characters* Pirandello described how his maidservant, Fantasy, admitted the insistent characters to his study. Similarly, in his speech on accepting the Hamburg Shakespeare prize, Pinter recorded 'I am aware, sometimes, of an insistence in my mind. Images, characters insisting upon being written.'[41]

There is a further area of common ground, that of Pirandello's theory of 'l'umorismo', or humourism,[42] which is related both to character and dramatic structure. For Pirandello humour is much more profound than the mere laughter of comedy, or the moral indignation of satire. The core concept is expounded in Pirandello's example of a grotesquely made-up old lady with an appalling hair-do, attempting to look like a young girl. In fact she looks like an 'exotic parrot', he tells us. The incongruity creates an 'awareness of the opposite' – what a respectable old lady should look like – which gives rise to comic laughter. But when a deeper 'reflection' arises in the viewer it makes us aware of the possible underlying cause of such an appearance (attempting to keep the love of a much younger husband, for example). Then we can no longer laugh. 'Reflection' has made us shift to a 'feeling of the opposite' which makes us respond with compassion, even though elements of the initial comic response may remain.[43]

Consider *The Birthday Party* and *The Caretaker* in the light of this. In Act Two of the former Meg enters for the party *'in evening dress'*,[44] which is immediately stressed in the subsequent exchange. Incongruously, Meg claims that her father gave it to her. The shift in action from Stanley's interrogation creates the laughter of relief which is increased by Meg's garish appearance: 'like a Gladiola',[45] as Goldberg says. In Pirandello's terms, we laugh from an 'awareness of the opposite', the disparity between intention and appearance, yet 'reflection' gives rise to the 'feeling of the opposite'. Meg's simple-minded delusion reminds us of the father who seemingly abandoned her as a child, and of her hope to please Stanley, the surrogate of her thwarted maternal longings. Comedy is deepened by the latent compassion of 'humourism'.

Again, consider the figure of Davies in Act Two of *The Caretaker*, trying on the *'deep-red velvet smoking jacket'*, and asking, 'You ain't got a mirror here, have you?'[46] The 'awareness of the opposite' is hilarious: the smoking jacket as synecdoche for that pre-war world of the sophisticated gentleman, glamour and romance – and Davies the tramp. But the inevitable 'reflection' gives rise to 'feeling of the opposite' by which the smoking jacket symbolises all that Davies is denied – status, friendship, love, comfort and so on. We still laugh at Davies as a stereotype of comic affectation here but this is ultimately displaced by the residual compassion for the plight of a human being at the close.

For Pirandello, as for Pinter, '[t]he humourist ... treasures ... ordinary events and common details ... all [of] which may appear trivial and vulgar',[47] but humourism allows these to shape the artistic structure. What Roger W. Oliver says of Pirandello, '[t]his conflict [of humourism] between surface appearance and deeper realities becomes the basis for both subject matter and dramatic technique',[48] is also true of Pinter.

Pirandello's work made a major contribution to modernism. Two other leading modernists, T. S. Eliot and James Joyce, directly influenced two of Pinter's plays, respectively *No Man's Land* and *Betrayal*.

T. S. Eliot 'I admire extremely', Pinter recorded.[49] In the early 1950s he joined a group touring London with a production of the choruses from Eliot's *The Rock* (1934).[50] Eliot's 'Aristophanic fragment' of the 1920s, *Sweeney Agonistes*, was regularly compared with the early Pinter for the common qualities of menace and banality, music-hall stylisation and the demotic. Eliot's Dusty and Doris exchanges are often compared with those at the opening of *The Birthday Party*; they make an even stronger parallel with those of Annie and Millie in *Night School*. Eliot speculated that perhaps the music-hall comedian would make the 'best material' to transform 'entertainment' to a 'form of art', but it was Pinter who fully realised this with such echoes of the cross-talk double-act of Goldberg and McCann in *The Birthday Party*. Similarly, the 'new form' which might be devised out of 'colloquial speech' that Eliot experimented with, for example at the opening of *The Cocktail Party*, is the celebrated hallmark of Pinter's whole *oeuvre*.[51] Goldberg and McCann's pursuit of Stanley to the seaside boarding-house has often been likened to the Eumenides' pursuit of Harry to the security of his family seat in *The Family Reunion* (1939). Again, an Unidentified Guest at *The Cocktail Party* (1949) leads to the jungle martyrdom of another guest: we do not know the precise fate of Stanley following his birthday party.

Pinter's blind Negro, Riley, in *The Room*, is arguably a burlesque of Eliot's Unidentified Guest who sings the music-hall song of the 'one-eyed Riley' and turns out to be Sir Henry Harcourt-Reilly. Pinter's Riley also brings a form of revelation, but it is existential rather than Christian. Elsewhere, as Katherine Burkman has hinted, *A Slight Ache* can be considered from one point of view – given Edward's displacement and the seasonal vegetative references – as a burlesque of fertility ritual as found in J. G. Frazer's *The Golden Bough* (abridged 1922) which contributed to the symbolism of Eliot's *The Waste Land* (1922).[52] But it was not until *No Man's Land* that Pinter indirectly confronted the informing beliefs of Eliot's dramatic world. For all the upper-class ennui of those conventional drawing rooms, Eliot is concerned with atonement and salvation.

Spooner overtly identifies himself with Prufrock, by repeatedly alluding to his lines – 'For I have known them all already ... And I have known'[53] – with 'I have known this before.'[54] The epigraph of 'Prufrock' from Dante's *Inferno*, Spooner's allusion to 'terza rima'[55] and the significance of Dante in *The Waste Land*, suggest a loosely parodic relationship between Spooner–Hirst as a mock Virgil–Dante, and the wasteland of Bolsover Street as reflecting Dante's third canto, but there are more direct correspondences to Eliot's dramatic work. Russell Davies has justly paralleled the drinks exchange between the Unidentified Guest and Edward in *The Cocktail Party*[56] but the greater correlation is between *The Elder Statesman* (1958) and *No Man's Land*.

In *The Elder Statesman*, after changing his name to Gomez, Culverwell returns to Lord Claverton's home where, as he knocks back the drink, he reveals his intention to pursue friendship, while at the same time reminding his host of the guilty secret of Oxford days: quite precise analogues for Spooner and Hirst in Act One. Again, Hirst's loneliness is kept at bay by his photograph album whereas Claverton's loneliness is exacerbated by his symbolic engagement book. In great contrast, Hirst at the close remains in his particular alcoholic circle of hell, Pinter thereby effectively rejecting any parallel to the epiphany of love vouchsafed to Claverton, just as Briggs and Foster's mock-antiphony parodies Eliot's liturgical mode.

In Pinter's next play we find a similar structural relationship: Acts One and Two of Joyce's Ibsenesque *Exiles* provide the genesis for scenes one and two of *Betrayal*. The direction of *Exiles* in 1970, a few years before writing *Betrayal*, not only demonstrated Pinter's lifelong admiration for all of Joyce's work but also brought into focus the preoccupation with male friendship and betrayal common to both writers which is reflected in the central conflict of each play. There are very many correspondences in verbal detail and dramatic situation. A few from each category are examined here, as further demonstration may be considered elsewhere.[57]

In *Exiles* Richard and Bertha return to Dublin and meet Robert and Beatrice once again, after nine years. Pinter's Emma admits to Jerry that she has confessed her adultery to Robert nine years after the affair began. Towards the end of Act One of *Exiles*, following the love overtures of Robert, Bertha is interrogated by her husband and reveals all that took place in the flirtation. In scene one of *Betrayal* the ex-lovers Jerry and Emma meet up in a pub and Emma reveals that not only are she and Robert about to separate, but that she revealed to him 'last night'[58] her affair with his oldest friend. In Act Two of *Exiles* Richard makes his way to Robert's cottage and confronts him with the betrayal: 'I know everything. I have known for some time … Since it began between you and her.'[59] Robert assumes that Richard was told 'This afternoon', but Richard has to disabuse him, 'No. Time after time; as it happened.'[60] In scene two of *Betrayal*, at Jerry's request Robert has arrived at his house, where he acknowledges that Emma 'didn't tell me about you and her last night. She told me about you and her four years ago.'[61] Robert expostulates with Richard, 'And you never spoke! You had only to speak a word.'[62] Jerry remonstrates with Robert, 'Why didn't you tell me?'[63] Richard leaves Robert with Bertha after the confrontation in Act Two. Eventually Robert hesitatingly asks, 'Did you tell him – everything?' 'Everything',[64] Bertha replies. Correspondingly, in scene one of *Betrayal* it eventually occurs to Jerry to ask, 'You didn't tell Robert about me last night, did you?' 'He told me everything. I told him everything', Emma answers. Staggered, Jerry asks twice, 'You told him everything?'[65]

In Act Three of *Exiles* Bertha expostulates with Richard, 'You are a stranger … A stranger! I am living with a stranger!'[66] In the longest speech of *Betrayal* Robert plays on relationship, title and names, and the idea of being a 'stranger': 'We could be, and in fact are most vastly likely to be, total strangers … I could very easily be a total stranger.'[67] At an early stage Joyce's Robert appeals to Richard 'for the sake of … our friendship, our life-long friendship'.[68] 'Your husband is my oldest friend',[69] Jerry reminds Emma.

Finally, all that is implicit in the buried homoerotic psychology of the men in *Betrayal*, is arguably made explicit in *Exiles*: 'You are so strong that you attract me even through her',[70] Robert says to Richard, who later acknowledges 'I longed to be betrayed by you and by her.'[71]

In conclusion, we can see the likely influence of Beckett, and the direct influence of Eliot and Joyce, on the genesis of specific plays, and the indirect influence of realist and experimental dramatic traditions. In some cases, Pinter's technique bears a fascinating resemblance to his predecessors. However, on closer analysis we find that each of Pinter's plays has its own character and accomplishment, and the totality of his drama, over nearly half a century, is of unique, unrivalled distinction.

NOTES

1. See David T. Thompson, *Pinter: the Player's Playwright* (London and New York: Macmillan, 1985), pp. 131–5.
2. All references to Pinter's plays are to the four-volume Faber edition (London, 1991), as follows: *The Room, The Birthday Party, A Night Out, The Dumb Waiter, A Slight Ache (Plays One); The Caretaker, The Collection, The Lover, Night School (Plays Two); The Homecoming, Landscape, Silence (Plays Three); No Man's Land, Betrayal (Plays Four).*
3. Pinter, 'Writing for Myself', *Plays Two*, p. ix.
4. *The Daily Mail*, 7 March 1964, p. 8.
5. 'New Comment', interview with Laurence Kitchin, 8 October 1963, BBC transcript, p. 10.
6. Quoted by Martin Esslin, *The Theatre of the Absurd* (Harmondsworth: Penguin, 1968), p. 23.
7. *The Financial Times*, 20 May 1958, p. 15.
8. *Plays and Players*, 7, 10 (July 1960), 15.
9. *The Manchester Guardian*, 29 April 1960.
10. *The Isis Review*, 14 May 1958, p. 27.
11. Eugène Ionesco, *Rhinoceros. The Chairs. The Lesson* (Harmondsworth: Penguin, 1976), p. 104.
12. *The Times*, 16 November 1959, p. 4.
13. See Eugène Ionesco, 'The London Controversy', *Notes and Counter-Notes* (London: John Calder, 1964), pp. 90–112.
14. *New Theatre Magazine* 11, pt.3 (May–June 1971), 3.
15. Harold Pinter, *Beckett at Sixty* (London: Calder and Boyars, 1967), p. 86.
16. 'New Comment', interview with Laurence Kitchin, 8 October 1963, BBC transcript.
17. Michael Billington, *The Life and Work of Harold Pinter* (London: Faber, 1996), p. 51.
18. 'Talking of Theatre', a joint interview with Donald McWhinnie, with Carl Wildman, 7 March 1961, BBC transcript, pp. 9–10.
19. L. A. C. Dobrez, *The Existential and Its Exits: Literary and Philosophical Perspectives in the Work of Beckett, Ionesco, Genet, and Pinter* (London and New York: Athlone Press, St Martin's Press, 1985), p. 333.
20. Nigel Dennis, 'Optical Delusion', *Encounter*, 15 (July 1960), 64.

21. Robert Brustein, 'A Naturalism of the Grotesque', *Seasons of Discontent* (London: Jonathan Cape, 1966), p. 182.
22. *Theatre World*, 56, 425 (June 1960), 8–9.
23. Robert W. Corrigan, 'The Drama of Anton Chekhov', in *Modern Drama. Essays in Criticism*, ed. Travis Bogard and William I. Oliver (London, Oxford, New York: Oxford University Press, 1965), p. 79.
24. Pinter, 'Writing for the Theatre', *Plays One*, p. xi.
25. Constantin Stanislavsky, *Building a Character* (London: Methuen, 1968), p. 113.
26. Pinter, 'Writing for the Theatre', *Plays One*, p. xiii.
27. John Russell Brown, 'Dialogue in Pinter and Others', in *Modern British Dramatists*, ed. John Russell Brown (Englewood Cliffs, NJ: Prentice Hall, 1968), p. 140.
28. John Mortimer, *The Evening Standard*, 31 May 1960, p. 12.
29. Anton Chekhov, *Plays*, trans. Elisaveta Fen (Harmondsworth: Penguin, 1982), p. 321.
30. *The Caretaker*, *Plays Two*, p. 15.
31. Thomas Postlewait, 'Pinter's *The Homecoming*: Displacing and Repeating Ibsen', *Comparative Drama*, 15 (1981), 195–212.
32. Adrian Noble, *The Guardian*, 12 April 1977, 'The Week', p. 7.
33. August Strindberg, *The Chamber Plays*, trans. Evert Sprinchorn, Seabury Quinn Jr, and Kenneth Petersen (New York: E. P. Dutton, 1962), p. 136.
34. August Strindberg, *Seven Plays*, trans. Arvid Paulson (New York, Toronto, London: Bantam Books, 1964), p. 70.
35. Irving Wardle, 'There's Music in that Room', in *New Theatre of the Fifties and Sixties*, ed. Charles Marowitz, Tom Milne, Owen Hale (London: Eyre Methuen, 1981), p. 131.
36. *The Independent*, 26 November 1993, p. 14.
37. Dobrez, *The Existential and Its Exits*, p. 333.
38. Pinter, 'Writing for the Theatre', *Plays One*, p. 13.
39. Luigi Pirandello, *Three Plays* (London: Methuen, 1985), pp. 85, 187.
40. 'Harold Pinter: An Interview' (with Lawrence M. Bensky) in *Harold Pinter: A Collection of Critical Essays*, ed. Arthur Ganz (Englewood Cliffs, NJ: Prentice Hall, 1972), p. 26.
41. 'Speech: Hamburg 1970', *Theatre Quarterly*, 1 (1971), 4.
42. Pirandello, *On Humour*, trans. Antonio Illiano and Daniel P. Testa (Chapel Hill, NC: University of North Carolina Press, 1974).
43. *Ibid.*, p. 113.
44. *The Birthday Party*, *Plays One*, p. 47.
45. *Ibid.*, p. 48.
46. *The Caretaker*, *Plays Two*, p. 40.
47. Pirandello, *On Humour*, p. 144.
48. Roger W. Oliver, *Dreams of Passion. The Theatre of Luigi Pirandello* (New York and London: New York University Press, 1979), p. 4.
49. Pinter, 'Talking of Theatre', p. 7.
50. See Billington, *The Life and Work of Harold Pinter*, p. 21.
51. For these and the following Eliot references I am indebted to Andrew K. Kennedy's helpful discussion in his *Six Dramatists in Search of a Language* (Cambridge: Cambridge University Press, 1975), pp. 108–15.

52. Katherine Burkman, *The Dramatic World of Harold Pinter: Its Basis in Ritual* (Columbus: University of Ohio Press, 1971), pp. 47–64.

53. T. S. Eliot, 'The Love Song of J. Alfred Prufrock', *Collected Poems 1909–1935* (London: Faber and Faber, 1961), pp. 12, 13.

54. *No Man's Land*, *Plays Four*, pp. 78, 121.

55. *Ibid.*, p. 139.

56. Russell Davies, 'Pinter Land', *New York Review of Books*, 25, 21/22 (25 January 1979).

57. See Ronald Knowles, 'Joyce and Pinter: *Exiles* and *Betrayal*', *Barcelona English Language and Literature Studies*, 9 (1998), 183–91.

58. *Betrayal*, *Plays Four*, p. 179.

59. James Joyce, *Exiles* (London: New English Library, 1962), pp. 73–4.

60. *Ibid.*, p. 74.

61. *Betrayal*, p. 185.

62. *Exiles*, p. 75.

63. *Betrayal*, p. 188.

64. *Exiles*, pp. 97–8.

65. *Betrayal*, p. 179.

66. *Exiles*, p. 136.

67. *Betrayal*, p. 222.

68. *Exiles*, p. 45.

69. *Betrayal*, p. 198.

70. *Exiles*, p. 78.

71. *Ibid.*, p. 87.

6

STEVEN H. GALE

Harold Pinter, screenwriter: an overview

Harold Pinter is one of the premier dramatists of the twentieth century; he also is a master screenwriter. In spite of the fact that he has written twenty-four filmscripts and in the 1980s and 1990s his artistic attention was focused almost exclusively on his screenwriting, relatively little critical attention has been paid to this large segment of his canon.

Since his first scripted film, *The Servant*, appeared in 1962, he has had numerous cinematic successes, in terms of both popular acceptance and critical acclaim, and he has won several prestigious awards for his work. Besides being entered in major festivals, Pinter's films have been listed among the year's ten best consistently, and he received both the British Screenwriters Guild Award and the New York Film Critics Best Writing Award for *The Servant* (1963), the Berlin Film Festival Silver Bear and an Edinburgh Festival Certificate of Merit for *The Caretaker* (1963), the British Film Academy Award for *The Pumpkin Eater* (1964), the Cannes Film Festival Special Jury Prize and a National Board of Review Award for *Accident* (1967), the Cannes Film Festival Golden Palm for Best Film and the British Academy Award for *The Go-Between* (1970), and a National Board of Review Best English-Language Film Award for *The Last Tycoon* (1976). His more recent films, *The French Lieutenant's Woman* (1981), *Betrayal* (1982), *Turtle Diary* (1986), *The Handmaid's Tale* (1990) and *The Trial* (1993) have received equal praise from reviewers. As a matter of fact, critics claim that Pinter's distinctive style and unmistakable writing ability have been responsible for the best work done by several of his directors (as I documented in *Butter's Going Up* well over twenty years ago).[1]

The breadth of Pinter's screenwriting talent is demonstrated in the range of his sources. Of his filmscripts, four are adaptations of his own dramas: *Betrayal*, *The Birthday Party* (1968), *The Caretaker* and *The Homecoming* (1969). Pinter has adapted one film from another dramatist's play, Simon Gray's *Butley* (1974). Fifteen of the remaining eighteen filmscripts are cinematic translations of other writers' novels (most of which were recommended to him by others such as director Joseph Losey): Nicholas Mosley's *Accident*, Adam Hall's *The Berlin Memorandum* (released as *The Quiller Memorandum*, 1966), Ian McEwan's *The Comfort of Strangers* (1990), John Fowles's *The French Lieutenant's Woman*, L.P. Hartley's *The Go-Between*, Margaret Atwood's *The Handmaid's Tale*, Aidan Higgins's *Langrishe, Go Down* (1978), F. Scott Fitzgerald's *The Last Tycoon*, Penelope Mortimer's *The Pumpkin Eater*, Marcel Proust's *À la recherche du temps perdu* (published but not filmed), Kazuo Ishiguro's *The Remains of the Day* (Pinter took his name off the 1991 project), Fred Uhlmann's *Reunion* (1989), Robin Maugham's *The Servant*, Franz Kafka's *The Trial*, Russell Hoban's *The Turtle Diary*, and Joseph Conrad's *Victory* (published but not yet filmed). Furthermore, he worked on a screenplay version of *The Diaries of Etty Hillesum*, a Holocaust narrative, in 1996, although the project did not go forward, but he did complete an adaptation of Isak Dinesen's short story 'The Dreaming Child' in 1997 and of Shakespeare's *King Lear* in 2000.

At least fifteen of his other stage plays, *The Basement* (1967), *The Collection* (1961), *The Dumb Waiter* (1985), the award-winning *The Lover* (1963), *Monologue* (1973), *No Man's Land*, *The Hothouse* (1982), *Mountain Language*, *Night School* (1960), *A Night Out* (1960), *One for the Road* (1985), *Old Times* (1991), *Party Time* (1992), *The Room* (1985) and *Tea Party* (1965), plus *Pinter People* (a cartoon compilation of some of his revue sketches, 1969), have been produced on television, some of them more than once. Indeed, the screenwriter has also written several television adaptations, including a filmed version of Elizabeth Bowen's *The Heat of the Day* (1989), and it is important to note that in answer to questions about the difference between his work in television and film, he said that he makes 'no distinction between working for television and feature film'.[2]

This blurring of the lines between film and television is typical of the author, and it is evident from early on in his writing, as is his interest in the cinema, which dates back to his childhood. While a student at Hackney Downs Grammar School in 1946, Pinter published a piece in the school literary magazine called 'Speech: Supporting the Motion that "In View of its Progress in the Last Decade, the Film is More Promising in its Future as an Art than the Theatre"' and in the autumn of 1947 he published 'Speech: Realism and Post-Realism in the French Cinema', also in *Hackney Downs School Magazine*.

While it seemed that this interest in film was sidetracked by Pinter's playwriting career, it was never far below the surface. As can be gleaned from the dates of plays and television productions cited above, the writer worked on television scripts at the same time that he was composing stage dramas. This is clearly evidenced in incidents of cross-over. Most notable of these cross-overs are the early plays that appeared on both television and the stage, some in one venue first, some in the other first. For instance, *The Birthday Party* was performed in the theatre in 1958 and then on television two years later. *ANight Out* was also telecast in 1960 and subsequently went on the boards in 1961. *The Basement*, originally titled *The Compartment*, was commissioned as one of three segments of a Grove Press film project, 'Project I: Three Original Motion Picture Scripts by Samuel Beckett, Eugène Ionesco, and Harold Pinter' but was never made into a film, although it was televised in 1967 and then staged in 1968.

One of the most obvious examples of the writer's ease in moving between the media is found in the opening scene of *Old Times*, when Anna is observed on stage but is not involved in the action as Kate and Deeley talk about her. Suddenly, she turns and joins in the conversation in midstream. Most critics were confounded by this manoeuvre. Did it mean that Anna was an imaginary character, they wondered, or was she part of Kate's dual feminine nature? In actuality, Pinter merely demonstrated an effective use of a cinematic device. By having Anna's figure on stage, he indicated that she was on the minds of the two other characters, but he also avoided a lot of unnecessary stage business – there was no need for the husband and wife to stop their dialogue and then go to the door where introductions would be made and then the trio would sit down to dinner, and so on. As in a movie, then, with this theatrical equivalent of a jump-cut Pinter simplified and skipped all of the small talk and unnecessary stage business in an instant so that he, and the audience, could focus on what is important in the meeting.[3]

Anumber of the screenwriter's sources are relatively undistinguished (*The Servant, The Quiller Memorandum*); several have been at least minor modern masterpieces (*The Go-Between, The French Lieutenant's Woman, Lolita*). His cinematic adaptations, however, have typically included the invention of characters, the creation of lines, drastic deletions and the selection of a vital thematic element in his source on which to focus. By examining only a few of the screenwriter's motion picture scripts in chronological order (*The Servant, The Caretaker, The Go-Between* and *The French Lieutenant's Woman*), it is easy to see where his genius lies and how he has developed over the years.[4]

The Servant was Pinter's first film and his first major cinematic success as well. Taken from Robin (Sir Robert) Maugham's 1948 fifty-six-page novella of the same name, the script demonstrates one of the screenwriter's primary traits: the ability to extract the essence from his source and then to expand that element to create a product that is true to its original while at the same time being superior to it. This particular project appealed to Pinter because the prose version dealt with the theme of dominance and subservience which appears repeatedly in his own stage plays from *The Room* on. As he told

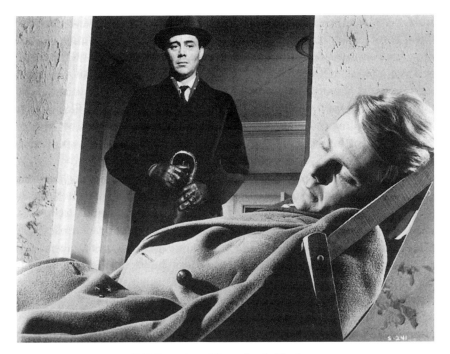

3 Dirk Bogarde and James Fox in *The Servant*

interviewer Lawrence M. Bensky, 'That's something of what attracted me to do the screenplay ... [the] battle for positions.'⁵ This theme becomes metaphorically and symbolically obvious almost from the beginning of the movie when the servant Barrett (played by Dirk Bogarde) is seen standing over his employer, Tony (James Fox), when they first meet. The early confrontation between the two men, when Tony invites his prospective manservant to sit down, is the first obvious indication that the characters are aware of the significance of the battle, for by forcing Barrett to take a seat, Tony temporarily enjoys a one-up position. The famous ball game on the staircase later on illustrates the shifting in positions beautifully, a shift that culminates in the party scene at the end of the film when Barrett is directing the action and Tony lies stupefied behind the bars of the cage-like banister.

Pinter wrote the motion picture script for director Michael Anderson, but he rewrote it when Losey decided to direct the film. This collaboration was to become one of the most effective in movie history. As Andrew Sarris concluded in *The American Cinema*: '*The Servant* and *Accident* have done more for Losey's general reputation than all of his other [twenty] pictures put together.'⁶ Losey and Pinter went on to work on *The Go-Between* and with

Claudia Bray they co-wrote the screenplay version of Proust's *À la recherche du temps perdu* (*Remembrance of Things Past*, which has been published as *The Proust Screenplay*, although it has never been filmed).

As significant as this first script was in terms of the writer's cinematic career, in terms of demonstrating his screenwriting technique it is even more important. He has taken a short tale about how a servant comes to dominate his putative master and turned it into an allegory of not only dominance but of the disintegration of a man's character. Pinter can do this because he has the ability to identify and isolate the essence of his source material. In this case, he focuses on Tony's weaknesses. That may seem a simple exercise, but the writer discards those elements of the novella which do not have a direct bearing on the meaning, and he emphasises and sometimes adds elements which reinforce the meaning. Given examples from cinematic adaptation as a genre, this is a noteworthy feat.

As a film, then, Pinter has improved on his source. Barrett is not even introduced until nearly one-sixth of the way through the book and there is no sense of conflict between the two men and no tracing of the breakdown of Tony's character in Maugham's less imaginative version. In contrast, Pinter focuses on Barrett from the movie's opening shot. The narrator is discarded and a secondary conflict grows out of the fiancée's relationship with the manservant, though the fundamental meaning of the movie centres on the theme of domination as related to the male characters. The basic difference between the novelist's approach and Pinter's is that in the first instance a story is related, a simple and brief recounting of something that has happened to a friend of the narrator. As a screenwriter, Pinter *demonstrates* the events taking place (the cinematic maxim is 'Don't tell, show'), leading his audience to a psychological understanding not only of what has happened but also why it has happened.

Everything in the novella is clear-cut and almost preordained because Barrett is equated with evil (like John Keats's Lamia, he is described as a snake) – he destroys from within 'by serving [his victim's] particular weakness'.[7] Vera represents lust and Tony symbolises the love for comfort and ease, a combination of sloth and gluttony. When Pinter turns these events into a psychological study (enhanced by the black and white photography), the story becomes interesting and moving.

The changes and additions gave Pinter some flexibility to pursue his characteristic interests, especially in exhibiting his love of tape-recorder-faithful dialogue and his special brand of humour (as in the oft-quoted 'gauchos'/ 'ponchos' exchange at the Mountsets') which revolves around miscommunications and wordplay. And, as John Russell Taylor pointed out, 'Tony's house is a sophisticated upper-class extension of the recurrent symbol in

Pinter's early plays, the room-womb which offers a measure of security in an insecure world',[8] so there are clear connections with his drama. The class-consciousness which underlies the action in *The Servant* ties the film to his later cinematic works as well. In truth, Pinter's work is clearly of a piece, it is all one, be it written for the stage or the screen – and while there are some technical differences due to the natures of the media, there are obvious technical carry-overs too.

Importantly, the alterations that Pinter effected in adapting *The Servant* established what was to become his basic approach to adaptation: 'I followed it [the novel] up. I think I did change it in a number of ways. I cut out the particular, a narrator in fact, which I didn't think was very valuable to the film, but I think I did change it quite a lot in one way or another, but I kept to the main core; at the same time the end is not quite the same ending that it was in the book. I must have *carte blanche* you know, to explore it.'[9]

Pinter's second film, *The Caretaker* (retitled *The Guest* when it was released in the United States) was based on his own stage play and thus does not illustrate the effect of selecting the essence of a work to be adapted that was apparent with *The Servant*. It does, however, display another kind of selection process, one which is important in the scenarist's development because it represents a realisation on his part of one of the major differences between writing for the stage and for the cinema.

Ironically, the author has had little experience translating his own theatrical productions to the silver screen, and *The Caretaker* almost did not make it. In spite of the play being an early success, there were problems in securing backing for a film version. The production cost of £30,000, with no guarantee of distribution, was privately financed by a group of backers which included Richard Burton, Leslie Caron, Noel Coward, Peter Hall, Peter Sellers and Elizabeth Taylor.

In this story of Aston (Robert Shaw) and Mick (Alan Bates), two brothers whose relationship is threatened by the intrusion of the tramp Davies (Donald Pleasence), Pinter faced a dilemma not present in the stage production:how to establish a claustrophobic psychological atmosphere. Director Clive Donner and cinematographer (later director) Nicholas Roeg helped with the construction of a set that replicated the cluttered milieu represented in the theatre and was emphasised by tight camera angles shot through the clutter on black and white film.

Pleasence, who had acted his part on stage (the other two actors had also played their characters in the stage version), reduced the plot to a six-word summary: 'boy meets tramp, boy loses tramp'.[10] For Pinter, this spare plot seemed cinematic. In 'Filming "The Caretaker"', an interview/article co-written by Pinter and Donner, he said, when you have two people standing on the stairs and one asks the other if he would like to be caretaker in this house, and the other bloke, you know, who is work-shy, doesn't want in fact to say no, he doesn't want the job, but at the same time he wants to edge round it ... Now it seems to me there's an enormous amount of internal conflict within one of the characters and external conflict between them – and it's exciting cinema.[11]

This is a natural conclusion, given the camera's ability to focus close up on actors' faces, for it is technically easier to convey internal conflict on film than on stage. Davies's shuffling dog-like back and forth behind Aston as he trails the brain-damaged brother down the street to the room in an early scene quickly and quintessentially captures the tramp's character. The small movements (smacking his hand with his fist, grimaces, nearly inaudible grunts and mumblings, and the like) reinforce this first impression.

Thus, for Pinter, the filming allowed him not only to capture certain elements that had been present in the play but to magnify them. So it is that the significance of the final glance between the two brothers is more emphatic (particularly the hint of triumph on Mick's part) because of the focusing ability of the camera. As Arnold Hinchcliffe has suggested,[12] this is crucial to understanding that in the end the two brothers reunite in order to expel the intruder. Like the fathers in *The Fantastics* who pretend that they want to keep their son and daughter separated in the hopes that this ploy will bring the children together, Mick must allow Aston to dismiss Davies in order to avoid having his brother take the tramp's side, which would have happened had Mick removed the menace, something which he is, of course, physically and psychologically capable of doing. On the stage there is only a slight implication of this motivation in the final scene, and the looks can easily be missed because there is nothing to direct the audience's attention specifically to the men's faces. On the screen, however, the expressions are carefully framed so that there can be no missing this brotherly exchange. Since the screen magnifies, less becomes more and a subtle glance takes on a significance that is diluted in the broader movements on stage, so the screen-writer can compress the action (and the time) in ways not readily available to the playwright.

But Pinter also wanted the audience to be aware that the play/screenplay extended beyond the physical bounds of the theatre/screen, and it was capturing the reality of the drama that delighted Pinter the most. While Davies may represent the existential Chaplinesque/Beckettian tramp on the road of life, he is also a *real* tramp who undoubtedly does 'stink the place out'. In screen parlance, there is another effect, called 'opening out', which is related to how the use of a camera can transform a play. In a review, Stanley Kauffmann emphasises the difference between the theatre and the cinema when he notes that in the film, 'at last, the work has been fully revealed'.[13] Pinter, again in 'Filming "The Caretaker"', agrees with this assessment:

> You can say the play has been 'opened out' ... that things ... crystallized when I came to think about it as a film. Until then I didn't know that I wanted to do them [films] because I'd accepted the limitations of the stage. For instance, there's a scene in the garden of the house, which is very silent; two silent figures with a third looking on. I think in the film one has been able to hit the relationship of the brothers more clearly than in the play.[14]

Obviously, filming *The Caretaker* was a learning experience for Pinter, and it is likely that he could truly come to comprehend the differences between stage and film only through translating one of his own works from one medium to the other. He turns this to his advantage over the rest of his career as a screenwriter, enjoying the creative freedom of writing for the screen (even if frustrated by the restrictions imposed by the business end of the profession – restrictions that ultimately led him to take his name off one script, *The Remains of the Day*, about which he is still bitter, and to try to remove his name from the credits of another, *The Handmaid's Tale*, which he has refused to publish and which caused him to demand contractually that he have final say in whether his name would appear in subsequent film credits). Pinter has commented on the effect of removing the limitations:

> What I'm very pleased about myself is that in the film, as opposed to the play, we see a real house [the movie was shot near his boyhood home] and real snow outside, dirty snow and the streets. We don't see them very often but they're there ... and these characters move in the context of the real world – as I believe they do. In the play, when people were confronted with just a set ... they often assumed it was all taking place in limbo, in a vacuum, and the world outside hardly existed, or existed at some point but was only half remembered. Now one thing which I think is triumphantly expressed in the film is Clive's concentration on the characters when they are outside the room.[15]

In addition to the entrance of Aston and Davies and the outside shed shot, the scenes to which the writer is referring include the opening with Mick parked in his van and the house in the background, which is followed by a sequence in which he enters the building, climbs the stairs and goes into the room, tracked by the camera, and the terrifyingly humorous scene of Mick driving the tramp around a traffic circle rather than down to Sidcup where he can 'recover' his papers.

Coincidentally, besides reflecting some of the dissimilarities in the two media with which Pinter is working, the opening out provides examples of how he approaches the differences. Because some of the action now takes place outside the room, dialogue must be added, cut, or rearranged to accommodate the new settings. Some dialogue is altered (the removal of lines from Aston's hospital monologue, for instance) due to the kind of flow of action demanded by film. Indeed, this becomes characteristic of Pinter's writing for the screen – he willingly substitutes pure action for words in many cases (particularly noteworthy is the condensation of Proust's 4,722-page-long novel, a task that he has called the most difficult in his life).

Six years after *The Caretaker* was released, Pinter completed the filmscript that brought him his most prestigious awards, his adaptation of L. P. Hartley's 1953 novel, *The Go-Between*. The third collaboration with director Losey, this film earned a best picture award at the 1971 Cannes Film Festival, winning a Palme d'Or, along with rave reviews which established his screen-writing reputation internationally.

In *The Go-Between*, the narrator, Leo, relates how he found his old diary and the memories that it evokes: in the summer of 1900 he stayed with a school chum in Norfolk where he was the go-between for a pair of lovers, carrying their messages back and forth; he discovered them making love, and the man committed suicide. In the epilogue, Leo returns to Norfolk and renews his acquaintance with the girl, who is now an old woman.

The screenplay is not an entirely faithful cinematic treatment of Hartley's novel, but as with Pinter's adaptation of *The Servant*, it was not meant to be. The major theme has been changed, subordinated really, and despite the accolades that it received, while it is a fine motion picture, *The Go-Between* is not as cinematically successful as some of his earlier films because the original is better in the first place, and because Pinter's choice of subject matter to emphasise is less compelling in the second place.

There are embedded in the film links to the playwright's dramas which deal with the subjects of memory, the past, the relationship between the two and their reality as they create the present or are created in retrospect by the present – in the manner of T. S. Eliot's 'Time present and time past / Are both perhaps present in time future, / And time future contained in time past' ('Burnt Norton') or Mary Tyrone's observation that 'The past is the present ... It's the future too' in Eugene O'Neill's *Long Day's Journey Into Night*. The themes in *The Go-Between* are the same as those that structure *Landscape* and *Silence*, two stage plays which Pinter wrote the same year that he wrote this screenplay (intriguingly, there is even a phrase in Hartley's novel, 'the landscape of a dream', which resonates with the title of the play that marked a major shift in Pinter's dramatic themes and style). Moreover, the plays of memory, in which the dramatist examines the workings of the mind and the interconnection between memory and time, are essentially capped by *Old Times*, which opened in the same year that *The Go-Between* was released.

There are clear indications in the British Library's Pinter Archives material (Box 21) that Pinter was wrestling with how to merge past and future. Among the materials is a draft outline, with chapter references to the novel, labelled 1–104 in ink, which is a scene chart that begins with chapter 2 of the novel (scenes 1–11) and concludes with '103, Mrs. M Leo Outhouse', the scene in which the young boy sees Marian and Ted making love, and '104 Return to Village'. Although there is a good bit of detail suggested about the scenes from the past, this outline includes almost nothing about the present scenes, how Pinter is going to handle the memory framework, and the like.

On three pages of yellow legal pad sheets, the author sketches a sequence that is his broad solution to the modern scene problem. It begins 'Split Epilogue into front and back – which consists of man's entrance into village into meeting with old lady.' A second note at the head of a major section is 'injection of present into boy's story/voice-over solitary boy scenes'. This is the impetus for the varied, restrained 'intrusions' of the present scenes into the memory scenes (i.e., the scenes from the past) that make up the bulk of the novel and the movie.

Pinter's treatment of the narrator in *The Go-Between* is different from that in *The Servant*. Where he discards the narrator in *The Servant* (the camera takes the narrator's place), he substitutes voice-overs in *Accident* and again in *The Go-Between*. The movement back and forth in time, which predates Pinter's work on his stage play, *Betrayal* (1978), and on his screenplay for *The French Lieutenant's Woman*, cannot be dealt with so easily, though. The techniques employed in *The Go-Between* (flashbacks, voice-overs) are fairly standard, and while they serve his purpose of transmitting thematic information, they are not what the writer was looking for. But his experimentation in trying to develop an acceptable approach to the dilemma of managing time in *The Go-Between* script surely led to his innovative and extremely successful method for *The French Lieutenant's Woman*.

Several elements embedded in the opening sequence of *The Go-Between* exemplify Pinter's approach to adapting Hartley's novel. To begin, the inter-cutting of past and present, which is Pinter's invention, and the use of voice-overs run through the film. Not only do these carry the thematic and plot threads of the original, but they also operate to emphasise the thematic points that the adapter wishes to focus upon, particularly the effect of events over time. Simultaneously, the absence of the narrator has an impact on the meaning of the film. Leo's reaction to Ted's harsh words in the kitchen is missing,[16] for instance, so we have to determine from the action itself what that reaction is instead of the narrator telling us.

Additionally, in the novel the theme of class is uppermost, with the introduction to adult sexuality almost assuming a secondary importance. This is partially because Leo is clearly aware of the class elements. He comments on them, and they are also reinforced by the descriptive passages and by the narrator's musings. Pinter has reversed the equation. Leo is still caught like Rosencrantz and Guildenstern in the midst of events that are beyond his understanding, but the action foregrounds the initiation theme. In turn, the class elements become secondary in part because they blend in as part of the setting, because they are not commented upon, and because many of Hartley's events, descriptions and conversations related to this theme have been deleted. This is integral to Pinter's technique: he pares things down, he combines, he condenses and he focuses on what he considers the major thematic element.

It is probable that it was the artistic freedom which Pinter found in screenwriting that allowed him to produce his greatest cinematic achievement, the screenplay for *The French Lieutenant's Woman*. There may be some disagreement about which of the sources for his cinematic adaptations is the best, but there can be no doubt that *The French Lieutenant's Woman* is his best screenplay. As Roger Ebert says, the script is 'both simple and brilliant'.[17] It is also the screenwriter's most inventive and imaginative screenplay, and both the film and the screenplay were nominated for Academy awards. In fact, it is the exemplar of Pinter's own declaration that, with screenplays, 'I don't just transcribe the novel; otherwise you might as well do the novel. In other words, these are acts of the imagination on my part!'[18]

John Fowles, whose 1969 novel of the same name served as Pinter's source, had not been 'happy' with previous movies made from his novels and had spent years trying to find the right director to turn *The French Lieutenant's Woman* into a film. As Fowles explained in a foreword to Pinter's published script, Karel Reisz had been involved with a difficult period piece (*Isadora*) and was not available, and Robert Bolt declined, on the basis that the novel was unfilmable. At this point the novelist and his agent, Tom Maschler, determined that they needed to look for a 'demon barber ... someone sufficiently skilled and independent to be able to rethink and recast the thing from the bottom up'; they also decided that Pinter was 'the best man for that difficult task'.[19] By happenstance, a development deal was offered to Fowles which included Pinter, but the novelist was not interested in the others involved in the proposed project. Then, in 1978, Maschler went back to Reisz, who now agreed – with the proviso that Pinter write the script.

Those components of Fowles's themes which probably attracted Pinter to this project were the manipulation of time and the exploration of the nature of reality (to some extent as related to art), which throughout his career occupied his attention in his own writing – dramas such as *The Lover*, *The Collection*, *The Homecoming*, *Landscape*, *Night*, *Silence*, *Old Times* and

No Man's Land – and virtually all of his filmscripts up to that time. In the script the screenwriter's interests are reflected in structure and theme alike. The challenge of the adaptation must have been irresistible.

Fowles's novel is extremely popular and highly acclaimed, but the very factors that make this so presented Pinter with an artistic challenge:how to capture the twentieth-century perspective from which the Victorian story is told, primarily through the vehicle of numerous authorial intrusions (foot-notes, references, poetry quotations, opinions, philosophical references, facts, descriptions) which flavour the novel. The alternating plotlines in the novel have a natural equivalent in cinematic parallel editing, but it is not the essentials of plotting that preoccupied the screenwriter. In an interview with Mel Gussow shortly after he finished the script, Pinter declared, 'The French Lieutenant's Woman. That's been bloody, bloody hard. It's a remarkable book. The problems involved in transposing it to film are quite considerable. It pretends to be a Victorian novel, but it isn't. It's a modern novel, and it's made clear by the author that he's writing it now. The whole idea had to be retained.'[20]

There were three major problems that Pinter had to confront in adapting this novel for the screen. The first of these troublesome concerns was the very complexity of Fowles's work which is generated by all of those authorial intrusions. The obvious technique of choice for accommodating these intru-sions would be the voice-over, but Pinter had concluded that this device was limiting. In fact, although he used voice-overs effectively, though only spar-ingly, in several of his earlier screenplays (most notably in The Go-Between), he chose to ignore the possibility in Lolita, where the nature of the original would seem to demand it.

The second dilemma was how to handle the dual ending of the novel. The first ending occurs in chapter forty-four with a short narration of how Charles contritely accepted a loveless marriage which he was doomed to suffer for the rest of his life in silent accord with Victorian tradition. In the second ending (which occurs in chapter sixty-one, over one hundred and thirty pages later), Sarah leaves. After years of searching for her, Charles, who has ended his relationship with Ernestina, finds Sarah, only to be rejected and left to rebuild his life existentially without her (or so the narrator suggests with his semi-hopeful references to a move to America and images of the sea – life goes on).

The third problem area was the normal dilemma of how to cut a novel-length story to fit within a typical film-length time limit, although Pinter had successfully managed this in his earlier adaptations.

To begin, in the script there has been an enormous amount of compression. The screenplay is equivalent to no more than about one-sixth of the length of the novel (the film has a running time of 124 minutes – Pinter cut more from his source in this adaptation than in any of his others, with the exception of *The Proust Screenplay*). This was accomplished by, among other things, eliminating the entire Winsyatt inheritance sub-plot and most of the Sam/Mary sub-plot.

Undoubtedly, the primary element of which Pinter can be proud is his execution of a *coup de cinéma* by replacing the narrator with a twentieth-century storyline and developing a film-within-a-film structure. What is interesting about the film version of *The French Lieutenant's Woman* is not the compression, cuts or alterations of the source material; what is interesting is what was added – though not the normal minutiae of details or dialogue – in the concept. Even though Pinter has admitted that the idea originated with Reisz,[21] it was the screenwriter who was responsible for the full realisation of the concept. The boldness and imaginativeness of this invention and its application brought an appreciative acknowledgment from Fowles:

> I am convinced now, in retrospect, that the only feasible answer was the one that Harold and Karel hit upon. We had all before been made blind to its existence by the more immediate problem of compressing an already dense and probably over-plotted book into two hours' screen time. The idea of adding an entirely new dimension and relationship to it would never have occurred to us; and quite reasonably so, with almost anyone but Harold Pinter.[22]

Pinter deserves Fowles's approbation, for he captures the essentials of the novelist's Victorian story, characters and era (which is all that many readers wanted when they went to the movie), but through the utilisation of the film-within-a-film construction he forefronts both the dual perspective and the underlying themes effectively.[23]

The paralleling of the two affairs as indicative of their respective societies serves to reveal the limitations of each, the constraint of the Victorians and the licence of the moderns, and the film-within-a-film technique is a perfect device to demonstrate this theme by juxtaposition. For instance, the proleptic technique – Mike and Anna sleeping together foreshadows what will happen when Charles and Sarah sleep together – is introduced easily and naturally in this format.

The intermixing of realities (and times) generated by the film-within-a-film allows Pinter to illustrate the subjective nature of reality. For example, else-where, Mike and Anna refer to a scene which they have just acted.[24] They have difficulty keeping straight which 'me' and 'you' they are talking about, the characters that they are playing or their actual selves. The intrusion of the Third Assistant is an abrupt reminder to the audience that there is a third reality (an idea reinforced by the character's title), that which the audience itself belongs to, which is entirely off screen, even though as viewers in suspended disbelief they may have been caught up temporarily in the duality being experienced by the on-screen characters.

An even more arresting example of Pinter's understanding of cinematic technique and his talent to use that knowledge effectively follows. It is a masterful scene created by Pinter that demonstrates how easily the fictional and the real sets of lives can become conjoined. Mike and Anna are rehearsing one evening in the empty billiard room of the hotel (shot 78):

ANNA: I'm looking at you.

MIKE: Yes, but now you come towards me, to pass me. It's a narrow path, muddy.

> *She walks towards him.*
> You slip in the mud.

ANNA: Whoops!

> *She falls.*

MIKE: Beautiful. Now I have to help you up.

ANNA: Let's start over again.

> *She goes back to the chair.*
> I've got my coat caught in the brambles.
> Suddenly you see me. Then I see you.

MIKE: Miss Woodruff!

> *She mimes her coat caught in brambles, tugs at it, walks along the carpet towards him. He steps aside. She moves swiftly to pass him, and slips. She falls to her knees. He bends to help her up. She looks up at him. He stops for a moment, looking down, and then gently lifts her. With his hand on her elbow, he leads her towards the window.*
> I dread to think, Miss Woodruff, what would happen if you should one day turn your ankle in a place like this.

> *She is silent, looking down.*
> *He looks down at her face, her mouth.*

ANNA: I must ... go back.

MIKE: Will you permit me to say something first? I know I am a stranger to you, but –

> *Sharp cut to:*

79. Sarah turning sharply. A branch snapping[25]

In the film, the called-for jump-cut takes place as Anna moves to pass Mike and she slips. The slip becomes a magnificently seamless slide into the Victorian story, a transition that carries the action immediately into the next sequence and the modern couple have become the Victorians. It is a beautifully efficacious cut used to weld the past and the present, the real and the imagined, together. The irony here, of course, is that even the 'real' lives are only reel lives on a silver screen.

Finally, solving the alternative endings problem was crucial. Pinter wanted to follow Fowles's lead with multiple endings and the possibilities that they engender, but the differences between each of those that the scenarist considered creates a unique meaning for his work. If Mike calls after Anna when she drives off from the cast's wrap party, as in the first instance, the movie is merely the story of two actors who have an affair, one of whom cannot admit that it has ended. If the tale ends with Charles and Sarah together in the studio, we are back in the Victorian story and the film no longer seems to have anything but a fictive grounding; the sense of any off-screen applicability is lost. Philosophically, the ending that Pinter chose is the most challenging, and it fits the thematic structure of the novel and film alike. The interjecting of a repeat of the happy-ending rowboat scene in the film itself draws the audience back into the Victorian story, yet it adds a sense of romantic unrealism to it, rather than being too pat like the studio ending. Mike is lost in a world between reality and illusion, and he cannot distinguish one from the other, but Anna escapes into reality, divorced from her role-playing, healthy and happy in the world of her real marriage and life outside the film. The dream-like repeat mirrors Mike's sensitivity at the film's conclusion, for even though he has lost Anna/Sarah, it is likely that he will live in a continuing fantasy instead of coping with reality, an ending foretold in Pinter's stage play *The Lover.*

In examining the progression of versions of the screenplay which are part of the archival material at the British Library, it is obvious that the screenwriter fine-tuned his material constantly and over a considerable amount of time in order to get what he considered the exact word or right combination or order of scenes. Sometimes he went back and forth between options several times before deciding on the final version. Just as obviously, it is not an accident that Pinter arrived successfully at the one approach which would accommodate all of the points of the Fowles novel cinematically. By the introduction of this new element in the form of a modern framework through the film-within-a-film, he retains the essence of Fowles's masterpiece – and at the same time makes the screenplay of *The French Lieutenant's Woman* a masterpiece in its own right.

Few of Pinter's contemporaries approach his success in moving between the media of stage and film – probably only Tom Stoppard and David Mamet, and possibly John Osborne. Despite his success, there can be no doubt that heretofore his contribution to screenwriting has not been recognised by scholars as being at the same level as his contribution to the theatre. Nevertheless, there can also be no doubt that he has made important contributions to the cinema, not the least of which has to do with the primary characteristics of his screenplays – in almost every case he has produced a script that was superior to his source and, more importantly, in virtually every instance that script is a work of art in its own right, one that stands by itself. That several of Pinter's works are now considered masterpieces of the cinema is an admirable and extraordinary accomplishment.

NOTES

1. Steven H. Gale, *Butter's Going Up: A Critical Analysis of Harold Pinter's Work* (Durham, NC: Duke University Press, 1977).
2. Pinter, in a letter dated 5 January 1991, in response to my letter to him of 22 October 1990, in which I asked, 'When you approach a script for television, such as *The Heat of the Day*, how do you view the project differently than when you are working on something that will be seen on a theatrical screen? In other words, are there techniques that you use differently for television and the movies? And, do you make a conscious distinction between television and the cinema in terms of how artistic, effective, valuable, important, or prestigious they are?'

    As he is with the theatre, Pinter has been fully involved with film-making, as a director (*Butley* and three television films) and as an actor (*The Caretaker, The Servant, Accident, Rogue Male, Turtle Diary, The Rise and Rise of Michael Rimmer, Mojo, Mansfield Park*, and in at least seven made-for-television films).
3. See my 'The Significance of Orson Welles in Harold Pinter's *Old Times*', *Notes on Contemporary Literature*, 13, 12 (March 1983), 11–12, for a full discussion of this scene.
4. Many of the scripts have been published. In addition, with the exception of *The Pumpkin Eater*, a myriad of versions of all of his scripts are available for perusal in the Harold Pinter Archives at the British Library. See Steven H. Gale and Christopher C. Hudgins, 'The Harold Pinter Archives ii: A Description of the Filmscript Materials in the Archive in the British Library', in *The Pinter Review: Annual Essays, 1995–96*, ed. Francis X. Gillen and Steven H. Gale (Tampa, FL: University of Tampa Press, 1997), pp. 101–42.
5. In Lawrence M. Bensky, 'Harold Pinter: An Interview', *Paris Review*, 10, 20 (Fall 1966), 30–1.
6. Andrew Sarris, *The American Cinema: Directors and Directions 1929–1968* (New York: Dutton, 1968), p. 96. Sarris also declared that 'Michael Anderson's career [thirteen previous films] is so undistinguished until *The Quiller Memorandum* that two conclusions are unavoidable, one that Harold Pinter was the true *auteur* of *The Quiller Memorandum*, and two that Pinter found in Anderson an ideal *metteur-en-scène* for his (Pinter's) very visual conceits' (p. 252). Actually, Pinter has worked with an impressive list of directors – besides Losey and Anderson, there have been Jack Clayton, Karel Reisz, Elia Kazan, Robert Altman, Paul Schrader, Jerry Schatzberg, David Jones and John Irvin – the consensus among film critics and scholars is that most of these have done their best work from his screenplays.
7. Robin Maugham, *The Servant* (London: Falcon, 1948; New York: Harcourt, Brace, 1949), p. 60.
8. John Russell Taylor, '*The Servant*', *Sight and Sound* (Winter 1963–4), 38–9.
9. Quoted in Arnold Hinchliffe, *Harold Pinter* (New York: Twayne, 1967), p. 128.

10. Quoted in Henry Popkin, *Modern British Drama* (New York: Grove Press, 1969), p. 24.
11. Pinter and Clive Donner, 'Filming "*The Caretaker*"', *Transatlantic Review*, 13 (Summer 1963), 17–26.
12. Hinchliffe, *Harold Pinter* (New York: Twayne, 1967).
13. Stanley Kauffmann, *A World on Film: Criticism and Comment* (New York: Dell/ Delta, 1966), p. 213.
14. Pinter and Donner, 'Filming "*The Caretaker*"', pp. 19–20.
15. *Ibid.*, p. 23.
16. Pinter, *Five Screenplays* (London: Methuen, 1971; New York: Grove, 1973), p. 311.
17. Roger Ebert, *Roger Ebert's Movie Home Companion 1989 Edition* (Kansas City and New York: Andrews and McMeer, 1988), p. 237.
18. Mel Gussow, 'A Conversation (Pause) with Harold Pinter', *New York Times Magazine*, 5 December 1971, p. 100.
19. John Fowles, 'Foreword' to Pinter's *The French Lieutenant's Woman: A Screenplay* (Boston: Little, Brown, 1981), p. viii.
20. Gussow, 'A Conversation', p. 53.
21. Michael Billington, *The Life and Work of Harold Pinter* (London: Faber, 1996), p. 272.
22. Fowles, 'Foreword', p. xi.
23. For those familiar with the commercial television version, the reaction may be one of confusion. Thirty minutes of 'extraneous' material was deleted by the televiser, to the detriment of plot, structure and theme.
24. Pinter, *The French Lieutenant's Woman: A Screenplay*, pp. 25–6.
25. *Ibid.*, pp. 30–1.

7

MARY LUCKHURST

Speaking out: Harold Pinter and freedom of expression

> Everyone has the right to freedom of opinion and expression; this right includes freedom to hold opinions without interference and to seek, receive and impart information and ideas through any media and regardless of frontiers.
>
> (Article 19, The Universal Declaration of Human Rights)

> Dear President Bush, I'm sure you'll be having a nice little tea party with your fellow war criminal, Tony Blair. Please wash the cucumber sandwiches down with a glass of blood.
>
> (Harold Pinter, the *Guardian*, 18 November 2003)

Two years after composing the above letter Harold Pinter was awarded the Nobel Prize for Literature. Many had thought that his outspoken views might preclude any chance of such an honour, but in the last decade the Nobel Prize judges have increasingly linked the award with a politics of human rights, and a championing of freedom of expression. In their citation the judges praised Pinter as a dramatist 'who uncovers the precipice under everyday prattle and forces entry into oppression's closed rooms'.[1] Pinter's insistence on speaking out, like other recent Nobel prize-winners, exemplifies the spirit of article 19 of the United Nations Universal Declaration of Human Rights. His blunt rage against the American/British invasion of Iraq had been made public in his poetry, in letters, and in speeches long before public opinion in the West turned anti-war; and his castigation of American imperialism has not ceased since the 1980s. In his controversial Nobel acceptance speech Pinter contended that 'the systematic brutality, the widespread atrocities, the ruthless suppression of independent thought' in communist Eastern Europe since 1945 have been fully acknowledged and documented, but that US crimes in the same era have scarcely been admitted, 'let alone recognised as crimes'.[2] He cited US support of right-wing military dictatorships, particularly in Latin America, as evidence of long-term criminal activity; and he attacked what he saw as the displays of 'absolute contempt' for United Nations charters, the Geneva Convention, international law and critical dissent in relation to the invasion of Iraq and the Guantanamo Bay detainees – acts for Pinter 'of blatant state terrorism'.[3] Over the course of fifty years, Pinter's political opinions have increasingly informed his theatre writing, and representations of human rights abuses have gradually become central to his project. The same major preoccupations that are manifest in his Nobel address – free speech, freedom of movement and the right to freedom from state aggression – are evident in early plays and crucial in the later ones. This chapter will explore Pinter's lifelong interest in representing the curtailing of freedom of expression.

The field of human rights is fraught with ideological controversy but in the aftermath of two world wars and the cold war, and the founding of institutions such as the United Nations, which is ever more concerned with humanitarian intervention, human rights issues now unquestionably play a prominent role in international politics.[4] Pinter was fifteen when the United Nations was founded and eighteen when the United Nations Universal Declaration of Human Rights was ratified in 1948. In the same year Pinter received his call-up papers for national service and exercised his own legal rights by registering as a conscientious objector. He went through a military tribunal, arrest, custody and a further trial, fortunately incurring nothing more than fines. It was an uncommon action at the time, particularly since Hitler was such a recent memory, but for Pinter it was an experience that taught him to be suspicious of politicians, was 'an early example of the corruption of a certain kind of bureaucracy' and the first major political decision of his life.[5] As a child who had witnessed the destruction of war in the East End of London, grown up with tales of death, disappearance and the concentration camps, and understood that his Jewish roots placed him among an ethnic minority, Pinter was one of the generation for whom the Declaration of Human Rights was created. The fact that he refers to the United Nations in his Nobel address is pertinent: if allowed to function according to its founding principles, he sees it as offering possible redress against the dominance of certain national and imperial agendas, but he is aghast that the United Nations has become subject to the very political oppression it seeks to overcome elsewhere. Kofi Annan was among the many who wrote to Pinter congratulating him over the Nobel award, praising him for speaking out: 'Throughout your career you have had the courage to be honest and outspoken on some of the most important and difficult issues facing humanity.'[6] Pinter replied in kind, writing of the debt he and many others owed to Annan.[7] Article 19 (see epigraph) sets forth a basic right for freedom of opinion and expression that Pinter has interrogated in differing ways throughout his theatrical career, but articles 5, 6 and 9 also provide interesting backdrops to Pinter's plays, especially those written from 1980 onwards.

Article 5
No one shall be subjected to torture or to cruel, inhuman or degrading treatment or punishment.
Article 6
Everyone has a right to recognition everywhere as a person before the law.
Article 9
No one shall be subjected to arbitrary arrest, detention or exile.[8]

Set out as fundamental ideals and ambitions in 1948, the Declaration of Human Rights has been of signal importance in many political negotiations and increasingly serves to define Western notions of 'civilisation', but the failure to implement this charter has, in recent years, been much more prominent than any success: Western democracies increasingly uphold it in principle while flouting in practice. Andrew Sullivan has argued that since the religious wars in the sixteenth and seventeenth centuries, 'The entire structure of Western freedom grew in part out of the searing experience of state-sanctioned torture' and he argues, like other contributors in Sanford Levinson's collection of essays on torture, that since 9/11 the West has come full circle by increasing levels of state intervention and state-sponsored torture in the name of the War on Terror.[9] Set against the mid to late twentieth century and current twenty-first century crises, Pinter's work is utterly of its time. He has steadfastly directed his gaze at a modern age of terror, surveillance and state control. Since the 1980s Pinter has consistently campaigned for freedom of expression and protested against torture, openly supporting organisations such as Amnesty International and PEN (and was part of the English PEN community who joined togther to form a body called Article 19 in protest at the *fatwa* issued against Salman Rushdie after the publication of *Satanic Verses*).[10] Many of his stage characters, however, are denied the right to speak out, some on pain of death: expressing an opinion contrary to the established line can have appalling consequences; speaking at all might be punished, outlawed or denied; and even the physical ability to utter words might be seen as too dangerous to permit.

Pinter has claimed that all his dramas are to do with 'terrorising through words of power – verbal power, verbal facility', but none is more so than his first professionally performed play, *The Birthday Party*.[11] The victim is Stanley, who is singled out for a visit by two interrogators, Goldberg and McCann, and is subjected to surreal rituals of verbal abuse both on- and off-stage. Stanley's annihilation is presaged at the end of Act Two, when Goldberg and McCann close in on him, the torch on his face, as he emits crescendoing, uncontrollable giggles and flattens himself against the wall.[12] The following morning, after a night of untold horrors with his persecutors, Stanley cannot control himself physically, has tried to screw the lenses of his glasses into his eye sockets, and has lost the power of speech. His torturers pointedly compare him to an animal.[13] Pinter concentrates the horror unflinchingly on Stanley's failed attempt at formulating words, which symbolises his complete subjugation and loss of autonomy:

GOLDBERG: What's your opinion of such a prospect? Eh, Stanley?
Stanley concentrates, his mouth opens, he attempts to speak, fails and emits sounds from his throat.

STANLEY: Uh-gug ... uh-gug ... eeehhh-gag ... (*On the breath.*) Caahh ... caahh ...
They watch him. He draws a long breath which shudders down his body. He concentrates.

GOLDBERG: Well, Stanny boy, what do you say, eh?
They watch. He concentrates. His head lowers, his chin draws into his chest, he crouches.

STANLEY: ug-gughh ... uh-gughhh ...

McCANN: What's your opinion, sir?

STANLEY: Caaahhh ... caaahhh ...[14]

In his stage directions Pinter represents the catastrophic collapse of Stanley's body through his abortive attempts to speak: drawing air and finding the strength to emit any sound at all calls on reserves and physical functions which have apparently been shattered. In the same way that McCann callously snaps his spectacles in half in Act Two, both Goldberg and McCann have 'broken' Stanley in body and spirit – a word often used to describe the purpose of torture.[15] The loss of vocal power and speech is particularly shocking because it reduces Stanley to the status of an absolute victim, unable to speak his pain and unable to protest. He is both his persecutors' captive and the prisoner of his own body.

In a letter to Peter Wood, director of the première, Pinter is clear that Stanley is 'neither hero nor exemplar of revolt': he is a man who briefly fights for his life but loses.[16] Stanley has no powers of self-analysis, Pinter explains: he 'cannot perceive his only valid justification – which is, he is what he is – therefore he certainly can never be articulate about it'.[17] If he had possessed self-knowledge, argues Pinter, Goldberg and McCann would either not have knocked at his door, or the play would have had a different 'articulate hero in its centre'.[18] Stanley lives through evasion, bluff and delusion, and proves no match for his accusers, but there is tragic poignancy in what Pinter calls 'Stanley's loss of himself'.[19] Stanley, then, in his fog of self-fakery and flight, has not lost freedom of expression since he never had any understanding of what authentic self-expression might be, but there is an argument, and Pinter pursues it, that in these last moments of traumatic utterance before he is removed from his day-to-day world to an infinitely worse place, he gains

4 Finbar Lynch and Paul Ritter in *The Hothouse*, directed by Ian Rickson, designed by Hildegard Bechtler, Royal National Theatre, 2007

momentary self-knowledge. These blood-curdling sounds are the last noises he will make in public, perhaps the last sounds he will ever make: the belated recognition of the loss of himself provides him with the only moments of self-perception he has ever had. Ironically, we are seeing Stanley in a moment of self-epiphany, but it is similar to the drowning man who sees the meaning in his life only as his lungs fill with water. Pinter writes of Stanley's exit with a brutal compassion.

> What else has he discovered? He has been reduced to the fact that he is nothing but a gerk in the throat. But does this sound signify anything? It might very well.

> I think it does. He is trying to go further. He is on the edge of utterance. But it's
> a long impossible edge and utterance [...] In the rattle in his throat Stanley
> approximates nearer to the true nature of himself than ever before and certainly
> ever after. But it is late. Late in the day. He can go no further.[20]

Stanley, then, stands on the brink of self-recognition but comes to it only momentarily and only through losing the very vocal power through which he might express himself. Political freedom of expression requires a bravery and a certainty of self which Stanley has never possessed.

Written in the same year as *The Birthday Party* was premièred, *The Hothouse* was not released for production until 1980. Set in a 'rest home', a cover for a secret state-run facility, where 'patients', known by number not name, are incarcerated and systematically forced to endure medical experiments, *The Hothouse* is a black comedy depicting the banal bureaucratisation of flagrant human rights abuses. It is run by Colonel Roote, an ageing despot, who is eventually murdered by an underling in a coup for power. The play presents only the staff and demonstrates what Amnesty International recognises as the necessary 'bureaucracy of repression' needed for rule by terror.[21] The real subjects are the invisible, wordless detainees who are eerily present in the intermittent soundscapes that Pinter has scored, and which director Ian Rickson exploited so effectively in his 2007 production at the National Theatre. Like Stanley, these patients are reduced to a small repertoire of vocal noises – sighs, screams, keens – that reverberate through the building. In Rickson's production these noises even unnerved Roote's staff, who froze, or looked round them for the source, or were momentarily silenced in mid-speech.

> Squeaks are heard of locks turning.
> The rattle of chains.
> A great clanging, reverberating, as of iron doors opening.
> Shafts of light appear abruptly about the stage, as of doors
> opening into corridors and into rooms.
> Whispers, chuckles, half-screams of patients grow.
> The clanging of locks and doors grows in intensity.
> The lights shift from area to area, rapidly.
> The sounds reach a feverish pitch and stop.[22]

Pinter's decision to embody patients only through vocal noise is interesting given the origins of *The Hothouse* as a radio play. But in the radio drama treatment he does include scenes of dialogue between staff and patients.[23] Removing patients from the stage as bodily presences heightens the spectator's imagination about what horrors they may be enduring, emphasises the secrecy and sinister qualities of the institution, and underlines the fact that detainees are denied the right to speak out. The play recalls the medical experiments practised by Nazi doctors in the death camps, and the terrifyingly meticulous bureaucracies deployed by both fascist and communist dictatorships in the twentieth century. The methods of torture and the medical terminologies also have echoes in testimonies published after the play was written, notably Alexander Solzenitsyn's exposés of the Soviet Union's systematic human rights abuses against political dissidents in psychiatric hospitals. Reports and testimonies of the medical abuse of political prisoners in the Soviet Union and in Latin American countries such as Chile and Argentina were particularly prevalent in the 1970s, which may well be why Pinter judged that the time was ripe for a production.[24] Not one of the institutionalised patients makes an appearance on stage, but the gradual demolition of the most recent staff recruit, the heart-stoppingly gullible Lamb, stands as its own symbol of what the unseen detainees are forced to submit to.[25] The torture and interrogation of Lamb by colleagues Gibbs and Cutts covers twenty pages, has some verbal echoes of the techniques of Goldberg and McCann, and sits at the heart of the dramaturgical structure – a grotesque insight into the real abuses of power behind the bluff language of officialese, the filing systems, and the discrepancies in Roote's diary-keeping. Under attack are Lamb's autonomy and identity, electroshock treatment leaving him in a state of 'catatonic trance'.[26] Lamb is left in a vegetative condition, but unlike Stanley, Lamb fails even to recognise his destroyers. The spectator is left in little doubt that the project of this facility is to break bodies and minds for the purposes of a totalitarian control over its subjects. The soundscapes suggest that the most effective way to break an individual's capacity to make any sort of political intervention is firstly to isolate them from the public sphere, and secondly to torture them with the purpose of destroying their ability to formulate words at all. Censorship is ensured in the most extreme way.

As Pinter sees it in his Nobel acceptance speech, Stanley and Lamb do not fulfil their obligations as citizens: they do not ask the fundamental question: 'What is true? What is false?'[27] Lamb does not question the ethics of what is happening in this secretive institution, reflect on the physical abuses taking place, or challenge the morality of his colleagues. Grotesquely obliging, he is an eager volunteer in his own destruction: he takes everything and everyone at face value and pays a high price. Stanley has been fleeing the truth about himself, but is only able to recognise this *in extremis* and when it is too late. Those who speak out against ruling ideologies must have both a profound knowledge of the self and must have willingly engaged in hard intellectual labour: it is the 'crucial obligation' of all citizens, Pinter argues, to apply 'unflinching, unswerving, fierce intellectual determination' in order 'to define the *real* truth of our lives and our societies'.[28] Lamb and Stanley have not worked for that fierce intelligence, nor understood why it might be politically important to do so, but Pinter suggests that the virtue of being human is that we can and must ask questions, and that with determination those powers of analytical clarity may, indeed must, be acquired.

A fierce intellect combined with the desire to speak out can result in an equally horrific fate as that of Stanley and Lamb, however. The difference is an insistence on political conscience and the desire to make some sort of intervention. Since the early 1980s Pinter has represented the loss of freedom of expression much more explicitly. His turn towards a more overtly political theatre can first be perceived in *One for the Road* (1984) and in *Mountain Language* (1988). As Billington has clarified, Pinter's decision to address these concerns unambiguously in his plays came out of pre-existing agendas, though the military coup in Chile in 1973 became his 'crux' moment for committing to greater activism.[29] In addition, the Conservative Party's regime under Margaret Thatcher from 1979 to 1990 also provided impetus for protest, especially in the arenas of foreign policy and civil rights issues (Pinter formed the June 20 Group opposing Thatcherism 'which was destroying so many institutions and convictions').[30] Pinter's involvement with PEN, which raises the profile of censored and imprisoned writers, and with Amnesty International increased substantially. Freedom of expression for Pinter also meant upholding the legal right to speak or not, and in 1992 he campaigned against the loss of the right to silence in the revised Official Secrets Act (in *One for the Road* the power of this right is demonstrated by Victor in the course of his first interrogation). In 1996 he objected to the government's extension of its own powers under the Prevention of Terrorism Act. Since 1984 the victims in Pinter's plays have been possessed of self-knowledge, are clearly in opposition to the status quo, and face torture and possible death as a result of their articulate protest. In *The New World Order* (1991), the 'blindfolded man' has no name and never speaks to his interrogators, a blackly comic duo called Lionel and Des. The blindfolded man may no longer be able to utter, be too terrified or have lost the will to speak, but there is no doubt about why he is in imminent danger.

> Before he came in here he was a big shot, he never stopped shooting his mouth off, he never stopped questioning received ideas. Now – because he's apprehensive about what's going to happen to him – he's stopped all that, he's got nothing more to say, he's more or less called it a day. I mean once – not too long ago – this man was a man of conviction, wasn't he, a man of principle. Now he's just a prick.[31]

The blindfold only emphasises the victim's powerlessness and the concealment of his face makes his emotions illegible to us.[32] He sits waiting for torture, perhaps death, resistance is impossible, his wife apparently due for her dose of violence from the same men. Pinter's prisoners of conscience from 1984 onwards point towards a larger picture of state oppression and abuse (Des and Lionel are 'keeping the world clean for democracy'[33]), and the issue is only in what manner and over what period of time they will be systematically broken down. It is noteworthy that the cover of Faber and Faber's *Plays Four*, which contains *One for the Road*, *Mountain Language*, *New World Order*, and *Party Time* (1991) – the dramas which most unrelentingly deal with loss of freedom of expression – represents a woman's gagged mouth.[34]

Pinter wrote *One for the Road* out of rage in a single night, and is clear that it has connections with earlier dramas: 'The world which the play inhabits had not only been on my mind for many years but I had actually expressed it in one way or another in earlier plays.'[35] Interestingly, the inspiration came out of a moment of his own speechlessness, a highly unusual experience for him. Pinter encountered two Turkish women at a party, one of whom worked at the Turkish Embassy. When he asked how they viewed 'the widespread torture that existed in Turkish prisons and police stations', they were not only unmoved by human rights abuses but sought to justify them on the basis that the victims of the torture were probably opposed to the ruling Turkish party.[36] Pinter's enraged speechlessness prompted immediate action: he left the party and returned home to write. His motive was as much to expose the injustice of censorship and torture as to try and capture the 'rhetoric' and 'nonsense' espoused by two women who could not see their complicity in the infringement of basic human rights or their own entrapment in an ideology that promulgated the existence of 'a fairy tale country, where some people are saved and some people are punished' for believing what they do and speaking out about it.[37]

The play depicts Nicolas in a series of one-to-one scenes interrogating three members of the same family: the father Victor, his wife Gila and their son Nicky. Victor is evidently a member of the intellectual class, for he is known for the 'cut and thrust of debate', and 'lots of books' have been found in his 'lovely' house, which Nicolas's soldiers have 'kicked around a bit'.[38] We learn little of how Victor may have been opposing what is apparently a religiously based totalitarian regime but he is certainly not one of the 'patriots' to whom Nicolas refers, and is wearing torn clothes and is bruised.[39] Victor's numerous silences in the face of Nicolas's taunts, threats and dark intimations about his wife and son emphasise the fact that the interrogation has nothing to do with the extraction of information or the eliciting of a confession, but is purely about destroying him and his family.[40] The process is its own state-sanctioned instrument of terror. Gila's interrogation convulses at the harrowing moment of her loss of control when she loses the ability to articulate words and starts screaming.[41] The dismantling of Gila has been effected through repeated rape and sexual humiliation, and her screaming externalises her mental and emotional agony. Elaine Scarry has examined the relationship between intense pain and the disintegration of language it incurs, 'bringing about an immediate reversion to a state anterior to language, to the sounds and cries a human being makes before language is learned'.[42] Real-life Turkish political prisoners gave testimonies that described unbearable screaming lasting for hours, so appalling that it could cause unconsciousness in those forced to listen to it.[43] In the last scene Victor appears before Nicolas once more, further brutalisation evident in the blurring and mumbling of his words and the difficulty he has in making himself understood.

> NICOLAS: I can't hear you.
> VICTOR: It's my mouth.
> NICOLAS: Mouth?
> VICTOR: Tongue.
> NICOLAS: What's the matter with it?[44]

Knowing a drink will cause him pain, Nicolas insists that Victor drinks. In the stage direction after he has drunk, *His head falls back*, Pinter describes a momentary movement of loss of self-control and of capitulation.[45] Although it is the only moment of visible collapse for Victor, it comes just before Nicolas informs him that he is to be released and that he might or might not see his wife again in a week's time, and it presages the beginning of what must be further internal collapse at the news of his son's apparent murder. With this information Victor's release is a bitter horror. The play ends:

> *Victor straightens and stares at Nicolas.*
> *Silence.*
> *Blackout.*[46]

The injury to Victor's tongue is a symbolic mutilation: the power of his protest has been in voice and language, and both are now damaged. The chilling silence at the end marks an atrocity which goes beyond Victor's powers of comprehension or expression. Victor's cataclysmic silence and Gila's screaming represent for each their objectification: the ultimate aim of their torture is to morph them from speaking political subjects into dehumanised automatons. Both have been forced over a boundary from which it is hard to return intact. Robert Cover argues that:

> Torture is designed to demonstrate the end of the normative world of the victim – the end of what the victim values, the end of the bonds that constitute the community in which the values are grounded. ... The logic of that world is complete domination, though the objective may never be realised.[47]

Pinter's performance as Nicolas at the Lincoln Center in July 2001 conveyed the sense of an overwhelmingly powerful physical presence – a man who even swilled and swallowed his drink with a deliberation that left no one in doubt that Victor and his family were to be enjoyed and consumed in the same way.

For Pinter agency, accountability and political conscience can be severely stretched, but the self is most in danger of destruction when speech is destroyed. Pinter explores this further through *Mountain Language*, in which the decimation of a people is represented through the prohibition of their own language. The denial of the right to speak a language becomes legitimised state torture and symbolically marks the beginning of genocide. *Mountain Language* was inspired by Pinter's trip to Turkey with Arthur Miller, and his encounter with torture victims.[48] The scenes are set inside and outside a torture camp, where the female Mountain people struggle to gain access to their incarcerated male relatives. At the end, a male prisoner collapses into a violent fit when he realises that his elderly mother has been traumatised to such an extent that she is now mute and unresponsive even though the language ban has temporarily been lifted. It is not clear what she registers any longer, whether she recognises her son, or knows who she is. A previous dialogue in voice-over between mother and son has emphasised the tenderness of a relationship which has been annihilated because they have been denied the right to speak to one another in their own language, the only language that the mother knows. The mother, then, is in a state reminiscent of Lamb's 'catatonic trance', the son is reduced to a writhing mass on the ground, able to emit only gasps. Lives, memories, relationships have been erased and two people are portrayed, in this moment, as something less than human. It is an image that many victims of torture would recognise: one sixteen-year-old Turkish girl has described how her persecutors accused her of not understanding the meaning of words (because she would not confess to crimes she had not committed). She was taken to a prison full of people who were 'distorted and deformed into other beings, anything but human. None of the men or women looked like or in the least resembled a human being.'[49] Pinter has spoken of the suppression of the Kurds and Kurdish language by the Turks as the initial idea for the piece, but the play has a much wider significance for him: it is 'about the suppression of language and the loss of freedom of expression. But I believe it also reflects what's happening in England today – the suppression of ideas, speech and thought.'[50]

In *Party Time* (1991) Dusty is married to one of the enforcers of 'peace' implicated in the state-sponsored terror and brutality imposed on 'dissidents'.[51] Dusty persistently undercuts the studious poise of partygoers by asking what has happened to her missing brother Jimmy. In an extraordinarily violent exchange with her husband it becomes clear that by speaking out she has sentenced herself to a grim end – quite probably, she implies, at her husband's instruction:

DUSTY: Perhaps you'll kill me when we get home? Do you think you will? Do you think you'll put an end to it? Do you think there is an end to it? What do you think? Do you think that if you put an end to me that would be the end of everything for everyone? Will everything and everyone die with me?

TERRY: Yes, you're all going to die together, you and all your lot.[52]

Dusty refuses to pretend that her brother never existed and to accept the political rhetoric that the country will be run 'on normal, secure and legitimate paths'.[53] Her defiance, her conscience and her sense of moral responsibility make her, in Pinter's terms, the ideal citizen. But her rationale that her oppressors' aim of absolute control is ultimately unrealisable, is more than artistic invention – similar statements from torture victims who have refused to compromise themselves have been well documented by Amnesty International.[54]

Jimmy's unearthly appearance at the close of the play is the final exposure of this sickeningly sadistic regime. His monologue seems to come from a parallel universe of the tortured and dispossessed. Alienated from himself, unable to connect with a past self or even his name, all his senses have shut down and he does nothing more than exist from moment to moment in a world that condemns him to a living death: 'The dark is in my mouth and I suck it. It is all I have.' 'What am I?' he asks, indicating his complete depersonalisation.[55] Pinter has described this juxtaposition of revelling champagne drinkers against military and police repression as 'an image of universal reference'.[56] Jimmy is part of the story behind the glitter, glitz and propaganda, and a story framed in recent productions against the War on Terror. Jimmy, Charles Grimes has argued, 'speaks, paradoxically, only to tell us he has no words and no existence, as Pinter comes as close as possible to creating a voice for the disappearance of voice'.[57]

It is no coincidence that Pinter's radio play *Voices* (2005) begins and ends with Jimmy's haunting monologue. *Voices* melds together a number of plays, and was musically scored by James Clarke. The play is a complexly textured soundscape of brutalisers and brutalised, but Jimmy's words and the actor's pain-filled voice act as a focusing lens and privilege the suffering, forgotten and oppressed with harrowing eloquence. In the after-show discussion Michael Billington spoke of *Voices* portraying a 'world of public terror, nightmare and persecution', which merges indissolubly with 'the private world of our daily life and its elements of treachery, betrayal and domination'.[58]

Unusually in his most recent stage play, Pinter chose to represent a policy-maker and implementer very close to the seat of power – a politician. *Press Conference* (2002) is a chilling performance of the totalitarian iron hand by none other than a Minister of Culture, who has assumed this role after tenure as the head of the Secret Police. He sees the two roles as identical, and the entire sketch is a satiric take on the Minister's rhetoric of cultural heritage and the need for vigilance, checks and safeguards against subversive forces. This amounts to a legitimation for state-sponsored torture and execution, including abduction and child-killing and the sexual violation of women – 'all part of an educational process'.[59] He espouses a need for critical dissent as long as it is never voiced, but reserves the right to search, arrest and torture dissident writers to 'keep our society free from infection'.[60] At the National Theatre première in February 2002, Pinter played the Minister with chilling joviality, inviting comparison with Tony Blair's smiling media appeal and his government's obsession with spin-doctoring and press control. What is noticeable in this play is the lack of any voice of protest, or indeed any individual expression of dissent. The press are represented as a pack (fourteen actors appeared in the première), the *dramatis personae* simply refers to them as 'press', and like puppets they laugh on cue, indulge in craven flattery and applaud at the end. The piece has the distinct feel of a piece of staged propaganda in itself, a show-press-conference perhaps. If not, it is the bleakest view imaginable of the state of freedom of expression and a terrible commentary on the conspiracy of power between those in government and those who control media outlets. Britain, Pinter has reminded us often, 'can easily employ totalitarian measures' – especially when seeking to combat terrorism.[61]

Many torturers, we know, do not think of themselves as evil, but as dedicated and patriotic guardians who believe that the end justifies the means. Pinter's zealous abusers of freedom of expression seem to gain increasing control as his plays progress, and by *Press Conference* even the broken and the traumatised have disappeared under the swell of state controls. Even the gasps, sighs and screams, as well as the coded voice-overs, have vanished. But though the battle may have intensified, and political spin continues to engulf policy-making, Pinter has not stopped pressing his case. Susan Sontag has argued that 'to designate a hell is not, of course, to tell us anything about how to extract people from that hell'.[62] Pinter is intent upon painting that hell precisely because it is incessantly glossed over, and with the passive agreement of many of his audience members. Sontag, like Pinter, cannot understand those who evade or deceive themselves about the intense suffering going on around them:

> Someone who is perenially surprised that depravity exists, who continues to feel disillusioned (even incredulous) when confronted with evidence of what humans are capable of inflicting in the way of the gruesome, hands-on cruelties upon other humans, has not reached moral or psychological adulthood.[63]

Pinter would make adults of us. And citizens. He would compel us to speak out.

NOTES

1. See www.contemporarywriters.com/news/pinterwinsnobelprize. Accessed 23 November 2007.
2. See Michael Billington, *Harold Pinter* (London: Faber, 2007), p. 434. This is a revised edition of *The Life and Work of Harold Pinter* (London: Faber, 1996).
3. *Ibid.*, p. 438.
4. Micheline R. Ishay (ed.), *The Human Rights Reader* (London and New York: Routledge, 1997), xiii–xiv.
5. Billington, *Harold Pinter*, pp. 23–4.
6. *Ibid.*, p. 425.
7. *Ibid.*
8. The United Nations Universal Declaration of Human Rights, in Ishay, *The Human Rights Reader*, pp. 407–12.
9. Andrew Sullivan, 'The Abolition of Torture', in *Torture: A Collection*, ed. Sanford Levinson (Oxford: Oxford University Press, 2004), pp. 317–27, (p. 319).
10. See Mel Gussow, *Conversations with Pinter* (London: Nick Hern, 1994), p. 86. See www.haroldpinter.org for further information on the organisations that Pinter supports.
11. See Ian Smith, ed., *Pinter in the Theatre* (London: Nick Hern, 2005), p. 83.
12. *Ibid.*, pp. 59–60.
13. Harold Pinter, *The Birthday Party*, *Plays One* (London: Faber, 1996), p. 78.
14. *Ibid.*, pp. 78–9.
15. 'Something broken can be put back together, but it will never regain the status of being unbroken – of having integrity. When you break a human being, you turn him into something subhuman. You enslave him. This is why the Romans reserved torture for slaves, not for citizens, and why slavery and torture were inextricably linked in the antebellum south.' See Sullivan, 'The Abolition of Torture', p. 319.
16. See Harold Pinter, *Various Voices: Prose, Poetry, Politics 1948–2005* (London: Faber, 2005), pp. 11–15 (p. 15).
17. *Ibid.*, p. 13.
18. *Ibid.*
19. *Ibid.*, p. 15.
20. *Ibid.*, p. 14.
21. See Duncan Forrest, ed., *A Glimpse of Hell: Report on Torture Worldwide* (London: Cassell, 1996), p. 141.
22. Harold Pinter, *The Hothouse*, *Plays One*, p. 319.
23. See Billington, *Harold Pinter*, p. 101.
24. See Eric Stover and Elena O. Nightingale, eds., *The Breaking of Minds and Bodies: Torture, Psychiatric Abuse, and the Health Professions* (New York: W. H. Freeman, 1985).
25. In the radio play synopsis Pinter refers to the patients as 'volunteers', but this label is dropped thereafter.
26. Pinter, *The Hothouse*, p. 328. Aston in *The Caretaker*, of course, undergoes electro-convulsive therapy which has left him physically and mentally damaged. Pinter's representations of medical intervention are not random here: after beating, electroshock torture is the world's most common form of physical abuse, see Forrest, *A Glimpse of Hell*, p. 139.

27. Billington, *Harold Pinter*, p. 431.
28. *Ibid.*, p. 442.
29. Billington, *Harold Pinter*, p. 287. For testimonies of the atrocities committed, see *Chile: An Amnesty International Report* (London: Amnesty International, 1974).
30. See Smith, *Pinter in the Theatre*, p. 101.
31. Harold Pinter, *The New World Order*, *Plays Four* (London: Faber, 1998), p. 276.
32. Amnesty International states that hoods are used to 'hide the identity of the torturer, and to increase psychological fears': see *Chile: An Amnesty International Report*, p. 63.
33. Pinter, *New World Order*, p. 277.
34. What is not in keeping with these plays is the hint of erotic pleasure that the woman appears to be demonstrating.
35. See Gussow, *Conversations with Pinter*, p. 86.
36. *Ibid.*, p. 94.
37. *Ibid.*, p. 87.
38. Harold Pinter, *One for the Road*, *Plays Four*, pp. 228–9.
39. *Ibid.*, pp. 223 and 232.
40. In totalitarian regimes, victims' family members are frequently tortured or killed to increase pressure on them and to terrorise members of their community.
41. Pinter, *One for the Road*, p. 239.
42. Elaine Scarry, *The Body in Pain* (Oxford: Oxford University Press, 1985), p. 4.
43. *Turkey: Testimony on Torture* (London: Amnesty International, 1985), p. 68. One victim reported that they reached a point where they could no longer breathe because they were screaming so much, p. 53. Another victim noted: 'They had us listening for hours to the cries of others being tortured', *Torture in Turkey* (London: Amnesty International, 1980), p. 8.
44. Pinter, *One for the Road*, p. 245.
45. *Ibid.*, p. 246.
46. *Ibid.*, p. 247.
47. Robert Cover, 'Violence and the Word', *Yale Law Journal*, 95 (1986), 1601.
48. See Gussow, *Conversations with Pinter*, p. 68.
49. *Turkey: Testimony on Torture*, p. 67.
50. *Ibid.*, p. 68. At the time of his interview with Gussow, Pinter suggested that it was the homosexual community then suffering oppression in England. Gussow, *Conversations with Pinter*, pp. 68–9.
51. Terry has similarities with Lambert and Matt in *Celebration*, who are strategy consultants 'keeping the peace' (London: Faber, 2000), p. 60.
52. Pinter, *Party Time*, *Plays Four*, p. 302.
53. *Ibid.*, p. 313.
54. For example, a tortured and dying husband told his wife: 'What does it matter if another bit of flesh and blood is gone? They cannot kill humanity.' *Turkey: Testimony on Torture*, p. 71.
55. Pinter, *Party Time*, p. 314.
56. See Smith, *Pinter in the Theatre*, p. 92.
57. Charles Grimes, *Harold Pinter's Politics: A Silence beyond Echo* (Teaneck, NJ: Fairleigh Dickinson Press, 2005), p. 125.
58. *Voices*, BBC Radio 3, 10 October 2005.
59. Pinter, *Press Conference* (London: Faber, 2002), p. 2.

60. *Ibid.*, p. 4.
61. Smith, *Pinter in the Theatre*, p. 103. See also Michael Ignatieff's *The Lesser Evil: Political Ethics in an Age of Terror* (Edinburgh: Edinburgh University Press, 2005).
62. Susan Sontag, *Regarding the Pain of Others* (London: Penguin, 2003), p. 102.
63. *Ibid.*

Pinter and Performance

8

RICHARD ALLEN CAVE

Body language in Pinter's plays

In the millennium year, Harold Pinter reached his seventieth birthday. Looking back over his achievements (as actor, pacifist, playwright, poet, critic, director, creator-adaptor of scripts that have sensitively translated the artistry of novelists into the medium of film, campaigner for civil liberties and freedom of speech), one is astonished at the sheer range and variety of endeavour to which he has brought a focused and profound commitment. Yeats, whom Pinter has long admired and studied, comes to mind as possessing a similar protean sensibility, which held to the belief that all creativity is both deeply personal and assuredly political. Fittingly there comes to mind the imperative that occurs in one of the many poems, 'An Acre of Grass', in which Yeats addresses himself as an old man: 'Myself must I *remake*'.[1] There was to be no quiet putting-out to grass, no cosy retirement for him; rather Yeats envisaged questing after 'frenzy', the energetic, satirical rage and insight of Timon, Lear and the elderly William Blake or Michelangelo. It would be a new manifestation of himself and yet one wholly true to old forms; there would be no loss of integrity in this transforming process. To view the four volumes of Pinter's *Plays* is to see manifold changes of subject matter, focus, linguistic register, conversational idiom, style and structure; yet the inspiring vision is always and uniquely recognisable as Pinter's.

Criticism has had to keep pace with those seeming changes of direction: since the late 1950s the plays have variously been claimed as fine examples of absurdism and of Freudian psychological theory applied to drama; they have undergone feminist revisioning and been championed for their meta-theatricality; and for the last decade they have been either praised or vilified for their confrontational political incisiveness.[2] In consequence there has been a tendency to view the plays as falling into 'periods', which can be conveniently labelled: 'comedies of menace'; 'the memory plays'; 'Pinter and politics'.[3] Yet, as Michael Billington admirably argues throughout his biography of the dramatist,[4] such categorising risks doing a disservice to the complexities of Pinter's artistry: politics (social, sexual and familial) as powerfully shapes the action of the early plays as *One for the Road* (1984); and it is absurd to view the Absurdism of *The Room* (written, 1957), *The Dumb Waiter* (written, 1957), or *The Birthday Party* (staged, 1958) as devoid of political insight. Every new play by Pinter causes us to look afresh at all his earlier work; apparent changes in Pinter's immediate thematic and stylistic preoccupations repeatedly appear on closer study to be developing qualities already present in previous plays; and so revivals are seen by reviewers as rediscoveries, as occasions for re-appraising seemingly familiar works in the light of the new.[5] Generally, it may be said, artists need to create the taste by which their work will be enjoyed; but, amusingly in Pinter's case, he seems continually to reshape the contexts within which his past work will be fully appreciated. Or one could reverse that proposition and claim that Pinter's plays have always been ahead of their time (and not locked within it, as is fast proving the case with most of the works of his contemporary, John Osborne). Perhaps this is because, as in the art of his admired Yeats, Kafka, Webster and Swift, he can distil a clear-sighted, politicised horror (even at times, disgust) into metaphor, symbol and myth. He can shape a poetry from outrage with no loss in social precision. And that would seem as true of *The Room* as of *Ashes to Ashes* (1996). What new perspectives on Pinter's drama have theatrical and critical contexts through the 1990s fostered? Or, to take the balancing proposition, what seemingly innovatory qualities have those changing contexts shown to be already latent within Pinter's invention? What in his work has offered itself most recently for discovery and re-appraisal?

The advent of physical theatre and concepts of physicalised performance in the 1990s coincided with (in part was the product of) developing theoretical formulations concerning the colonised and post-colonised body; the gendered, the feminist and the queer body; the politicised body; and the postmodern body. All these have taught us how to *read* both social and performing bodies and how to discriminate in the process between the performing and the performative; how to be alert to the individual body's shaping under acculturating influences; how to determine the degree to which that body is *constructed* by external forces. Much of this theorising has developed to varying degrees from earlier critical preoccupation with the male *gaze* and its prescription of values by which the female body was to be presented for its pleasure and judgment; theories of the *gaze* deconstructed what was deemed a socially privileged method of control over women. Control over others, whether private or state-sanctioned, has of course been an on-going theme in Pinter's work. It may seem perverse to write of the importance of *body* language in plays that formerly have chiefly been admired for their *verbal* artistry: their finely judged use of idiom; the disciplined rhythm, the pauses, silences, timing and pacing of lines like musical phrases, which build in such works as *Old Times* (1971) and *No Man's Land* (1975) into structures of an almost symphonic complexity; the equally musical preoccupation with timbre in intimating subtextual complexities. Yet actors' body language can equally well convey subtextual complexities (and do so in ways quite distinct from what may be read into the spatial relations between performers in a given playing space).[6] If Pinter taught audiences in the 1990s to appreciate the importance of body language throughout the range of his plays, it is as much through his choosing to act in and direct revivals of his own earlier works as through new writing. Harold Pinter as actor especially has been a revelation.[7]

Reading through the collected reviews of his most recent stage performance as Harry in *The Collection* (directed by Joe Harmston at the Donmar Warehouse, 1998), one is struck by the constant reference to the impact of Pinter's *presence*, variously described as 'massive', 'commanding' and 'domineering'.[8] This was not an instance of the dramatist asserting privilege in the situation to hog the limelight: Pinter's making a powerful, enveloping, charismatic figure of Harry was a conscious choice in the process of characterising the role. Pinter has a big-framed physique (the fact was somewhat accentuated by the far slenderer build of the other three actors in the piece, Lia Williams, Douglas Hodge and Colin McFarlane); but the surprise came with the way Pinter offset that bigness with a mannered grace of movement; his Harry had elegance, panache; and this carefully sustained delicacy became a correlative for the super-subtle workings of the character's mind. Of all the characters, Harry as an ageing homosexual has most to lose if his protégé, Bill, were to leave him. Bill may, or may not, recently have had an adulterous fling with Stella; and he appears to excite hitherto repressed homoerotic yearnings in James, Stella's husband, when he arrives at Harry's house, seeking to establish what exactly has happened respecting his wife. How stable on the one hand is Bill's sexuality and on the other his affection for his mentor? Harry runs a fashion house, specialising in *haute couture*; James and Stella provide fashionable chic in the rag trade; Bill has privileges and the run of a moneyed household, but only through association with Harry. Pinter the playwright has a wonderful sensitivity to class discriminations and the surprising areas of experience in which they operate. Homosexuality, it is claimed, is often perceived as a threat to Establishment mores because relationships often bridge class divides (Wilde's case is generally cited by way of example: he, being middle-class and an Oxonian, consorting with both the son of a peer and working class rent boys). Such a bridging of classes operates with Harry and Bill, yet Harry is quick to remind Bill of his origins with ugly directness ('there's nothing wrong with slum slugs in their place'[9]) and of his material good fortune when Harry's own emotional security is threatened. (The play was a remarkable *tour de force* of honesty and courage in its

5 Harold Pinter as Harry in the Gate Theatre's production of *The Collection*,
part of the Pinter Festival at the Gate, April 1997

negotiating of such territory when staged in 1962, some years before the legalising of homosexual acts in Britain.)

What impressed about Pinter's performance was the way the commanding stance and the physical urbanity were offset by a constant wariness, indicated by a sudden but subtle turn or angling of the head (this sugar daddy was alert to every gesture or word that hinted at his losing his toy boy). The need for and the cost of this meticulous control were sensed on but two occasions when the 'cool' front relaxed: one, when – in the words of the *Observer* reviewer – he signalled 'his allegiance to his partner merely by a casual, practised massage of the neck';[10] the other when he (hilariously) wrestled and wrenched at a newspaper in sheer desperation at Bill's refusal to 'come clean' over the issue of Stella and James. These moments registered as more than conventional stage business because, isolated and unexpected in being in marked contrast to this Harry's prevailing restraint, they took on the status of physicalised metaphors: both indicated a depth of affection, although the first had an ambiguity (there was a certain take-him-by-the-scruff-of-the-neck quality to the gesture that hinted at mastery) and the second a manic energy, both of which were at once touching and sinister. It would be easy to caricature the role, given a certain bitchiness in Harry's representation (his petulance about the ill-fitting stair-rod and the wrong placing of his juice on the breakfast tray), and to overlay the performance with a wealth of camp or effeminate mannerisms. Pinter in playing the role resisted this possibility; he chose instead to deploy the physical attributes of his performance to focus an audience's attention on the uneasy power-structuring within the relationship between Harry and Bill. In this it exactly parallels the condition of the 'straight' marriage between James and Stella. The possibility of a one-night fling between Stella and Bill, whether genuine or imagined, gives those two seemingly subordinate partners access to a degree of freedom within their respective committed relationships to equalise the power balance. Both find the weak spots in their partner's possessiveness and end the play in positions of advantage. Pinter's performance was wholly attuned to this inner psychological dynamic in the production; and it was his subtle physicalising of the role that gave an audience imaginative access to that subtextual life of the drama. The rich sonorities of Pinter's voice were familiar from his playing earlier in the decade as Hirst in *No Man's Land* (Almeida, 1992) and Roote in *The Hothouse* (Chichester and the Comedy Theatre, 1995); the revelation in this revival of *The Collection* was the telling degree to which Pinter the actor was a joy to *watch*.[11]

This reading of Pinter's performance as Harry was considerably influenced by the physicality of the acting style Pinter himself educed from his actors in the revival of *The Caretaker*, which he directed at the Comedy Theatre in 1991.[12] Body language contributed extensively to shape further implications to what was spoken. The use of the actors' hands was particularly noticeable. Aston's seemed bony and contorted and they were continually held in positions that drew attention to their angularities, especially an odd placing of them on the knees, which intimated much about the character's past in a mental institution before he chose to reveal such facts in confidence to Davies (Donald Pleasence). The whole image conveyed by Colin Firth's body and Pinter's constant positioning of Aston on the peripheries of the acting space, as if seeking the comforting proximity of a wall or solid piece of furniture, suggested a troubled, insecure individual, prone to self-consciousness and a fear of making connections with others. Davies's hands by contrast were invariably clenched into fists that made short, stabbing, pugilistic gestures randomly into the air about him to accentuate his speech. Life for this man was a seemingly endless fight against circumstance; consciousness and stance were almost permanently alert to the need to be self-protective. There were moments when the guard slackened (as with the gift of the tobacco and then the smoking jacket) when a relaxed expansiveness suffused his whole person, suggesting a growing ease and security with Aston, with the room, with his new-found position as 'caretaker'; the whole body expressed rapture with this sudden access to a long-hoped-for sense of sheer bliss; but with this consummate ease of being, Davies's nastier prejudices began to flourish; mind and body were alarmingly at variance. Mick (Peter Howitt) rarely showed his hands: they were generally tucked into the side pockets of his leather jacket, giving him a confident swagger; instead he used his head and shoulders to emphasise his words, project an idea, challenge a listener. Howitt's positioning of his head was sinuously flexible; there was nothing bullish about the stance or overall body-image.

Equally potent in this production were the postures suggestive of concentrated watching. Mick established this visual theme in our awareness at the very start of the performance. When we first saw him he was seated studying and appraising the contents of the room; a door without banged to, and his body was at once caught up into a position of alert attentiveness; hearing voices, he rose and moved stealthily to the door, which he closed with silent precision behind him. The play opened with a protracted sequence of mime. Pinter and his actor had the confidence to allow this to run for a considerable amount of playing time, as Howitt drew the audience's attention to all important elements of the setting (the disposition of the two beds, the bucket, the Buddha) and in the process invited them to engage imaginatively with his role. However naturalistically done, silent mime requires an audience to focus on body language: to observe and, in observing, to read and to interpret. What we observe in this instance is a character who is himself watching and listening, activities which begin to carry disturbingly sinister connotations, given the feline grace of Mick's movements.

Speakers throughout the play have a need of listeners, and listeners in this production were also shrewd and physically intent watchers. Aston watched Davies, ever hesitant over talking about himself, since to talk is to reveal, which is to render the self vulnerable to another; only late in the play do we learn why he is so fearful. (Time and again in this production the performance invited one extensively to interpret the significance of what one saw, before offering an explanation to confirm or challenge what one had extrapolated from one's perceptions.) When eventually Aston talked, trying to share with Davies the pain, the obscene loss of dignity he suffered while undergoing shock treatment, Firth's Aston let his whole posture steadily slump downwards as if it were retreating into itself; and never once did he look at Davies eye-to-eye. Aston may have hoped for fellow feeling, but Davies watched him here as elsewhere only with an eye to the main chance. As Aston reached the end of his revelations about his past, Davies's whole posture was transformed into that of a stealthy predator poised for the attack. The published text here asks for a gradual fading of the light till '*by the close of the speech only* ASTON *can be seen clearly.* DAVIES *and all the other objects are in the shadow.*'[13] In Pinter's production the physical collapse of Aston was marked by a seeming growth in stature of Davies, seen largely in silhouette but, nonetheless, an unmistakable presence, rather than a figure disappearing steadily into shadow. That image, held briefly to allow an audience time to read the implications of the body language before a blackout signals the end of Act Two, gave a powerful impetus to the final episodes. Howitt's Mick seemed always to be watching others in the way of studying and appraising them, just as he had observed the room at the start of the play; his eyes seemed half-hooded by the lids and brows, but the pupils were diamond sharp; 'eagle-eyed' would be the fitting metaphor. Meticulously he watched the effect of everything he did on Davies; the forms of taunting were less horseplay than tactical strategies; a brilliant intelligence was watching events closely the better to plan the next move.

When *The Caretaker* was first staged in 1960, reviewers commented on the rare combination of the witty and the sinister. In Pinter's own revival these elements were certainly in place, but were offset by an exploration of the text for a counter-theme to do with *taking care*. The complexities of care and of caring (the moral challenges and imperatives, the burden of responsibility entailed, the potential for intricate forms of emotional and psychological blackmail) inspired a range of plays from Pinter throughout the 1980s: *A Kind of Alaska* (1982), *Family Voices* (1981) and even *One for the Road*, where Nicolas, the torturer, repeatedly excuses what he is doing on the grounds that it is all for the future well-being of his victims in society. Mick seems to be taking care after his own brusque fashion of his brother, Aston, who has been 'in care'; and Aston, for a short time, proffers care to Davies. Aston in this production was definitely progressing towards mental health, after his traumatic experiences when insti-tutionalised; his very invitation to Davies to come home with him appeared a significant step in his rehabilitation. All would doubtless be well, were Davies tenderly sensitive to Aston's state of mind: Aston needs delicate handling; but Davies is dangerous in his brutishness, his truculence, his self-obsessions and prejudices, as Mick's strategies quickly expose:

MICK: Now come on, why did you tell me all this dirt about you being an interior decorator?

DAVIES: I didn't tell you nothing! Won't you listen to what I'm saying?
> *Pause.*
> It was him who told you. It was your brother who must have told you. He's nutty! He'd tell you anything, out of spite, he's nutty, he's half way gone, it was him who told you.
> MICK *walks slowly to him.*
MICK: What did you call my brother?
DAVIES: When?
MICK: He's what?
DAVIES: I ... now get this straight ...
MICK: Nutty? Who's nutty?
> *Pause.*
> Did you call my brother nutty? My brother. That's a bit of ... that's a bit of an impertinent thing to say, isn't it?
DAVIES: But he says so himself!
> MICK *walks slowly round* DAVIES' *figure, regarding him, once.*
> *He circles him, once.*
MICK: What a strange man you are.[14]

Cornered by Mick, physically and psychologically, Davies tries to recover some vestige of status by damning his benefactor. But as the Sermon on the Mount admirably advises: judge not, lest ye be judged. It would be too easy to interpret Mick's closing in on Davies and then his slow circling about the man as menacing; it was in Howitt's performance more an act of judgment and of shaming; a long, last, searching scrutiny to detect if any redeeming features were apparent. Retribution comes quickly as Mick curtly dismisses Davies from his 'caretaking work', tossing a half-crown at his feet by way of recompense (thirty pence, old-style: an ironic and derisory parallel with the treacherous Judas's fee). When a stunned Davies tries to remonstrate, Mick picks up the statue of Buddha, which has throughout perched incongruously on the stove amidst Aston's things, and shatters it: a Buddha, the symbolic representation of endless patience. Aston, on entering shortly afterwards, seemed in this production wholly unperturbed by the breakage; facing his brother, he sustained a direct and unwavering eye-contact for the first time in the play; and a faint smile suffused each of their faces. This is an enigmatic series of reversals, in which the most perplexing (on a *reading* of the text) is the breaking of the statue. The moment is often played as if Mick were regaining his customary self-control by channelling impulses for even greater violence into this one symbolic gesture, an act that is at once a triumphant release of a pent-up anger and a warning to Davies against further provocation. Here, urged by Pinter's direction to be open to the complex signification of the body in movement and stasis, we responded more to the *sequence* than the

6 Rupert Graves and Michael Gambon in *The Caretaker*, directed by Patrick Marber, The Comedy Theatre, 2000

individual incident within the flow of action: the verbal and then the physical rejection (epitomised by the tossed coin with all the biblical resonances that releases), the contained violence, the expression of feeling that intimates a deep bond between the brothers, Mick's immediate departure. Given the context of *caring* that this production had steadily built up, Mick's momentary loss of control and of patience reached beyond violence or menace: it was more an anguished frustration that the longstanding burden of being his brother's keeper (which he had hoped to pass to Davies, since Aston had elected him to share his life) had inexorably been returned to him now that Davies had proved hopelessly inadequate to the task. There was momentary rage against Davies and against Aston, against circumstance and himself; but it was *contained* destruction, a burst of anger that in its steely control implied

Mick's acceptance of his lot. The smile was in part the token of that acceptance; but it also intimated new levels of understanding, trust and compatibility between the brothers. It is difficult to convey the impact of that steady gaze, which contrasted so starkly with the evasive or aggressively staring looks which had previously obtained between the characters. In promptly going, Mick generously left Aston to discover the power within himself to determine Davies's fate.[15] In this staging we watched Aston's slow progress to maturity under his brother's watchful gaze; Mick was an unobtrusive presence, guiding without directing that progress.[16]

Pinter's production brought *The Caretaker* close to the territory explored in *A Kind of Alaska* with its awareness of the acute moral and emotional hazards of taking on the care of another; and it did so chiefly by evolving a coherent subtext through the body language deployed by the actors. There is of course a danger in rooting an interpretation in what many would see as the minor signifiers in a theatrical performance. It must be stressed, however, that the physical details described here were not privileged over other important signifiers in the production (vocal timbre, rhythm, spatial relations); overly to have emphasised them would have resulted in crass thematic simplifications. Rather the opening mime for Mick presented the body in stillness and motion as a prime medium of expressive communication and established a mode of reading the subsequent performance, to which the physicality of the actors made a distinct contribution. It could further be argued that this mode of interpretation risks, consciously or unconsciously, ascribing specific intentions to the director, which cannot be fully verified; and that it relies exclusively on one spectator's perceptions (even though they may have been clarified over several viewings of the production and checked against the responses of contemporary reviewers). Perceptions certainly are relative to the individual spectator. But circumstances make it impossible for a spectator, well versed in Pinter's work as texts and performances and in the chronology of his creative output, to approach a revival of an early play without bringing to the experience perceptions tutored by an awareness of his more recent writing and a sensibility shaped by current theatrical practice (which frequently does lay stress on the body as a site of cultural reference). And those same influences (biographical and cultural) must to some considerable degree shape Pinter's approach to directing one of his own early achievements. Rather than being an exercise in nostalgic excavation, his production has to be seen as a spirited *re*-creation. Over thirty years had passed between the initial production and Pinter's revival; three decades' experience cannot be denied (particularly by a writer for whom during that period the elusive nature of the past and the vagaries of memory had exerted an increasingly potent fascination). In the world of fine art, retrospective exhibitions tend to reveal certain paintings as unexpectedly seminal for their place within the artist's development. Pinter's staging of *The Caretaker*, in subtly linking his creative past and present, took on a quality akin to such a retrospective, in which the unexpected feature was the attention paid to body language. This insight seemed to open up a whole new way of engaging with the range of Pinter's plays in performance, which encounters with the plays as printed texts generally overlook. What levels of signification can be read elsewhere in the canon into hands, mime, physicalised metaphors, contained violence (the forms in which body language shaped spectators' response to this revival of *The Caretaker*)?

Pinter's most recent play, *Ashes to Ashes*, begins by asking us to *imagine* a relationship defined only though body language; the focus of the scenario that Rebecca's words evoke is on a man's hands: 'Well … for example … he would stand over me and clench his fist. And then he'd put his other hand on my neck and grip it and bring my head towards him. His fist … grazed my mouth. And he'd say, "Kiss my fist."'[17] Rebecca is responding to questions from an interlocutor, Devlin; he prompts her to continue and she informs him that she would indeed kiss the man's fist, which he would then open, offering now the palm to her lips. The scene suggests a display of male dominance but, noticeably, Rebecca's account is wholly factual (no judgmental language intrudes). She tells how she invited the man to put his hand around her throat, which he did, holding it there 'very gently, so gently' (the shift from the loosely descriptive 'very' to the precisely qualitative 'so' suggests that the delicacy of his touch was sufficiently distinctive for it even at this precise moment to be *present* to Rebecca's perceptions through imaginative recall).[18] Asked by Devlin whether the man exerted no pressure, Rebecca responds, as if from the depths of memory, revealing how he put just enough pressure so that her head would begin to move backwards 'gently but truly', till the movement, by engaging more and more of the spine, caused the whole body to move backwards at the same pace, 'slowly but truly'.[19] Within a style that has till now been so matter-of-fact, the reiterated word 'truly' invites attention. Rebecca has admitted that the man 'adored' her (that was evident to her in the quality of his touch) and 'truly' suggests an equally wholehearted response encompassing an absolute trust, a commitment of her total self to him and to her experience of that moment in time. Devlin's imagining of the scene stays resolutely within the bounds of the physiologically factual; having thought through and sensed the consequences of her body's subtly changing position, he asks: 'So your legs were opening?'[20] Her intimations (implicit within that one word, 'truly') of emotional fulfilment are reduced by his question to a lurid image of sexual availability.

The episode demonstrates admirably the creative ambiguities that Pinter can find in body language. In Devlin's final question we can perceive the decided limits of his imagination; on the other hand, because the phrase is repeated, it cannot be easily dismissed. However the passage evolves, one cannot forget that powerful opening image of the man's fist and the accompanying command that Rebecca kiss it. The lack of any qualifying epithets leaves one unsure whether this is sadistic display or erotic power game. Only after the image has had time to develop in an audience's imagination is the idea of Rebecca's willing compliance introduced. Devlin's eventual brutishness serves to recall the other man's *potential* for brutality as captured in that graphic opening image. How much of that potential was apparent to Rebecca, if she 'truly' opened herself to the man? Significantly Devlin's next question is, on the face of it, a surprising shift of ground: 'Do you feel you're being hypnotised?'[21] Rebecca is uncertain how to answer ('When?'), because uncertain of the situation to which the question applies (whether now with Devlin or formerly with the man). The question prompts the audience to read a different interpretation into Rebecca's scenario from either hers or Devlin's. The force of that unexpected present tense ('Do you feel ...') invites one to question whether Rebecca is still under the influence of the man's seductive power. Later the play shows Rebecca struggling to reconcile her private understanding of her relationship with the man, whom she eventually describes as her 'lover', with her increasingly shocked discovery of his fascist behaviour in public life, where his self-aggrandisement and brutality are displayed before her, seemingly for the same approving acquiescence which she brings to their intimacies together. How morally different is such acquiescence from the slavish obsequiousness of the workforce in the man's factory ('He told me afterwards it was because they had such great respect for him. ... They had total faith in him. They respected his ... purity, his ... conviction'[22])?

Pinter ensures that this graphic opening sequence of images involving a man's hands and a woman's face stays firmly in the spectator's mind by having Devlin suddenly change his tactic: 'Look. It would mean a great deal to me if you could define him [the man] more clearly.'[23] Rebecca is unsure what this new term, 'define', means in the context; and Devlin explains:

> Physically. I mean, what did he actually look like? If you see what I mean? Length, breadth ... that sort of thing. Height, width. I mean, quite apart from his ... disposition, whatever that may have been ... or his character ... or his spiritual ... standing ... I just want, well, I need ... to have a clearer idea of him ... well, not a clearer idea ... just an idea, in fact ... because I have absolutely no idea ... as things stand ... of what he looked like.[24]

The speech with all its hesitations tended to elicit laughter in performance at Devlin's expense, because those opening images had created so powerful a sense of the man's presence through his body language that the details Devlin now asks for are rendered redundant and meaningless. The man lives in Rebecca's imagination and her words have brought him forcefully into the audience's imagination too (noticeably in the episode it is only Rebecca's person and body language that live in Devlin's imagination). It has been a perfectly judged exposition: the audience now know all about the man, or as much as they need to know to engage with the rest of the play. Yet it is an exposition in which we have been invited to visualise body language in response to the simplest words. *Ashes to Ashes* is to interrogate the relationship between sexuality and power, between private and public codes of behaviour; Pinter has found the means through body language to engage his audience experientially with a disturbing ethical quandary, which the subsequent drama will address.[25]

Towards the end of *Ashes to Ashes* Devlin begins to enact the movement patterns described in the opening moments of the play: he presents his fist to Rebecca, grips her neck and brings her head towards it, opens the fist to present now his palm to her lips, places his hand on her throat and begins to tilt her head backwards. Though she is wholly passive, she refuses to join in enacting the scenario, speak her lines or be in any way compliant; instead her consciousness is totally absorbed by a memory of abandoning her child, seemingly to save her own life; and Devlin removes his hand from Rebecca's throat. There is no explanation; what structures of meaning one may read into this episode to some degree depend on how one till now has chosen to interpret Devlin's role. Is he perhaps 'the man', the one-time 'lover', displaced from Rebecca's affections on account of her growing political awareness of his nature? Is he a new, would-be lover finding it increasingly impossible to touch Rebecca physically or emotionally, because of her fixation with the past, with her old lover and the traumatic consequences of that former relationship? Is he, perhaps, an interrogator from some new regime, trying to prove by some devious tactics her role as collaborator with members of the former political establishment? Or is he a psychiatrist trying by drastic means to break into a patient's trauma in order to begin to channel her mind's experience into a process of healing? Because Devlin's precise identity is not determined, all such interpretations remain possible, allowing the enigmatic body language to take on metaphoric resonances. The indisputably common factor in the various interpretations, however, is Devlin's gender as male, and the various possible ways of interpreting his role all define forms of male intrusion into a female psyche to control and shape that woman's future. There is a coherence within the creative ambiguities of this conclusion which makes *Ashes to Ashes* theatre poetry of the highest order.[26]

Since *The Dumb Waiter* several of Pinter's plays have moved inexorably towards some moment of activity, which seems to take into itself all the implications resonant within the foregoing drama and to resolve them into a potent physicalised image with which the drama then concludes. When Gus stumbles into the room, an utterly broken figure, stripped to his shirt and denuded of his holster and gun, and Ben promptly levels his gun at him, all the nervy tensions of the play and the half-hearted rehearsing of the killers' normal routine take on new meaning; and the long-held stare between the men on which *The Dumb Waiter* ends invites us completely to rethink what till then we have reacted to as black comedy. Or consider the concluding moments of *No Man's Land* when Hirst, accepting that all four men have 'changed the subject' and 'for the last time', raises his glass with the words, 'I'll drink to that', and invites the others to join him.[27] Pinter's final lighting instructions are always crucial; and he asks here for a *slow fade*, in which we view four men with uplifted glasses in a room darkened by the closing of all the curtains. The men's body language suggests a convivial *bonhomie* and yet the raising of glasses has occurred with such frequency throughout the action that the gesture now has the status of a tired, automatic routine. We have learned, moreover, the extent to which each of the men is trapped in an obsessive private hell, from which none of their varying cultural or social ambitions will save them and which drink confirms rather than assuages ('the great malt which wounds'[28]). Creativity eludes their solipsistic psyches and they drink to compound their misery and vulnerability. That gesture with the raised glass which seems to affirm social concord and elation, we know in that final fading image is to be read as emblematic of futility and self-betrayal. More complex still is the image that concludes *The Homecoming* (1965). Ruth displaces Max from his seat at the centre of the stage; Joey crosses the space to curl at her feet and lay his head in her lap; Lenny moves to stand behind (but to one side of) them and looks down, watching her; Max collapses then moves subserviently towards her on bended knees; Ruth's poise is consummate. It is a black parody of the traditional groupings of a Nativity scene or those countless paintings entitled 'Madonna and Child with Saint and Donor'. There may be solicitude in Ruth's stroking of Joey's hair, but we know that gesture comes at a price. Ruth's action in taking centre-stage has redefined passivity (hitherto expressed in her quiet, feminine elegance) as power and control; she is now the still nucleus around which the men will move at her bidding. Yet is seizing that power a token of her victory or defeat? Has she retained her autonomy or become the embodiment of the men's erotic fantasies about her? Is she, perhaps, *acting*, playing with the roles expected of her the better to protect her inner independence? To what extent for Ruth are sex and gender elements of masquerade which she pursues to safeguard a social and financial security? And how can we reconcile any of this, if true, with the sense, accumulating throughout the play, that she possesses an integrity which none of the men can rival? Again: all these interpretations are possible, since none is confirmed. Each presents an equally disturbing insight for audiences into sexual politics within the home and the consequences of strict, traditional constructions of gender. As the actors move into their final positions on stage, we watch a physicalised metaphor come into being.

These episodes deploy body language in the careful shaping of a final tableau. In *Old Times* (1971) the tableau is preceded by a sequence of extended mime. Superficially, it enacts a situation described earlier in the play by Anna, which she introduces with the gnomic observation: 'There are things I remember which may never have happened but as I recall them so they take place.'[29] The memory, as she rehearses it, tells the story of a man who was first marginalised and then wholly displaced from the room she once shared with Kate ('It was as if he had never been'[30]). Throughout her account Anna preserves the conventional past tense of narrative; Kate, observing this, tersely breaks Anna's control of the prevailing mood ('You talk of me as if I were dead'[31]). Noticeably she again reverts to the subject of death in the long speech which precipitates Kate and Deeley into that final mime: 'I remember you [Anna] lying dead.'[32] She speaks of enacting symbolic death-rituals in turn over each of their bodies. Throughout the ensuing mime Kate stays seated, utterly still, despite any efforts to establish contact with her that Anna and particularly Deeley try to make. Friend and husband enact their displacement from the centrality of Kate's presence: Kate remains upright, completely self-possessed, Anna is left lying on a divan, while Deeley slumps in a chair. The physical (the body language and positioning) has by the end become the correlative of the psychological, emotional and spiritual conditions of the three characters. What impresses in seeing as distinct from reading this conclusion is that Anna and Deeley are the agents of their own dissolution; Kate plays no directive role in their being marginalised; they are the shapers of their own fates. For much of the play they have sought to impose contesting interpretations on Kate's identity and past; their increasing urgency in doing this implies a desperate need to shape a role for Kate, which will somehow confirm their own troubling existences. Resisting the intrusive intentions of their intimacy, Kate shows them that their identities are compounded of nothing beyond a will to gain power over her; they have no inner resources whatever, no depth. In that ending, she looks out confidently into a future; but they lie or slouch, eyes unfocused, locked in the past. The lighting intensifies '*full sharply*' to '*very bright*' on that final grouping in Pinter's stage directions, which repeat what must be the final postures of the three performers.[33] Interestingly, the text gives no directive for a curtain, fade or blackout.[34]

Those raised lights seem in performance to etch the final tableau deep in one's memory till it takes on the status of an icon or what James Joyce would have termed an epiphany, an experience which is startling in its immediacy and profoundly illuminating for its symbolic and psychic relevance. With all the closing tableaux discussed, we are confronted by a similarly powerful, sustained image. It is as if in each of these plays the action reaches a point where words are no longer capable of holding together the intricacies of meaning that are being evolved and the body alone through the language of movement can give due weight to the fullness of experience being represented. The late Martha Graham, the American dancer-choreographer, was fond of reiterating the phrase: 'Movement never lies.'[35] In these plays movement and ensuing stasis create what is sensed as an apt ending but in so physicalised and poetic a form that it resists closure. As enacted symbol or physicalised metaphor, these tableaux hold multiple possibilities for a resolution in a deft poise without endorsing any one as definitive. By bringing audiences to focus their attention on body language and its potentials for significance within the larger stage picture (the closed curtains and array of bottles in No Man's Land; the disposition of the divans and chair in Old Times; the brilliant lamps in an otherwise darkened space in Ashes to Ashes), Pinter contrives a strategy whereby, in resolving the action into an icon of richly allusive intensity, he opens the play up beyond the performance to the enquiring imagination. A refined use of body language in these instances ensures the plays an after-life for audiences, as subject for debate or what Yeats would term 'excited reverie'. Movement may never lie, but neither does it conclusively determine meaning.

Relying on the suggestive powers of body language also allows Pinter to contain the representation of violence in his plays. At a time when the presentation of violence on the screens of cinemas and televisions has achieved an unparalleled ferocity, inventiveness and, through camera-trickery, a seeming naturalism, the impulse to contain violence onstage might seem a retrograde, even prissy step. But in the theatre such action is more immediately direct in its impact on an audience's imagination, because of the actual physical presence of the actors enacting the violence within the same space as the audience. Too literal a representation risks either implicating an audience in voyeuristic responses or inducing nausea in them (these are risks which Edward Bond, Sarah Kane and Mark Ravenhill have notably had difficulty in negotiating at times in their plays). The fundamental issue is what one wishes to achieve creatively through the representation of violence and how one focuses an audience's awareness on that specific end rather than the means to its achievement. Pinter in a number of his plays deploys body language (as in Stanley's final appearance in The Birthday Party) as the means to encourage his audience to register horror at the *consequences* of violence. He controls the experience meticulously so that he can move that audience through shock to psychological, moral and political insight. Jimmy, for example, whose sudden appearance concludes *Party Time* (1991), has been the victim of unimaginable torture. He is the reality, the product, the true cultural expression of the political elite, whom we see elsewhere in the play vacuously partying to celebrate their supposed superiority and absolute right to rule. Jimmy's approach is several times signalled during the party by a dimming of the illumination within the room as the light beyond a partially opened door intensifies to blinding proportions. He finally appears like a frail ghost seen (*'thinly dressed'*) in silhouette against the burning whiteness of that 'beyond', as the door swings fully open. What we see is a man's shape totally devoid of characterising detail, a body reduced to a point where it is recognisable only by its outline, the exact correlative of his inner condition. Jimmy recalls he once had a name but it is a thing of the past. Now all that his consciousness is aware of is its own processes of closing down till existence coheres for him about a desperate longing for the comfort of darkness:

'Sometimes a door bangs. I hear voices, then it stops. Everything stops. It all stops. It all closes. It closes down. It shuts. It all shuts. It shuts down. It shuts. I see nothing at any time any more. I sit sucking the dark.'[36] Those present tenses are relentless. Consciousness may be shutting down but the shutting *off* is endlessly protracted through time and the hope for extinction has become the man's only means of sustenance. The shape framed in the doorway is, nonetheless, recognisably human and speaks out of his abject condition to the humanity he still shares with the audience. This is a powerful visual metaphor for a terrifying situation, but the chosen mode of representation ensures that the audience, while registering the brutality being inflicted on Jimmy, focuses imaginatively on how a sensibility copes with such inhumanity. The outrage is that anyone should be forced so to cope. However degraded Jimmy may be by the regime that governs the world of the play, the character has not lost dignity in Pinter's representation. Body language is here refined to its simplest, yet Pinter invests it with a disturbing and profound eloquence.

This is similarly the case with the portrayal of the Elderly Woman in *Mountain Language* (1988). Waiting to see her imprisoned son, she has been harassed by guards and their dogs, one of which has savaged her hand. Finally allowed to see her son, she is prevented from speaking to him, since her mountain language has been officially banned; the son tries to reason with the guard who surveys their encounter, but in vain. When the son claims a common humanity with the guard (by remarking that he too has a family when the guard refers to his 'wife and three kids'), the soldier promptly summons his superior ('I thought I should report, Sergeant … I think I've got a joker in here'). A blackout followed by a change of scene and of characters ensues after the arrival of the Sergeant, questioning 'What joker?'[37] In Pinter's production for the National Theatre, when we returned to the cell the disposition of the three figures (Elderly Woman, Prisoner, Guard) exactly paralleled how we first saw them: woman and son sat either side of a bare table, while the guard had his back to them. The table was carefully angled so that the Prisoner's face was in quarter profile and the mother, opposite him, was all but full-face towards the audience. The differences were subtle (and took time to register) but profound: the son's spine was held rigid and the head slightly tilted upstage; a thin trickle of blood ran from his temple and ear; the mother's eyes and features, which formerly registered loving warmth, were now simply blank. Though the prisoner began to tremble and fell eventually to the floor, the mother's once expressive face sustained a dead stare. We did not need to see the violence done to the Prisoner, we could read every detail in the catatonic state of the woman who had witnessed it all: she had watched her son victimised merely for genially claiming kindred, which gave him a history and an identity other than the neutered category of prisoner. Here the bestiality of an authoritarian system is experienced imaginatively by the audience through observing the consequences of its efforts at control. Instead of staging the violence realistically *in action*, Pinter elects to offer us a staged image of its outcome, where words in part create a context but where chiefly we read the bodies of the characters for what those bodies reveal of their immediate experience: the son collapsed, the mother witless, the guard indifferent.

In *One for the Road* (1984) we see two victims of torture in periods of respite when they are subject to interrogation. They are a husband and wife; and their body language intimates the nature of what till now has been unremitting physical abuse. Victor's movements are (in every sense of the word) painfully slow, and by the time we see him in a second scene at the close of the play he has virtually lost control of his body: urged to drink, he can barely hold the glass; when he attempts to sip, the head rolls back. It is hardly surprising from what his body intimates of his treatment that, late in his first interrogation, he begs to be killed. Gila with her torn clothes and bruised skin has, as her answers to Nicolas, the interrogator, confirm, been systematically raped; but, unlike her husband, she is upright, held tightly determined in that position of self-control, we realise, by some inner core of rage through which she preserves a last sense of an inviolate selfhood. Where Victor flinched and cringed back into his seat away from Nicolas's gesturing with his hands ('I wave my big finger in front of your eyes. Like this'[38]), Gila reveals a provocative and confrontational self-possession. But it proves dangerous to reveal anything of one's inner being before an individual like Nicolas, who takes insidious pleasure in playing a cat-and-mouse game with her, raising her hopes of release only to consign her promptly back to yet more of her recent experiences till she too is fully broken like Victor: 'You're of no interest to me. I might even let you out of here, in due course. But I should think you might entertain us all a little more before you go.'[39] Given Gila's physical appearance, the nasty *double entendre* of 'entertain' exactly places Nicolas's sadism.

Between Victor's first interview and Gila's, Nicolas talks with their son, Nicky; he is unmarked physically, curious, wholly open and direct: a beautifully realised portrait of a trusting child. Nicky's natural behaviour and movement patterns betoken an innocence, a complete correlation between inner and outer selves in him, that contrasts markedly with the compulsive drinking that makes Nicolas's suave manner so suspect (what repressions in the interests of his job require such constant recourse to the whisky to make them bearable?), Victor's habitually fearful responses and Gila's studied control.[40] The sheer difference of the child's body language emphasises the degree to which the torturing of his parents is both a physical and a psychological invasion: Nicolas is seeking to gain absolute mastery of Victor and Gila by controlling their responses, their sensibilities, values, and the ways these inner, cultural qualities are manifest in the body's motion. He is marking, deconstructing and reshaping them till their bodies are fitting emblems of his power.

In *Surveiller et punir* (*Discipline and Punish*)[41] Michel Foucault records how early in the nineteenth century the spectacle of *public* torture and execution, where the bodies of criminals were literally inscribed with the marks of justice, was largely abandoned in Europe, being deemed barbaric for its display of Law and the Establishment as violent; instead, it was the trial that became the spectacle as public demonstration of an exercise of right reason; and penal 'correction' was displaced to the privacy of prisons. In modern society correction (Foucault argues) is an unknown factor experientially; sentences are abstract formulations, which rarely engage the imagination. What Pinter has done in his late plays is to bring torture and correction into the public eye again to reveal them as demonstrations of power not justice. 'Correction' implies a bringing into line with some standard, some pattern of behaviour which is deemed *correct* (or *right*) by the ones who effect the correcting. Hiding away such politically motivated procedures does not render them any less barbaric, any less shaming for the perpetrators than the dramas on the scaffold in the past; the hiding away is an admission of shame, a fear of judgment (one recalls Nicolas's compulsive drinking). Pinter in these plays engages with the subject of torture situating it rigorously within the larger context of political ethics; but always the focus of his theatrical representation of this debate is the suffering body, which is the chosen site for these

exhibitions of power and control: the victim's body (Jimmy's, the Elderly
Woman's, Victor's, Gila's) in the process of being reduced to a political cipher
becomes paradoxically the most potent of moral signifiers.

Few contemporary theoretical accounts of the politically inscribed body
have carried their analysis to the conclusions that Pinter bravely requires an
audience to experience in *One for the Road*. Never more frighteningly than in
this play has Pinter demonstrated the extent to which the bodies of his
characters carry his meaning. Justly Pinter has been celebrated for his verbal
artistry, but that is an artistry that centres on duplicities, evasions, manipu-
latory strategies. Equally, it could be argued, Pinter deserves to be celebrated
for an artistry that centres on the revelatory capacities and poetic immediacy
of body language. Movement – in Pinter's plays, as in Graham's dances –
never lies. The body *speaks* truths, which the voice would often seek to deny.

NOTES

1. W. B. Yeats, *Collected Poems* (London: Macmillan, 1961), p. 347. (My emphasis.)
2. The volume of criticism on Pinter's plays is considerable. A representative selection
   of titles that would illustrate this point would be: Martin Esslin, *The Theatre of the
   Absurd*, rev. edn (New York: Doubleday/Anchor, 1969) and his *The Peopled
   Wound: The Plays of Harold Pinter* (London: Methuen, 1970); Lucina P.
   Gabbard, *The Dream Structure of Pinter's Plays: A Psychoanalytic Approach*
   (Cranbury and London: Associated University Press, 1976); Margaret Croyden,
   'Pinter's Hideous Comedy' in *A Casebook on Harold Pinter's The Homecoming*
   ed. John Lahr (New York: Grove Press, 1971), pp. 45–56; Elizabeth Sakellaridou,
   Pinter's Female Portraits (Basingstoke and London: Macmillan, 1988); Katharine
   Worth, *Revolutions in Modern English Drama* (London: G.Bell and Sons, 1972);
   David T. Thompson, *Pinter: The Player's Playwright* (London and New York:
   Macmillan, 1985); Richard Allen Cave, *New British Drama in Performance on the
   London Stage: 1970–1985* (Gerrards Cross: Colin Smythe, 1987); Susan Hollis
   Merritt, 'Pinter and Politics', in *Harold Pinter: A Casebook*, ed. Lois Gordon (New
   York and London: Garland, 1990); and the various sections of Katherine H.
   Burkman and J. L. Kundert-Gibbs (eds.), *Pinter at Sixty* (Bloomington and
   Indianapolis: Indiana University Press, 1993).
3. These are the titles of several chapters within a recent study of Pinter's drama,
   (D. Keith Peacock, *Harold Pinter and the New British Theatre* (Westport, CT:
   Greenwood Press, 1997).
4. Michael Billington, *The Life and Work of Harold Pinter* (London: Faber, 1996).
5. The most notorious example of this was the wholesale turnabout effected by many
   newspaper reviewers, who damned *Betrayal* when first staged by Peter Hall at the
   National Theatre in 1978 but totally revised their view when the play was revived
   by David Leveaux at the Almeida in 1991. Their embarrassment was clearly still
   rankling in 1998, since most referred to their lapse of judgment when reviewing the
   play for a third time on its revival by Trevor Nunn at the National Theatre.
6. David T. Thompson may appear to be embarking on a discussion of body language
   in the final chapter, entitled 'Revaluation: Movement and Dialogue', of his study,

Pinter: the Player's Playwright; but throughout his discussion of movement he is preoccupied only with spatial relations between characters and basic actions such as sitting and standing; and he rather rapidly moves on to discussing the speakability and rhythm of Pinter's lines, which occupy nineteen of the chapter's thirty-one pages.

7. The reference is to Pinter's recent work as an actor under his own name and not to his early career, when he adopted the stage name of 'David Baron'.

8. The range of reviews can be found in *Theatre Record*, 7–20 May 1998, pp. 617–22.

9. Harold Pinter, *The Collection* and *The Lover* (London: Methuen, 1963), p. 43.

10. *Theatre Record*, 7–20 May 1998, p. 620.

11. Pinter had previously played Mick in *The Caretaker*, Law in *The Basement* and Deeley in *Old Times*.

12. A longer, differently focused critique of Pinter's production of *The Caretaker* is included in my essay, 'I Sessanta Anni di Pinter degli Anni Novanta', in *Teatro inglese contemporaneo*, ed. Carla Dente Baschiera (Pisa: Edizioni ETS, 1995) pp. 27–57. I am grateful to the editor for permission to reproduce some of that material here.

13. Harold Pinter, *The Caretaker* (London: Eyre Methuen, 1962, reprinted 1973), p. 54.

14. *Ibid.*, p. 73.

15. From the page it might seem as if the play ends in a state of stasis with Aston refusing to look at Davies and Davies whingeing desperately in the hope of remaining in the shelter of the room. But Aston has rejected Davies's plan for changing their beds and his proffered help in putting up the projected shed in the garden; more significantly he has actually *faced* Davies to utter his final dismissive accusation, 'You make too much noise' (*ibid.*, p. 77). Moreover there was in Pinter's production a marked change in the characters' body language compared with the close of Act Two: Aston may have had his back to Davies and to the audience but it was his stance now that was confident, whereas it was Davies who seemed to be collapsing into himself. Writing about Pinter's helpful presence in rehearsals for two of his plays which she directed, Carey Perloff observes how instructive it was for her and her cast when Pinter took to the stage and demonstrated points of acting. Her chosen example is of him showing 'why ... it is *potent* to act with one's back to the audience' (Carey Perloff, 'Pinter in Rehearsal', in *Pinter at Sixty*, ed. Burkman and Gibbs, p. 7. My emphasis.). Given the fact that Davies has recently drawn a knife on Aston, Aston's positioning himself with his back to Davies argued not only for a new confidence but considerable presence, tenacity and will-power.

16. This was a valuable revision of the traditional reading of the role of Mick as decidedly macho. The doctor, Hornby, in *A Kind of Alaska* (1982) in his lifetime of devoted care of Deborah, possesses a quality that is feminine, even maternal in its concern: 'I have nourished you, watched over you, for all this time. ... I have never let you go.' (See Harold Pinter, *Other Places* (London: Methuen, 1982), pp. 34–5.) There is no loss of masculinity in the portrayal. Peter Howitt's Mick possessed such a quality but without minimising the butch elements in the role.

17. Harold Pinter, *Ashes to Ashes* (London: Faber, 1996), p. 3.

18. *Ibid.*, p. 5.

19. *Ibid.*, p. 7.

20. *Ibid.*

21. *Ibid.*
22. *Ibid.*, p. 25.
23. *Ibid.*, p. 11.
24. *Ibid.*, p. 13.
25. Pinter also invites us to imagine body language in relation to qualities of touch in Beth's account of her visit to the beach with her 'true love' in *Landscape* (1969).
26. Pinter has several times referred to the formative influence in his early years of reading John Webster's plays with his schoolmaster, Joe Brearley (see, for example, his 'speech of thanks' on receiving the David Cohen British Literature Prize in 1995, which is reproduced as the Introduction to *Harold Pinter: Plays Four* (London: Faber, 1996), pp. ix–xi). This closing section of *Ashes to Ashes* (written and staged a year after Pinter's receipt of the Cohen award) deploys an echo effect where a disembodied voice repeats crucial words from Rebecca's speeches, as if it were the ghost of the abandoned child speaking within her consciousness, or a shocked 'higher' self in Jungian terms registering disbelief at her own pragmatic callousness. The technique recurs in Elizabethan and Jacobean drama but is used most memorably in Webster's *The Duchess of Malfi*, where an Echo warns the Duchess's husband, Antonio, in tones that remind him of his 'dead wife's voice' to 'fly his fate', implying certain death if he carries out his plan of trying to meet on peaceful terms with his vicious brothers-in-law. The Duchess has died by strangulation, after being systematically tortured by one of her brothers, Ferdinand. The hands on the throat, the veiled hints of a torture that is administered as somehow for a woman's 'good', the echo, the forcible seizing of a baby from its mother's arms, these motifs appear in both plays. Webster's tragedy lies as a significant intertextual echo within Pinter's play, reminding us that after nearly four hundred years of cultural refinement certain styles of masculinist sadism still obtain in the sexual and political arenas.
27. Harold Pinter, *No Man's Land* (London: Eyre Methuen, 1975), pp. 93–4.
28. *Ibid.*, p. 32.
29. Harold Pinter, *Old Times* (London: Eyre Methuen, 1971), p. 32.
30. *Ibid.*, p. 33.
31. *Ibid.*, p. 34.
32. *Ibid.*, p. 71.
33. *Ibid.*, p. 75.
34. For a fuller discussion of the closing mime and tableau, see my article, 'Dance and Stylised Movement as Visual Codes in Drama: A Crisis in Interpretation', in *Verbal and Non-Verbal Codes in European Drama*, ed. Marta Gibinska (Krakow: Krakow University Press, 1996), pp. 81–105.
35. Martha Graham, *Blood Memory: An Autobiography* (New York: Doubleday, 1991), p. 4.
36. Harold Pinter, *Party Time* (London: Faber, 1991), p. 38.
37. Harold Pinter, *Mountain Language* (London: Faber, 1988), pp. 34–5.
38. Harold Pinter, *One for the Road* (London: Methuen, 1984), p. 33. The play was simultaneously published in two formats by Methuen that year: one, in the New Theatrescripts series, contained only the text; the other, a revised edition, also included photographs by Ivan Kyncl of Pinter's original production and a 'conversation' between Pinter and Nick Hern, entitled 'A Play and its Politics'. All references here are to the latter edition.

39. *Ibid.*, p. 74.
40. A shift of tense in Nicolas's final reference to Nicky – 'Your son? Oh, don't worry about him. He *was* a little prick' (*ibid.*, p. 79, my emphasis) – intimates the child has been exterminated. The casualness of the reference conveys Nicolas's callousness exactly.
41. See Michel Foucault, *Discipline and Punish: The Birth of the Prison*, trans. Alan Sheridan (London and Harmondsworth: Peregrine Books, 1979). Particularly relevant as influencing my argument here is the first section entitled 'Torture'.

9

MICHAEL PENNINGTON

Harold Pinter as director

In the theatre, some trades are like carpentry, their virtuosity more or less subsumed in the thing made: a lifetime of experience of things other than wood may lie in the joints and dowels, the grain and the glue, but it is the accommodation and proportion of the finished chair that the carpentry draws attention to. Other tasks are like the making of stained glass, which may be as devotional and also as practical, but which cannot but broadcast the flair of the design, the particular vision of the artist. If good acting starts as an example of the latter case, and at its very best approaches the inspired anonymity of the former, then directing and writing, safeguarding and requiring each other, are of the former. It is perhaps no accident that Arthur Miller has a passion for woodwork comparable to his energy as a playwright.

The three jobs are certainly specialised, seeming to call for different profiles: it is rare to find two of the talents in the same person, leave alone three. We do not know if Shakespeare was a good actor, and there was no such thing as a director in his day; Molière's entrepreneurial skills (or at least his understanding of patronage) are beyond doubt, but it seems that his desire to be a tragedian was at odds with an inevitably comic stage persona, and so the writer in him had little competition. Chekhov delivered brilliant brief insights, usually in letters to his wife, into how his plays should be acted, but I think he would never have had the patience or forbearance to co-ordinate the traffic of a whole production, so those qualities were reserved for his writing instead: and history is silent on his acting potential.

In the case of Harold Pinter, a big surprise arrives. He has dominated our dramatic landscape as a writer for over forty years; but he started life as a professional actor at the age of nineteen, and soon afterwards toured Ireland for five seasons in Anew McMaster's company, playing a repertoire of everything from the Greeks to Shakespeare to Agatha Christie. From his delightful memoir of these days, *Mac*, you can see that he was from the start touched by the endless practical accommodations of rehearsing five plays in two weeks and then of touring one-night stands, as well as by the very old, rhapsodic tradition of heroic theatre embodied by this last great actor-manager – one who, having called for his false teeth and a drop of whiskey, could reminisce all day about Sarah Bernhardt and Mrs Pat Campbell before stepping out as Oedipus or Othello – when he would display

> ... gestures complete, final, nothing jagged, his movement of the utmost fluidity and yet of the utmost precision: [he] stood there, dead in the centre of the role, and the great sweeping symphonic playing would begin, the rare tension and release within him, the arrest, the swoop, the savagery, the majesty and repose ... He acted along the spine of the role and never deviated from it ...[1]

Pinter played first support to McMaster, and sometimes the lead (Iago, Jack Worthing, a single performance of Hamlet), so even then his own acting required no apology at all.

As a director, he has, to date, mounted some twenty productions in London, including the premières of six plays by Simon Gray, and works by writers as diverse as Coward, Joyce, Mamet and Tennessee Williams, as well as the film version of Gray's *Butley*, and four television productions for the BBC. Again, there is obviously no question of his gifts, but some difficulty in defining them, so thoroughly does he efface himself in his attention to another author's text and in his careful handling of his collaborators – this is the carpenter in him. Into the apparent vacuum many trade anecdotes flood – all of them amusing, in general affectionately told and most of them partly true. For myself, I have been directed by Pinter only once, and to some extent I too have to report in anecdote, with, I hope, readable space between its lines.

I had always wanted to work with Pinter, in one way or another. But apart from a production of *The Dumb Waiter*, which I put on myself at school, it had not come up, though there had been some talk of my being in the film of his *Betrayal*. In fact I had barely met him, though, since no one is quite a stranger in our industry, there had been the warily courteous acknowledgements across canteens and parties of those who have not yet worked together but might do some day. Then, in 1994, my agent called me in the melancholy tone reserved for another stage offer with no commercial advantages: to go to Dublin to play in the Gate Theatre's Pinter Festival, a three-week celebration of the plays that would set the town alight while stretching the Gate's own resources to their maximum, both financially and practically. There were to be three new productions of full-length plays – *Betrayal*, *Old Times* and *Moonlight*, preceded in a 6 pm slot by three of his shorter works – *The Dumb Waiter*, *One for the Road* and *Landscape*. I was being asked to play the interrogator from hell in *One for the Road*, a brilliant extemporisation written as if on a single enraged breath by Pinter on the subject of state-authorised torture. Good as the idea was, it was not enough for me in my current mood – I had not done any Pinter before and wanted to be more fully involved. If they were going to do *Old Times*, could I please play Deeley in that as well? The hesitations in reply were not, I think, so much artistic as practical – the plays opened one day after another after rehearsing side by side for only three weeks. I offered to work at all times of night and day, shuttling between two worlds, two rooms, two casts and two directors: I took it on myself to learn and deliver both performances to standard within the time. Agreed.

When Pinter had been asked about this I am told he signalled his approval by snapping his fingers with a cry of 'Pennington!', then making a gesture which was compared by my imaginative informant to that of Donald Pleasence when he created the role of Davies in *The Caretaker*, when he speaks of getting to Sidcup – I hope it was less frustrated. Though Pinter was – obviously – deeply involved in the Dublin event, neither of my shows was to be directed by him; he was set instead to do *Landscape* with Ian Holm and Penelope Wilton. The whole Festival was both grand and a little Saturnalian: across Grafton Street stretched a banner announcing 'The Pinter Festival' (can you imagine it in Bond Street?) and it was conducted in a spirit of affectionate revelry (and a slight hint of fit-up) perhaps consistent with Pinter's Irish roots. It took Michael Billington, critic of *The Guardian* and Pinter's biographer, to comment on the obvious fact that for Dublin's Gate to be the first to do such a thing was a reproach to the English theatre, who might have rewarded Pinter's achievements in this way years ago. True; but this special glorification of a living author is something we don't do much, perhaps for fear he might get too big for his boots, or one of those other English sins.

Pinter invited me to lunch with Kevin Billington, the director of *Old Times*. We did not talk much about the play – it was more an actors' meeting, awash with anecdote, enthusiasm and the third bottle; Billington had the pleasant impression that we were getting on well, and I felt I had shaken a hand I had long wished to. Two days later, Pinter rang on quite another matter, to offer me the world première of Ronald Harwood's new play about the great conductor Wilhelm Furtwängler, *Taking Sides*, which he planned to direct the following year. Having read it, I had to do some nifty footwork with other commitments, but swiftly made myself free.

The Dublin Festival, meanwhile, was a success (three years later there was another) – excellent work all round. Harold liked the two productions I was in, pointing out only that in the climactic speech of *Old Times*, when Deeley's emotional pressure flowers into a wild arabesque about 'the Edgware Road gang':

Old friends. Always thinking. Spoke their thoughts. Those are the people I miss. They're all dead, anyway I've never seen them again. The Maida Vale group. Big Eric and little Tony …²

I shouldn't keep one hand in my pocket. I said that this was a feeble attempt by the character at insouciance. He said that that might be, but it looked too much like the real thing. Point taken, and my first acting note from Harold Pinter.

Taking Sides opened during the 1995 Chichester season, before transferring to the West End, where it ran for six months and could have continued. Daniel Massey played Furtwängler, a final triumph in his career and his last stage work before his untimely death in 1998. Pinter is very loyal to his collaborators – Tom Rand did the costumes, and under Mick Hughes's lighting, Eileen Diss designed the bombed-out Berlin perspective in which the American security forces pursued their denazification programme in 1946, an enquiry that focused on Furtwängler's motives in staying in Hitler's Germany when many of his contemporaries – Bruno Walter for instance, and Otto Klemperer – emigrated. Special attention was paid in the play, as in history, to his relations – perhaps collaborative, perhaps creatively Faustian – with the Third Reich: Furtwängler used his influence to intercede for many Jewish musicians and helped them escape, but he also played concerts for the Party Congress in 1935 and Hitler's birthday in 1942. What is history's judgment on him? It depends, as Harwood says in his introduction, on what side you take.[3]

I was playing the American interrogating officer, Major Arnold, who had, like the other allies, survived the horrors of discovering the death camps while they moved as liberators towards Berlin during the preceding months. He had, as he said, 'seen things with these eyes', and was in no mood to listen to a lot of 'airy-fairy' talk about art being above 'politics', still less to Furtwängler's ambiguous justification of his own position: to Major Arnold it was simply a matter of good and evil. In this fine play a dangerous theatrical alchemy threatened: the persecuted artist always looks good – after all, if you watch a play you enjoy art – and his walking conscience less so. Dollops of Furtwängler's Beethoven recordings punctuated the action, rather emphasising the problem; however, Harwood was careful to place throughout the play markers of Major Arnold's subtle agony, culminating in a desperate account of his nightmarish experiences at the end. Still, many people, fifty years after the event, found it difficult to see beyond the defensive boorishness that was, so to speak, Arnold's front face; and ultimately the confusion caused the *New York Times* critic to denounce the London theatre as being in the grip of anti-American prejudice. So I had my work cut out. Pinter and Harwood chose Massey for his exceptional ability to enter the spirit of the artist, and myself for what they saw as my lack of sentimentality as an actor, and Pinter adjudicated on the result with his fellow writer, welcome, open and collaborative, at his side. The cast also included Gawn Grainger as Furtwängler's second violinist, only in that post because of the vacancies caused by the disappearance of the Jews (and thus, in Arnold's eyes, entirely culpable); Suzanne Bertish as the widow of a young Jewish pianist Furtwängler had helped to escape but who then died in Auschwitz; Geno Lechner as Arnold's enforced secretary, a German music lover whose father had been part of the conspiracy to assassinate Hitler; and Christopher Simon as a young Jewish lieutenant working under Arnold whose parents had disappeared in the death camps.

I worked hard on the play before we began, and not only on the accent. Since there are roles far enough away from you that they need particular research, I combined an American holiday with a trip to West Point to talk to and, as much, to observe the military historians there: a charming group of men who on the one hand assured me that the historical detail was right, and who on the other privately fascinated me by not being able to name the exceptional bird-life that hovered over the Hudson River outside, on the basis that they were military historians, not ornithologists. These pleasant soldiers seemed unable to walk, even off-duty, without marching. I had taken care not to tell Ronald Harwood before the event that I was going to check up on his research, and when I congratulated him on his accuracy, his look was a little old-fashioned – we were not as close friends then as we are now. I went to see Harold on the eve of rehearsals and expatiated on what I'd learned – he poured me generous glasses of wine and seemed attentive and pleased.

As we began to rehearse Pinter outlined his approach, which was utterly practical. We would read, stage, practise, find out as we went. The play was sufficient to itself, accurate enough to its period; he trusted his designer, and we were not to be distracted by any minutiae of history that obscured its strong impulse. In the face of this gentle put-down, I remembered that there are some forms of research that an actor should keep to himself. By now Massey knew intimately all Furtwängler's recordings, but I suppose he had not made as much fuss about it. There is an entertaining story of Alan Ayckbourn, as a young actor playing in the first revival of *The Birthday Party*, asking Pinter for some background to his character and being told by the author to 'mind his own business' (it is not quite accurate, but enjoyed still by all parties) – I realised that in displaying my West Point wares, I was not allowing Pinter the director to mind his own business. I made no more comment on the background to the play, or its substance, except to recommend a more American word for the male sexual organ than the English, a suggestion that was taken up with delightful formality. Around this time, I considered showing Harold, in an off-duty moment, an apprentice critical work I had written at university, published in *Granta* magazine in 1963: it

7 Michael Pennington and Daniel Massey in *Taking Sides*, directed by Harold Pinter,
the Minerva Studio Theatre, 1995

8 Michael Pennington and Daniel Massey in *Taking Sides*, directed by Harold Pinter, Criterion Theatre, 1995

was trailed on the cover as 'Pennington on Pinter', rather as if we were equals, and inside it the undergraduate counselled the writer (with *The Caretaker*, *The Collection* and *The Birthday Party* behind him, not to mention the screenplay of *The Servant*) on his best way forward: 'Pinter has shown ... that he belongs to this sphere [the theatre 'moment']; now, after three consecutive exercises for broadcasting, what is needed from him is a more complete commitment to the medium which best rewards his powers ...'4 On reflection, I decided against.

Ronald Harwood, an old friend of Pinter's (they met playing together in Donald Wolfit's *Lear* in 1953 – indeed Harwood enjoyed a relationship with Donald Wolfit not unlike Pinter's with McMaster), has described these rehearsals: 'No one creates a pleasanter, more agreeable atmosphere … His care and precision, his affection for the actors was marvellous.'[5] Exactly. We worked, as I think Pinter often does, in a solid four- or five-hour block in the middle of the day, a system in which you achieve as much as in an eight-hour day punctuated by breaks – the blood sugar remains relatively constant, and concentration fairly steady. Sometimes even that period was cut a little short if our best work seemed to have been done for the day – a confident feeling of time in hand can be as helpful as anxious exhaustion, especially when there are lines to learn in the evening. Pinter was unfailingly courteous and sensitive to the author on one side of him and the actors on the other – in fact I doubt if he would ever be sharp to an actor except in the case of laziness, since he is one of us and understands the job. There was in any case no laziness – a sense of industry, unobtrusively introduced into the room by the seriousness of the subject, the quality of the writing and Pinter's gentle authority, possessed everybody concerned. He lived in the present: actors are constantly fretting that they are 'not there yet', or even as close as they would wish, and he always reassured, saying that tomorrow was another day. There was a desk on either side of the stage and a chair for Furtwängler and the other witnesses in the middle, and thus the usual meticulous concern about angles and precise positioning. The whole proceeding was scrupulous and unassuming; there was no theorising, and rehearsals were conducted with an unoppressive punctuality, an uninhibiting sense of discipline. As well as his sympathy towards his actors, Pinter is celebrated for his dislike of intrusive noise: it is said that he once objected to a fly buzzing in a rehearsal room, that he tried to get the traffic stopped on another occasion, and that he spent many hours, when directing Simon Gray's *Rear Column*, in establishing the precise dimensions of the fully grown male turtle in order to deduce the necessary size of the crate in which two of them were to arrive at the beginning of the play (they are then forgotten until the end). I suspect his sense of humour would have softened his position on the traffic and the buzzing fly, and the enquiry about the turtle is an honourable and professional one; but there is no doubt, as you would expect, that this is a man who appreciates the value of silence, and the explosive effect of the right word dropped into it. Sadly the noise on this production that awoke his ire was that of a great crash which turned out to be his own parked car being reversed into outside the building. He was unusually considerate to the stage management, the cats who sometimes get kicked, only occasionally testing them, tongue a little in cheek – as when an assistant was sent to stop a conversation in the yard outside. We were rehearsing in a sports centre, and we certainly had no rights outside our own room, but perhaps an impossible assignment like this is a helpful rite of passage for a young stage manager.

The delicacy of a director's relationship with the writer can be imagined, and then doubled if the director is a fellow writer as well. The script was not altered at all in rehearsal, except for one instance so subtle that I thought at first the difference only existed in Pinter's ear. In the second act, Arnold makes a deal with the second violinist, whom he has discovered to have been a Party member despite all his protestations. In return for information about Furtwängler's dealings with the Party, Arnold will give him a job as janitor in the building and thereby keep him warm and fed. The violinist then attributes anti-Semitic remarks to the conductor, claims that he sent Hitler a birthday telegram and used to have his critics conscripted, suggests that his private life contains scandal, and finally refers to Furtwängler's professional jealousy of Herbert von Karajan, on which point the scene closes. Pinter was sure these charges were in the wrong order, and that the hint about his private life should come last. To leave the audience suspecting the artist of a sexual peccadillo rather than professional malice was, he pointed out, not just a matter of old-fashioned suspense but of the verbal rhythms supporting it. Compare the alternative curtain lines:

RODE: Yes, ask him about von Karajan. And you may notice, that he cannot even bring himself to utter the name. Furtwängler refers to him as K.[6]

or

RODE: Oh, and ask him about his private life.
ARNOLD: His private life?[7]

Musically and theatrically, there was no contest.

We moved forward in a thoroughly conventional way. There was, I think, only one passage which had to be dismantled for experiment and discussion. Towards the end Arnold and Furtwängler finally face each other down, gloves off, their separate crises evident:

FURTWÄNGLER: I know that a single performance of a great masterpiece was a stronger and more vital negation of the spirit of Buchenwald and Auschwitz than words. Human beings are free wherever Wagner and Beethoven are played ...
(ARNOLD: *grabs the baton from his desk, stands trembling before* FURTWÄNGLER, *and snaps it in half* ...)
ARNOLD: ... Have you ever smelled burning flesh? I smelt it four miles away. Four miles away, I smelt it. I smell it now, I smell it at night because I can't sleep any more with the stench of it in my nostrils ... You talk to me about culture and art and music? You putting that in the scales, Wilhelm?[8]

This moment where the bottled-up tensions explode forms a logical and, you might say, satisfying climax to the play. You know where you are when this happens in the theatre – it is the showdown. The scene is written with great sincerity – it encourages the actors to give it all they have, ferociously committing themselves to the emotions. In its very satisfactoriness, though, lurks a problem, all the greater for the fact that this is a very serious issue that goes far beyond the *angst* of two individuals created for the theatre, one of them imaginary, their prototypes now claimed or forgotten by history. Since everyone is in some way affected by the Holocaust, the audience needed the space to consider it, the right to experience their own feelings, and the warm feeling of individual catharsis seemed increasingly out of place as we played the scene for all it was worth. One detail was simple enough – the sound of Furtwängler's baton snapping was pitiful in the midst of it all: the gesture was too petty, a nut being cracked by a sledgehammer, so it was cut. The broader question was less easy to resolve. Harold stressed a theatrical conviction – that always what mattered to him was not unruly emotion but the way it resolved itself into what, and what only, had to be said: many times, the exact form of what is written leads you to the content, and you should reveal only so much emotion as is needed to frame proportionate words. Actors are wary of a line like this, taking the intellectual point but sensing that it polices them too much – and indeed an audience too attuned to theatrical cliché may feel let down by such severity. But the suppression of emotion, or rather its rechannelling, is a chronic human activity, and the theatre reflects that, just as it occasionally offers release from those restraints. At this point in rehearsals Harold, with exceptional instinct, could only report an unease, a jarring sound on his ear, an unworthy feeling of surfeit – as the most demanding audience we would ever meet, he was not happy.

He asked us to sit and speak the scene through devoid of emotion, so that he really heard the argument and had enough breathing space to absorb it. Dan Massey did not see the point of this, feeling that there is no such thing as language without emotion, especially this language, and that the exercise was artificial. He felt disempowered, fearful of having his impulses deconstructed, and he felt it strongly. A rather fruitless wrangle ensued about the rights and wrongs of even trying the experiment; we eventually did, since that was all it was. I found the experience rather barren but not a waste of time. Shortly after, Harold did something which, as he said, he had never done in a rehearsal before – bring in a piece of his own writing that was apropos and read it to the cast. It was a passage from *The Dwarfs*, and it certainly settled the debate:

> The trouble is, you've got to be quite sure of what you mean by efficient. Look at
> a nutcracker. You press the cracker and the cracker cracks the nut. You might
> think that's an exact process. It's not. The nut cracks, but the hinge of the

cracker gives out a friction which is completely incidental to the particular idea. It's unnecessary, an escape and wastage of energy to no purpose. So there's nothing efficient about a nutcracker.[9]

Or about the wrong kind of acting. The result of the argument was thus not an immediate revelation but a talisman that guided us until the final performance months later – a warning, in fact, to prefer efficiency to bravura. From this point Massey moved towards what he finally offered as Furtwängler at this moment – a ruthlessly precise study of himself and an atrocious sense of compromise: the speech ends with a declaration that he was wrong and should have left Germany in 1934, at which point he retches and is taken ingloriously away. It was a fine and brutal piece of acting that left you with no comfort. In a way I proceeded in an opposite direction – eight questions follow each other in Arnold's speech and they are there not to elicit an answer, or to ask for understanding, but as dispassionate weapons, not so much hectoring as insinuating, even delicately polite: 'Have you seen the crematoria? … Have you seen the mounds of rotting corpses? … You putting culture and art and music against the millions put to death by your pals?'[10] The emotion was there all right, laid into the subtly musical repetitions in the writing: '… I smelt it. I smell it now, I smell it at night … I'll smell it for the rest of my life',[11] but the prime aim was to leave the audience space to smell for themselves the feculence of Arnold's night terrors. It was like reining in a runaway horse, but not so successfully as to disguise the power of the beast; and the whole method was determined by the director's small unease many weeks before.

Preparing its final shape, Pinter kept attending to the grain of his wood. I think we felt ushered rather than directed into place, and I mean that as a compliment. As the opening approached, his notes became highly selective – less of a pause there, more of an emphasis there, a warmer tone perhaps, even a counterpoint between the line said and the manner of its saying. For instance, a phrase such as 'he'll wait until hell freezes over' can be played quite gently, since the image is aggressive enough as it is; and a pause for silent action – the pouring of water, the giving of a cup of coffee – should never be rushed, but take the time it takes: these are all points that actors recognise but sometimes forget as anxiety closes in. He typically gave one well-placed character note, carefully phrased, at each session, though I sensed there were other things he might have said but decided not to for the moment. At one point Geno Lechner was becoming too hostile towards the Major – so she should remember that her every thought and action is coloured by the humiliating fact that she represents a newly conquered nation. He warned Chris Simon of a parallel danger. In a scene where Wills thanks Furtwängler for changing his life with a performance of Beethoven's Fifth Symphony, the lieutenant says that the conductor 'opened a new world for me ... More than a world. Like waking from sleep ... You showed me a place where there was – an absence of misery.'[12] Pinter pointed out that Wills could only have survived his terrible losses, Nazism, his life as a soldier, by developing a toughness which would keep this speech from sentimentality. Just as Arnold had to be viewed in the context of the time, not from a nineties liberal standpoint, he was reminding these younger actors (one a post-war German herself, the other inclining towards the tones of a contemporary college kid) of a memory which to them could only be second-hand – exactly what their parents' generation had survived, that precise state of affairs. Meanwhile, an observation to me that I tended to overplay and slur my accent in the opening minutes before settling down easily into it, as if I was anxious about its authenticity (I was – I knew we would be playing to many American visitors) in fact gave me confidence. Dan – a little swifter sometimes please, particularly in angry response. Gawn should remember that Rode is in every way second violinist material, and never suggest, in his passion for the music, a greater talent than he has. As Tamara, Suzanne should remember that although her part consists of one highly emotional scene, she must, however keyed up for it, still have some objective sense of folding it into the overall momentum of the play. As we opened in Chichester, whatever truculent determination was in Pinter was applied to our interests only – he fought and won an exceptional victory in having the sale of Smarties banned from the theatre confectionery, since the rattling of their tubes during the action was seriously distracting – a triumph for art in a theatre which, like all others, has to be interested in its merchandising.

We transferred to the Criterion in London, a smaller stage which presented one or two sightline problems; I was summoned, together with Massey and Harwood, to inspect it before the deal was struck to play there, which was almost spoiling the actor. During the summer and autumn of the run, it seemed for a moment that Harold, in some exemplary way, was in control of the London theatre in all his guises – he was himself playing in a revival of his early work *The Hothouse* round the corner at the Comedy, and *Old Times* was running at the Wyndhams. Still, he studied the performance report of *Taking Sides* each day and would be on the phone if anything seemed to be amiss – a most unusual attentiveness. Towards the end, Massey became ill and the understudy, Stuart Rayner, went on: Harold came down and gave him just enough guidance – no more than he could handle – to get him through the gruelling experience. Geno Lechner's understudy went on too; and the director came as close to scornfulness as he ever did when she opined that Arnold was brutalising, even harassing her, in the play: the whiff of sub-feminist distortion maddened him for a moment, as did any form of judgmentalism on any character – one reason why it was easy to play Arnold for him.

On *Taking Sides* we had a sense that we were special, long before the show was in any sense a success, and everyone in it did their best work (as did the cast of *Twelve Angry Men*, which Pinter went on to direct the following year). You are entitled to ask how that came about, but the fact is that there is not so much to say. There is no special flourish to Pinter the director, no particular methodology, no exotic rehearsal practices. He is certainly first class, one of the very best I have known, but his obligation to nothing but the work in hand can make him seem almost invisible: instead of tiresome panache, there is only a healthy practicality, and a hatred of sentimentality. His sense of the weight and meaning of language is of course absolute – of the weight and meaning of a gesture too;[13] as an actor you have his undivided attention all the time, and he always goes to the heart of the matter.

He is also very selective in what he does – at the time of writing, he has never directed a classic, if you discount Jean Giraudoux's *The Trojan War Will Not Take Place*: never, indeed, returned to his roots with Anew McMaster. It is surprising – John Webster, as much as Shakespeare, delighted him as a young man, and he writes movingly of his English teacher, mentor and lifelong friend Joe Brearley, with whom he regularly walked from Hackney Downs to Bethnal Green yelling favourite passages at the trolley-buses. Certainly the phantasmagoric energy of *The Duchess of Malfi* and *The White Devil*, the controlled grotesquerie of its poetry, would seem very close to Pinter's literary sensibility. Perhaps he distrusts the inevitable flamboyance and expressionism involved in the putting on of such plays; at any rate, not being a career director, he does not need to consider the question and can continue to do what appeals to him. The public, as a consequence, has the pleasant feeling that any project he takes on is precisely what he believes in. It will, in fact, be whatever allows him to exercise the special precision that releases meaning and illumination; but it should not suggest that he is a miniaturist.

Pinter has spoken of 'this perilous fact of life which theatre is all about', of the theatre as a 'dangerous activity', and in describing himself as a director he could, of course, be speaking as actor, and perhaps writer, as well:

> I hope I'm both spontaneous and meticulous, you can be both things at the same time … I think directing plays can be quick and slow at the same time … you don't know where you're going, but you've got to find out, and then when you find out you don't know what the next step is going to be either … you've got to keep your feet, but it's very precarious.[14]

On the other hand, speaking of his writing, he has said: 'I've got an animal in the middle of the play which has to be held by the author. But I like the animal, by the way. If it wasn't for the animal, there'd be nothing there at all'[15] – and for 'author' you could say 'director' or 'actor'. His best acting performances – such as Colonel Roote in *The Hothouse* – suggest through the lightest of touches and a beguiling sense of comedy a quite alarming measure of violence; as a director he is able, by operating like a watchmaker, to release the energies of the most horrifying events of the twentieth century. Controlling the animal until it has to be released, so that it comes out of its lair at exactly the right size, the right colours and proportion and making the authentic noise, is his effort as playwright, screenwriter, director, performer, as well as poet, polemicist and prose writer. If some characteristics are set aside as he directs – the performer's assertiveness disappearing in the discreet handling of other actors, the edginess of the writer softened by good humour on the floor – the triple persona is obviously driven by a unified sensibility. He is, as it turns out, at home in both carpentry and stained glass – to quote Shakespeare in a rare moment of self-disclosure, an entire theatre man whose 'nature is subdu'd/To what it works in, like the dyer's hand'.

NOTES

1. Harold Pinter, in *Mac*, in *Harold Pinter – Various Voices* (London: Faber, 1998).
2. Harold Pinter, *Old Times, Plays Three* (London: Faber, 1997), p. 307.
3. Ronald Harwood, Introduction to *Taking Sides* (London: Faber, 1995).
4. Michael Pennington, *Pinter Now and Then*, published in *Granta Magazine*, 1963.
5. Quoted in Michael Billington, *The Life and Work of Harold Pinter* (London: Faber, 1996), p. 365.
6. Ronald Harwood, *Taking Sides*, in Ronald Harwood, *Plays Two* (London: Faber, 1995), p. 43.
7. *Ibid.*, p. 42.
8. *Ibid.*, p. 64.
9. Harold Pinter, *The Dwarfs* (London: Faber, 1990), p. 93.
10. Harwood, *Taking Sides*, p. 64.
11. *Ibid.*, p. 64.
12. *Ibid.*, pp. 34–5.
13. Interestingly, Michael Billington attributes this in part to Pinter's observation of actors like McMaster and Donald Wolfit, whose sense of the potent gesture tactically chosen Pinter much admired: 'In a Pinter play, the movement of a glass from one side of a table to another or the simple crossing or uncrossing of a pair of legs becomes the equivalent of Wolfit's cloak' (Michael Billington, *The Life and Work of Harold Pinter*, p. 47).
14. Interview with Mireia Aragay and Ramon Simó, quoted in *Harold Pinter – Various Voices*, p. 79.
15. *Ibid.*, p. 73.

10

PETER HALL

Directing the plays of Harold Pinter

A distinguished dramatist once surprised me by lamenting the plight of Harold Pinter. 'All other dramatists', he announced, 'can go off and write any type of play they please – farce or history, polemic or romance. But Harold Pinter has to write a Harold Pinter play. It must be hell for him.'

This was an affectionate joke, but a joke which expressed a truth. Pinter's plays are instantly recognisable and particular. 'Pinteresque' is a word that has entered the language. His voice – whether it be combative cockney, or expressing the unexpected associations and leaps of memory – is very much his own. His content – the unknown threat, the confrontation in the confined space, whether it be territorial, or the personal tensions of the subconscious – has hardly changed in forty-five years. The threats have always been political, metaphors of power. Pinter is the champion of tolerance and compassion in the brutal jungle of life, the seeker after clarity in the confusions of memory.

The presence of imminent violence, of a breakdown bound to happen, haunts all his plays. Speech is at cross-purposes and combative; charm is possessive; concern contains a hidden mockery; even love is often a violation.

But all these threats are subtle – never palpable. Above all, they are ambiguous. Tension may finally explode when a man's head is split open by a blow from a walking-stick. But before this, the demands of social conduct have been observed in their full contradictions. To mock someone, to take them on, only scores points if the hatred is disguised with charm, and the hostility with wit. The victim must never be sure that the antagonist is his enemy.

In his early years, Pinter was often categorised as part of the theatre of the absurd. Nothing could be more misleading. The absurdists (and Ionesco remains their leading exponent) sought to illuminate by incongruous juxta-positions or improbable shocks – which were usually justified by a grain of truth. But Pinter in comparison has always been truth itself. Underneath his confrontations, hidden in the enigmas of the back stories of his plays, there is always a perfectly credible and recognisable pattern of human behaviour. It may be disguised (it usually is), but beneath all the ambiguities is something utterly coherent and lifelike. Yet it is never obvious; audiences delight in unravelling puzzles.

A Pinter play confronts us as dispassionately as the mask of Greek drama. The enigmatic expression is neither sad nor cheerful, because it is both. Once the text is heard against it, it becomes tragic or comic by turns. Play and mask have an apparent calm that hides a turbulent and passionate emotional life which may erupt at any moment. What is hidden is felt by the audience, even though it may never be revealed. It remains one of the particular miracles of live theatre that this instinctive communication is always present. An audience can therefore sense what an actor is feeling, without the actor having to *show* that feeling. But the inner feeling must be specific and true. He must experience it, even though it does not need to be stated or revealed. Paradoxically, the mask does not hide, it exposes. So does the play.

So while directing Pinter is always about preserving ambiguity – in performance, set, costume, action – and only rarely showing emotion, directors and actors must always know very clearly *what* they are hiding. Ambiguity can never mean not knowing.

All dramatists are vulnerable to their directors; but since the text remains for other directors to interpret later, the written word is finally preserved. But Pinter's plays, like Beckett's (because both contain such rich under-texts, and what is said is rarely what is meant), are particularly susceptible to vagueness and generalisation. On the stage this leads easily to pretension, and sometimes to absurdity. If an actor observes a Pinter pause without deciding why it is there and what hidden process is going on inside him, then the result can be a pretentious moment that leads to the wrong kind of laughter.

Similarly, the director must be even-handed with his audience and take care that the enigmas that are at the heart of every Pinter play are clearly presented. The audiences must be able to construct their own view of the past. Once the audience have pieced the story together, they can judge it. They may come to slightly different conclusions as they consider, for instance, what happened in Leeds in *The Collection*. There is often no certainty about memory, and even no absolutes concerning truth. So a director who tells the back story, so that there is no room for interpretation or for ambiguity, may have simplified the play and betrayed his author. He must present all the evidence dispassionately. But above all, he must avoid making a statement.

This is frequently a difficult task. One of my chief memories of directing Pinter is weighing the dramatist's frequent, anxious question: 'Isn't that a bit of a statement that you are making?' The revelations in the plays come slowly and must be handled delicately. This is a world of secrets, where past actions are constantly reconsidered and revalued. Above all, in the plays of the great middle period (*The Homecoming* and *Old Times* through to *Betrayal*) the principal metaphor of life is presented by the enigma of woman. A man can never, it seems, quite understand the mystery of femininity.

The process of work on a Pinter play must therefore preserve the ambiguity, while developing a clear understanding of *what* is to be hidden. I believe that Pinter is essentially a poetic dramatist. He and Beckett have brought metaphor back to the theatre, where Eliot and Auden failed. Although he revels in the vernacular rhythms of the London cockney, he is equally at home with the antithetical understatements of the English upper classes. The precision of his texts, and the form and rhythm of his lines, hold the audience in a formal grip as strong as Shakespeare or Beckett.

Pinter is a great screenwriter:this is his craft. He constructs with precision. But as a dramatist he also works like a poet, because his text is as considered as a poet's. This the director must understand. To direct Pinter requires a rigorous respect for the form and an insistence that the actors understand and respect it. They cannot be sloppy, inaccurate or approximate in the use of his words. Above all, they must listen to his rhythms. There are, of course, finally as many ways of saying a line as there are human beings. But within that infinite freedom, there is only one shape, one rhythm to a Pinter line – and that is Pinter's. The task of the actor is therefore formal and a little like a musician's. Instead of deciding what the character is feeling and then inflecting what he says accordingly, the actor must first consider the line that is to be said and the shape and rhythm of it. The line is a given – rather like the notes of a musical phrase. What must the actor feel in order to make this shape the expression of truth?

Pinter has to write a Pinter play because his form and style are so personal, and the actor has to subdue his idiosyncrasies in order to serve this style. Pinter works as a poet. In fact, having on occasion been very close to him, I have been aware how many of his plays have been genuine inspirations, seizing him completely until they are finished. Yet he is a consummate craftsman and never hands a play to a director that is not considered down to the last comma and pause.

Pinter's pauses have become, journalistically, his trademark, and it is easy to denigrate them, even to think that they are meaningless – to think that the characters have nothing to say because they say nothing. This is never true. Pinter can be read quickly, jumping over the pauses. Actors can do the same. But the unsaid in Pinter is as important as the said; and is frequently as eloquent. He once rang me up and announced a rewrite: 'Page thirty-seven', he said (I found page thirty-seven). 'Cut the pause.' There was a smile in his voice as he spoke, but he was nevertheless dead serious. It was like cutting a speech. The placing of the pauses, and their emotional significance, have always been meticulously considered. His imitators do not understand this. He often uses nearly colloquial speech patterns. But by the use of silence and of pauses, he gives a precise form to the seemingly ordinary, and an emotional power to the mundane. It is a very expressive form of dramatic speech.

There are three very different kinds of pauses in Pinter: Three Dots is a sign of a pressure point, a search for a word, a momentary incoherence. A Pause is a longer interruption to the action, where the lack of speech becomes a form of speech itself. The Pause is a threat, a moment of non-verbal tension. A Silence – the third category – is longer still. It is an extreme crisis point. Often the character emerges from the Silence with his attitude completely changed. As members of the audience, we should *feel* what happens in a Pause; but we can and should be frequently surprised by the change in a character as he emerges from a Silence. The change in him is often unexpected and highly dramatic.

These three signs in the text all indicate moments of turbulence and crisis – the Three Dots, the Pause and the Silence. By their use, the unsaid becomes sometimes more terrifying and more eloquent than the said. Pinter actually *writes* silence, and he appropriates it as a part of his dialogue. The actor who has not decided what is going on in this gap will find that his emotional life is disrupted. The pause is as eloquent as speech and must be truthfully filled with intention if the audience is to understand. Otherwise the actor produces a *non sequitur*, which is absurd and makes the character ridiculous. I have always supposed that Pinter gained confidence in this technique because of Beckett's use of pauses. Certainly Beckett is the first dramatist to use silence as a written form of communication. Shakespeare's: 'Holds her by the hand silent', in *Coriolanus*, is the only other moment of complex drama that I know where words are deemed inadequate.

The Pinter actor must understand that the silences, whether short or long, are moments of intense emotion. And although the characters are hiding what they are feeling, they must feel it nonetheless. The same goes for the reader. He should join the actor in deciding what emotions are being contained.

The basis of much of Pinter is the cockney 'piss-take', much beloved of London taxi drivers. To take the piss out of someone is to mock them, to make them insecure. It is a primary weapon in the jungle of life. But the successful piss-taker must not let those from whom he is taking the piss, *know* that he is taking it. If this happens, he loses face. His mockery should be masked by grace and concern. The hostility is deeply hidden, the malice carefully concealed. Lenny, in *The Homecoming*, consistently makes his father uneasy by staring pleasantly at him. Or by simply ignoring him. He insults him with infinite charm and care. He converses with great concern. This is a master taker-of-piss.

Furthermore, there is underneath Pinter's dialogues a constant seething melodrama, filled with strong hates and forbidden lusts. Beneath the mask of speech, there are high passions, which the actors must know, and yet almost never reveal. To show your feelings in Pinter's world puts you at a fundamental disadvantage. You are weakened once your antagonist knows your motives.

Very occasionally, these feelings come to the surface. They either become too hot to hide, or they are suddenly goaded into revelation. Then the violence – which has been hidden, though evident – suddenly erupts and a catatonic fit seizes the violater.

This underlying violence has to be confronted in rehearsal. It is therefore necessary, as part of the work, to go through each scene exposing the crude emotions as if the actors were playing in a melodrama. They expose their passions completely and are encouraged to show their hatreds and their loves in extreme terms. They find out what the character *wants*. The selfish desire to exist, to be gratified, is the beginning of all acting – just as it is the beginning of existence.

Having found these strong emotions, the next task is to hide them completely – contain them, bottle them up. But now the actors know what they are hiding. Once again, if this process is not followed, the pauses are empty and the dialogue abstract. The words and the pauses govern the passions and hide them. But both the words and the pauses must be *earned*. Unless the audience can follow the hidden emotions through the pause and under the verbal choices, they cannot understand the journey that the character is making. The vacillations will seem unmotivated, even ridiculous. There is a danger then that the audience will laugh *at* the play, rather than with it.

For me, directing Pinter breaks down into a pattern of rehearsals with clear objectives. They are all designed to preserve the ambiguity. This means knowing clearly what is meant and then not overstating it – mostly, indeed, hiding it. It begins with the design.

Since Pinter's world deals with a precision that is masked in understatement, the set must do the same. 'Making a bit of a statement' is once more the danger. The designer may pre-empt the interpretation. A set which is too colourful, which has too much character, or is too naturalistic in detail, will stop the play reverberating. It says too much. On the other hand, Pinter is *not* abstract. A room in North London is a room in North London. But it is a surreal room – realer than real. And that which is not necessary should not be there. In *The Homecoming*, all the action occurs in the arena of the room – a defined, protected place of uneasy security – uneasy, because it is open to invasion at any moment. This room has already been opened up; a wall has been knocked down. There has already been a violation of the space ('*An old*

9 From left to right: Greg Hicks, Nicholas Woodeson, Warren Mitchell, and John Normington in *The Homecoming*, directed by Peter Hall, The Comedy Theatre, 1991

house in North London. A large room, extending the width of the stage. The back wall, which contained the door, has been removed. A square arch shape remains. Beyond it, the hall. In the hall, a staircase, ascending up left, well in view').

We learn later that the room has been opened up, 'to make an open living area'. There are no secrets in this place, everything is 'well in view'. It is a public area where this all-male family fights out its battles between the father and his sons, in full view of each other. There is no door to shut. The metaphor of the set is clear: it is a dangerous, exposed place.

Yet everything that is on stage, from the large, dominating father's chair (the insistent, but now impotent ruler of the family) to the huge, visible staircase which Teddy will use to lead his bride to their bedroom in the middle of the night, is used and useful. Nothing is there for decoration. The precision and discipline of Pinter, where less is consistently more, must be translated into the design. Decoration is misleading. Atmosphere can be too strong.

Pinter wrote *The Homecoming* for the Royal Shakespeare Company at the Aldwych Theatre. He was worried initially by the largeness of the stage. Would it have sufficient claustrophobia, sufficient tension? The 'open living area' came from responding to the strengths of the wide stage. So the Aldwych, in some sense, provoked the image of *The Homecoming*.

I record this to remind any director that Harold Pinter is a man of the theatre, even before he is a great dramatist. He is a director himself, and an actor who understands the processes of acting. What he asks for in his plays is not asked for lightly. So design, lighting, sound and above all the performances must be ambiguous.

For the director, the work with the actors has three distinct stages, though they of course often overlap. The first stage must be a study of the text. The form and the rhythm of Pinter are as particular as the iambic rhythms of Shakespeare. The Silences and the Pauses and the Dots have to be learned precisely and differentiated, and the repetitions of all the antithetical phrases have to be pointed and understood. Pinter, even at his most cockney, is a precise rhetorician. His characters love contradiction and paradox. And so should his actors. All this is a formal, technical work process. *Hearing* the rhythm of the line is essential. So is accuracy. We are not dealing here with understated, naturalistic dialogue that has no resonance.

I have found that the most useful guide to directing a living playwright's work is to listen carefully to how he speaks. Not his dramatic speech, but his speech as he goes about the ordinary business of living. The tone of his voice is inevitably never far away from the dialogue in his plays. Whether it be Pinter's assertive, staccato phrases, that are frequently followed by sudden silences; Stoppard's dry, yet highly illuminating quips, that deflate even as they help you to understand; Shaffer's infinitely antithetical qualifications; David Hare's cryptic and sudden dialectic challenges; or the rueful and very comical repetitions of Samuel Beckett, they all help us *hear* the writer. It is invaluable knowledge for the rehearsal room and one of the undoubted benefits of working with a living writer.

Pinter came into a theatre which was dominated by seemingly 'real' dialogue, but dialogue that was frequently sloppy and imprecise. Many actors in the early years found the discipline of Pinter unbearable. But just as in the classics, they have learned over time to respect his form and his craft. His lines have a shape and an economy, which the actor cannot ignore. If he tries to make Pinter more 'naturalistic' by ignoring his pauses, chopping up his lines and denying his rhythms, he simply ruins the potency of the writing. His form must be assimilated and endorsed. Finally, of course, the actor must and will make the lines his own – just as a great pianist makes the phrase his own. But the phrase is still Pinter's, if the actor has done his work properly.

After the formal text work, I move to rehearsals which concentrate on the psychological processes of the characters, and what they want. The methods of Stanislavsky are cautiously brought into play and the natures of the characters are considered. I stress 'cautiously', because this process cannot result in improvisation, or alteration of the dialogue, or the pauses, or the shape of the text. If the actor feels uncomfortable with the text once he has found his motives, then the motives are wrong, not the text. A conductor would be surprised if one of his first violins rose from his desk and said 'I can't play this A flat: I don't feel it.' But many actors believe themselves justified in questioning a line, if they feel that their character wouldn't say it. Occasionally, of course, this can be a valid objection. But the danger is that however true the actor's instinct may be, what he wants to represent may be less original than what the author envisaged. So, the actor has to accept that when he is dealing with a major dramatist, it is usually the character that the actor has created that is wrong, not the line. If Harold Pinter is asked what something means in rehearsal, his usual response is to ask another question: 'What does it say?'

The next process of work is to release the melodrama that lies underneath the text. It is not fanciful to see the suppression of emotion as one of the great strengths of English literature. From Jane Austen to Oscar Wilde and then on to Noel Coward and Harold Pinter, many varieties of the stiff upper lip are evident. When characters in Oscar Wilde feel unbearable emotional conflict, they break into epigrams in order to preserve their equilibrium. When Noel Coward's characters care too much, they rise above it with a quip. Pinter's characters have a new kind of stiff upper lip. Their animosities are concealed by charm and restraint – an understatement that often verges on the malicious. These hot passions have to be understood and then resolutely masked.

The melodrama rehearsals are very hard to sustain, because the emotions unleashed by the actors are frequently so extreme that they verge on obsession, if not hysteria. Yet the actor must explore them, and chart them as the journey of his character. Then he must hide them, suppress them, contain them. His emotions have to be felt with great intensity at every performance. The audience will know what is hidden. Most actors yearn to let some of this emotion out, to reassure the audience by telling them what they are feeling. It is an anxiety to communicate, but it is not only unnecessary, it is dangerous. It can easily look like special pleading – asking the audience to understand. If the actor feels the emotion and hides it, the audience will apprehend it.

So once the passions have been unleashed, they have to be controlled. And in the next stage of rehearsals, it becomes a fault, a demonstration of failure, if one actor can recognise the naked emotional needs of the other. The form is now used as the means of containing the emotion.

The staging – the physical life of a Pinter production – also needs the same restraint as the acting and design. Excess must always be avoided. Too much movement blurs the text and reveals emotional weaknesses in the characters. Stillness leads to concentration and accentuates the potency of the dialogue. The glass of water in *The Homecoming* becomes a symbol of the sexual contest between Ruth and Lenny. Who will actually touch it? Who will actually drink it? Uncle Sam takes an apple (the only life-enhancing thing in that arid room), and it becomes a symbol of violation, an assertion of ordinariness. (I found, incidentally, that the apple had to be green. Redness made a statement.) There is something elemental and quite precise about the staging of any Pinter play. The moves seem to be written into the text, if the motives of the characters are clearly understood. The sudden outbursts of violence and the sudden movements only have their full effect if they are set in stillness – just as the silences are defined by words.

Done flexibly and with humanity, all these disciplines can make a life on stage which is completely convincing. It can, of course, also add up to something mannered, self-consciously restrained and inhuman. Then the production has failed. But my experience is that if the form is respected, there is a moment of release when the actors dance to their own tunes, although they are still dancing to Pinter's. The play becomes theirs. It is like learning a complicated dance, or a difficult duel. When the technical form is completely mastered, then the performer makes it his own and lives it. But that interpretation, although it should be free, has by the very disciplines imposed on it, the capacity to vary from Pinter's requirements by only an infinitesimal amount. But this variance born of the individual response of the actor is finally what makes the play live. The play is still Pinter's, but it transcends Pinter.

T. S. Eliot wrote in 'Poetry and Drama': 'A verse play is not a play done into verse, but a different kind of play … The poet with ambitions of the theatre must discover the laws, both of another kind of verse and of another kind of drama.' I would go further. I believe that no play is worth our attention unless we can describe it in the widest terms as a poetic play. Only the poetic play makes metaphors rich enough to persuade the audience to play the essential dramatic game of make-believe, and have its imaginations fired by the actor. I do not mean a play that uses poetry in the literary sense, but a play that achieves metaphorical strength by using all the vocabulary of the theatre. Word, action, visual image, subtext, all combine to make something *dramatically* poetic. In our age of the screen, provoking the imagination is the unique strength of theatre – the imaginings that are encouraged by a live performance. Poetic theatre can deal with the widest subjects, the most improbable transitions. We can imagine that we are anywhere. We can imagine the heights and depths of feeling. Though verse is not a prerequisite of this metaphorical potency, form is – because it represents the means to encourage a metaphorical interpretation of the play's language or action. Or both. Pinter is pre-eminently the playwright of form, and his director must honour that.

The great plays have always been and always will be poetic plays. Pinter's stage is a metaphor. His form is complex and intensely studied. And it is his form which makes his dialogue crackle with theatricality. He can be a very lyrical writer, particularly when he deals with memory. He can be a very funny writer – his sense of the ridiculous is part of his very being. But above all, his form allows him to explore the instinctive hostilities between human beings. They fight duels not with swords, but with words and silences. He has restated that the theatre's strength is metaphor, and by doing so, has been able to demonstrate that its primal potency is always invested in language. His director must celebrate the ambiguity by charting and then hiding the strong emotions. He must trust the audience to understand, even when they are dealing with contradictions. And above all, he must make his actors as precise as the singers of Mozart. Yet that precision must paradoxically also be a means of expressing their own particularity. 'The opposite is also true', said Marx. (Groucho, not Karl.) And this is true of directing Pinter. It is not easy; but it is not easy to direct any great dramatist who deals with the contradictions of living.

11

CHARLES EVANS

Pinter in Russia

In the market revolution sweeping through Russia, theatre has played its own part. Musicals, foreign adaptations and zippy updated classics have long since replaced the stodgy orthodoxy of Soviet times. There is also a strong interest in the work of Harold Pinter. At first sight, the reasons seem clear: first, the advent of *Glasnost* in the mid-1980s liberated an interest in work which, though sometimes privately circulated, could not generally be seen onstage during the Soviet years; secondly, the pro-Western impulse, following major social and political reform, concentrated this interest on English-speaking writers; thirdly, in a time of rapid and bewildering change, Russians found in Pinter's work in particular a strong echo of their own situation. Yet, on closer analysis, these reasons raise further questions. Were Pinter's plays never to be seen in Russia before 1985? Was the 'pro-Western impulse' in itself sufficient to account for an interest in the work of Harold Pinter? What precisely in their own situation do Russians find echoed in Harold Pinter's plays? In addressing these questions, this chapter falls into two parts. First, I shall give a critical account of a number of notable Pinter productions which ran in Moscow between 1972 and 1994, focusing on one famous early production. Concurrently, I shall try to set each production in the context of the tumultuous social and political events of the period. Second, I examine the line of development which links these productions; that is, how they interrelate a particular understanding of Pinter's work with changing attitudes to the unfolding events of recent Russian history.

From 1991 I began to spend extended periods in Moscow, researching Russian theatre. Increasingly, I was distracted from Russian drama and drawn towards the often more influential Russian-language productions of English and American plays. Perhaps paradoxically, they seemed to give more insight into current moods and preoccupations than the home-grown drama of the period. In particular, there seemed to be a sudden focus of interest in the work of Harold Pinter,[1] and, as an English theatre specialist, I found myself a *de facto* consultant and reference point for students and critics alike. Intrigued by this (as it then seemed to me) unlikely fascination, I began to seek out all the Russian productions of Pinter plays that I could find. At the same time, using the good offices of an extensive network of friends and colleagues in the Russian theatre, I undertook the task of tracing the development of Pinter plays in Russia, from productions of Soviet years right up to post-*Glasnost* Pinter. It would of course be impossible to identify all the productions that were mounted in this period. Many were amateur, some performed in secret, others based on hand-copied translations, nearly all containing mistakes or incomplete. But my researches pointed increasingly to six main Pinter projects, not all successful in production and some eccentric in interpretation, but which were in a sense landmarks and, taken together, comprise a distinct line of development in the Pinter canon.

The first, and arguably most successful, of these was the famous early production of *The Caretaker*, a semi-clandestine underground (*podpole*) production in a similar sense to the underground dissemination of dissident novels or poetry ('*Samizdat*'). This production, in various venues and with a changing cast, ran intermittently between 1972 and 1987. I spoke with many Muscovites who recalled it, most – but not all – connected with the professional theatre. Of all the Pinter productions that I could trace, this one seems to have made the most lasting impression on those who saw it. In 1989, just two years after *The Caretaker* had finally ceased to appear, there was a celebrated production of *The Dumb Waiter*. Again, two years later, in 1991, the Creative Studio of the Theatre Workers' Union staged a 'Pinter Evening'. In the following year, 1992, the young Moscow director Andrei Rossinsky staged *Betrayal* at the Laboratory Theatre. In 1993 a new group, known as The Erotic Theatre of Moscow and directed by Irina Gavrilina, staged a production of *Landscape*. Completing this set of six Pinter productions, and bringing us full circle, was Gregori Zalkind's production of *The Caretaker*, staged at the (then) Krasnaya Presnya Theatre.[2] This production, which I saw in November 1994 (though it premièred earlier than this), was perhaps, in a sense I hope to make clear, the most Russian of the six productions considered.

Let us now look at each of these six productions in more detail, beginning with the underground production of *The Caretaker* of 1972–87. It seems to me that this remains the most important production of a Pinter play to be staged in Russia. This is not only because it proved the most durable and lasting, and hence became the most widely known; nor even because it effectively set the standard for those which followed. It is also because it was the most honest, the most questing, production – one which did not set out with an easy answer to the problems of identity and power contained in the play, but which adapted, changed and evolved in a constantly renewed search for answers. The production has an interesting provenance. In 1970 the noted Russian tragi-comic actor Alexei Zaitsev played in a small experimental production of *The Caretaker* in which the two brothers, Aston and Mick, were played by the same actor. Intrigued by the play, Zaitsev drew the attention of another actor, Yuri Afsharov, to it, suggesting that he and Afsharov should collaborate on a full production of the play. The production was realised, and, for the following fifteen years, several times per week and in widely varying venues, it followed an extraordinary and precarious existence. It played in libraries, basements, studio theatres and university rooms, sometimes to large audiences, sometimes to a mere handful of spectators, usually acclaimed, often misunderstood, invariably enjoyed. On occasion it was taken out of Moscow, and one friend recalls a performance as far afield as Odessa in about 1975. At least until the 1980s, performances were rarely advertised and news of performances was spread by word of mouth only. During the whole fifteen years of the run, the roles of Aston (played by Afsharov) and Davies (played by Zaitsev) remained constant, but four different actors appeared in the role of Mick (one of these being Yuri Pogrebnichko, of whom more later).

In what context, social and political, was the production playing? We should remember that, at least up to 1985 and the accession of (then) General Secretary Gorbachev, the Soviet system, although already reflecting the stresses and strains of corruption, overstretch and economic decline, was still largely intact. The bureaucracy of Communism, with its control over all aspects of Russian life, including the arts, continued in place, even after the faith – and even the sympathy – of the people had been forfeited. Under these circumstances, how did the production survive the Soviet years? At first sight, it seems astonishing that it did so. Russians have always seen *The Caretaker* in a special way, one which, initially at any rate, radically challenged the idea of 'New Soviet Man'. This concept, an integral element of Communist ideology (and propaganda) from the earliest years of the Revolution, is a seductive one and has exercised a powerful influence on the Russian people. 'New Soviet Man' is, essentially, Man reborn, in a sense similar to the evangelical Christian idea of 'born again', as honest, unselfish and hard-working, placing the interests of the New Communist Society above his own. Furthermore, it is the proletarian working class which, historically, is the agent through which this radical transformation of society is made possible. Thus, a play depicting a member of the vanguard working class as deceitful, selfish and lazy, particularly when he is also attractive and amusing, was excitingly seditious. In this sense (and in the same way as Bulgakov's good-for-nothing Sharikov in *Heart of a Dog* thirty-five years earlier), Davies, the central character of *The Caretaker*, could be seen as personifying a radical rejection of a cardinal tenet of Communist belief. It is not surprising, therefore, as the Moscow dramatist, and Pinter translator, Viktor Denisov[3] has said, that the authorities 'made difficulties' for the production. But, by Soviet standards of censorship, they could hardly be counted as serious. Certainly none of those who discussed the production with me could recall any systematic attempt, official or unofficial, to suppress it. So why did it go unscathed, and for so long? First, in an unlikely collection entitled *Seven English Plays*, *The Caretaker* had already been published in the 1960s, and so was theoretically available in print even if difficult to find. Second, it is clear that, during the years 1972–87, both ideologically and in practice, Communism was progressively loosening its hold on the lives of the Russian people, so that, once the play had begun its run, it became steadily easier for it to continue. Thirdly, even if that grip had not loosened, the production was seen by comparatively few. Its appearances were intermittent; its audiences were (mostly) small; it visited few cities outside Moscow. Furthermore, when it did appear, its appeal was to the intelligentsia, a fringe element, and not to the public at large. Thus, it seems probable that the authorities simply did not bother to censor – a censorship which might in any case have attracted more attention than simple connivance. But I believe there is a fourth reason why the production survived, which has more to do with the way in which the play was interpreted. It is of course difficult so many years later and in such changed times to evoke the particular feel and mood of that (or any) production. But, having talked to those who saw or acted in it, I believe that a characteristic of the production was the careful avoidance of specificity of time or place. Yuri Afsharov, now a tutor at the Shchukin Theatre School in Moscow and still a practising actor, played Aston throughout the production's long life. He maintains a strong interest in English theatre, relishing recent roles in Osborne and Wilde at Moscow's Satiri Theatre. He talked to me at length about that original production of *The Caretaker* in Moscow, which he remembers well. He recalled the way that Mick was played, 'slow, methodical and yet fussy, like a detective'; and he has a particular memory of Aston's long monologue at the end of Act Two, the 'detached' way in which this speech had to be delivered and how much he enjoyed playing it.[4] But, above all, Yuri Afsharov recalls that the events of the play, as presented in that production, could have been happening anywhere in the world and at any time. Yuri has strong views about universality, how the great plays – and the roles within them – achieve greatness by transcending particular times, places and periods (he was critical of the Royal Shakespeare Company's *Coriolanus* which, for him, dulled the point of the play through its specific French Revolutionary setting). Yuri emphasised the indeterminacy of their treatment of *The Caretaker*, how the production presented a Davies, a setting and a situation which could have existed in any society and in any country. It is clear that this approach to the play blunted its edge as a perceived attack on the Soviet system and thus (perhaps inadvertently) ensured its survival.

If this production was, as I have maintained, the most important production to come out of Russia, in what way did it begin a line of development through the six productions under scrutiny? Certainly, it set the standard, introducing a writer still unknown to most Russians and at a time when it was not altogether safe to do so. But, just as importantly, in a country and a theatre tradition in which the director often dominates the playwright and a Dodin, Lyubimov or Viktyuk can leave an indelible, perhaps even distorting, signature on a production, the early Russian *The Caretaker* was refreshingly open-minded. Indeed, it seems to have developed an organic life of its own. Yuri himself talks of the way in which the play changed in subtle ways during its run, the alterations in its internal balance as new Micks came and went, the impact of different venues and audiences. It all sounds very un-Russian – more like actors' theatre than the more characteristic directorial hegemony of the Russian stage. Above all, what characterised this first major production of Pinter in Russia was that it was non-committal, leaving open the meaning of the play, declining to use it as comment or propaganda. To put the point another way, the production was essentially exploratory.

The next noteworthy production of Pinter in Moscow came in 1989, again initiated by the actor Alexei Zaitsev. Zaitsev recruited the services of the director Mikhail Makeev, and together they undertook a production of *The Dumb Waiter*.[5] The year was critical to the production, the year in which the dramatic news images of the dismantling of the Berlin Wall provided a focus and symbol for the collapse of Communism worldwide. In Moscow, the forces of *Glasnost* and *Perestroika* released by President Gorbachev were in full flower. In places like the Arbat, in response to the new spirit of openness, a great wave of irreverent artists, satirical balladeers and guitarists, political poets and street-corner debaters delighted and shocked Muscovites and tourists alike. At the same time, radical economic reform transformed the marketplace and goods never before seen in Moscow (at least publicly) began to flow into the shops and stores. The only shadow over this new scene was the prediction by 'the pessimists' (as they were then invariably characterised, usually with amusement) that the situation could not last, that Russians were living in a fool's paradise, that there would be hard times to come. News from Beijing that the fledgling Democracy Movement had been brutally crushed in Tiananmen Square seemed to confirm the pessimists' fears of a backlash. Despite this, the mood overall was one of optimism and promise, tempered only slightly by nagging premonitions of trouble ahead. A curious public consciousness emerged from all this, one of conspicuous jollity shot through with a spirit of black comedy. In concerts, on television and in the pages of the arts magazines, this new spirit was generally reflected in the light-hearted work of satirists such as Zhvanetsky and Khazanov. But in the serious theatre *The Dumb Waiter*, with its blend of the unfamiliar, the comic and the threatening, caught the mood more precisely. As interest developed in the production, it became increasingly innovative and experimental, at least by Moscow standards. At one stage, as debate about the meaning of the piece intensified, Zaitsev and Makeev decided on a kind of Pinter–Shakespeare composite. Scenes from Shakespeare's *Richard III* were cut into *The Dumb Waiter* in an effort to illuminate it. A Moscow friend who saw the production recalled that 'the killing scene' from *The Dumb Waiter* was one which for him acquired particular resonance. During this time it was of course nearly impossible to buy the text of the play. Indeed, it has never been easy to find texts of Pinter's plays in Russia, whether in translation or the original. By 1998 English text editions were beginning to appear in the specialist English-language bookshops. But the only Russian versions of Pinter texts I have been able to find during exhaustive searches in Moscow are a collection of five published by Raduga in 1988 (with an illuminating introduction by Mikhail Shvydkoi)[6] and *The Dumb Waiter* (in a version by Viktor Denisov) published by Samara in 1991,[7] both gifted by Moscow friends. It was certainly not possible to find such texts on general sale in 1989. The general result is that most Russians who know Pinter know him, not from studying the text, but from seeing performances. After the performance, with no text to refer to and only a memory of what they saw and experienced, they retain more the sense of mystery and unease than quotations and references. So, as with the first Pinter production, *The Dumb Waiter* remained open to a variety of interpretations. Perhaps the main feature of this second Pinter venture was the attempt to suggest an interpretation by relating it to another play already known to Moscow audiences.

Two years later, in 1991, came the third major Pinter production. But the climate of opinion in which the play was produced had changed considerably. By now, the pain of economic reform was part of everyday life: as controls lifted, prices were rocketing, there was a booming black market and foreign currencies were taking over from the devalued rouble. Optimistic early faith in the reforms was beginning to falter. It was the year of the failed coup, when, for the first time, there was a major challenge to democratic reform. On 19 August of that year Boris Yeltsin took his famous stand outside the White House and an estimated 50,000 Muscovites prepared to defend it against anticipated attack by the army and gathering forces of opposition from the Right. The mood of the time was well portrayed in Richard Nelson and Alexander Gelman's collaborative play *Misha's Party* – though the play worked better in its English version than when translated to Moscow. Perhaps there was a sense in which the play was too sure of itself, for the time was above all one of political tension and uncertainty. In the theatre, it was as if, tiring of the endless debates over their social and political future, Muscovites consciously turned their backs on practical problems and retreated into the world of the spirit. In this year the Creative Studio of the Theatre Workers' Union set up a number of theatre workshops, each headed by a director, one of whom was the celebrated Vladimir Klimenko. I had the opportunity of seeing what I was told was the 'Pinter Evening'. There was no public announcement, or any kind of advertising of this event, and I came to know of it only through the word of a young Muscovite then acting as my theatre guide, the drama critic Ekaterina Novikova. She telephoned one evening with an invitation to attend a 'private' theatre event. We went together to an anonymous-looking Moscow block where we were ushered into a small bare hall. The set consisted of a few chairs and an old-fashioned tripod camera. A tape played soft background noise of rain and storm. The audience consisted of ten to twenty people seated on a row of chairs to one side. Despite the inauspicious setting there was an extraordinary atmosphere of excitement and a sense of real occasion, almost that of a conspiracy. Before the curtain there was the unmistakable buzz of anticipation, at the interval excited discussion broke out and after the performance discussion turned into argument and controversy. Significantly, though it was already 1991, the whole evening had a forbidden and semi-clandestine air about it. In fact, and despite the excitement and my own expectations, the event was a major disappointment. I had been told that the evening would comprise a linked series of scenes from early Pinter work, subsequently commented upon by a 'guest director'. But this was not how the scenes appeared to me. I could see no plan or pattern in the passages that were selected. The cast wandered about the set speaking dialogue fast and softly, at times almost privately. They engaged for long periods in what seemed to be acting exercises – dancing, striking poses, engaging in rituals (like washing one actor's feet and legs). There was no attempt to place the dialogue in any kind of setting or context, no connection between characters so that lines could be used to communicate or attack or evade, no build-up of any tension or situation. Instead, we had long silences, stylised movement and slow-motion dancing. The feeling grew on me that we were watching the display of a collection of tricks and gimmicks – perhaps not out of place as loosening-up exercises for first-year drama students, but in no sense meriting the title 'Pinter Evening'. My notes from the time conclude with the words 'pretentious and silly'. Afterwards, I made a half-hearted attempt to engage an intense young Russian director in discussion about the evening, suggesting alternative approaches to a Pinter text. I recall indicating that the doom-laden style, as well as the obscurantism, were classic Pinter production pitfalls, even suggesting that humour had some valid place in this work. But it was clear that I made no impression at all on the director or his associates. I had an eerie sense of advocating caution to someone who was uncritically in love. What particularly struck me at the time, from productions such as this and the awe-struck response of friends and critics of normally sound judgment, was the curious and uncritical mystique building up around the name of Harold Pinter. We had moved, at this point in the development of Pinter's work in Russia, into a deeply – and, I would say, misleadingly – reverential stage.

The next production of the series came in 1992 and, significantly, was of a rather later Pinter work, *Betrayal*, by the Laboratory Theatre of Andrei Rossinsky.[8] A year after the failed coup, the atmosphere in Moscow had now undergone a transformation. There was a new spirit in Moscow. Many called it a new spirit of enterprise – though for others 'exploitation' was the more appropriate word. Certainly there was a whole new class of young, eager and often ruthless entrepreneurs committed to the business of making money fast and without too much concern for the methods. Everyone seemed to call himself a 'businessman', but this was a catch-all term that could mean anything from street-corner purveyor of junk jewellery to international import–export dealer. A new business elite was beginning to emerge, often of great wealth and power. At the same time, as more and more prices were freed from control and the big price rises of April 1992 had their effect, the less well paid began to experience genuine economic hardship. Opinion was polarising fast, as Russians realised, perhaps for the first time, that the transition period would be long, fraught and perhaps even dangerous. Some politicians, such as Zhirinovsky, were already speaking of the West's 'robbing Russia', and the contemptuous description of aid requests as 'the Russian begging-bowl' seemed to catch the widespread sense of national humiliation. In this climate, it was not surprising that interest shifted to a different kind of Pinter play, set in a different world from *The Caretaker* and *The Dumb Waiter*. Theatre friends, noticeably less enthusiastic than in the days of *The Caretaker* and *The Dumb Waiter*, took me to see what was for them the new Pinter. The world of *Betrayal* had arrived, perhaps in a double sense. Ironically, we went to see the new production at one of the ubiquitous Houses of Culture, in this case a warren of rooms and corridors in a grandiose building once attached, Soviet-style, to the Moskvitch car plant. But I had seen interesting work there, including a bold and lively account of Voynovich's *Ivan Chonkin*. The theatre studio is cosy (seats for perhaps 150), well raked and has a good house feeling. The director was then Andrei Rossinsky, and it would be difficult to find a keener or more committed exponent of Pinter's work in

Russia. Rossinsky first came across Pinter at the end of the 1960s, when he was lucky enough to find a copy of the text of *The Caretaker*. Rossinsky regards Pinter as 'one of the greatest drama writers of this century' – though his knowledge of Pinter's work is of course restricted to what is known in Russia, which does not include much published after 1980. He speaks fondly of *The Caretaker*, which he thinks holds something special for many Russians and has become for them something like 'a Pinter visiting card'. But his conversation returns constantly to *Betrayal*, to his own production of it and his plans for future Pinter ventures. The production itself was ambitious, and undeniably rough at the edges. Certainly the facilities at the Theatre Laboratory were restricted, as was stage space, and this was even more apparent in the videotape of the production, which Rossinsky had me bring back to London to present to the author.

Yet certain features distinguished this production of *Betrayal* from others I had seen. In the first place, Rossinsky had well-developed views about the role and state of language both in Pinter's work and at this critical point in his country's development. It is certainly clear that, in the 1990s, many Russians were in the process of rediscovering the beauty and richness of their language after the Orwell-like distortions, jargon and neologisms visited upon it by the ideology of Marxism-Leninism. But of course such a revival cannot take place overnight, and in the streets, markets, buses and apartments, Moscow was a place in which two parallel languages could be heard, both of them Russian. Rossinsky was particularly sensitive to this and referred constantly to Russia's 'problem of two languages'. It is clear that his admiration for Pinter is closely related to this problem. He explains that, in declaring Pinter to be 'one of the greatest dramatists of this century', he means not only that Pinter is 'a great explorer of situations', but also that he employs a particular 'bright language'. Asked to define this language, he responds that it is 'the language of civilisation', 'the language of high quality' and 'the language that was lost to Russians during the Revolution'. It is not difficult, he maintains, to appreciate this language when involved in a production of a Pinter play, when studying it on the page, or when – as an actor – using and projecting it. The difficulty lies in showing this richness and complexity to spectators who use a language which has been impoverished by the dogmas of Marxism-Leninism, are increasingly exposed to pop music and soap operas with a Western context (along with much anglicised Russian) and have no incentive to rediscover the Russian of pre-Revolutionary times. As a result, today's theatregoers are only able to 'look for events' and cannot see 'the turning of the language itself'. On this view of Pinter's art, it is clear why Rossinsky sees the focus of a play like *The Caretaker*, with its brutal power struggle, as being on situation, while the focus of *Betrayal*, with its silky and coded game of sexual ownership, is on language. This explains the production's careful, sometimes even unnatural-sounding, emphasis on the words spoken, which made the production oddly emphatic and demonstrative, arguably impeding the pace as the plot unfolds (or refolds).

But there was a second feature of Rossinsky's production that was striking. This had to do with Rossinsky's view about the kind of society which *Betrayal* presents and its relationship with developing events in Russia. For he asserts that those close to art in Russia 'have some premonition that Russians will need Pinter in the near future'; and the reason is that the characters in a play such as *Betrayal* have reached a level of civilisation which makes them 'forget their animal origin' and that Russians 'will come to this problem only tomorrow'. In support of this, Rossinsky argues that it is not by chance that the two men in the play are a publisher and a literary agent. It is inconceivable, on his view, that they should be (say) two bus-drivers, and the interchange can only take place on a 'higher level of civilisation'. This view of Pinter, it seems to me, carries the danger (among others) of making the writer appear heavy and didactic; and Rossinsky does indeed seem reluctant to address the question of humour in Pinter. In conversation with me he was happy to remark that he had seen only two or three spectators laugh during his *Betrayal*, but most 'had tears in their eyes'. Rossinsky certainly does not accept the often expressed view that, in charting the tragedy and comedy of small events, Pinter bears some affinity with Chekhov. He sees Pinter as something at once deeper and more mysterious. He does not simply concede, but sees as imperative, that the average Russian playgoer should find Pinter complicated, watch his plays 'with great stress' and often not even understand what is happening.[9] He does not believe that the receding order of events in *Betrayal* creates any difficulty: various dramatists had used the technique during Soviet times (Vampilov, for example) and Russians have no difficulty with the form. Rather, it is the language which creates the difficulty, and which holds the key. In this sense, what marks out Rossinsky's *Betrayal* is that it is essentially a linguistic production.

In 1993 came the fifth, and perhaps least auspicious, Pinter venture in Moscow. Following Rossinsky's *Betrayal*, with its rather self-consciously delivered text, interest shifted to what actually lay beneath these lines. Was it possible that the exchanges, even the most banal-sounding, held a secret? As Denisov sees it, 'We have to attend to every word, pause, nuance, maybe even just a semi-tone.'[10] But a resolve to clarify whatever meaning lies buried in the text can become an urgent desire to exteriorise it, often with destructive results. So it was with the 1993 production of *Landscape* undertaken by The Erotic Theatre of Moscow under the direction of Irina Gavrilina. By this time, the appearance of a group so named, unthinkable in Soviet times, caused no surprise in Moscow. Alongside the glitter of shops packed with Western goods and the razzmatazz of new-style promotions and services came the sleazier face of unrestrained capitalism: the rise of pornography, prostitution, drugs and violence. But changes were taking place on a broader front. It was the year of Russia's first democratic elections, the new Constitution was published – and, significantly, in October came the second coup, when armed opposition to the reforms arose within the White House itself, and was duly shelled into submission. The theatre reflected the new mood of anarchy and permissiveness. There was an upsurge of violent and negative pieces, often incorporating nudity and obscenity for their own sake, recalling the period in London theatre immediately following the abolition of the Lord Chamberlain's censorship function. Gavrilina's production of *Landscape* followed the trend. By most accounts, it was little more than an exteriorisation – and, so many said, cynical marketing – of the sexual undercurrent running through the piece, rather like Roman Viktyuk's treatment of *The Maids* or *Lolita*. No one could deny, of course, that both Beth and Duff generate powerful erotic images in the play; but to turn these images into actual naked bodies, to translate the shifting interdependent images of recollection and invention into hard stage pictures, is counterproductive – unless the objective is simply to fill the theatre. Writing as drama critic of Moscow's *Nezavisimaya Gazeta* (Independent Newspaper), Denisov said exactly that. He also remarked dryly to me that audiences at the production consisted largely of 'old men with binoculars'. In its neglect of the dream-like indeterminacy of Beth and Duff's exchanges, and its countervailing determination to make graphic and explicit every sexual reference in the text, this production can only be called exploitative.

We come to the sixth Pinter production, the last of the series. This was a production of *The Caretaker* staged in the main house of the (then) Krasnaya Presnya Theatre. Initially directed by Gregori Zalkind, it was, following his death, taken over by Yuri Pogrebnichko. It is tempting to speculate with what excitement Pogrebnichko, in changed times, came to a work which he had first met in the 1980s, and again took on the role of Mick. I was first able to see the production in November 1994. It was a fascinating, sometimes shocking, time to be in Moscow, as that once prim city increasingly assumed its tawdry capitalist trappings; and it was marked above all by a general crisis of confidence among the Russian people. In economic terms it was the year of the great rouble crash when many, even modestly placed, Russian savers and investors experienced at first hand the downside of a capitalist economy. Socially and politically, there was a major preoccupation with the soaring crime rate, not just the growing incidence of low-level street crime, but the increasing power and influence of organised criminal activity on a massive scale. At the same time, there were ominous signs that the country was sliding towards war in Chechnya, and already speculation about the possibility (or not) of parliamentary elections in the following year. In this uncertain climate, it was perhaps not surprising to see *The Caretaker* make a reappearance, albeit in a rather different style to the earliest Moscow version. The twin hands of Zalkind and Pogrebnichko had fashioned a production which combined a modern, and indeed strikingly Western, reading with certain persistent Russian (or Soviet) features.

Let us begin with the Western aspects. Here was certainly an open-ended production, neither serving an ideological cause nor seeming to debunk one. Davies was his own man, enigmatic maybe, idiosyncratic certainly, but always an individual, never coming over as a mere symbol designed to negate the idea of New Soviet Man. He was a Davies, too, who conveyed with his shifting eyes and vague, fluttery gestures the sense of an unnamed danger offstage, one never quite identified. Finally, the production increasingly had an ease about it, almost that of a comedy, as the audience, quiet at first, settled to the comic possibilities of a down-and-out offered gratuitous help and hospitality. In these respects, the production followed well-established principles of Pinter interpretation: a not-quite-defined atmosphere, lingering sense of menace, overlap of real and imagined (with no clear borderline) and a recurring light-comic counterpoint. Yet, to the Western observer, there were persistent Russian variations, perhaps even aberrations. The first surprise was the size of the set. The whole of the massive stage area at floor level, occupying the full width of the building, was in use; and the clutter (stove, ex-Army communication set, beds, coat-rack, blankets, bucket, boxes etc.) was spread to every corner. The resulting impression was curious: more an unused hall or warehouse, with its suggestion of black-market dealings, than an evocation of bedsit land. The second surprise came from Davies. He was in some ways the usual archetypal social casualty: he was often confused, he wandered and stuttered, he was afraid of something unnamed. Yet in other ways he was a curiously impressive, even powerful figure. He was, first, the cleanest Davies I have ever seen, his clothes neat and free of stains, perhaps suggestive of second-hand welfare handouts but certainly not sleeping rough. There was no question, either, of a loss or disintegration of personality: he was able to produce, Soviet-style, a neat-looking packet of personal documents, perhaps explaining why the Sidcup references went by in a puzzled-seeming audience silence. Then there were the simple living skills, conventionally the first to deteriorate in a broken-down personality, but which, in this case, seemed to have suffered little impairment. Thus, this Davies used a coathanger dextrously, undressed with ease, tied bootlaces without undue effort. Finally, his neatness, his carefully kept personal documents, his social know-how, all combined to suggest someone well able to cope with life at this level, ready to do whatever was necessary in the present moment, whether agreeing, disagreeing, playing the clown, acting friendly or being aggressive, to help him survive in the world. He was in all these senses streetwise. This was a Davies, one felt, who had dropped out deliberately, not fallen out accidentally. From this came the third surprise of the evening. For this Davies, as in no other production I have seen, emerged as a dominant member of the trio. His lines seemed to grow out of a peasant cunning, neutralising Mick's veiled threats. He was capable of unnerving Aston, using fast talk or physical proximity to confuse him. Even at the close, facing eviction, this Davies had more words, more fight, more tricks, to call on. Would Mick or Aston ever be able to shake him off? This was, in summary, one of the most original renderings of a Pinter text that I have seen in Russia. It very nearly turned prey into predator.

I now turn to the second part of the chapter. What line of development can be traced through these six landmark productions, and in what way do they reflect changing attitudes to Pinter's work and to unfolding events in Russia? Let us return to the first production, to the famous *podpole* version of *The Caretaker* by Zaitsev. I have already indicated that the production was above all one which left the meaning of the play open, that there was no Russian-style directorial imposition, that the production essentially developed an organic life of its own. It was in this sense an exploratory production. That was exactly what one might expect, and it provided a baseline (as well as a standard) for what followed. Denisov reports its director, Zaitsev, as declaring that he loved the play – but doubted if he understood it. There was no reason why he should. After years of Stalin's 'Socialist Realism', what could he make of a play which embraced no cause, urged no moral and gave centre stage to a sly, inarticulate, opportunist drop-out? So Zaitsev and Afsharov simply let the play have its head. But audiences knew what to make of the play. As Communism crumbled, Russians were more than ready to see that ideas like 'New Soviet Man' were ideological fictions; that human nature was more complex and fascinating than the idealised Communist Party member; that a confused tramp was just as worthy of our attention as a hero of the Soviet Union. Zaitsev sensed that there was something in *The Caretaker*, though he was unsure what it was. Muscovites found that something. In a critical period of reflection and rethinking, Russians used the play to rid themselves of the ideological baggage of 'New Soviet Man'.

The Dumb Waiter was, in all senses, a different story. The year 1989 was a strange one in Russia, combining the celebration of *Glasnost* and *Perestroika* with the disturbing half-knowledge of events in Tiananmen Square. Against this background, the new production of *The Dumb Waiter* moved on from

Zaitsev's *The Caretaker* in two important ways. First, the play was well chosen to catch the new public mood in Russia, which was one of enormous excitement and optimism tempered with nagging doubts that the reforms were simply too good to be true. In conversation, friends classified themselves as either optimists or pessimists: there seemed to be no other option. *The Dumb Waiter*, with the appealing simplicity of one winner and one loser, both subject to an unseen and inscrutable authority, seemed to echo the situation exactly. So this production of a Pinter play much more nearly matched a situation familiar to Russians than *The Caretaker* had ever done. Yet, secondly, this very familiarity threatened to impoverish what a Pinter production had to offer. For, where the meaning of Zaitsev's production of *The Caretaker* had been left in decent obscurity, allowing audiences to draw their own conclusions, the changed climate did not allow *The Dumb Waiter* to go uninterpreted. As the production gave rise to open debate and argument, the famous Shakespearian inserts were made into the production, in the belief that this would somehow make the text clearer. It was an indication how, at this point, the new generation of Russians was not only polarising politically, but also beginning to adopt in the theatre a dangerously literal approach to a Pinter text, demanding precise explanations and decoding.

Between 1989 and 1991 the line of development of Pinter productions changed sharply. If *The Caretaker* had served to debunk a lingering ideological relic, and *The Dumb Waiter* had effectively symbolised what followed, each in its own way making a contribution to the social and political debate, then 1991 marked a new approach to Pinter. It was a time when Russians, weary of political turmoil and upheaval, looked to their theatre for the world of the spirit. For Pinter in Russia, this could only mean what one might call the 'arty' stage. Thus, the era of the 'Pinter Evening' had arrived. When the Theatre Workers' Union staged their Pinter excerpts, shrouding the evening with impenetrable mystery and symbols, it was not an attempt to laud obscurity for its own sake. Rather, it was an attempt to move beyond politics, an affirmation that there was more to man than his political relations, however difficult it was to define that missing dimension. The result was bound to be in some sense arty, even pretentious. A Moscow friend remarked to me that Russians had had all the realism which they wanted on the streets; now they went to the theatre only for poetry. So Russians went publicly to see work such as Nina Sadur's *Weird Woman* (available in print since 1989 but only now onstage), and perhaps more privately to see the work of Harold Pinter. Both gave them a non-realist and apolitical world. I write 'privately' in the case of Pinter because, surprisingly, as if still living in the *Samizdat* era, many directors continued to promulgate their Pinter productions by word of mouth only, avoiding any public announcement or advertisement. It was true that funds for programmes or posters were short. But, rightly or wrongly, the belief lingered that, in 1991, the authorities could and would move against unapproved or subversive writers. In a curious sense, I think, Russians needed to believe this. There was an overriding need for a focal point around which the anti-materialist forces could gather; and it would, in the Russian tradition, have more appeal if it were secret, or, better still, persecuted. So, for a time, Pinter became a champion, and in two senses. First, he came to stand for those strange (even mystical) forces which operate between human beings, which lie in some sense outside politics, which can be charted but perhaps never understood. Secondly, he came to be seen, even in 1991, as the voice which so spoke against the ethos of the day that he had to remain semi-clandestine. He had become the secret writer who wrote openly. He was the *Samizdat* writer in an era of no *Samizdat*. He was, with all the distortions that can follow, the voice of spiritual rebirth.

But this 'spiritual' approach to Pinter, if we may call it that, did not last long. By 1992 there was a new mood in Moscow. The world of the businessman, the new entrepreneur, the import–export dealer, had arrived; and, with it, a lifting of price controls – and the first great wave of price rises. In a Moscow which had at first welcomed the arrival of the foreigner, Western influences and investment, attitudes had hardened. 'Our love affair with the foreigner is over', a Moscow friend remarked to me. Even in the theatre, the expectation was growing that work should be clearer, establish its credentials, in a new sense pay its way. In a Russia in which the arts had lived a life apart, subsidised and protected, the era of commercial theatre had arrived. Musicals like *Jesus Christ Superstar* came into town; Viktyuk sensationalised *Lolita* and *The Maids*; new theatres like Spartak and the Okay made their pitch for the tourist market. Not surprisingly, while the interest in Pinter continued, a harder attitude to his work was discernible. The absurdity of a power struggle between two brothers and a tramp had been left behind. The open violence of a killing contract no longer applied. The vague aspirations of unlocated Pinter characters in a compilation of woolly excerpts lacked definition and purpose. Russians wanted something more. It was time for Pinter to appear in a new form, in a play in which believable characters in recognisable time and space had something to say about the lives and problems which preoccupied Russians. Rossinsky's production of *Betrayal* caught the moment. In a Russia linguistically divided by old Russian and new Russian, *Betrayal* seemed to focus on language. In a Russia struggling to accommodate the new business class, *Betrayal* presented a social elite. In a Russia shedding formal standards of conduct, *Betrayal* explored values in personal life. For the first time, critics who had associated Pinter with the spiritual yearnings of a Sadur or the

10 Set of *The Caretaker* at the (then) Krasnaya Presnya Theatre, November 1994

self-indulgent wordplay of a Shipienko saw in him a writer from whom Russians could, in difficult times, draw practical lessons for the New Russia.

But, to a Russian critic such as Denisov, to understand Pinter is always to solve a mystery or uncover a secret; and, for Russians impatient for clarity in uncertain times, perhaps the weakness of *Betrayal* was what they saw as its encrypted form. So, meeting this new demand, in 1993 came the most decrypted – and, arguably, most distorted – of any of the six productions. It played to a Moscow in the grip of political and criminal violence, and in which the glitter of Western goods and services was matched by prostitution, pornography and the beginnings of the drug culture. The thrusting capitalist Moscow of 1993 had little time for restraint, ambiguity or (least of all) spirituality. So The Erotic Theatre of Moscow gave theatre-goers what they seemed to want: a Pinter production which was short, clear, simple and sexy. It was like the instant coffee which was now widely available, or the hamburgers and pizzas which Muscovites assumed were genuine nourishment. It had to be fast, require no effort, offer an immediate charge to the senses. And so *Landscape*, with its beautiful drifting indeterminacy of recollection and invention, its gentle interweaving of the real and the imagined, was turned into voyeuristic pornography. Gavrilina's production had Duff and Beth generate onstage the objects of their monologues, which at once destroyed the ambiguity, neutralised the eroticism and subordinated the text. The production chose to ignore the subtext in order to exhibit the meaning, and in doing so lost it. It was a classic case of baby and bath water.

But 1994 was a year in which, chastened by the rouble crash and alarmed by prospects of a colonial war, Russians drew back from the brash optimism of unrestrained capitalism. In the theatre, too, it was as if Muscovites paused for breath. In 1994, *The Caretaker* at the Krasnaya Presnya Theatre was suddenly the place to be. It is not a big theatre, nor was it packed when I attended the production in November of that year. But, like no other Russian audience of Pinter that I had seen hitherto, this audience watched, laughed, saw, understood. Now, across the twenty-two years since Zaitsev's first effort, with all the oddities, aberrations, good intentions and best efforts of the intervening productions, Zaitsev's original and the Zalkind/Pogrebnichko production link up. Zaitsev's underground production of *The Caretaker*, for all its rough edges, cast changes and fit-up history, had at least the great merit of allowing the play to speak for itself. But, speaking for itself, it was not always understood. For Russians in the transition period during which it played, it seemed to hint at something, act as a harbinger, suggest truths (and tensions) which did not exist in the Communist world. This was its fascination. In attempting to hunt down these elusive truths in the years and the productions that followed, there were, as we have seen, cul-de-sacs, dead ends and short cuts which led nowhere. But the Zalkind/Pogrebnichko production was triumphantly back on track. For a start, this production allowed the play its own organic life. There was no ideology, no extraneous material, no unnatural speech emphasis, no exteriorisation of subtext. The dialogue, as it was spoken, was trusted to do the work. But it was also, in an important sense, the first genuinely Russian production. With no imposition from actor or director, it was transmuted into a Russian play. Davies came to life in a distinctive Russian way, had Russian habits, spoke and acted like a Russian. The set looked and felt like something familiar to Russians. Perhaps most importantly of all, the life and rhythm of the play took on a typical Russian meaning: it seemed to favour the underdog. So, as I write, does the New Russian struggle, against a background of competing forces, religious, commercial and spiritual, to find his new identity. *The Caretaker* is a universal play, and came across as such in 1972. By 1994 it was a universal play filtered through a Russian prism. And the line of development is complete.

Except, of course, that the line of development is never complete. There will certainly be other Pinter productions in Moscow, newer Pinter plays, differing versions in bigger and more influential houses. Since 1994 there have already been a number of new productions, though perhaps not so clearly related to the critical years which I have tried to describe. Two of the most interesting have been at the lively (and recently renovated) Nikitsky Vorot Theatre, where a vigorous production[11] of *A Slight Ache* has been included in its repertoire; and again at the Krasnaya Presnya Theatre, where the promising young actor-director Vladimir Khrabrov staged one of the most imaginative productions of *Landscape* that I have seen,[12] and had two other Pinter plays in rehearsal.[13] Two more recent productions are both more interesting and more contentious. At the little Armen Dzhigarkhanyan Theatre, a production of *The Homecoming*, directed by Sergei Gazarov and with the theatre founder and noted actor Armen Dzhigarkhanyan playing Max, provides an extraordinary evening of squalor, confrontation and emotional outpourings.[14] Most recently of all, Vladimir Mirzoev has mounted an independent production of *The Collection* in a Chinese-Buddhist setting which takes us even further from conventional notions of a Pinter play.[15] These latest productions must await their turn for more considered examination elsewhere. Certainly, they make important statements, contribute new ideas, arouse controversy in a way that the fledgling efforts could not hope to achieve. It would be a pity, though, if the six earliest productions, together with the route they charted, were entirely forgotten. They stand for a period when Russian theatre, emerging from the ideological shadows, was first dazzled by the bright light of Pinter, stumbled uncertainly for a time, then triumphantly turned his beam upon themselves. The early torchbearers, good and bad, deserve to be remembered.

Postscript 2008

In the years between 1972, when the semi-clandestine underground performance of *The Caretaker* first appeared, and 1994, when the Zalkind/ Pogrebnichko production finally gave it a genuinely Russian production, there was a clear line of development. Each new Pinter production was a landmark, signalling the advent of a new mood or attitude in the swiftly changing scene. Pinter productions were in this sense used, given a particular interpretation which reflected contemporaneous events, rather than probing each play's own meaning and resonance.

The following years saw a number of maverick, even eccentric, Pinter productions in which directors appeared to struggle to find the Pinter voice independent of developing events in Russia. One was a production of *A Slight Ache*, with a French director, and a slightly altered title, which opened at the Nikitsky Vorot Theatre in February 1999. It was a noisy production, with shouted lines and musical inserts, which strained to find the meaning of the piece (though it had settled into a quieter and more effective interpretation when I revisited it a year later). It shared the weakness of another misconceived production, *The Homecoming* at the Dzhigarkhanyan Theatre, in which the theatre founder and celebrated actor Armen Dzhigarkhanyan played Max. These productions were passionate and at times violent, not cool and ironic, both making the subtext explicit and thereby dissipating its impact. In both productions the approach suggested more affinity with, say, Tennessee Williams than Samuel Beckett. A production of *Landscape* by the young actor-director Vladimir Khrabov, at about the same time, found the stillness and unspoken sadness between Beth and Duff; but again the direction was uncertain enough to feel the need to unpack or expand the play, to include extra explanatory characters, to incorporate songs and poetry. In an interview in 2000, the director Vladimir Mirzoev asserted that Russians needed a key to unlock Pinter, that without some extra device they could not understand his plays; he had to inject more 'vitality' into his own Pinter productions, otherwise Russians would become bored and leave. So, in his production of *The Collection*, the play has a spectacular Chinese-Buddhist setting (based on James's single reference to 'a collection of Chinese pots') and an explicitly sado-masochistic relationship between Harry and Bill. The production is full of actions which seem gratuitous, based on half-hints and passing references in the dialogue, all made explicit in scenes which are comic, or shocking, or both. In all four of these productions, there was a reluctance to let the text speak for itself.

In the early years of this century, as the new Russia has emerged, there is a mixed and changing scene in all areas of life. The market economy has expanded ruthlessly, and the gap between rich and poor has visibly widened. Members of the upper house of parliament are no longer elected, but appointed, and new political parties are not normally allowed. Most media outlets, including national television, are controlled by the state, and few newspapers are truly independent. Internet access is limited. Whether from government or mafia threat, investigative journalists put their lives in grave danger. Russians are routinely travelling abroad in unparalleled numbers. Some have become the new Russian super-rich, and, at the same time, the Russian intelligence services have expanded operations at home and abroad. In foreign policy, Russia demands respect, to be taken seriously as a world power. Above all, under the leadership of President Vladimir Putin, the government began to assume (or resume) an authoritarian role in the lives of its subjects, often reminiscent of the Soviet regime; and this change of direction, as President Putin imposed order over chaos and criminality, enjoys broad popular support, despite a growing dissident movement. No longer an economic weakling still emerging from the slogans and rhetoric of a failed ideology, and despite the progressive erosion of democratic freedoms, the Russian people are more confident, assertive and ambitious than ever before.

This is a changed Russia. How has the new authoritarian climate affected the theatre of Harold Pinter in its capital? In marked contrast to the early years, when productions predominantly adopted a deeply reverential approach, in this new assertive Russia the first impulse seems to have been to take his theatre less seriously. A striking example of this was provided at the Sphere Theatre in early 2003, with an in-the-round production of *The Lover*. Significantly, it was paired with a short Dario Fo piece in what was clearly presented as a comic double-bill. *The Lover*, second on the bill, was presented as near-farce, in which every possible reference in the text was the starting point for dance, mime, tricks or songs, and occasionally audience participation. It was as if the production was looking for a Mirzoev-style 'key', and the key was knockabout comedy. As two examples: the opening sequence was a kind of dance, with synchronised crossing and uncrossing of legs, accompanied by music and rhetorical questions to the audience; when the bongo drum appeared, the scene turned suddenly oriental, with Richard in kimono (plus sword) and Sarah transformed into a geisha. Apart from a quiet closing scene, in which the production briefly explored the couple's faltering attempts at a compromise future, it was fast, stylised and mimetic, in the same style as the Fo piece which preceded it. A few of the audience left; most appeared to enjoy these pieces as an evening of fun. Another example of this new light-hearted approach to a Pinter text could be found at the small out-of-town Art House in February 2004 where the director, Vadim Tukvatulin, staged a production of *Landscape*. Tukvatulin is an ex-pupil of the respected actor and drama tutor Yuri Afsharov who, from the outset, has played a major role in the presentation of Pinter in Russia – and, as we shall see, continues to do so. But the style of Tukvatulin's *Landscape* was very different from the early productions of Afsharov's *The Caretaker*. It presented a decrepit old couple bickering in a run-down country house; incorporated frequent sound effects (opening with thunder and lightning, going on to birdsong, rain, passing train, barking dogs); used many props (such as a doll for Beth's baby); had costume changes (from cook and butler to white silk nightclothes); mixed fierce, wild declaimed reminiscences with calm voice-over. The production was mobile (when usually still), comic (when usually serious), fast (when usually slow), and played in real time (when usually lost in dream-like indeterminacy). At times, such as when Duff appeared, holding umbrella, in battered dinner jacket with red rose in button-hole, *Waiting for Godot* came inescapably to mind; at others, such as when Beth piled sugar non-stop into Duff's coffee, it could have been Whitehall farce. It became clear, in a subsequent interview, that Tukvatulin shared Mirzoev's view that a particular style had to be found to make Pinter acceptable to Russian audiences, that some kind of key was needed or audiences would find the plays boring, and leave. This key was designed to 'unpack' the text, and Tukvatulin's key was to fill the plays with illustrative jokes at every opportunity. Both *The Lover* at the Sphere and *Landscape* at the Art House took this approach, if in different ways. Certainly, Pinter productions in this zany and free-spirited style could not have been found in Russian theatres until these later years.

Other developments in Russian Pinter have been more interesting, and perhaps more controversial. In December 2001 I heard from Yuri Afsharov, the original Aston in the 'visiting card' production of *The Caretaker* in the 1970s, that the impresario and director Vladimir Rudy was staging a new and innovative production of the play. I saw it in rehearsal at the Mayerkovsky Theatre and was immediately struck by a radically different approach to the text. Rudy, who headed the theatre company Art Plus, told me that the time had come for Russians to rethink *The Caretaker*, not least because the general attitude to drop-outs and the dispossessed had changed as Russia had grown more prosperous. The question was not 'what were they now' but 'what had they been'. The dominant feature of Rudy's production was his determination to give it a kind of timeless universality, a concept always close to the heart of Yuri Afsharov, who had played Aston in the original Moscow production. As a private venture, lacking funding and a fixed venue, Rudy's production has had only intermittent performances. But in performance, at the Mikhail Chekhov Art Studio in March 2002, it was one of the most distinctive versions of the play that I had seen. Yuri Afsharov certainly took the character of Davies in a new direction. He now had provenance. He was dishevelled and broken-down certainly, but with attempts at self-justification, touchy, reaching for a lost dignity, growing in authority, most intriguingly of all somehow suggesting a reputable (one is tempted to say *pre-Revolutionary*) past. This contrasted with an Aston who was half-witted, waif-like, gullible (and deeply moving); and a flashy Mick who strutted the stage bombastically (and was a clear weakness). The set, by the designer Maxim Abrezkov, was striking: a rickety contraption of cords supporting an overhead mesh of white translucent panels, suggesting a tent or ship's rigging, with spindly steel chairs and frames as furniture. Davies was clad in a tattered enveloping patchwork of robes and shawls which could come from anywhere (suggesting, if anything, the Middle East), Aston in short jacket and baggy trousers vaguely suggestive of a child's school uniform, and Mick in red shirt and black leathers. There were frequent sound effects, including a repeated eerie double ping, an orchestrated or sung Chopin prelude at climactic passages and threatening percussion at moments of menace. The production had great pace, and the audience, closely attentive, laughed frequently. At the curtain, even by Moscow standards, it was received with acclaim. I spoke to a number of theatregoers about the production. One described the evening as 'ghastly'; another felt that it was the first Pinter play that he had ever understood. What emerged principally was a bold venture to take *The Caretaker* out of a specific time and place, pushing the interpretation in an absurdist (and universal) direction. Despite eccentricities of staging and effects (and a grossly histrionic Mick), and perhaps principally through a bravura account of Davies by Yuri Afsharov, it was (and is) a production to be seen and pondered.

There is another development, at least potentially, of Pinter's work in Russia. When I talked to Harold Pinter about Russian productions of his plays, he commented more than once that early plays were constantly produced, but later work rarely presented; and with Pinter's encouragement I took a copy of *Celebration* to Moscow, and placed it in the hands of Alexander Doroshevitch. Doroshevitch is a noted film and theatre academic, and the translator of the first *The Caretaker* in Moscow (the translation which was also used in Vladimir Rudy's production). I met Doroshevitch again in Moscow in March 2003. He had seen the Rudy production of *The Caretaker* and spoke warmly of it. It had, he said in his precise English, 'kept something of the inflections, movements and feelings of the original production'. He added, in an echo of Rudy's observation about drop-outs: 'Of course nowadays we understand Davies much better.' Doroshevitch had not then completed his translation of *Celebration*, but was satisfied that his translation to date was 'not bad'. Interestingly, he felt that the content applied well to modern Moscow (though, ominously, he had had to make occasional inserts to make this clearer). I had the same reaction from Vladimir Rudy, who, enthusiastic to produce the play, commented to me that 'it sounds exactly like a picture of Moscow today'. For all the skill and English fluency of Alexander Doroshevitch, it is difficult to believe that the nuanced slang and colloquialisms of *Celebration* can translate successfully into another language and culture; but in London the following year he presented me with a copy of his translation. In 2007 I heard that it had been published in the quarterly *Sovremennaya Dramaturgiya* (Modern Drama), a specialist journal with a small circulation, accompanied by a short article. Doroshevitch was already working on a translation of *The Hothouse*, believing that this work too was 'very up to date now'. In the context of the new Russia, it would be surprising if versions of *Celebration* and *The Hothouse*, as comment on social and political trends respectively, did not at some time appear on the Moscow stage.

Another prominent Pinter enthusiast in Moscow is the director Evgeny Mikeev, who is currently undertaking a new production of *The Dumb Waiter* at his Three Comedies Theatre. The production has some similarities with Vladimir Rudy's *The Caretaker*, most obviously in the spare stage setting, again by Maxim Abrezkov; but the production is not yet ready for public performance. With this exception, and a Pinter compilation by the touring Byelorussian Theatre from Minsk, little work by Harold Pinter has appeared in Moscow, and interest seems to have waned. Indeed, the critic (and director of the Bibliographical Centre at the State Library) Yuri Friedstein described the theatre scene as 'totally dead as far as Harold Pinter is concerned'. Recent developments have been in publishing: a collection of earlier plays released by the St Petersburg publishers Amphora; and Doroshevitch's *Celebration* in *Sovremennaya Dramaturgiya*, possibly to be followed by *The Hothouse*. Mikeev has also proposed, with the backing of the Ministry of Culture, a Pinter Festival, to be held in Moscow in August 2008, which may revive interest in Pinter's work in Russia. Opinions in Moscow differ widely on reasons why so little Pinter work now appears there. The Moscow-based drama critic John Freedman suggested to me that ' Russian perceptions of Pinter don't fit Russian reality any more', implying that, as Russia has emerged from the shadows, the Pinter moment has passed. Mikeev believes that 'Russians now feel free of specific Russian frames', believing that Pinter drama is now more attractive and up to date, has a universality not previously perceived. Conversely, Vladimir Mirzoev claims that the major theatres are not keen to produce Pinter simply for fear that Pinter plays 'would not be understood or [would] bore the Russian audience'.

After Soviet Communism, and the turbulent period of transition which followed, Russia has entered a new phase of confidence and self-assertion. In this new mood, interest in the questioning images and slippery language of Pinter plays has faded. It remains to be seen how soon the theatre of Harold Pinter, in interpretations which seek out the social and political undercurrent, will return to enrich the Russian stage.

NOTES

My main thanks are due to Natasha and Pietr Jukovsky, whose friendship and support I have valued over many years. Many Russian friends and colleagues, principally Yuri Afsharov and also Viktor Denisov, contributed help and ideas. The tireless efforts of my friend Oleg Stashkevitch opened many theatre doors. I am grateful to Birgit Beumers, of the Department of Russian Studies at the University of Bristol, who made many helpful suggestions. In Moscow, I have received invaluable help and advice from my friend and colleague John Freedman, theatre critic of the *Moscow Times*. Finally, I acknowledge gratefully the financial help and assistance given by the British Academy and the Leverhulme Trust.

1. This was part of a broader interest in the theatre of the absurd in general. During this period, it was often easier to find productions, and texts, of Samuel Beckett than Harold Pinter. But that is another story.
2. The theatre has since been renovated and renamed. It is now the Theatre Okolo Doma Stanislavskovo (Theatre By Stanislavsky's House) – known simply as the Okolo Theatre.
3. Viktor Denisov's *Six Spectres of Lenin on a Piano* premièred at the Laboratory Theatre in 1993. His collection of short plays was published in 1998. His translation of *The Dumb Waiter* appears in *Five Dramatists Under One Cover* (Moscow: Samara, 1991). He also completed translations of *The Lover* and *The Homecoming* for publication in the theatre magazine *Sovremennaya Dramaturgiya* (Modern Drama).
4. Yuri Afsharov later reprised Aston's monologue as part of a televised tribute to the director Gregori Zalkind.
5. According to one commentator, Zaitsev and Makeev gave themselves the name 'Ulysses'. This would have been appropriate, but I have been unable to corroborate it.
6. The collection is called *The Caretaker and Other Plays*. The other plays are *The Collection, Landscape, No Man's Land* and *Betrayal*. In 1993, when I had the pleasure of interviewing him, Mikhail Shvydkoi was Deputy Minister at the Ministry of Culture of the Russian Federation. Shvydkoi contributed a (still) useful chapter on English theatre after 1945 in *A History of Foreign Theatre* (Moscow: Prosveshchenya, 1977).
7. The collection has the title *Five Dramatists under One Cover*. The other writers featured are E. E. Cummings, Edward Albee, Sam Shepard and Tennessee Williams.
8. At the time of writing, Rossinsky has left the Laboratory Theatre and is setting up a new theatre in Moscow.
9. Conversation with the author.
10. Conversation with the author.
11. A little too vigorous, as I saw it. The French director had the actors play most of the lines *fortissimo*, even in the early exchanges. The result was monotonous, with

little feeling for the charged subtext. The respected critic Svetlana Novikova wrote an insightful review of the production in Moscow's *Theatre Courier* (March 1999) entitled 'Don't Make Boredom Boring'.

12. There was a striking and effective contrast between Beth and Duff. Beth maintained a dream-like stillness and fixation, while Duff achieved a casual, in-the-present psychological realism. I was less keen on the intercut poems and songs.

13. At Vladimir Khrabrov's invitation, I attended rehearsals of *Old Times* and *The Dumb Waiter*. Both plays were scheduled for production in late 1999 or early 2000 but had not yet found theatres.

14. At a post-performance reception in March 2000 I talked with Armen Dzhigarkhanyan and Sergei Gazarov about the production. Both defended their highly naturalistic approach to the play's text and my references to irony and subtext appeared to fall on deaf ears.

15. Vladimir Mirzoev provokes strong reactions. From his production of *The Birthday Party* at the University of Michigan in 1992 (during five years in Canada) through to Gogol's *The Government Inspector* (produced under the title *Khlestakov*) in 1996, his productions have been startlingly original: insights for some, outrage for others.

Author's note: I record with sadness that Natalia Mikhailovna Jukovskaya, my Russian friend and mentor for many years, died in Moscow on 14 June 2007 after a short illness.

12

ANTHONY ROCHE

Pinter and Ireland

During the 1990s and 2000s Dublin's Gate Theatre, under the artistic direction of Michael Colgan, staged a series of festivals celebrating the achievement of two of the century's greatest playwrights, Samuel Beckett and Harold Pinter. Both involved productions of individual plays performed by Irish practitioners or by foreign artists long associated with the playwright, backed up by seminars and debates. But there were differences. One playwright, Beckett, was recently dead when the Festival of his dramatic works was first staged in 1991; the other, Pinter, was alive and present throughout all three of his, directing on two occasions, acting on one. It is possible to stage all of Beckett's plays on the one occasion, as was done in 1991; whereas even with a Pinter Festival in 1994, another in 1997 and a third on the playwright's seventy-fifth birthday in 2005 there still remain key works unperformed and an element of choice colours each occasion.[1] But a third factor relates to Ireland and the decision to stage a festival of a dramatist's work. The staging of all of Beckett's plays in Dublin by a predominantly Irish theatrical group was an important step in the establishment of Beckett as an Irish (as opposed to an English, French, international or non-specific) playwright; the adoption of Irish accents by Ben Kingsley and Alan Howard in Peter Hall's revisiting of *Waiting for Godot* in 1997 may be taken as confirmation of the extent to which Beckett's Irishness is now universally conceded. The same was even more the case in 2006, the centenary of Beckett's birth. But Pinter is English and cannot even claim the Irish ancestors that might have got his plays produced at the Abbey Theatre. Michael Colgan rightly argued that he regarded Pinter as one of the greatest living playwrights and one he wished to honour, by mounting productions of plays of classic status that had rarely received professional Irish productions. But there also has always been, as Colgan would have known, an Irish strand to Pinter's career to which the Pinter Festivals at the Gate would contribute. There are two aspects to this relationship I wish to consider in this chapter: first, Pinter's career as an actor in Ireland in the early 1950s with the troupe of Anew McMaster; and second, the impact on his theatrical practice of such Irish playwrights as Beckett and Yeats, and the early Abbey Theatre.

The greatest interest in the second Pinter Festival centred on a production of *The Collection*, since the playwright himself was to take the role of Harry, the older man warding off the threat to his hold on the younger Bill in the play's shifting *ménage à quatre*. Pinter has returned to acting with some regularity in recent years; but this was to be the first time he had acted on Irish boards in over forty years. The part calls for '*a man in his forties*'[2] but the casting of the then 66-year-old Pinter added force to the older man's need to hold on to the younger. Pinter also brought a great deal of vocal and physical relish to the part, a reminder of his charisma as a performer. The production was also important for the unprecedented extent to which it brought together Irish and non-Irish practitioners. In the 1994 Festival, the productions had tended to break into Irish and non-Irish productions of Pinter, in which the Irish actors often seemed uncomfortable in their roles while the English appeared to find readier access to Pinter's words and world. A production like *Landscape*, directed by Pinter himself and starring Ian Holm and Penelope Wilton, might as well have been produced in and for London. But the overall effect of that Festival was invaluable for the exposure it afforded both Irish actors and audiences to the shock of Pinter's theatrical language; and there seemed a greater degree of familiarity and welcome for the 1997 event. With *The Collection* Pinter as actor meshed with the three Irish principals (Gerard McSorley, Frank McCusker and Ingrid Craigie) under the direction of Alan Stanford, an Englishman long resident in Ireland. Perhaps placing Pinter in connection to Ireland suggests the concept of theatrical hybridity.

Harold Pinter announced in a diary entry in 1951 that he had landed his first proper job as an actor: 'I'm going for a six-month tour in Shakespeare to Ireland next month. An Irish actor-manager called Anew McMaster.'[3] But McMaster was English, not Irish, born in Birkenhead not Monaghan (as he claimed).[4] This discovery underlines the extent to which Anew McMaster's greatest performance was the important daily masquerade of being Irish and finding the language to match, so well reproduced for us in Pinter's wonderful 1966 memoir, *Mac*: 'Look out the window at this town. What a stinking diseased abandoned Godforgotten bog ... But you see one thing the Irish peasantry really appreciate is style, grace and wit.'[5] In this, McMaster emulated his brother-in-law, Micheál MacLiammóir, who translated himself from the Alfred Willmore born in London into an Irishman with Gaelic-speaking Cork parents. As Christopher Fitz-Simon puts it: 'Anew McMaster claimed for himself the town of Monaghan as his birthplace, and Warrenpoint, County Down, as the scene of his earliest memories.'[6]

His two-year stint with McMaster, for all that he had had spells at RADA and Central, may well be said to constitute Harold Pinter's true apprenticeship in the craft of theatre, with Mac as mentor. Their relationship is epitomised by Pinter playing Iago to McMaster's Othello:

> One of the greatest moments of theatre I have ever experienced was when Iago is probing Othello and he goes slightly too far ... When I said, as Iago, 'With her, on her, as you will,' Mac turned, and the next moment he was strangling me as he said the line, 'Villain, be sure thou prove my wife a whore.' It was the most incredibly dramatic gesture. In fact I can still feel his hand round my throat![7]

This passage was reproduced in the programme for the 1997 Pinter Festival and shed light on that occasion, when Pinter once more took to an Irish stage, now acting in one of his own plays, but one which bore the unmistakable imprint of the earlier experience. For *The Collection* can be seen as a modern-day *Othello* with a distinct homoerotic subtext in which the men speculate about the vexed question of a wife's fidelity. Occasional eruptions of violence break the veneer of good manners and verbal restraint, notably when a cheese knife becomes a potentially lethal weapon and when James echoes McMaster's line as Othello in saying: 'When you treat my wife like a whore, then I think I'm entitled to know what you've got to say about it.'[8] Pinter's plays have often been seen, to adopt Christopher Innes's succinct formulation, as 'a struggle for the acting-space, in which the character who dominates is the actor who up-stages the others'.[9] This 'struggle for the acting-space' is what most often comes across in accounts of Pinter's stint as an actor with McMaster in Ireland. Here is Pinter's verbal recollection of the actor-manager whose insecurities permit others to threaten him with getting the upper hand:

> He undercuts me, [Mac] said, he keeps coming in under me. I'm the one who should come under. I'm playing Hamlet. But how can I play Hamlet if he keeps coming under me all the time? The more under I go the more under he goes. Nobody in the audience can hear a word. The bugger wants to play Hamlet himself, that's what it is. But he bloody well won't while I'm alive.[10]

It is worth noting in this context that Pinter got to play Hamlet precisely once, at a Thursday matinée.[11] The ruthless undercutting and the verbal bragga-docio of McMaster found its way into one of Pinter's greatest theatrical creations, the role of Max in 1965's *The Homecoming*. There the same contradictory mix of disgust and respect that McMaster displays in the earlier quotation about the Irish environment (bog and peasant) among which and to whom he played is expressed by Max about the memory of his dead wife. And there is a character called Mac in the play, verbally invoked by Max as a kind of *alter ego* in one of his fantastic monologues:

I used to knock about with a man called MacGregor. I called him Mac. You
remember Mac? Eh? *Pause.* Huhh! We were two of the worst hated men in the
West End of London. I tell you, I still got the scars. We'd walk into a place, the
whole room'd stand up, they'd make way to let you pass. You never heard such
silence. Mind you, he was a big man, he was over six foot tall. His family were
all MacGregors, they came all the way from Aberdeen, but he was the only one
they called Mac.[12]

But in the domestic space of *The Homecoming* no male authority goes
uncontested and, while Max insists on his throne-like chair and wields his
stick, he does so in the face of his sons' opposition. The above speech becomes
a monologue rather than a dialogue when Lenny, to whom it is addressed,
refuses to confirm Max's memory of Mac. Silence operates and is interpreted
within the monologue as a tribute to the impressive presence of Mac and
Max; but the hostility implied by Lenny's repeated silences emerges explicitly
when the monologue has run its course: 'Plug it, will you, you stupid sod, I'm
trying to read the paper.'[13] The play's opening exchanges between Max and
Lenny operate by means of mutual undercutting in which neither is prepared
to give ground. Like the young male Turks in the theatrical 'family' of Anew
McMaster, the three sons in *The Homecoming* may lust to play the tragic lead
but the older man still has his hands around their throats if they come too
close to doing so. Whether Shakespeare or melodrama, the subtext of each
night's performed play, especially for the players themselves, must have
existed in the moves and counter-moves as each sought to wrest theatrical
power from the other. One imagines an aged male mentor with thrusting
young sons enacting dramas of jealousy, lust and revenge.

It is to this sojourn in Ireland in the early 1950s that Pinter owes the
discovery of what may well be his single greatest literary influence, the writing
of Samuel Beckett. In a year or so, the Paris première of *En Attendant Godot*
would occur and Beckett's drama would begin to exert its Copernican influence on the development of world theatre. *Waiting for Godot*'s London
production in 1956 is a milestone in the development of English theatre,
and cannot but have had a major impact on Pinter as a nascent dramatist;
and the play's director Peter Hall was to become a crucial onstage interpreter
of both dramatists. But I think it significant that Pinter discovered Beckett
prior to the appearance of *Waiting for Godot* and as a specifically Irish writer
in the English language – again, something that the Parisian début of a play in
French was apt to conceal. While in Ireland, Pinter first encountered Beckett's
writing as follows:

One day I came across, I stumbled across, a poetry magazine called *Poetry
Ireland* edited by David Marcus in which I found a fragment of Beckett's *Watt*. I

was stunned by it but I couldn't get hold of this David Marcus because the magazine telephone never answered so I never found out who this man Beckett was. I went back to London and no library or bookshop had ever heard of Beckett. Finally I went to the Westminster Library and asked them to burrow in their records and they came up with a book that had been in the Battersea Reserve Library since 1938 and that was *Murphy*. After a couple of weeks, I got it, pinched it and still have it … I suddenly felt that what his writing was doing was walking through a mirror into the other side of the world which was, in fact, the real world.[14]

The language here is that of epiphany but also of personal discovery, an unearthing of buried treasure. It establishes the grounds on which the writing of Samuel Beckett first made its impact on a young man looking for a distinctive sense of self and style. And Beckett is not the only writer cited as mattering most to Pinter who turns out to be Irish. There was his excited discovery of Joyce's *Ulysses* at eighteen, and in 1970 Pinter was to direct an acclaimed London production of Joyce's one play, *Exiles*. He has a lifelong and oft-proclaimed passion for the poetry of Yeats, which even makes its way into several of the plays. And the importance of Beckett's writing to Pinter has been frequently and well attested to, not least by the author himself. What I wish to stress is that the context of the discovery indicates Pinter's immediate awareness of Beckett as an Irish writer, from the fragment of *Watt* published in *Poetry Ireland* to the pilfering of a copy of Beckett's first, and most Irish, novel, *Murphy*. Many of the writers Pinter was attracted to lay outside the English tradition – Kafka, for example. It was perhaps to be expected that a modish young Englishman in the early 1950s would steep himself in Continental literature. What is more unexpected is that the major writer he is importing into England from abroad, to enlarge the cultural boundaries of a post-war provincialism, should come from Ireland rather than, say, from France.[15] If Pinter was in Ireland bringing Shakespeare to the masses, he was clearly working on his own agenda; and the cultural exchange was two-way.

Pinter's memory of his first literary encounter with Samuel Beckett in a journal of Irish writing is not entirely accurate. One might question why a poetry journal should publish a fragment of prose, even if that prose scarcely adheres to the norms of fiction. But a scan of *Poetry Ireland* for the period up to and through Pinter's time in Ireland reveals that no fragment of *Watt* was published therein. In the April 1949 issue (no. 5) of *Poetry Ireland*, however, there appeared three poems by Samuel Beckett; the poems were in English, but were all credited as 'From French originals by the author' and 'With acknowledgements to the author and to the editors of "Transition", Paris'. These poems feature as three of the 'Six Poèmes 1947–1949' in the 1977 John Calder *Collected Poems* and are the three for which Beckett has provided translations into English. The *Poetry Ireland* provenance reveals that Beckett's own translations of these three poems date from the same period, and that the wish to see them published in an Irish context may well have occasioned the act of translation. Pinter's reference, to both *Poetry Ireland* and its editor David Marcus, shows that he was familiar with the journal. It seems reasonable to assume that he read these poems at this time, a time of his life when he was writing steadily as a poet, and that Beckett's poetry had an impact on him.[16] The three poems are (published in this order): the nine-line 'my way is in the sand flowing' ('je suis ce cours de sable qui glisse'); the fifteen-line 'what would I do without this world faceless incurious' ('que ferais-je sans ce monde sans visage sans questions'); and the following well-known quatrain: 'I would like my love to die / and the rain to be falling on the graveyard / and on me walking the streets / mourning the first and last to love me' ('je voudrais que mon amour meure'). The line from the three that must immediately strike any reader or audience of Pinter is the following (from the second poem): 'what would I do without this silence where the murmurs die'. There is clearly, as has long been recognised, a shared poetics of silence in the drama of Pinter and Beckett. What is striking is to come across it adumbrated in the poetry of both writers, a genre for which neither is renowned, at an earlier stage than expected, and to view the transition into drama as the need more fully and acoustically to establish a zone in which silence is an abiding presence.

The dominant influence in the early poetry of Pinter was Dylan Thomas. And while Beckett may be said to continue the Celtic connection, the spareness and strangeness of his writing counters the floridity of that association. The jaunty rhythm and alliterative runs of 'I Shall Tear Off My Terrible Cap' from 1951 show the strong influence of Thomas in the year Pinter moved to Ireland. 1953's 'Poem', which begins 'I walked one morning with my only wife / Out of sandhills to the summer fair', does indeed, as Michael Billington has said, 'seem to be in the world of Yeats and Synge – a world of peasants, shawls and summer fairs – [with] even a faint echo of "The Lake Isle of Innisfree"'[17] and may well suggest why Pinter did not need to stay any longer in Ireland. He also does the obligatory Aran Islands poem, as Wallace Stevens had before him, though it is notable in Pinter's poem how the three Aran Islands retain their isolation, mystery and separateness, refusing to yield their secrets to the observer:

> Aran like three black whales
> Humped on the water,
> With a whale's barricade
> Stares out the waves.

Aran with its bleak gates locked,
Its back to the traders,
Aran the widower,
Aran with no legs

Distended in distance
From the stone of Connemara's head,
Aran without gain, pebbled
In the fussing Atlantic.   (1951)[18]

But it is in another poem from the same year, 'The Irish Shape', which Pinter has made widely available in *Various Voices*, that the presence of Beckett and a different sense of Ireland from the above are registered. The poem is bereft of specific Irish references other than one iteration or outlining of 'the Irish shape'. It expresses the same doomed romanticism and unfurling, twisting syntax as the three Beckett poems, reflecting: 'Not for this am I for nothing here, / But for that only I remain from her. / … But for that only and the Irish shape.' Behind the question of why the speaker remains in Ireland is a larger existential dilemma, as he enumerates in the last three lines those fragile qualities which secure his minimal presence in the world:

Only for this mirror and this all spring's time,
Only for the passing of the sea below,
Only for the silence, for her eyebrow.   (1951)[19]

The image of 'this mirror' recalls the terms in which Pinter expressed the shock of recognition he experienced on first reading Beckett: 'I suddenly felt that what his writing was doing was walking through a mirror into the other side of the world which was, in fact, the real world.'[20]

This brings us back to the fragment from *Watt* which Pinter said he had come across in *Poetry Ireland*. That fragment of Beckett's prose fiction appeared rather in a sister publication, *Irish Writing*, co-edited by the same David Marcus and which, in 1953, absorbed *Poetry Ireland* as a supplement rather than a separate publication; this may well have been the cause of Pinter's confusion.[21] An 'Extract from *Watt*' by Samuel Beckett was published in *Irish Writing* no. 17 (December 1951), edited by David Marcus and Terence Smith. The extract ran to six pages, beginning 'It was about this time that Watt was transferred to another pavilion'. In terms of the novel as a whole, which was not to be published until 1953 even though completed in 1945, these pages come at the very beginning of Part Three of *Watt*'s four sections.[22] It marks a notable transition, shifting from Watt's account of his time spent serving in Mr Knott's house to a later occasion on which he met the narrator to whom his story was transmitted. The face-to-face encounter between the two is described in the following terms: 'suddenly I felt as though I were standing before a great mirror, in which my garden was reflected, and my fence, and I … so that I looked at my hands and felt my face, and glossy skull, with an anxiety as real as unfounded'.[23] On his first glimpse into Beckett's fictional world, Pinter appears to have divined in the meeting between the narrator and Watt a kind of literary *alter ego* or *doppelgänger* for himself: 'What I seemed to be confronted with was a writer inhabiting his innermost self.'[24]

Much of the exchange between Watt and the narrator hinges on difficulties of communication. For 'Watt spoke as one speaking to dictation, or reciting, parrot-like, a text, by long repetition become familiar.'[25] In this, his last text to be written in English before he turned to French, Beckett is writing English as though it were a foreign language and certainly not a medium for self-expression, either on the part of what may be deemed 'characters' or a self whose very existence is problematic. What the three Irish writers valued by Pinter – Joyce, Yeats and Beckett – have in common with writers like Kafka is their modernism and their strangeness. The difference is that they are writing, not in French or German, but in English; and the nature of the translation involved is cultural rather than linguistic. In Irish writing in English, language is rarely transparent, a straightforward means of access to an accepted social reality. Indeed, for any Irish writer (whatever their knowledge or ignorance of Gaelic), the English language is apt to be both 'so familiar and so foreign', as Joyce put it in *A Portrait of the Artist as a Young Man*:

> The language in which we are speaking is his before it is mine. How different are the words home, Christ, ale, master, on his lips and on mine! … His language, so familiar and so foreign, will always be for me an acquired speech. I have not made or accepted its words. My voice holds them at bay.[26]

The lack of a shared socio-political context in which the meanings of words can be agreed upon is no less true of Pinter's plays. Each of his speakers exerts his or her authority over the words they speak, as much to assert their own sense of self as to deny the listener immediate access to the meaning of those words. This principle could be illustrated from almost any of Pinter's plays, but if I choose to discuss 1969's *Landscape*, it is because in it I discern an 'Irish shape' and Beckettian presence which may help to explain why Pinter chose to direct it in Dublin for the first Festival in 1994. *Landscape* consists of two monologues by a man and a woman, Duff and Beth, which interweave but rarely match up with each other. Duff claims that they are man and wife, together the sole employees of a Mr Sykes with the task of keeping his house in order. The declared aim was to 'live in Mr Sykes' house in peace, no-one to bother us'.[27] The fastidious detail with which Duff elaborates on their

11 Ian Holm as Duff and Penelope Wilton as Beth in the Gate Theatre's production of
Landscape, part of the Pinter Festival at the Gate, May 1994

12 The full cast of the Plays, Poetry and Prose readings with Harold Pinter on stage at the Gate Theatre as part of the Pinter75 Celebration 2005

domestic duties brings us back to the world of Beckett's *Watt* and his description of the sharing of duties in Mr Knott's house with one other person. The vein in which Beth speaks is more lyrical, as she describes approaching a man on a beach who may be her lover: 'He lay above me and looked down at me. He supported my shoulder. *Pause* So tender his touch on my neck. So softly his kiss on my cheek. *Pause*'.[28] This reverie recalls in several key details the erotic monologue in the punt on which the elderly Krapp fixates as he replays the tapes of his past in Beckett's 1957 play, *Krapp's Last Tape*: 'I asked her to look at me and after a few moments – [*Pause.*] – after a few moments she did, but the eyes just slits, because of the glare. I bent over her to get them in the shadow and they opened. [*Pause. Low.*] Let me in.'[29] These were words Pinter himself was to speak when he played the part of Krapp at the Royal Court in 2006. In *Landscape* the same entreaty is increasingly urged on Beth by Duff, but he is as effectively shut out from her inner reverie as the remembering Krapp is from the woman with whom he shared the punt. Both plays are fuelled by regret, Duff's for his unfaithfulness, Krapp's for the life he has lived. In *Landscape* Pinter is bringing together two strands of Beckett's writing, the prose exactitudes of *Watt* and the lyrical dramatic monologue of *Krapp*, and listening to them attentively like replayed tapes. Duff's long speech about the gong, like Watt's pedantic elaboration of the

13 Stephen Brennan, Janie Dee and Donna Dent in *Old Times* at the Gate Theatre as part of the Pinter75 Celebration 2005

rituals of Mr Knott's household, becomes less actual and more surreal as it continues, the words increasingly usurping any pre-existent social reality as they assert a verbal frenzy of baffled desire:

> I booted the gong down the hall. The dog came in. I thought you would come to me, I thought you would come into my arms and kiss me, even ... offer yourself to me. I would have had you in front of the dog, like a man, in the hall, on the stone, banging the gong, mind you don't get the scissors up your arse .... you'll plead with me like a woman, I'll bang the gong on the floor, if the sound is too flat, lacks resonance, I'll hang it back on its hook, bang you against it swinging, gonging, waking the place up, ... bang your lovely head, mind the dog doesn't swallow the thimble, slam – *Silence*.[30]

In Pinter's most dramatically adventurous and emotionally probing examination of sexual and emotional infidelity, 1978's *Betrayal*, another Irish writer plays a crucial role: W. B. Yeats. Explicit references to writers in the texts of Pinter's plays are rare, even when the characters of his later plays become more upwardly mobile. The three characters of *Betrayal* are all involved in the world of London publishing, and so it would not be out of character for them to drop authors' names into their conversation. And we hear a great deal about an (Irish?) writer called Casey, a novelist who – like

Godot – never actually appears but who is verbally summoned when one of the characters wants to antagonise another. But the play has a series of sustained references to W. B. Yeats which is crucial to the emotional and, I shall argue, to the dramaturgic subtext of the play. The references cluster round a holiday Robert and Emma spent in Venice, where a trip was proposed to Torcello, where Robert claims he read Yeats in the dawn. According to Emma, the trip never took place. The first exchange on the subject of Yeats occupies the close of scene two:

> ROBERT: Have you read any good books lately?
> JERRY: I've been reading Yeats.
> ROBERT: Ah. Yeats. Yes.
>
> *Pause*
>
> JERRY: You read Yeats on Torcello once.
> ROBERT: On Torcello?
> JERRY: Don't you remember? Years ago. You went over to Torcello in the dawn, alone. And read Yeats.
> ROBERT: So I did. I told you that, yes. *Pause* Yes. *Pause* Where are you going this summer, you and the family?
> JERRY: The Lake District.[31]

The suggestion is that Wordsworth, Coleridge and the Lake District are a good deal safer than Torcello and Yeats. For while Yeats may have claimed he was the Last Romantic, and may be regarded as such in his hopeless idealised love for Maud Gonne, a serious reader of Yeats – as Pinter has always been – knows that Yeats is the poet of sexual betrayal.[32] After all, this is the man who wrote (in a letter to Lady Gregory) scarcely a month after his marriage to Georgie Hyde-Lees in September 1917: 'I have betrayed three people.'[33] He was not only referring to his new wife but to Maud and her daughter Iseult, to both of whom he had proposed marriage (and been rejected) in the months before. In the sexually more explicit poems Yeats wrote in the second half of his career, the encounter of a man and a woman in the act of love is likely to be troubled by the presence of a third: either a lover from a past life or the projection of an idealised counter-self to the beloved. In 'An Image from a Past Life', the male speaker tries to reassure the woman that there is nothing to fear, but she has the final word which suggests there is much to be afraid of in 'the hovering thing night brought me'.[34]

It is appropriate, then, that the textual ghost of Yeats should be invoked by the three lovers who are caught in a round of mutual self-deception in their adulterous triangle.[35] The Venice holiday for Robert and Emma turns out to be the occasion on which her affair with Jerry comes to the surface and Emma declares 'We're lovers.'[36] The discovery is framed by the proposed trip to Torcello, which they first visited 'six months after we were married'.[37] By the time Robert closes the scene by repeating 'Tell me, are you looking forward to our trip to Torcello?',[38] the emotional axis has shifted and the question is hollow and rhetorical. But Robert has also mentioned his own relationship with Jerry, begun when they were undergraduates and editors of poetry magazines. Where now Jerry and Emma exchange clandestine letters, then Jerry and Robert exchanged 'Long letters about … oh, W. B. Yeats, I suppose'.[39] As in the scenario of a Yeats poem outlined above, the image of Jerry is present to both lovers, but each has cast him in the image of their own desire, and so the ground has been well laid – via the mediumship of Yeats – for Robert to wind up with: 'I've always liked Jerry. To be honest, I've always liked him rather more than I've liked you. Maybe I should have had an affair with him myself.'[40] But if Yeats as poet of sexual betrayal has a contribution to make to the play, so too does Yeats as dramatist. For he contributes, I believe, to the dramaturgically most innovative and ethically and emotionally most probing feature of Pinter's *Betrayal*, the decision to reverse the chronology in unfolding the development of Jerry's affair with Emma. Each of the play's nine scenes is dated, from the 1977 of scene one to the 1968 of scene nine, the present as much historicised by this means as the past. The first two scenes are in fact progressive, as first Jerry and Emma and then Jerry and Robert discuss the end of the affair. The play begins to reverse chronology with scene three (1975); what has ended scene two is the lengthy discussion of 'reading Yeats' referred to earlier. It is the reference to Yeats, then, which immediately precedes and, I would argue, initiates the reversal of time. Anyone who has been 'reading Yeats' widely, and the reference may remind us that Yeats wrote extensively in prose and drama as well as poetry, would have come across the concept of the 'dreaming back'. In his prose philosophy *A Vision* Yeats describes the process whereby the spirit of someone who has just died 'in the Dreaming Back … is compelled to live over and over again the events that had most moved it; there can be nothing new; but the old events stand forth in a light which is dim or bright according to the intensity of the passion that accompanied them.'[41] The scenario of the 'dreaming back' envisages people who are forced to relive the details of their life, bathed in the retrospective light of everything that has occurred since and with the moral burden of much greater knowledge than the ignorance they could claim at the time. Yeats himself was aware of the potential of the 'dreaming back' for drama, and utilised it in several of his plays. In *The Dreaming of the Bones*, for example, a young IRA man in the present encounters the ghosts of two adulterous lovers who have betrayed not just the husband but Ireland, by letting the invader in; he refuses to forgive them and so the cycle of violence remains unbroken. In *The Only Jealousy of Emer* a wife is forced to confront her husband's infidelities as he lies on his deathbed.

'Every event so dreamed is the expression of some knot, some concentration of feeling separating off some period of time ... and the dream is as it were a smoothing out or an unwinding.'[42] The scenes of *Betrayal* separate off some period of time in the three-way relationship between the characters and allow for a concentration of feeling – perhaps because of this very technique a greater degree of feeling than is always associated with Pinter. In scene three, for example, when Jerry remarks how difficult it is for the two lovers to meet, Emma ruefully reflects: 'You see, in the past ... we were inventive, we were determined, it was ... it seemed impossible to meet ... impossible ... and yet we did. We met here, we took this flat and we met in this flat because we wanted to.'[43]

And indeed we are going to see, in subsequent scenes of Pinter's version of the dreaming back, these words of Emma become embodied in the less jaded, more daring, earlier stages of their relationship. But we have also just seen the later, full deterioration of the affair, where the lack of possibility mirrors the further waning of desire, and we bring that knowledge as a layer to the reading of Emma's speech. There may even be some anticipation of it in what she says. Clearly these three people are not in the strict sense ghosts and do not consciously have an awareness of what the future will bring. The actors playing the three roles do, not just because they have read the entire script, but because they have played out the end of the relationship first and bring the knowledge of that, the scent of that future decline, to the playing of the earlier scenes. The audience are the ones who most fully occupy the role of revenant, witnessing each scene of the 'unwinding' of the dramatic event in its intensity, bringing the knowledge of future events to a reading of each scene's 'present' which – far from conferring a detached god-like perspective – enforces a great empathy with what is gone through. In a sense, the characters themselves seem the more detached; it is as if the audience goes through the emotions on their behalf.

The notable development in Pinter's playwriting career after 1978's *Betrayal* has a possible Irish connection. Whereas earlier he had mixed shorter and longer plays, Pinter's plays of the eighties and early nineties are all short and extremely concentrated – unsuitable for commercial presentation and even difficult to stage in the subsidised theatre. They resemble what used to be called one-act plays but they recall even more the short, concentrated plays staged at the Abbey Theatre early in the century by Yeats, Lady Gregory and Synge. Although occasionally performed at the Abbey, the most sustained outings of these one-act plays in Ireland remained the amateur drama festivals held throughout the country, where Pinter might well have seen some of them in the 1950s. The earlier playwright of international repute who had 'progressed' towards shorter and shorter pieces was, of course,

Samuel Beckett; but he in turn was familiar with this Irish tradition.[44] It is out of the uncanny similarities between Pinter's 1988 *Mountain Language* and Lady Gregory's 1906 *The Gaol Gate* that these speculations arise. Both plays share the same central situation and characters: two women, one elderly, one young, who come to a prison to visit a husband and/or son imprisoned within. The chief brunt of the encounter is between the women and the prison authorities, or at least the functionaries who control access. The lack of communication between the two sides is starkly stated in the Pinter: 'Now hear this. You are mountain people. You hear me? Your language is dead. It is forbidden. It is not permitted to speak your mountain language in this place. You cannot speak your language to your men. … This is a military decree. It is the law. Your language is forbidden. It is dead.'[45]

These are precisely the terms of Lady Gregory's play. The women in *The Gaol Gate* have come from a mountainous region, as their comments about the claustrophobia their imprisoned man will be suffering make clear: 'He that was used to the mountain to be closed up inside of that!'[46] It turns out that the prisoner Denis Cahel has already been executed. The Gatekeeper's account is as brutal, in its own folksy way, as the speech of Pinter's guards: 'Those that break the law must be made an example of … A long rope and a short burying, that is the order for the man that is hanged.'[47] The women have come too late because they were unable to interpret the language of the official letter in which they were sent the news: 'I wish we could know what is in the letter they are after sending us through the post. Isn't it a great pity for the two of us to be without learning at all?'[48] While Lady Gregory wrote in both Irish and English and translated between the two languages, her play never specifies that the women are more fluent in their native Gaelic than the recently imposed officialese of English. What both plays want to stress is the political implications of two different kinds of English being spoken and the two different orders of reality they connote: one hierarchical and brutal, the other communal and interactive; what they dramatise is the colonial process by which one is imposed on the other. When the elderly woman in Pinter's play speaks, it is in 'a strong rural accent'[49] and in a language that the guard cannot understand and opposes violently. When the lighting changes, and we tune in to the exchanges between mother and son in the mountain language, it speaks in precisely the terms of *The Gaol Gate*, of a community which waits to welcome him home:

> The baby is waiting for you. … When you come home there will be such a welcome for you. Everyone is waiting for you. They're all waiting for you. They're all waiting to see you.[50]

> The child he left in the house that is shook, it is great will be his boast in his father! All Ireland will have a welcome before him.[51]

The alignment of the two plays suggests a rereading of Lady Gregory as a much more political writer than has heretofore been recognised; but it also shows how alert and original as a witness, an interpreter of the Irish dramatic movement, Pinter is. He certainly knows these works and writers from the inside, and can read well beyond such simplistic constructions as 'peasant drama', seeing through the Celtic tracery to the dramatic, psychic, poetic and political possibilities at their core. At the same time, as an outsider, he is freer to make of them what creative use he will, and in particular is not caught within the limits of an imposed tradition.

The contemporary Irish playwright Frank McGuinness stressed these 'contacts with Ireland' in 2004 when University College Dublin, under the auspices of the National University of Ireland, conferred the degree of Doctor of Literature (*honoris causa*) on Harold Pinter. Pinter was awarded the honorary doctorate on 16 June, the hundredth anniversary of the day on which James Joyce's *Ulysses* was set. Indeed, the Bloomsday readings and performances were well under way at various city-centre locations as we gathered at Number 86, St Stephen's Green, for the conferring – the doors Stephen Dedalus and Joyce had entered when they were undergraduates just over a century earlier. In his remarks, Frank McGuinness particularly foregrounded Pinter's association with Joyce and, as one playwright speaking about another, a natural emphasis fell on *Exiles*, the one play Joyce wrote, and on the profound ways in which Pinter's direction of that acclaimed 1970 production may have influenced his own art:

> This production illuminated the complexities and silences at the heart of Joyce's *Exiles*, placing it where it belonged in the forefront of European literature. Its influence nourished later plays by Harold Pinter, most especially *Betrayal* and *Old Times*. Both are plays of enormous secrets ... As with the characters in *Exiles*, the characters of *Old Times* and *Betrayal* have suffered some sorrow, leaving them to bear the effects of that sorrow's wounds. The doubt and wound Joyce identified at the strange, sore heart of *Exiles* disable Pinter's lovers too, and his plays diagnose and dissect the rough condition of erotic desire.[52]

In his closing remarks, McGuinness linked Pinter with Joyce through a shared credo of disobedience, 'non serviam', since 'art in a democracy never, ever bows to the logic and lies of authority'. In above all acclaiming him for his 'conscience' McGuinness sounded a political note all too rarely heard in Irish discussions and celebrations of Pinter. At the lunch afterwards, Pinter was asked about the play he was currently directing, Simon Gray's *The Old Masters*. He spoke of his admiration for the actress Barbara Jefford who appeared in it and who had played Molly Bloom some thirty-seven years earlier in Joseph Strick's film version of Joyce's *Ulysses*.

In 2005, the Gate Theatre staged a third Pinter Festival, to coincide with and to celebrate the playwright's seventy-fifth birthday. The two main productions, perhaps prompted by the Joycean associations suggested by McGuinness, were *Old Times* and *Betrayal*. Both mixed Irish and English actors and directors as before. Michael Barker-Caven, an English director who lived and worked for many years in Ireland, placed English actress Janie Dee as the enigmatic centre of *Old Times*, flanked by two Irish actors playing her increasingly baffled and enraged husband Deeley (Stephen Brennan) and the vivacious Anna (Donna Dent). The Scottish director Robin Le Fevre, who has directed many Irish plays in both Ireland and England, cast English-born Irish-resident Nick Dunning as the husband Robert in *Betrayal* opposite another Irish duo – Cathy Belton as the wife Emma and Risteard Cooper as the lover/friend Jerry. Dunning memorably conveyed the wounded doubt assailing Robert in his features as much as in what he said, bringing a measure of the audience's understanding to the most potentially unsympathetic of the play's three characters.

But the highlight of the 2005 Pinter Festival was undoubtedly the reading of the playwright's most recent work for the stage, *Celebration*. In large part, this was due to the fact that because it was a one-off reading rather than a full production of however many weeks or months, and because it was intended as a celebration of its author, Michael Colgan was able to assemble a cast that not even the most munificently funded theatre could reach to. Onto the stage of the Gate at 6 pm on Saturday 8 October strode Michael Gambon, Penelope Wilton, Derek Jacobi and Sinead Cusack to occupy Table One; Jeremy Irons and Janie Dee sat opposite each other at Table Two; while standing by to serve were Stephen Brennan and Donna Dent (from the casts of the two plays being staged) as Richard and Sonia and Stephen Rea – returned at last to the Irish stage – as the waiter. The reading was superbly directed by Alan Stanford, English-born Irish-based actor-director who had done so well by the mixed cast of *The Collection* some eight years before; and because the play is set in a restaurant, with most of the actors seated for most of the time, the reading was half way to being a production. If ever a presentation demonstrated that there are no small acting parts or roles, it was this one as each member of the ensemble got the full measure of each line and traded it with their partners in a stunning, witty ensemble. And this was the event's other main attraction: it was a Pinter play largely unknown to the audience, who would have had no opportunity to see it staged heretofore in Ireland. Bearing in mind it was recent, they may well have expected a sombre, explicitly political work, rather than the uproarious comedy to which they were treated. It became clear that this is Pinter's most Wildean comedy long before the waiter makes the observation that his grandfather 'lost' his grandmother, intended not as a euphemism for her death but as a comically literal fact: 'he lost her somewhere. She disappeared, I think, in a sandstorm. In the desert.'[53]

The play's present is a satirically adept dissection of wealthy City of London types at the turn of the millenium. But the play's present-time horizon is cut across by vertical invocations of the past and anticipations of the future. That past is insistently familial – at some point, every single character talks about their father and their mother, who were frequently at cross-purposes if not at each other's throats, 'fucking up' their offspring in diverse ways (the play has an inspired Oedipal riff on mothers and sons wanting to fuck each other). These family reminiscences extend further back, in certain cases, to grandparents, who generally assert a more benign presence and have transmitted a more positive family legacy, After a while, the serving staff get in on the act. Richard talks of how his restaurant was inspired by the old-fashioned country pub he was brought to by his father – nostalgia for a rural England commodified by capitalism. Sonia mainly fantasises out loud about foreign men but does report factually when asked about her upbringing: 'I was born in Bethnal Green. My mother was a chiropodist. I had no father.'[54] But each of them is topped by the Waiter. On three occasions during the play, Stephen Rea approached the diners in a sideways deferential manner and interjected a Pinter set-piece about his grandfather. The ostensible *raison d'être* is that he happened to overhear a famous cultural name or group being discussed (T. S. Eliot, American cinema of the thirties) and is able to weave his grandfather into the mix by asserting that his forebear knew them all personally. Rea began each speech with a tone of sweet reasonableness which he never quite lost even as the lists grew more fantastical. The first monologue culminates with the assertion that his grandfather was James Joyce's godmother. The second establishes the Irish ethnicity of American film stars and gangsters of the 1930s. The third mentions a diverse range of characters from Yeats and Pound through to Franz Kafka and the Three Stooges. The Irish strain or shape in the Waiter's monologue was beautifully brought out in Stephen Rea's interpretation and made the references to Joyce and Yeats in particular a comically refracted tribute by Pinter to their enhancement of his artistic self. And as the other actors exited to leave the play's last word with the Waiter, it was clear which of the many stars on stage had slyly slipped *Celebration* into his pocket and walked off with it. The Waiter's closing speech returns to his grandfather and in doing so makes it clear that the play's main subtext is a facing up to death: 'My grandfather introduced me to the mystery of life and I'm still in the middle of it. ... He left it behind him and he didn't look back.'[55]

These lines bore on Pinter's presence at the 2005 Festival and the question of his participation in it. He was originally announced as one of the readers for *The Pinter Landscape*, the readings from his poems, prose and plays scheduled for Sunday 9 October at 4 pm. But in the event his name was replaced on the programme by that of other readers. And the Harold Pinter who made his way with Antonia Fraser to their seats in the stalls before the reading was a significantly frailer figure than the man who had visited Dublin sixteen months earlier for the UCD conferring. At the start of the second half Pinter had left the stalls and was seated on stage, at the centre-inmost point of the half-moon of assembled readers. When the reading had apparently concluded and the applause began, Pinter raised his hand. He said he wished to read a poem about his wife and their short visit to Paris after they began their relationship over thirty years before. In absolute silence, the poem 'Paris' was delivered directly to Antonia Fraser in the audience: "She dances in my life. / The whole day burns.'[56]

The response was tumultuous. Four days later, he won the Nobel Prize for Literature and was interviewed on the doorsteps of his London home. A cap worn at a jaunty angle half concealed a bandaged wound. It was the result of a nasty fall at Dublin Airport which resulted in four hours in hospital and nine stitches in his head. As he recalls: 'One moment I was enjoying life greatly after the most wonderful weekend that left me very moved. The next moment, I was flat out in hospital thinking that, with all my other illnesses, I was going to die.'[57] But the rumours of his death proved greatly exaggerated and he appeared on television on 14 October, bloodied but unbowed, to discuss his Nobel Prize. An oft-quoted phrase of Beckett's seems an apt way to conclude the highs (and lows) Pinter experienced on his seventy-fifth birthday in Dublin: 'I can't go on, I'll go on.'

NOTES

1. The first Pinter Festival ran from 2 to 21 May 1994 and featured productions of *Betrayal, Old Times, Moonlight, The Dumb Waiter, One for the Road* and *Landscape*. The second Pinter Festival ran from 7 to 27 April 1997 and featured productions of *The Collection, Ashes to Ashes, A Kind of Alaska* and *No Man's Land*. The third Pinter Festival ran from 30 September to 19 November 2005 and featured productions of *Old Times* and *Betrayal*; readings of *Family Voices* and *Celebration*; and *The Pinter Landscape*, a reading of poetry, prose and extracts from the plays.
2. Harold Pinter, *The Collection, Plays Two* (London: Faber, 1991), p. 108.
3. Michael Billington, *Harold Pinter* (London: Faber, 1996; rev. edn 2007), p. 36.
4. *Ibid.*
5. Harold Pinter, *Mac*, in *Various Voices: Prose, Poetry, Politics 1948–2005* (London: Faber, 2005), pp. 26–7.
6. Christopher Fitz-Simon, *The Boys: A Double Biography* (Dublin: Gill and Macmillan; London: Nick Hern Books, 1994), p. 16. 'The Boys' refers to MacLiammóir and Hilton Edwards, who co-founded Dublin's Gate Theatre in 1928.
7. Mel Gussow, *Conversations with Pinter* (London: Nick Hern Books, 1994), pp. 110–11.

8. Pinter, *The Collection, Plays Two*, p. 119.
9. Christopher Innes, *Modern British Drama: The Twentieth Century* (Cambridge: Cambridge University Press, 2002), p. 347.
10. Pinter, *Mac, Various Voices*, pp. 27–8.
11. Billington, *Harold Pinter*, p. 39.
12. Pinter, *The Homecoming, Plays Three*, pp. 16–17.
13. *Ibid.*, p. 17.
14. Billington, *Harold Pinter*, p. 43.
15. For a study which argues that the 1930s, 1940s and 1950s in Ireland were less culturally impoverished than has been assumed, see Brian Fallon, *An Age of Innocence: Irish Culture 1930–1960* (Dublin: Gill and Macmillan, 1998).
16. Cf. Pinter's statement to Mel Gussow: 'It was in 1949 when I started to read Beckett.' Gussow, *Conversations with Pinter*, p. 32.
17. Billington, *Harold Pinter*, p. 42.
18. Pinter, 'The Islands of Aran Seen from the Moher Cliffs', in *Collected Poems and Prose* (London: Faber, 1991), p. 13; see also Pinter, *Various Voices*, p. 129.
19. Pinter, 'The Irish Shape', in *Various Voices*, p. 135.
20. Billington, *Harold Pinter*, p. 43.
21. Pinter corrected the reference in his 1995 'Speech of Thanks' for the David Cohen British Literature Prize: 'in I think, 1951, [I] read an extract from Beckett's *Watt* in a magazine called *Irish Writing*'. See Pinter, *Various Voices*, p. 61.
22. The 'fragment of *Watt*' comprises pages 149–62 of the published novel, to the paragraph concluding 'that is perhaps something, perhaps something': Samuel Beckett, *Watt* (London: John Calder, 1963). The final page of the fragment published in *Irish Writing* does not appear in the published novel. It runs as follows:

> So we began, after so long a time, to walk together again, and to talk, from time to time.
> Continuing then, when he had told me all this, then he loosed my hands from his shoulders, and backwards through the hole went back, to his garden, and left me alone, with only my poor eyes to follow him, this last of many times to follow him, over the deep threshing shadows backwards stumbling, towards his habitation. And often he struck against the trunks of trees, and in the tangles of underwood caught his foot, and fell to the ground, on his back, on his face, on his side, or into a great clump of brambles, or of briars, or of thistles, or of nettles. But ever he picked himself up and unmurmuring went on, towards his habitation, until I saw him no more, but only the aspens, and the yews. And from the hidden pavilions, his and mine, where by this time dinner was preparing, the issuing smokes by the wind were blown, now far apart, but now together, mingled to vanish.

23. Beckett, *Watt*, p. 157.
24. Billington, *Harold Pinter*, p. 43.
25. Beckett, *Watt*, p. 154.
26. James Joyce, *A Portrait of the Artist as a Young Man* (Harmondsworth: Penguin, 1965), p. 205.
27. Pinter, *Landscape, Plays Three*, p. 175.
28. *Ibid.*, p. 187.
29. Samuel Beckett, *The Complete Dramatic Works* (London: Faber, 1986), p. 223.

30. Pinter, *Landscape*, p. 187.
31. Pinter, *Betrayal*, *Plays Four* (London: Faber, 1998), pp. 36–7.
32. Cf. Harry White in his article, 'Ireland and the Irish in Pinter', in Programme for The Pinter Festival, 2–21 May 1994: 'Yeats [is] the poet of betrayal above all others.' In addition to Yeats's presence in *Betrayal*, White also examines: the Irishman McCann in *The Birthday Party*; the discussion of the film *Odd Man Out* in *Old Times*; and Pinter's screenplay of Aidan Higgins's novel, *Langrishe, Go Down*.
33. *The Letters of W. B. Yeats*, ed. Allan Wade (New York: Macmillan, 1955), p. 633.
34. W. B. Yeats, *The Poems*, ed. Daniel Albright (London: J. M. Dent/Everyman, 1994), p. 227.
35. A crucial reference to Yeats occurs in the text of Pinter's 1971 play, *Old Times*, when Anna lays territorial claim to her old friend Kate by epitomising their earlier life in London thus: 'more often than not [we] sat up half the night reading Yeats'. Kate's husband Deeley responds to the challenge by remembering how he first met Kate at a screening of Carol Reed's film about a dying IRA man in Belfast, *Odd Man Out*. The Irish references emerging on both sides of the equation help create an aura of sexual and romantic contest. Harry White sees it as 'Pinter's use of Ireland as a vital trope for the past'('Ireland and the Irish in Pinter').
36. Pinter, *Betrayal*, p. 69.
37. *Ibid.*, p. 67.
38. *Ibid.*, p. 73.
39. *Ibid.*, p. 68.
40. *Ibid.*, p. 72.
41. W. B. Yeats, *A Vision* (London: Macmillan, 1937), p. 226.
42. *A Critical Edition of Yeats's 'A Vision'* (1925), ed. George Mills Harper and Walter Kelly Hood (London: Macmillan, 1978), p. 227.
43. Pinter, *Betrayal*, p. 41.
44. On this subject, see Katharine Worth, *The Irish Drama of Europe from Yeats to Beckett* (London: The Athlone Press, 1978).
45. Pinter, *Mountain Language*, *Plays Four*, p. 403.
46. Lady Gregory, *The Gaol Gate*, in *Selected Plays of Lady Gregory*, chosen and introduced by Mary FitzGerald (Gerrards Cross, Bucks.: Colin Smythe, 1983), p. 137.
47. *Ibid.*, p. 141.
48. *Ibid.*, p. 138.
49. Pinter, *Mountain Language*, p. 405.
50. *Ibid.*, p. 408.
51. Gregory, *Selected Plays*, p. 142.
52. Frank McGuinness, Introductory Address, on the occasion of the conferring of the degree of Doctor of Literature, *honoris causa*, on Harold Pinter, 16 June 2004, University College Dublin/National University of Ireland. Copy of the address supplied by the Conferring Unit, University College Dublin. This and the following quotation are from the address and are quoted with permission.
53. Harold Pinter, *'Celebration' and 'The Room'* (London: Faber, 2000), p. 66.
54. *Ibid.*, p. 28.
55. *Ibid.*, p. 72.
56. Pinter, *Various Voices*, p. 179.
57. Billington, *Harold Pinter*, p. 421.

13

JOHN STOKES

Pinter's late tapes

O Rocky Voice,
Shall we in that great night rejoice?
What do we know but that we face
One another in this place?
                                    W. B. Yeats, 'The Man and The Echo'.

I remember an unusually long silence before the performance began – a shared mood of anticipation, an extended moment for intellectual and emotional preparation – and then again when it was over, another long shared silence – time to recoup, absorb, and to wonder at what we had witnessed. Harold Pinter's season acting the main, the only, part in Beckett's *Krapp's Last Tape* ran for a mere ten performances at the Royal Court in October 2006 but it was destined for theatrical history from the moment it was announced: 'This man in this play at this time', as the critic of the *Times Literary Supplement* would put it.[1] He might have added 'in this place' as the Court was celebrating fifty years as the home of the English Stage Company.

When Pinter appeared in front of us it was clear just how much the recent illness had left its marks (as, no doubt, had its cure), molesting the face and impeding the body, all too fitting a Beckettian touch. Even the electric wheelchair was both a surprise (one hadn't, perhaps, realised the full implications of his illness) and a reminder of *Endgame*'s Hamm, of the kind of prop favoured by a playwright who was never afraid to make comedy out of disability. Not that there was much space for comedy now. Omitted from this production were not only Krapp's desperate pacing round his room, but the opening banana routine, the comically clumsy rewinding of the tape (Pinter simply used a second machine) and the songs. What remained was skeletal. Beckett himself once described Krapp in animalistic terms as being 'like a tiger in a cage' and 'a badger in his hole',[2] but Hildegard Bechtler's dusty set was almost a graveyard, more like a dead-letter office, a foul rag-and-bone shop of the heart.

Knowing what was expected of them the critics lived up to their responsibilities, worked hard to do justice to the terrible bravery that drove the writer to become an actor once more, and to point up, firmly but tactfully, the obvious parallels between his condition and this particular role:

The ravages of Pinter's battle with cancer are staring you in the face as he sits wheelchair-bound, and every word he speaks comes as from the grave, deep and rasping. The combination of frailty and tenacity is terribly moving. At one point, when the wind rattles the attic's shadowy window, he glances over his shoulder and you feel his mortal fear. At the same time you feel this man will give Death himself a fierce run for his money when he comes knocking.[3]

And again,

In the extraordinary opening moments, everything happens without words; little groans and coughs and puffs, all projected as effortlessly as if that lantern face was in close-up on a screen … He uses none of those baneful Beckettian trademarks – no wild hair and no whimsy – but brings to his delivery of the lines part of what his plays have brought to the theatre, a sardonic and delighted attention to everyday life. He makes the words 'dirty little rascal' sound unfathomably and unprecedentedly filthy; when he grooves on the word 'spool', he does so with a delight which seems to surprise himself as well as the audience. You often feel that you're suddenly seeing in three dimensions, as if two slides – a Beckett/Krapp and a Pinter – are being superimposed on each other.[4]

Michael Billington, the critic who because he is Pinter's trusted biographer knows him best, urged some caution, insisting that 'this is a performance, not an exercise in self-revelation'. Nevertheless,

At two precise moments, Pinter looks anxiously over his left shoulder into the darkness as if he felt death's presence in the room. This is the moment that will linger longest in the memory. It is impossible to dissociate Pinter's own recent encounters with mortality from that of the character … And the final irony of an unsparingly honest performance is that when Krapp talks of 'the fire in me now', it is followed by a long, agonised silence as a death-bell distantly tolls.[5]

Not that everyone approved of the bells in quite this way: 'If these interpolations suggest another world, they sentimentalise and diminish what Beckett wrote.' Untrue to Beckett meant untrue to Pinter: 'With Pinter in the part, now, it is about last things.'[6]

Pace Billington, few missed the moment when Krapp swept the tape boxes off the table in what looked like a burst of Pinterish rage, 'a last look back in anger'.[7]

The accident happens with such naturalness, it's as if a muscular spasm had occurred. It's followed by a volcano of wrath such as might have quelled Pinochet or Bush. The audience laugh – it looks for a minute as if Pinter has suddenly blasted his way out of Beckett and is using his own script – before recognising this as Beckett to the letter.[8]

14 Harold Pinter in Samuel Beckett's play *Krapp's Last Tape*, directed by Ian Rickson, Upstairs Theatre, Royal Court, 2006 © John Haynes / Lebrecht Music & Arts

As the play got underway it became clear how the arbitrarily imposed stop and start of the tape machine fractured sentences into units of meaning, leaving us with the compacted ambiguities of short phrases, a modernist technique that the two playwrights share. In a TV interview given in 2006 Pinter had said that the play's last line, 'I wouldn't want them back' is 'what's called irony'.[9] In performance he delivered the line in an unemphatic, almost anti-climactic, way which released the irony very slowly indeed. After all, what drew the younger Pinter to Beckett in the first place was that he didn't 'want philosophies, tracts, dogmas, creeds, way outs, truths, answers, nothing from the bargain basement'.[10] This performance certainly wasn't in the business of giving answers.

Ambiguities still lingered. Is it 'irony' that Krapp 'wouldn't want them back' because the false promise of youth has now been replaced by some kind of reality? Or is it that he wouldn't want them back because his life is now closer to its ending and he couldn't bear to start all over again? The *TLS* put the matter in reverse: 'Yet with each step forward, the resignation is harder, because less remains ahead ... Not wanting to go back is not quite the same as being glad that it is over.' Astoundingly, as if to underline that very point, Pinter did something entirely unexpected at the curtain. 'With a show of strength, he rises to his last legs and walks to the exit.'[11] There could have been no more painfully physical a representation of the battle between acceptance and resistance which so often accompanies the fact of mortality than that first and last walk from the stage.

And yet Pinter's Krapp was merely the latest professional appearance in an acting career that goes back over half a century. In the course of it he has frequently established close links between man and role, bringing something unmistakable whatever the occasion, whatever the play. Of course, his performances wouldn't have had such an impact had he not been so physically and vocally distinctive – and no one has caught that body language, interpreted those speaking gestures, better than his friend Simon Gray, the playwright whose work he has sometimes directed. Gray's published journals cover some twenty years between 1985 and the recent past. Already in the first volume Pinter is pictured as 'composed and powerful in black',[12] with the walk of 'a key figure in the Mafia or a prosperous undertaker'[13] who normally 'stands or sits bolt-upright'.[14] Throughout the journals Pinter's voice is usually somewhere to be heard: 'gravely muttering',[15] 'developing the husky rasp'.[16] Sometimes Gray hears within it mixed messages: 'His voice is naturally dark and gravelly, but here it was darker, gravellier, which gave his utterance a hint of ambiguity.'[17] Gray does more than recreate surface characteristics: he gives us inklings of how vocal tones and physical mannerisms betray underlying, if often contradictory, emotions. He writes of Pinter's 'boiling reasonableness'[18] and of his 'ferocious geniality'.[19] When Pinter recuperates after illness Gray notes him 'walking with a willed step … so bravely determined'; he registers the 'feeble but obstinate tread'[20] that whole audiences were to observe at the curtain of *Krapp's Last Tape*.

Isolation and risk are the twin conditions that Pinter habitually ascribes to the act of writing. 'The author stands alone on a sheer cliff', he has said. 'Others can sympathise, but none can share his unique brand of vertigo.'[21] This might equally well describe his own style of acting which has the same sort of edginess. Acting, as he has also said, 'is a precarious and testing activity'.[22] With both pursuits, writing and acting, the excitement is to do with not knowing what lies ahead and with an awful freedom. The effectiveness of acting is often said to depend upon what is withheld, but there are very few revealed facts in a Pinter play. There are instead mysteries, gaps, uncertainties, absences, emptinesses, possibilities, what the director Sam Mendes calls the 'secret play' that an actor may possibly know but need never disclose to the audience or even, in rehearsal, to his or her fellow actors.[23] Pinter's acting is without any obviously discernible subtext and it is essentially solitary – which is not say that the process that has brought it into being has not been collaborative or that solitary characters don't interact with others on their own terms.

Actors in a Pinter play need, therefore, to have an air of speculation, of the extempore, about them, need to be ready to take a verbal perambulation around the possibilities. They must sample and appreciate the opportunities for nostalgia, for humour, for threats. This doesn't necessarily make for a comfortable experience for the audience or for the other characters. 'I loved the innate brutality of this confrontation', Pinter remarked in 2007 about a workshopping of No Man's Land, comparing it implicitly with the classic, but more tightly controlled, rendering by Gielgud and Richardson.[24] Performance offers opportunities for cruelty and for bullying. When Gray first read Pinter's One for the Road in 1984 he was immediately struck by 'the ghastly richness of Harold's monster, the seemingly unmotivated switches of mood from bantering playfulness to self-righteous rage followed by a joke that he genuinely wants to share with whichever victim is immediately in his presence'.[25] The cliché may insist that all bullies are cowards, but this is far from the case in the theatre of Harold Pinter where bullies (and whole nations) are simply men who have reached a terrifying level of freedom.

What makes Gray an exceptionally good critic of Pinter the writer, as well as a dedicated chronicler of the man and his life, is not just that he is a fellow playwright but that he is very conscious of the differences between their two approaches. His own characters, he says, are kept 'on a tight rein', whereas Pinter's characters, 'though seemingly locked in habits and circumstances, always have an ultimate freedom from thisness and thatness which is likely to express itself in an aria of free-wheeling lunacy, sometimes comic, sometimes frightening, but never needing justification'.[26] 'Free-wheeling lunacy' has implications for the actor too.

Although Pinter's acting style has intensified in recent years, the element of danger appears to have been there from the start and it can even be seen and felt in his performances in work by other writers. His performance in a TV production of Huis Clos directed (by Philip Saville) in 1965 has something of the brooding sexiness of all those would-be British Brandos of the day such as Alan Bates, Richard Burton, Robert Shaw and Richard Harris. Indeed, the production as a whole marks a distinct cultural moment. It's filmed in black and white, of course, has a Miles Davis soundtrack and a spare, rather stylish, 'contemporary' setting far from the Second Empire paraphernalia that Sartre asked for. It is cool – and so, up to a point, is Harold Pinter. His shrugging delivery of 'Hell is other people' and 'well, let's get on with it' at the close is more English than French. Certain gestures or mannerisms noticeable then are still apparent forty years later. They already convey the uncertainty of the moment and the possibility of going in different directions. In Huis Clos we see the head set slightly to one side, the narrowing of the gaze, the stroking of the bottom lip. There are silences, of course, though at this early stage they are thoughtful rather than menacing: pacing not pausing. But already Pinter has developed the habit of putting certain words in quotation marks by slightly raising his voice – and the voice itself, though naturally lighter than today, is already unmistakable in its mixture of precision and portentousness.

Where does it come from, that carefully enunciated, sometimes actorish diction? A leftover from his otherwise highly unsatisfactory RADA training? Or is it local and indigenous, Hackney *hauteur*? It's certainly true that, as Dickens knew, East London speech (at least of previous generations) can be curiously correct. And Pinter can, when he wants to, turn on a much heavier Cockney style, especially now that his voice has become harsher, thicker. In 1997 he's entirely convincing as Sam Ross, the gay gangster in the film of Jez Butterworth's *Mojo* which is set in 1950s Soho. No trace of posh here, only soft-centred brutality; when, in blue silk dressing-gown, he leans over and asks a sexy teenage pop singer, 'What are yer, tickles or slaps, eh?', we know exactly what he intends. As Max, the aging father, in the radio broadcast of his own *The Homecoming* in 2007,[27] he's also satisfyingly crude. But Pinter is always especially good when there's a call to counter coarseness of expression with an attempt at social respectability. As Goldberg in the 1986 TV production of *The Birthday Party*, directed by Kenneth Ives, he's a *faux* English gentleman in cravat and blazer, a genial outgoing Jew respectful of his family, and a lady's man 'past fifty'. There is masculine swagger even in the buttoning and unbuttoning of his jacket and professional pride in the smoothing of his lapels – though the exact profession remains obscure. A hand, often the right one, opens in a seeming invitation that might easily become a demand; a finger points in a helpful but commanding way; by the end of the play the fist is occasionally clenched. These gestures say something about the dominant emotions but not necessarily how and why they might have originated.[28]

Since even Simon Gray (who is no actor) sometimes finds himself describing his own behaviour as Pinter-like ('I ... turned on my heel, Harold-style'),[29] it's not really very surprising that characters in recent revivals of Pinter's plays should have become increasingly like their creator. *That's Your Trouble*, a sketch in *Pinter's People*, a collection of revue sketches and other short pieces that the comedian Bill Bailey compiled at the Haymarket in 2007,[30] featured a Pinter lookalike in black clothes and dark glasses. Both male roles in a revival of *Betrayal* at the Donmar in the same year[31] were more vehement than in the previous productions, with Sam West as Robert, in particular, hinting at a violent potential. West's delivery with its repetitions, savourings and implicit underlinings of certain words had a recognisable air of tension and self-awareness. He may well, consciously or not, have felt an impulse to model himself on the author, born perhaps out of personal familiarity with the man. Somewhat earlier West had written an excellent piece for *The Guardian* on the experience of recording the radio production of *The Homecoming* with Pinter and of hosting a personal appearance in Sheffield. Pinter, he said, 'is terrifying as Max, and fairly terrifying as himself'.[32] Even in situations of polite personal encounter Pinter's presence, for all the warmth and geniality to which his friends frequently testify, can be worrying.

These and other revivals have been prompted not only by admiration and affection for a playwright now in his seventies and often in poor health, but by a recognition that what makes them classics is that they confront recurrent situations. Many productions have adopted a realistic or period style which makes the dramatic events seem simultaneously familiar and strange at the same time. The Sheffield Theatre's production of *The Caretaker* opened with the pizzicato sound of heavy rain which immediately justified the presence of that famously suspended bucket;[33] Hildegard Bechtler's set for the *The Hothouse*, which stretched deep into the Lyttleton's interior, was instantly recognisable in its institutional ugliness;[34] Peter Hall's production of *Old Times*[35] had a set all in brown, a colour fashionable in the early 1970s when the play was written (even if for one critic it was like watching 'three little people in a jar of Nescafé').[36] The compendium of sketches, *Pinter's People*, had a decidedly period production style with a music track based on the jazz of the late 1950s and early 1960s (bass playing by Charles Mingus and yet again muted trumpet in the manner of Miles Davis). *Betrayal* at the Donmar was likewise set in the 1960s or 1970s, evoking the décor of that early TV production of *Huis Clos*, although symbolically more adventurous. Gauzy white drapes delineated time as well as space, acting like veils of memory with specific dates projected upon them.

The days of baffled incomprehension are long past, replaced by a more knowing appreciation. As Lee Evans, star of *The Dumb Waiter* at the Trafalgar Studios,[37] remarked, the play was 'relevant in the present climate. It seems as though we're losing control. People live in fear, particularly in London, and we needn't. We're being told to be fearful of something, and I don't think that's very healthy. It's healthy for the people in charge, that's how they control us.'[38] A sense of the political 'elsewhere' that permeates the domestic 'here' can even be felt in the late squib *Apart from That* which, with its repeated tag-line of 'Are you all right?', is ostensibly about the banalities of mobile phone use, but hints at what is very much not 'all right', specifically perhaps the war in Iraq.

For whatever reason, the director of *Pinter's People* decided to fill out *Apart from That* with comic business by setting it in a hospital. A bed-ridden woman whose hand is in a sling fails to reach for the phone. A male patient linked up to a drip has similar problems: as he turns around the hospital garment he is wearing opens at the back to expose his bare behind. The verbal motif of 'losing you' is stressed to the utmost but without very great effect. In this instance, it was the sketch that lost its relevance; it had actually been more impressive when Pinter had read it with Rupert Graves as part of a television interview.[39] Fortunately, early sketches written in the 1950s and 1960s about the absurdities and frustrations of city life retained, even increased, their pertinence in 2007. This was especially true of *Victoria Station*, a farcical foreshadowing of urban paralysis. Themes of class (*Tess*) and of race (*Request Stop*) are also as recognisable as ever while the overtly political pieces such as *Press Conference* and *The New World Order* spoke directly to an audience conscious of wars in Afghanistan and Iraq and of the weasel words of governments. Realism and relevance apparently reached a far greater pitch, however, with the 'site specific' production of a collage of *The New World Order*, *Mountain Language* and *One for the Road*, staged in the Brighton Town Hall, again in 2007. This started in the Council Chamber but eventually moved to a lower level: 'As we descend into the building's labyrinthine depths, we witness the way the state's dirty work is conducted underground', wrote Michael Billington.[40]

Revivals don't simply reverse time so much as bring the past up to date whilst, at the same moment, returning us to an earlier period. By reorienting temporal processes they sometimes reduplicate structural possibilities within the text. 'That first last look in the shadows after all those in the light to come wrings the heart':[41] Samuel Beckett's response on first reading *Betrayal* (he must surely have been thinking of the last scene) confesses his awareness, professional and instinctive, of how theatrical narratives, although they have the formal ability to reverse and divert events, can never halt time's underlying, its inexorable, forward progress.

In a great performance a single exchange of looks can sometimes remind us of this generic truth, and sometimes that look is directed at an audience. When the critics faced Pinter in *Krapp's Last Tape* they found themselves, above all, subjected in return to Pinter's unique gaze. For some the look was directed beyond them at a distant empty place: 'He's a haggard, brooding, near-Gothic horror, his eyes in half-shadow glaring into the void with bitter rage.'[42] For at least one critic, though, it was much more close to home:

> An old-fashioned curtain fell away. There, on an almost bare, twilit stage, and fixing me, a mere six feet away, with a confident glare of his significant eyes, was Mr Pinter himself. He sat in a dressing-gown and an electric wheel-chair, at a desk on which stood tin boxes, an antique tape-recorder and a vast accounts book. Pinter said nothing – at some length. I lowered my eyes. I was too close for comfort.[43]

There is obviously a difference in perception here between the critic who sees Pinter gazing into a void and the critic who sees Pinter 'fixing me, a mere six feet away, with a confident glare of his significant eyes'. It's a difference, though, as much to do with Pinter's ambiguous presence as with the subjectivity of the individual.

Theoreticians often feel a need to stress the 'face to face' aspect of live theatre, of bodies – performer and spectator(s) – in close proximity to one another but occupying different spaces. This is never a simply reciprocal relationship but, as Alan Read has described it, one of 'disposition', meaning that it is unstable and provisional because it has as its essential precondition the presence of 'the other', whether mutually acknowledged or not.[44] As Pinter would seem to understand it, the relationship between performer and spectator, self and other, goes beyond even the 'dispositioned' being always potentially dangerous, combative. He says of his early days:

> I always thought acting was a kind of contest with the audience at that time. It was either them or us, you know. Who was in charge? And, to a certain extent, that has remained with me all my professional life in writing plays. That I had an idea of what would shut up an audience through being an actor. It hasn't always worked by the way. You can't regulate an audience. You can't tell an audience what to do. But you've got to keep your end up.[45]

Quite remarkably, Pinter's combative gaze, his glittering eye, has survived the transfer of the Royal Court performance of *Krapp's Last Tape* to a TV broadcast (and thereby to anyone who chose record it on tape or disc) and the dissemination of his Nobel acceptance speech on the internet (where it is available to anyone who cares to log on to the appropriate site). In these very different circumstances the 'face to face' encounter involves one face looking out at innumerable other faces without their being in the same, the 'real', time and place at all. It is, nonetheless, a two-sided affair in that the viewer can turn away, replay, pause, fast forward, close the website, or switch off altogether, while the viewed retains the authority of a kind of permanence or fixity, inviolate unless deliberately erased or allowed simply to decay – which can sometimes happen. Pinter's videoed performances are, in fact, palpable demonstrations of the postmodern realisation that live and recorded performances, rather than being the totally distinct entities that one might assume them to be, are closely intertwined – that what we assume to be permanently frozen records have their own temporal life and, conversely, that live occasions can actually gain immediacy and presence from the fact of their being recorded.[46]

The video of the Nobel speech appeared online before the TV broadcast of the Beckett performance. To watch the two recordings now is to become newly conscious of mortality and the passing of time, to experience a kind of *Krapp's Last Tape* of the video, and now digital, age. Viewing the Nobel film retrospectively, whilst the wheelchair and blanket may now look proto-Beckettian,

Pinter's brows seem quite bristly, his face almost healthily red, the bottom lip rather full. Relatively speaking, and in comparison with the later appearance in *Krapp*, this performance, for all the raggedness around the edge of the voice, comes over as a moment of great moral and physical assertion. In order to explore the abuses of political authority carried out by others Pinter has to draw upon his own full authority as a performer and in this he unquestionably succeeds. The achievement is reinforced by the presence of a blown-up photo of him as a younger man while simple camera movements move between profile and, for the greater part of the time, full face.

Of course, an acceptance speech is a performance of a different order from a dramatic role. And yet Pinter's Nobel address has some, if not all, of the qualities of his purely theatrical appearances. Delivered not from a podium but from a TV studio, the speech might easily have taken on the air of a desperate communication from an absent leader, a guerrilla leader even. The BBC foolishly compounded that risk by barely reporting or relaying the speech. Circumstances might therefore have conspired to make Pinter appear even more embattled than he actually was, and an occasion of public recognition, obscured by claims and counter-claims, turned into yet another row about media censorship. Thanks to technology, the delivery of the Nobel speech was not only a refusal to be silenced (politically or physically), it has remained a public performance.

There is a moment late on in his delivery when Pinter invokes the ways in which moral certainties, and by implication the tenets of fundamentalist religion, can work together to endorse state power. He does so in the theatrical style of those mock public speeches, more blatant even than the real thing, which reveal their underlying cynicism through a transparent display of supposed rationality. The pseudo speech runs from 'God is good. God is great. God is good' through to 'We are a great nation' and finally to 'You see this fist? This is my moral authority.'[47] Although he is making a similar political point Pinter traces a kind of reverse pattern to the 'Fugal Chorus' from Auden's *For the Time Being*:

> Great is Caesar: He has conquered Seven Kingdoms.
> The Seventh was the Kingdom of Popular Soul:
> Last night it was Order – Order, tonight it is Hear – Hear:
> When he says, You are happy, we laugh;
> When he says, You are wretched, we cry;
> When he says, It is true, everyone believes it;
> When he says, It is false, no one believes it;
> When he says, This is good, this is loved;
> When he says, That is bad, that is hated.
> Great is Caesar: God must be with Him.[48]

Auden's fascist authority is abstract, although inspired by the Caesar of the gospels; Pinter's implicit emperor is immediate, George Bush. This would seem to be a more straightforward target but it brings its own challenges. Rightly resisting the theatrical temptation to assume a full American accent Pinter, the experienced actor, implies inflections that are well known to any-one who listens to news broadcasts, creating the kind of parodic effect whereby one performance exposes the duplicities of another. As he had remarked earlier about Tony Blair: 'Blood is dirty. It dirties your shirt and tie when you're making a sincere speech on television.' The real corruption of the presidential speech lies in the fact that its ghost-writer, ventriloquised by Pinter, is at least half aware of his own manipulations.

The Nobel speech also contains some of those commonplace, slightly antiquated but still forceful phrases which are familiar from the plays and relished by actors: 'a man's man' (of the American president), 'It has to be faced, right here, on the spot', 'one fell swoop', 'a frozen silence', 'the greatest show on the road'. Pinter has always had a fascination with everyday idioms, with commonplace language whose effectiveness is borne out by its longevity. Gray records many such instances: 'stopped me dead in my tracks',[49] for example, and 'suddenly smote my forehead'.[50] Pinter's alertness to such phrases in conversation makes them newly contagious, reinforces their power. 'Sometimes when I talk to Harold I find myself using unfamiliar words and phrases. He liked this one, and repeated it. "Top-notch you say. That's terrific".'[51] Elsewhere Gray records rather similar moments when the process operates in reverse. 'Harold has a phrase that would cover my reaction to this, rather a dead phrase, actually, that nevertheless comes to such life in his mouth – "It took my breath away!" – I found myself saying, Harold style: "You've taken my breath away!"'[52]

Performers, including Pinter himself, can make much of these phrases because they are gestural and because they imply physicality. One in par-ticular resonates in the Nobel speech: '[The United States] puts its cards on the table without fear or favour'. The card-playing trope, which is repeated later, produces a powerfully evocative visual image. Ironically but tellingly, Gray records Pinter making exactly the same gesture when playing Bridge with his wife: 'Harold made a movement, an emphatic putting-down-a-card-take-that! kind of movement.'[53] In the context of the Nobel speech the favourite phrase implies not only the triumphalism of American politics but, recipro-cally, the competitive nature, the declarative frankness of Pinter in full oppo-sitional flow. As he delivers the Nobel speech typical hand gestures accompany his words: the half-clenched fist (fully clenched at the end when he becomes the brutal enemy), the indicative finger held slightly aloft, and the clasped hands of self-composure.

About halfway through, a transition from the art of the playwright to American imperialism and the current war in Iraq is marked by a pause, too easily described as Pinteresque, that may admit, or at least fail to conceal, an intellectual shift at this point. He had begun by going back to a statement he made nearly fifty years ago which has been much cited by academic critics ever since:

In 1958 I wrote the following:

'There are no hard distinctions between what is real and what is unreal, nor between what is true and what is false. A thing is not necessarily either true or false; it can be both true and false.'

I believe that these assertions still make sense and do still apply to the exploration of reality through art. So as a writer I stand by them but as a citizen I cannot. As a citizen I must ask: what is true? What is false?[54]

The development of the Nobel speech as a whole depends on this initial distinction between art, defined as relative, subjective, hypothetical at most, and politics, which are absolute and undeniable. Paradoxically enough, it is this distinction that has enabled Pinter (and his critics) to insist that his art has always been political since the freedoms of art, though undeniably real in themselves, are always accountable to the reality of actual experience.

When Gray commented on the 'seemingly unmotivated switches of mood' in *One for the Road* he went on to note that here was 'a study in the absolute power of someone who's gone beyond absolute corruption on to complete freedom of spirit. Which is complete vacancy'.[55] Not simply an insight into the technical demands that Pinter makes upon an actor, this takes us to the very heart of his performative ethics. 'Complete vacancy' implies an absence of all moral values amid an infinity of possibilities. It is this terrifying void that Pinter counters in his Nobel speech and he does so by contrasting the contingency of plays with the fixity of political morality. The politics to which Pinter has always been opposed are invariably based upon false certainties such as 'God is good' – which is not to say that no certainties exist at all.

There's an extraordinary moment at the very end of the speech:

When we look into a mirror we think the image that confronts us is accurate. But move a millimetre and the image changes. We are actually looking at a never-ending range of reflections. But sometimes a writer has to smash the mirror – for it is on the other side of that mirror that the truth stares at us.[56]

Not 'discard' the mirror or 'turn away' from it, we should note, but, typically, to *smash* it, to make a gesture of violent affirmation. And, as we should also register, to have the truth then stare back at you. In Pinter's view to see beyond yourself is to go beyond theatre, a salutary fact for all who admire his art. When he says that 'theatre raises our consciousness of the lives we actually lead'[57] he means our awareness of what we too often ignore or deny about the world which theatre represents.

It is so obviously a truism that theatre distorts and refracts the world that much theatre (even the theatre of Samuel Beckett) acknowledges and pre-empts accusations of reflective falsity by incorporating them within its own processes, by exposing illusionistic techniques. Pinter's take on this has always been unusual: his theatre has never been anti-illusionist because it has never seriously toyed with illusion in the first place. It is rather a theatre of formal and existential freedom, at liberty to go wherever it pleases. But this solipsistic and relativistic freedom is dangerous. It can be wilfully ignorant and mindlessly cruel. It can even offer the kind of 'vacancy' that fascism feeds upon and so, sometimes, it must be rejected, smashed, to let the facts stand revealed. That is why in these, his late tapes, Pinter goes beyond acting and becomes ineradicable.

NOTES

1. Jim McCue, *Times Literary Supplement*, 20 October 2006.
2. The phrases are quoted by Susannah Clapp in her *Observer* review, 22 October 2006. They originate in a letter from Beckett to Rick Cluchey and the San Quentin Drama Workshop in 1977. See Dougald McMillan and Martha Fehsenfeld, *Beckett in the Theatre*, vol. 1, *From 'Waiting for Godot' to 'Krapp's Last Tape'* (London: John Calder; New York: Riverrun Press, 1988), p. 298.
3. Kate Bassett, *Independent on Sunday*, 22 October 2006.
4. Clapp, *Observer*.
5. Michael Billington, *Guardian*, 16 October 2006.
6. McCue, *TLS*.
7. Nicholas de Jongh, *Evening Standard*, 16 October 2006.
8. Clapp, *Observer*.
9. Interview with Kirsty Wark, BBC 2, *Newsnight*, 23 June 2006.
10. Harold Pinter, *Various Voices: Prose, Poetry, Politics 1948–2005* (London: Faber, 2005), p. 45.
11. McCue, *TLS*.
12. Simon Gray, *An Unnatural Pursuit* (London: Faber, 1985), p. 87.
13. *Ibid.*, p. 62.
14. *Ibid.*, p. 56.
15. *Ibid.*, p. 76.
16. Simon Gray, *Enter a Fox* (London: Faber, 2001), p. 42.
17. Simon Gray, *Fat Chance* (London: Faber, 1995), pp. 69–70.
18. Gray, *An Unnatural Pursuit*, p. 126.
19. *Ibid.*, p. 159.
20. Simon Gray, *The Smoking Diaries* (London: Granta, 2004), p. 94.
21. Harold Pinter, Foreword, to Gray, *An Unnatural Pursuit*, p. 15.
22. *Newsnight* interview.

23. Sam Mendes interview in Ian Smith, *Pinter in the Theatre* (London: Nick Hern Books, 2005), pp. 218–30, p. 220.
24. *Working with Pinter*, Channel 4, 26 February 2007.
25. Gray, *An Unnatural Pursuit*, p. 54.
26. *Ibid.*, p. 41.
27. Radio 3, 18 March 2007.
28. Richard Cave describes the 'body language' that is inscribed in Pinter's plays and productions in chapter 8 of this volume.
29. Simon Gray, *The Year of the Jouncer* (London: Granta, 2006), p. 169.
30. Haymarket Theatre, 1 February 2007.
31. Donmar Warehouse, 31 May 2007.
32. *Guardian*, 17 March 2007.
33. The production opened on 11 October 2006 at the Crucible Theatre in Sheffield and later moved to the Tricycle Theatre in Kilburn.
34. Lyttelton Theatre, 18 July 2007.
35. Opened at the Theatre Royal, Bath, in April 2007 and then toured.
36. Rhoda Koenig, *Independent on Sunday*, 15 April 2007.
37. Opened 2 February 2007.
38. *Guardian*, 22 January 2007.
39. *Newsnight* interview.
40. *Guardian*, 16 May 2007.
41. Programme note to *Betrayal*, Donmar Warehouse.
42. Bassett, *Independent on Sunday*.
43. De Jongh, *Standard*.
44. Alan Read, *Theatre and Everyday Life* (London and New York: Routledge, 1993), p. 91. Also see ibid., p. 153. These ideas have been extended and developed in interesting ways by Nicholas Ridout in *Stage Fright, Animals and Other Theatrical Problems* (Cambridge: Cambridge University Press, 2006), especially pp. 70–1.
45. *Working with Pinter*.
46. See Philip Auslander, *Liveness: Performance in a Mediatized Culture* (London: Routledge, 1999).
47. *Guardian*, 8 December 2005.
48. III Fugal Chorus, 'For the Time Being', in W. H. Auden, *Collected Poems* (London: Faber, 2007), p. 373.
49. Gray, *An Unnatural Pursuit*, p. 69.
50. *Ibid.*, p. 139.
51. Gray, *Year of the Jouncer*, p. 43.
52. Gray, *Enter a Fox*, p. 86.
53. Gray, *Year of the Jouncer*, p. 282.
54. *Guardian*, 8 December 2005.
55. Gray, *An Unnatural Pursuit*, p. 54.
56. *Guardian*, 8 December 2005.
57. *Working with Pinter*.

Reactions to Pinter

14

DREW MILNE

Pinter's sexual politics

Introduction: delimiting 'the political'

Pinter's theatre is a theatre of images involving domestic violence, territorial struggles and linguistic conflict. As the conflictual range of responses indicates, the dramatic syntax of these images remains paratactic, both generically and linguistically, difficult to articulate as tragicomedy or through the existing grammar of social relations. Events and relationships are framed within socially intelligible and dramatically 'powerful' situations in ways which resist the dramatic conventions of naturalism or realism. The tension between rhetoric and grammar enables a figurative diversity of conversation which has come to seem recognisably 'Pinteresque', a comically pregnant moment of conversation which dwells in a menacingly tragic absence of social recognition. The enigmatic particularity of dramatic images is both a principle of dramatic construction in Pinter's work and a key dynamic in performance. Precise theatrical presentation makes it difficult to describe or narrate the suggestive power of these images in non-dramatic or non-theatrical terms. As Pinter himself put it: 'To supply an explicit moral tag to an evolving and compulsive dramatic image seems to me facile, impertinent and dishonest.'[1] To interpret his plays symbolically or allegorically also does violence to Pinter's precise art. But to the extent that his images generate metaphors of more general concerns, they need to be considered as socio-political representations of power.

Based principally on *The Birthday Party*, *The Caretaker* and *The Homecoming*, Pinter's reputation was fostered in opposition to the forms of political theatre which emerged in the 1950s and persisted into the 1970s. Many British playwrights of this period were socialists, engaged in theatre as a political forum. Among Pinter's attractions for the critical establishment was the way his work appeared to scorn such approaches and could be seen as the continuation of dramatic art as something above and beyond politics. Recent critical discussions, above all since *One for the Road* (1984), have revised such perceptions of the apolitical quality of Pinter's plays. *One for the*

Road suggested a new political emphasis on the use and abuse of power. Early plays such as *The Birthday Party*, *The Dumb Waiter* and *The Hothouse* now appear more evidently political. Questions nevertheless remain as to the political specificity of Pinter's work.

One for the Road: political revisionism and formal negativity

In an interview published with *One for the Road*, Pinter suggests that his earlier plays, far from being apolitical, worked as political metaphors, implicitly critical of the abuse of authority. He claims, significantly, that *One for the Road* is not itself a metaphor.[2] Many of Pinter's sketches, such as 'Applicant', involve processes of physical and mental torture which can be seen to underlie longer plays such as *The Dumb Waiter* or *The Hothouse*. Pinter nevertheless claims that the metaphorical situations of torture in his earlier work have become more explicitly factual: 'The facts that *One for the Road* refers to are facts that I wish the audience to know about, to recognise.'[3] The play, however, remains elusive about geopolitical contexts which locate 'facts' about the use of torture. Political ambiguity is revealed by the way Nicolas uses cricket metaphors. This suggests English contexts, not least cricket as a favoured idiom of the English civil service. But intimations of a totalitarian regime do not invite readings of the play in relation to political torture in the north of Ireland. Pinter's indifference to political specificity is confirmed by comments in the same interview: 'militarily, this country [i.e. Britain] is as much a satellite of America as Czechoslovakia is of Russia. Now the terms are not quite the same but the structures are the same. The relationships aren't quite the same, but so what ...'[4] This is hardly an illuminating factual basis for political theatre. It is doubtful whether conflicts in Pinter's work can be distilled as political 'facts'. Rather, his plays generate new kinds of ambiguity in relations between dramatic situations and the abstract framing of political 'facts'.

Pinter's authorial revisionism nevertheless displaces his earlier quasi-Beckettian mode of modernist dissidence, exemplified by his claim that: 'I'm not committed as a writer, in the usual sense of the term, either religiously or politically. And I'm not conscious of any particular social function.'[5] Despite refusing specific commitments, Pinter insisted on a kind of abstracted realism in his work: 'I'm convinced that what happens in my plays could happen anywhere, at any time, in any place, although the events may seem unfamiliar at first glance. If you press me for a definition, I'd say that what goes on in my plays is realistic, but what I'm doing is not realism.'[6] Ambiguity of realistic content without contextual significance is held together by a theatricality which foregrounds language and power.

Pinter's plays remain enigmatic and indeterminate compared with the political specificity usually associated with political drama. Political drama has conventionally dramatised conflicts as metonyms of more general concerns, using metonyms to represent social contradictions so that they can be understood politically or, more often, socially. Pinter's images undermine such conventions and modes of representation. Read as tragicomedies of misrecognition, his plays seem determined to resist the familiar terms of political recognition. The interpretative movement from part to whole continually breaks down, turns aside or reveals new twists in the games of misrecognition so artfully played by Pinter's characters.

Audiences often project the authorial intentionality of the playwright or the director, but divergent audience response is constitutive of theatre. The specific indeterminacy of meaning in Pinter's plays is achieved through the negation of inferred, naturalist subtexts, a process which nevertheless depends on naturalist conventions for its intelligibility. Apparent openness to different kinds of interpretation works to exclude naturalist interpretations focused on socio-political intelligibility. The negative dependence on naturalism works in turn to resist non-naturalist interpretations appropriate for symbolist or allegorical plays. In Raymond Williams's provocative formulation, Pinter's domestication of modernist dramatic idioms constitutes 'a naturalism at once confirmed and emptied of content'.[7] Power is shown to depend on gestures and turns of phrase which are characterised as being of local but unrepresentative significance. Pinter's persistent interest in the English language as it is used in London, for example, inhibits generalisations about such idioms as metonyms of London politics, while nevertheless provoking speculations about the limits of local political frames.

Attempts to contextualise local idioms in more universal terms reveal a gulf between specificity and abstractions of the political. *Mountain Language*, for example, addresses the suppression of ethnic minorities, in particular their language, in a play advertised as a parable about torture and the fate of the Kurdish people. Turkish politics may have prompted the play, but the desire to read this into the play is confounded by the play's details. Abstract moral pathos can be inferred and then generalised, but any more politically nuanced understanding of nationalist politics and language would need to consider English as a global and imperial language involved in comparable processes. Resistance to political contextualisation extends beyond authorial statements to the formal negation of contextless and site-specific art. Pinter's concrete images suggest that the language of political abstraction needs to be resisted and that this resistance to politics is political.

The politics of speech acts: language games as power-plays

The wit with which Pinter observes the cut and thrust of conversation provides no comfortable meta-language with which to describe the politics of everyday life. Even the attempt to categorise relationships in Pinter's plays somehow misses the sense of situation and on-going redefinition that forces analysis to address moments of language in use. Often the status of friends, relatives and enemies is precisely what characters cannot quite control or confirm. In such dynamics, the illumination of dead metaphors can be used not to reanimate speech, but as a threatening form of violent or comic literalism, as in *The Homecoming* when a character appears to refuse the norms of conversational implicature:

> MAX: When Dad died he said to me, Max, look after your brothers. That's exactly what he said to me.
> SAM: How could he say that when he was dead?
> MAX: What?
> SAM: How could he speak if he was dead?[8]

The comedy trope of the double-act highlights a peculiarity in Max's speech. But given that Sam is Max's brother, recognition of motivations behind his 'witty' deflection suggests a more sinister resistance to conversational recognition. Their 'relationship' in the play hinges on the accumulation of such moments, right through to Sam's last-gasp 'revelation' in his final line. Dramatic wit plays with the deadness of conventions which motivate the dramatic relation between speech habits and psychology. Apparently innocent structures of conversational implicature are dramatised as coercive moments of misrecognition with no comfortable rules for dialogue or negotiation, either for the characters or for the audience. Beyond a formal concern with language games and speech acts, the plays show desires at work in this kind of formal concern. Rather than formalising a drama of speech acts, Pinter offers something more like a Wittgensteinian interest in disabusing believers in the context-free truth of words. It becomes no less tricky to maintain belief in the ability to ascribe internal psychological states or private languages of intentionality.

Pinter's stylised dialogue often involves a grim humour that relishes the dark sensuality of the demotic. While this is one of the pleasures of Pinter's work, the tenor is to show how all language games are implicated in assertions of power. Context almost invariably reflects badly on pleasures of linguistic precision. Many of his more violent and unpleasant characters have a penchant for the twisted or punctured idiom, often in the strategic use of obscenity. In *The New World Order* (1991) Des provides an uncharacteristically explicit account of such precision, an account which then implies a converse suspicion as to the authoritarian mindset involved.

> DES: You called him a cunt last time. Now you call him a prick. How many times do I have to tell you? You've got to learn to define your terms and stick to

them. You can't call him a cunt in one breath and a prick in the next. The terms
are mutually contradictory. You'd lose face in any linguistic discussion group,
take my tip.[9]

This kind of reversal is significant, not least in the violence of gender confusion
in distinguishing 'cunt' and 'prick'. The obscenity of both terms reflects indifference to biological accuracy and to civility. As a politics of language abuse,
the obvious implication is an insistence on a kind of linguistic hygiene, but such
moments of reversal undermine the implied moral high ground. Formal dexterity with speech acts is not to be taken simply as a virtue. The dramatisation of
such micro-politics of power nevertheless risks confirming a generalised ni-
hilism rather than articulating struggles for recognition, freedom and justice.
There are few signs in Pinter's plays of progressive resolutions which might
suggest how language could be used truthfully rather than abused in some
eternal recurrence of the will to power. Whatever the wit of Pinter's observation
of conversation, the plays show no mercy to wit's complicity with violent
evasions of good-humoured discussion or argument. The conditions of formal
possibility are dramatised to make 'wit' a critical question about forms of
power in the performance of language. Herein lies the necessity of Pinter's
interest in dramatic form rather than representational narrative.

From politics to sexual politics: between metaphor and metonymy

Pinter's politics might then be compared with the anti-enlightenment and
anti-representational analyses of power associated with Friedrich Nietzsche
or Michel Foucault, analyses which remain profoundly sceptical about political progress. The political instability of Nietzschean dissidence might help
to explain why Pinter's work remains politically awkward. Pinter's public
pronouncements suggest more conventional liberal concerns regarding justice
and human rights, though his hostility to America and its support for various
right-wing regimes has brought him close to socialist positions. The separ-
ation of art and politics is a disabling legacy of cold war aestheticism of which
Pinter has become increasingly critical. Pinter's use of his status as a writer is
more the public conscience of an active citizen than a continuation of his
dramatic work by other means. His plays nevertheless continue to show a
marked reluctance to move beyond pessimistic analyses of the abuse of
power. As Ruby Cohn has suggested: 'it is by his bitter dramas of *de*human-
ization that he implies "the importance of humanity"'.[10] If Pinter's 'political'
drama amounts to more than a negatively implied humanism, it is through the
micro-politics of dramatic form. The difficulty of moving beyond micro-
politics to a politics of the personal unhinges the political generalisations of

humanism's supposed gender neutrality. The human condition is not male. Perhaps unintentionally, Pinter's predominant focus on male characters reveals conflicts of sexual difference as the micro-politics of social being.

Understanding Pinter's images politically involves articulating these images both concretely and as metaphors, metaphors whose representative qualities are indirect and resonant rather than realistic or explicit. Two distinct phases of Pinter's work – from *The Birthday Party* to *The Homecoming* and from *One for the Road* to *Ashes to Ashes* – can be read as dramatisations of violent and authoritarian forces. But political contextualisation requires more than recognising opposition to authoritarian language use as a generalised 'political' theme. Distinctions need to be drawn to explain the contexts out of which these plays were first written and might now be performed, and to explain why Pinter's plays for so long seemed apolitical. Retrospective politicisation of Pinter's work also has pitfalls. A politically nuanced reading needs to recognise how some plays – such as *No Man's Land* and *Betrayal* – might have no great political significance and might be distorted by insisting otherwise. There are Proustian intimations of the disturbances of family memory in plays such as *Family Voices*, *A Kind of Alaska* and *Moonlight* which are misconstrued if their lyrical meditations are too quickly collapsed into political representations.

The sequence of supposedly political plays from *One for the Road* to *Party Time*, however, raises a number of questions as to the purposes behind Pinter's persistent dramatisation of misogyny. These plays seem designed to make admirers of Pinter's work uncomfortable by confronting audiences and readers with the politics of complacency and cynicism that coexist with the global realities of torture and oppression. Scenes of explicit violence in these plays seem designed, moreover, to show how the political abuse of power is not abstract or metaphorical but part of the micro-politics of everyday life. The abuse of metaphor itself is often a condition of physical and verbal violence in Pinter's plays. Particular metaphors are shown as metonyms of the micro-political language games of power. This critical oscillation between metaphor and metonymy begins to specify the difficulty of describing the politics of sexual politics in Pinter's work.

The tortuous incivility of Nicolas's interrogations in *One for the Road* involves a structural imbalance in the treatment of male and female victims. The savage parody of male camaraderie Nicolas inflicts on Victor extends to a series of obscene references to his wife, Gila. Gila is the victim of unseen terrors, including rape, but her interrogation proceeds not through the insinuations of male bonding, but through a brutal oscillation of obscenity and patriarchal misogyny. The play's concluding confrontation between Nicolas and Victor leaves Gila as an object in Nicolas's grotesque account of the 'brothel' in which she appears to have been raped. In *Mountain Language* women are again subjected to physical and verbal abuse. The action is ambiguous, but a young woman is seen being made to prostitute herself to the military, apparently to save a male prisoner, a sacrifice which silences the elderly mother more effectively than the brute force of military bullies. In *The New World Order* the tortured male victim is again subjected to obscene misogynist discussions of what the torturers will do to his wife. In *Party Time* the stage is dominated by sexist men who silence the questions of their wives regarding the 'round-up' proceeding offstage. Misogyny is also projected through two female characters who engage in obscene character assassinations of a 'nymphomaniac slut' also described as a 'bigtitted tart'.[11] The dominant currency of violence in these plays is misogynist abuse and connections between rape, prostitution and female submission. Analysis is repeatedly forced to confront unspeakable logics, but such repetitions exceed the justifications suggested by more explicitly political frames.

The focus on male authoritarianism in these 'political' plays provides only mute or submissive forms of resistance. Political realities are drawn on only to be aestheticised in a dramaturgy of sadistic power games which blocks analysis of the contexts metaphorically evoked. Without a more politically articulate critique of patriarchal power, Pinter's representation of male power games risks celebrating misogynist wit, offering a training school in forms of everyday authoritarianism that defeats the imagination. Greater dramatic resourcefulness is given to those who abuse power. The devil's party seems stronger and more compelling. It might be insisted that the plays are symptomatic of realities with which we are complacently complicit. But by precluding analysis of such realities as socially specific metonyms, Pinter's metaphorical displacement of reality into power games reveals an ideological faultline in the metonymic status of misogyny. The difference between understanding struggles between men and women as individual or human concerns comes into conflict with the interpretations of such relationships as micropolitical metaphors. This begins to specify the politics of sexual politics in Pinter's work.

Looking back in anger: dramatising misogyny

In a society in which the power of the image is politically significant, not least through the commodification of sexuality, Pinter's dramatic images have a poetic quality which resists political mediation. These images often depend, however, on the assumption of male perspectives whose structural blindspots form the basis of unrecognised political exclusions. Many of Pinter's plays concern male-centred perspectives focused on struggles of male bonding and female exclusion, themes which can be traced back to Pinter's semi-autobiographical novel *The Dwarfs*. This does not make the plays inherently misogynist. At issue is the critical dramatisation of the abuse of power. Drama's 'objectivity' as a collective and public form reveals gendered perspectives subsumed within objectivity. Where the structure of Pinter's plays excludes a political understanding of women's agency then the status of women as objects of abuse, fear and desire is not simply objective. This is all the more significant where misogynist structures of representation become generalised metaphors for the abuse of power. Unacknowledged structures of misogyny motivate the oscillation between metaphor and misogyny in Pinter's plays, and this becomes the condition of possibility for Pinter's dramatisation of sexual politics.

The need to specify dramatic form is revealed by Pinter's poem 'American Football'. In a short essay about this poem, 'Blowing up the Media', Pinter discusses how the poem's outspoken combination of politics and obscenity was a response to the 'triumphalism, the *machismo*, the victory parades' that accompanied the 'end' of the Gulf War: 'This poem uses obscene words to describe obscene acts and obscene attitudes.'[12] The poem, however, risks reproducing the obscenity it hopes to criticise. The final lines read:

> Praise the Lord for all good things.
> We blew their balls into shards of dust,
> Into shards of fucking dust.
> We did it.
> Now I want you to come over here and kiss me on the mouth.[13]

Insofar as the poem makes more than a punk gesture of spleen against the media consensus celebrating the USA, it is through the movement from the 'we' to the 'I' in the final line. But without the social context of utterance provided by dramatic form the crude analogy between football and war depends on its own kind of macho irony or sarcasm. This is only 'powerful' to the extent that Pinter is willing – as an expression of political anger – to lend his authorial voice to the obscene use of the lyric first-person voice of poetry. Said in a play, the politics of the line could be deployed differently.

The expression of protest through male anger suggests long-term affinities between Pinter and the so-called angry young men of 1950s drama. The gestures of the poem 'American Football' bear comparison with the final lines of Pinter's first published poem 'New Year in the Midlands' (1950): 'Watch / How luminous hands / Unpin the town's genitals – / Young men and old / With the beetle glance, / The crawing brass whores, the clamping / Red-shirted boy, ragefull, thudding his cage.'[14] While his early poems bear comparisons with poets such as Dylan Thomas, W. S. Graham and George

Barker, Pinter's shift from poetry to drama might be seen as a way of controlling confused impulses which otherwise vitiate the often inarticulate anger of British drama in the late 1950s.[15] Usually within shifts in class politics, the explicit drama in such plays often focuses on gender conflicts: all too often, the enemy in sight is a wife or girlfriend. As Raymond Williams argues in relation to Pinter:

> What was present as an intense disturbance in Strindberg, and again often in Lawrence, has hardened to something that is taken for granted, and that commonly resists explanation … what is characteristic about the abuse of women is that it is in pseudo-critical terms; not a fusion, but a displacement … To an ordinary kind of sexual disturbance, something is added: the disturbance as metaphor.[16]

The confusion of class and gender in the pervasive influence of Lawrence is symptomatic of the late 1950s and early 1960s. Strindberg, perhaps most notably in *The Father*, suggests how dramatisation of male–female conflicts might be developed against the grain of Ibsen's proto-feminist realism to naturalise structures of misogyny. Strindberg's misogynist sexual politics remain provocative, but the micro-political dynamics of power are structured around the absence of the struggles for freedom and self-consciousness dramatised by Ibsen. The *unheimlich* in the drama of Ibsen and Strindberg is often dramatised to think the unthinkable thought of the family itself as the repressive force which makes the home unhomely. Pinter's plays offer a more mute and claustrophobic account of the room as a scene of unhomely conflicts between individuals. Pinter shares the characteristic displacement of anti-Establishment impulses into disturbed sexual politics developed by other angry young male dramatists, but has perhaps a more awkward sense of misogyny within the post-Lawrentian sensibilities of the 1950s and 1960s.

In whatever genre, political metaphors generated out of dramatisations of male rage and violence, however ironic, need to articulate political connections between macho language and patriarchal power. In an opinion piece entitled 'Oh, Superman' broadcast in 1990, Pinter claims that: 'US foreign policy can still be defined as "kiss my ass or I'll kick your head in". But of course it doesn't put it like that. It talks of "low intensity conflict".' He describes the situation as one of 'disease at the very centre of language, so that language becomes a permanent masquerade, a tapestry of lies'.[17] Pinter suggests that 'we' are obliged to develop an intense critical scrutiny of the way we use language. And yet without a theory of the micro-politics of language, Pinter's own description of US foreign policy remains rhetorical and politically inarticulate.

Pinter's recent politics continue to engage with a critique of male violence and authoritarianism which has its roots in the drama written by men in the

1950s and 60s, drama which often used violence to shock bourgeois audience complacency. Notoriously in plays such as Edward Bond's *Saved* and *Lear*, violence is portrayed as part of what Bond called an 'aggro-effect', in a kind of crude Brechtian estrangement. This use of sex and violence has persisted in the work of many socialist playwrights, notably in the work of Howard Brenton and Howard Barker, but the shock-effect of male violence often vitiates political analysis in favour of inarticulate provocations. The critical task is to specify the political connections involved in moving beyond the inarticulacy of male anger. In this sense, Pinter's work can be understood as a long-term and indirect displacement of the class struggles of the 1950s, struggles displaced by dramatic forms which relied on unacknowledged structures of misogyny. This could be traced from Pinter's work on screenplays such as *The Servant* to his interest in David Mamet's play *Oleanna*, which he directed in London, and his admiration for the sexually violent work of Sarah Kane.

The Homecoming: misogyny as critical reception

The awkward status of misogyny is confirmed by reconsidering Pinter's critical reception before political revisionism emerged in Pinter studies. Martin Esslin's influential reading of Pinter sought to legitimate the displacement of politics into poetic images. Comparing *The Room* or *The Dumb Waiter* with *The Birthday Party* he states the contradiction between realism and poetic metaphor as though it were resolved in the latter: 'The situation which forms the starting point for the action is far more realistically treated, at least in its tangible, external detail, and thus acquires considerably greater power as a poetic metaphor.'[18] This approach relies on a highly selective sense of the relevant level of interpretative detail. Complicity with political stereotyping is revealed, for example, by Esslin's description of McCann as 'the brutal Irish terrorist'.[19] More significant is Esslin's use of psychoanalysis: 'Meg, with her crushing combination of motherliness and senile eroticism, is a mother-image seen from the viewpoint of an Oedipus complex ...'[20] The structural principle at work here is to see the female characters in *The Birthday Party* as projected facets of the male protagonist. Stanley's attempts to strangle Meg and rape Lulu are then figured as: 'the same, immensely complex, immensely relevant, and immensely *true* poetic metaphor for a basic human situation, an existential archetype embodied in a play like *The Birthday Party*'.[21] Similarly, Esslin reads the dramatisation of a misogynist nightmare in *A Night Out* as 'an elegant and subtle set of variations on the theme of man's confrontation with aspects of the feminine principle'.[22]

As such, these plays offer either a metaphorically critical relation to the violence represented, or an aesthetically stylised legitimation of violence as a dramatic form of ambiguity. This is not an either/or which admits its complicity with what is portrayed. Rather, according to Esslin:

> The ambivalence of our social selves, the coexistence in all of us of the primeval, amoral, instinct-dominated sensual being on the one hand, and the tamed, regulated social conformist on the other, is one of the dominant themes of Pinter's writing: above all the oscillation of the image of woman between that of mother/madonna/housewife and that of the whore/maenad.[23]

The most complicated exemplification of such patriarchal stereotyping is *The Homecoming*. The play has generated wildly divergent interpretations, not least through the tension between naturalist subtexts and more metaphorical or poetic possibilities. For Esslin the play achieves 'the perfect fusion of extreme realism with the quality of an archetypal dream image of wish fulfilment'.[24] But whose wishes are fulfilled? Ruth's acquiescence as the working mother, sexual provider and prostitute for a group of sadistic and misogynist men might fulfil the wishes of this profoundly dysfunctional 'family'. But does the play provide any basis for generalising the play as an image of family life? Esslin goes so far as to claim that 'The very ease with which Ruth is persuaded to take up a life of prostitution and to become a readily available sexual partner for Joey and Lenny seems, if the play is seen as a dreamlike myth, the most natural thing of all …'[25]

Even where productions of the play attempt to make this seem 'natural' this has not been evident to audiences. Esslin's own account reveals the difficulty in portraying the role of Ruth with any sense of active, proto-feminist agency:

> the character of Ruth *must* be a passive one: she is the object of male desires and, being an image in a dream, yields to these desires without putting up any resistance. Yet the play must also function on the realistic level; and here Pinter's success in making Ruth a credible character even when seen as a real person and not just the passive object of archetypal desires, is a virtuoso achievement.[26]

This is particularly revealing as an account of the structural misogyny at work in the play. As a projection of a male misogyny, the credible absence of convincing psychological intentionality with which to motivate Ruth becomes a virtuoso achievement in the mystification of patriarchal fantasy. Esslin's 1990 review of a recent production congratulates the actress playing Ruth for leaving it open 'whether deep down she is an omnivorous nymphomaniac or a frigid iceblock, a potential prostitute from an excess, or from a total absence, of sexual appetite'.[27] It is difficult to perform Ruth as a positive image of female self-determination, since her power depends on her recognition and confirmation of the misogynist fantasy within which she is forced to perform.

Other critics suggest that *The Homecoming* offers a choice between seeing the play as a Strindbergian meditation on the misogynist nightmare of the whore/mother stereotype, or as an Ibsenite dramatisation of a woman asserting her independence in a modern doll's house of female exploitation. Elizabeth Sakellaridou, for example, suggests that: 'By agreeing to satisfy the household's sexual needs (while driving a hard bargain and remaining a "tease"), Ruth also gains a paradoxical independence, since by becoming a whore she is able to break free from the straitjacket of the philosopher's lowly wife.'[28] The freedom of the whore is an unlikely feminist revision of the critique of bourgeois marriage as a property relation which legalises prostitution. Attempting to resist such a critique, Sakellaridou's supposedly feminist reading confirms the terms of Esslin's conflation of metaphor and realism: 'Ruth's centrality does not yield only a strong archetypal figure of the Earth Mother or the Bitch-Goddess, operating on a mythic and ritualistic level alone – as many critics believe – but also a very interesting realistic female character ...'[29] Sakellaridou even suggests that Ruth speaks with authority and self-confidence, to the extent that she blends 'the two polarities of mother and whore into one harmonious whole'.[30]

Whereas Esslin highlights the structural passivity of Ruth as an object, Sakellaridou's emphasis on Ruth's rational self-determination makes her acquiescence to misogynist structures into a positive image. What emerges from the accounts of both Esslin and Sakellaridou is how the play's form undermines the possibility of interpreting the image in positive terms without making significant concessions to implicitly misogynist structures of identity. The dramatisation of male paranoia could be traced back to Strindberg and the passive centrality of Lulu in Wedekind's *Pandora's Box*, and beyond that to the fear of powerful women in Greek tragedy. The violence of the domestic homecoming could in turn be traced back to the patriarchal ambiguities of Aeschylus' *Oresteia*. Pinter, however, uses the central female character as an enigmatic and implausible sphinx around which to create a web of misogynist bonding and political economy, but without the metaphysical theodicy of sexual difference through which Greek tragedy makes such questions critical.

'Kiss my fist': sex, gender and politics in *Ashes to Ashes*

The metaphorical resonance of sexual politics in Pinter's dramatic images can be approached retrospectively through his recent play *Ashes to Ashes* (1996). Less overtly political than his work after *One for the Road*, *Ashes to Ashes*, along with *Moonlight*, appears to return to more private conflicts of desire and memory. Conflicts of language nevertheless dramatise micro-political implications in male–female relationships.

Ashes to Ashes revolves around the description and enactment of a physical and linguistic gesture. This combination of action and word is introduced by Rebecca at the beginning of the play. She tells Devlin, her interlocutor, how an unnamed man would stand over her, clench his fist: 'And then he'd put his other hand on my neck and grip it and bring my head towards him. His fist ... grazed my mouth. And he'd say, "Kiss my fist".'[31] Rebecca narrates how she kissed his fist, then the palm of his opened hand: 'I said, "Put your hand round my throat." I murmured it through his hand, as I was kissing it, but he heard my voice, he heard it through his hand, he felt my voice in his hand, he heard it there.'[32] Although more is said by Rebecca, the described moment remains ambiguous and darkly suggestive. Descriptive precision makes the underlying motivation all the more imprecise and resistant to psychologisation.

Although there are some contextual indicators, notably that the play is set in the present, a lightness of contextual suggestion was evident in the production directed by Pinter. Rebecca might be telling Devlin about a former or current lover, or she might be narrating a dream, an imagined or desired experience, perhaps even a moment from a film or book. The mental and physical relationships between the two central characters remain in a critical and unstable state. Towards the end of the play, the actions and words that make up the opening gesture are repeated but with important variations. Devlin clenches his fist and asks Rebecca to 'Kiss my fist.' When she does not move, he instructs her: 'Speak. Say it. Say "Put your hand round my throat."'[33] But she does not speak or move. The transfer of power is ambiguous. Devlin seems to fail to take the place of the man narrated, imagined or desired by Rebecca. But the way he touches Rebecca motivates the context of Rebecca's final narration, as if his actions extract a confession from her, though this might also be her way of torturing him.

The movement from a described combination of word and action to the enactment of this combination dramatises 'kiss my fist' as a speech act. The play suggests intentionalities which might motivate this as an act between two specific dramatic characters. Context, however, remains suggestive rather than naturalised or realistic. The play's central speech act acquires a metaphorical resonance which invites reflection on the experiential and social contexts which make such gestures intelligible. As a representation the play is metaphorical, offering an image of dramatic power that can be understood as a metonym of the more general mediation of power in society. If 'kiss my fist' is read as a private drama of sexual desire, then the image works as a metaphor for physical violence and sexual desire within patriarchal heterosexuality. The image resonates as a metaphor for the male-dominated structures through which authoritarian masculinity is desired or rejected by women. If the speech act is understood as a less sexual and more explicitly political drama, then the image works as a metonym for the language of authoritarian male domination. The difficulty of distinguishing physical and sexual abuse comes into focus if 'kiss my fist' is understood as a metaphor or a metonym.

Within the framing of gesture in *Ashes to Ashes* the fist remains male, while female response to the gesture is varied. Rebeccca takes issue with Devlin's assumption that the man she describes tried to murder her by suffocating and strangling her, suggesting instead that he felt compassion for her and adored her. The play thus flirts with the misogynist commonplace that women love to be dominated, while showing how Rebecca uses this to undermine and disorient Devlin. In a reversal familiar from *A Slight Ache* and *The Lover*, the play dramatises sexual role-plays between Rebecca and Devlin, but there are structural imbalances in the roles available. The most profound disturbance seems to come from the idea of women accepting the role of whore and then demanding to be recognised as such. The whore seems to persist as a dramatic trope throughout Pinter's work, but the reasons for this remain ambiguous. Either these dramatic forms of misogyny are understood as particular pathologies of misrecognition and perverted sexual fantasy, or as structural generalisations about the disturbing assumptions of power in male–female relationships. Either way, male-defined power remains structural.

Rebecca's desire for authoritarian male power is projected through her chillingly disjointed story of a man who 'used to go to the local railway station and walk down the platform and tear all the babies from the arms of their screaming mothers'.[34] Michael Billington provides a political context for this by claiming that such images in the play came from Pinter's reading of Gitta Sereny's biography of Albert Speer.[35] Billington reads the play as a perverted love story and as an evocation of the cruelty of state power: 'Pinter is not writing specifically about the Nazis, but about the umbilical connection between the kind of sexual Fascism so graphically described in the opening scene and its political counterpart; about a world of brute masculine power and naked submission.'[36] The difficulty, however, is the extent to which connections between the personal and the political are 'umbilical', either in Pinter's play or in reality.

In an interview discussing the politics of *Ashes to Ashes*, Pinter concedes that he thinks that men are more brutal than women, and that his plays express a male point of view. He also explains that he wrote *Ashes to Ashes* out of the 'images and horror of man's inhumanity to man' which have haunted him since the end of the Second World War.[37] Contradictions between masculinity and humanism are evident here. The script of *Ashes to Ashes* indicates that both Devlin and Rebecca are in their 'forties' and thus born after 1945. The play thus dramatises the way holocaust imagery haunts subsequent generations. The imaginative juxtaposition of holocaust 'memories' with female desire for misogynist authoritarianism nevertheless leaves political responsibility disturbingly ambiguous. Critical judgment of the broader political implications and responsibilities of desire is further complicated by performance dynamics. Power between male and female actors can be performed as a gendered structure or as a more temporary process in which power shifts moment by moment. Whatever the qualities brought to the play by individual actors, dramatic tension between the actors seems necessary to sustain the play. The unexplained 'echo' of the final section breaks down any naturalist basis on which to motivate this tension. Tensions between implications and suggestion structure ambiguities in which audiences have to engage their own perspectives.

Ashes to Ashes remains prismatic, a generator of politically indeterminate interpretations which highlight the gendered assumptions of audiences, but without providing terms by which different perspectives could be judged. This confirms the structural gulf between politics and sexual politics in Pinter's work as a whole. The movement from power as a dramatic structure to an understanding of how power relations might be interpreted as political metaphors remains incomplete. However resourceful, Pinter's plays remain complicit with the misogynist structures of sexual difference through which power is reproduced. The violence of torture and the exposure of authoritarian desire provide a critique of power which falls short of political articulation. Pinter nevertheless dramatises particular forms of the abuse of power in language. The structural blind-spots of these forms are most apparent in the misogyny which determines his drama's spoken and unspoken conditions of possibility. But it remains an important question whether the structural blind-spots of sexual difference can be overcome politically.

NOTES

1. Harold Pinter, 'On *The Birthday Party* II' (1958), *Various Voices: Prose, Poetry, Politics 1948–1998* (London: Faber, 1998), p. 18.
2. Harold Pinter, 'A Play and its Politics: A Conversation between Harold Pinter and Nicholas Hern', *One for the Road* (London: Methuen, 1985), pp. 7–8.
3. *Ibid.*, p. 11.
4. *Ibid.*, pp. 21–2.
5. Harold Pinter, 'Writing for Myself' (1961), *Plays Two* (London: Faber, 1996), p. x.
6. *Ibid.*, p. ix.
7. Raymond Williams, *Drama from Ibsen to Brecht* (Harmondsworth: Penguin, 1968), p. 374.
8. Pinter, *The Homecoming, Plays Three* (London: Faber, 1997), p. 37.
9. Pinter, *The New World Order, Plays Four* (London: Faber, 1998), p. 275.

10. Ruby Cohn, 'The World of Harold Pinter' (1962), in *Harold Pinter: 'The Birthday Party', 'The Caretaker', and 'The Homecoming'*, ed. M. Scott (London: Macmillan education, 1986), p. 25.
11. Pinter, *Party Time, Plays Four*, p. 290.
12. Pinter, *Various Voices*, p. 217.
13. *Ibid.*, p. 182.
14. *Ibid.*, p. 132.
15. See, for example, Michelene Wandor, *Carry on, Understudies: Theatre and Sexual Politics* (London:Routledge, 1986); and Lynne Segal, 'Look Back in Anger: Men in the 50s', in *Male Order: Unwrapping Masculinity*, ed. R. Chapman and J. Rutherford (London: Lawrence & Wishart, 1988).
16. Williams, *Drama from Ibsen to Brecht*, pp. 368–9.
17. Pinter, *Various Voices*, pp. 212–13.
18. Martin Esslin, *Pinter: The Playwright*, 4th edn (London:Methuen, 1982), p. 80.
19. *Ibid.*, p. 82.
20. *Ibid.*, p. 88.
21. *Ibid.*, p. 90.
22. *Ibid.*, p. 98.
23. *Ibid.*, p. 140.
24. *Ibid.*, p. 154.
25. *Ibid.*, p. 159.
26. *Ibid.*, p. 160.
27. Martin Esslin, '*The Homecoming* Reviewed', in *The Pinter Review*, ed. Francis Gillen and Steven H. Gale (Tampa, FL: University of Tampa Press, 1990), pp. 88–91.
28. Elizabeth Sakellaridou, *Pinter's Female Portraits: A Study of Female Characters in the Plays of Harold Pinter* (London: Macmillan, 1988), p. 69.
29. *Ibid.*, p. 107.
30. *Ibid.*, p. 109.
31. Pinter, *Ashes to Ashes, Plays Four*, p. 395.
32. *Ibid.*, p. 396.
33. *Ibid.*, p. 428.
34. *Ibid.*, pp. 406–7.
35. Michael Billington, *The Life and Work of Harold Pinter* (London: Faber, 1996), p. 374.
36. *Ibid.*, p. 377.
37. Pinter, *Various Voices*, p. 80.

15

YAEL ZARHY-LEVO

Pinter and the critics

> To a great extent my public image is one that's been cultivated by the press.
> That's the Harold Pinter they choose to create.
>
> (Interview with Stephen Moss, 4 September 1999, in *The Guardian*)

In this chapter I deal with a particular public image of Harold Pinter – that of Pinter as playwright. This image was first constructed by the press, and specifically by theatre reviewers, in the early phases of Pinter's writing career, and has since been further cultivated by the reviewers in the later phases of his career. Pinter, however, while well aware of the reviewers' construct of his dramatic work, does not appear to have remained passive in the face of it. Rather, he has chosen a unique response, seemingly collaborative at first, but ultimately trapping the critics in their own confined space.

In this overview of Pinter's career, presenting the 'Pinter' construct on the one hand, and the playwright's mode(s) of response on the other, I have chosen to focus on three highlights: first, the consolidation of the construct throughout Pinter's process of acceptance by the critical community and his 'semi-collaborative' response; second, Pinter's unpredictable poetic move, manifested by his mid-career play *A Kind of Alaska*, and the reviewers' response in this case; and third, Pinter's late play *Ashes to Ashes*, the culmination of his overtly political plays and yet another mode of poetic response to the critics, together with the critical reaction it elicited. This chapter examines in particular the London productions of Pinter's plays, and consequently the reviews appearing in the London press.

The reviewers' conduct in the case of Pinter exemplifies the tactics of criticism in general. Elsewhere I have suggested that theatre reviewers can be perceived as institutional agents with regard to a new theatrical product.[1] Serving as mediators, endowed with institutional authority, one particular function of reviewers in the theatrical field entails providing an initial 'legitimation' for playwrights whose acceptance into the theatrical canon has not yet been determined. Throughout the reception process of a new playwright the reviewers seek to meet two major conditions: to find an affiliation for the new dramatist; and, once affiliation is achieved, to embark on a strategy of promotion. The strategy of promotion is designed to market the playwright's particular means of theatrical expression, resulting in the emergence of a dramatic construct as an integral part of the

249

reception of any new playwright, and as such is not unique to Pinter. However, the components and process of forming the construct differ in each case.

The process of Pinter's initial critical reception can be seen as comprising three major phases: the unfavourable responses to his first professionally produced play, *The Birthday Party*, in 1958; the altered critical perceptions that emerged between 1959 and 1964; and the third phase, from 1964 to 1965, that culminated in his admission into the theatrical canon.

Four major strategies[2] are employed by reviewers during the reception process of a new playwright. Use of the first strategy – comparison – can be perceived as legitimising a new play by comparing or affiliating it to already-established forms of drama. Whereas the critical means to affiliate consist in references to the past, the second strategy – forecasting – can be perceived as a critical marketing tactic that incorporates reference to the future.[3] Use of the second strategy thus aims to achieve legitimation of the playwright through presenting the new play as a promise of future dramatic achievement, possibly even as a potential paradigm.

With respect to the paradigm, the forecasting strategy is linked to a third strategy, employed in some cases – that of name-giving. The latter serves a constitutive function by supplying a reference point.[4] The new and unfamiliar dramatic product is thus assigned a label by the critics that is perceived as referring to a set of given attributes. The fourth strategy – formation of a package of attributes – characterises the new dramatist's work. In the early stage of reception the reviewers devise an initial package, which is subsequently formulated into the playwright construct, comprising an aggregation of the traits recurring in the works that typify the dramatist in terms of influences and innovation. This construct is seen as the dramatist's trademark, serving the reviewers to further market the plays and the playwright. Formulation of the playwright construct is essential in facilitating the critics' function as mediators, which is to make the work accessible and locate the dramatist within the perceived overall theatrical tradition.

The first London production of a Pinter play, *The Birthday Party* (19 May 1958), was attacked and rejected by most reviewers to such an extent that the play was taken off after only a week's run.[5] The reviews reflected the critics' difficulty in identifying its dramatic style or in associating this with any established dramatic model. In their attempt to locate the play, in terms of influences or affiliation, within the framework of British or European theatrical traditions, the reviewers compared it to Ibsen's plays on the one hand, and to those of Osborne, Beckett and Ionesco on the other.[6] But Pinter's play, which at that stage did not fit any existing classification or meet the familiar and accepted theatrical criteria, was pronounced by the reviewers obscure, delirious, oblique, enigmatic and puzzling,[7] and dismissed as a theatrical failure.

One influential drama critic, Harold Hobson of *The Sunday Times*, did voice his support of Pinter's theatrical talent, but his review was published too late to save the fate of the production.[8] Hobson employed the same strategy of comparison as that of the other critics, but in order to prove an opposite contention. He compared Pinter to several dramatists whose first works had also received unfavourable, or even scandalised notices, such as Beckett, Shaw and Ibsen. Acknowledging himself to be alone in his conviction of Pinter's talent, Hobson presented the critical rejection of Pinter's first play as a sign of the dramatist's genius. He prophesied that, although such bad notices might influence the box office in the short term, Pinter's dramatic talent, as in the cases of his great predecessors, would eventually be recognised by the other critics. Hobson's means to promote Pinter's first play illustrate the use of two of the above-noted basic strategies employed by reviewers when encountering new dramatists: namely, comparison and forecasting.

In contrast to their reviews of Pinter's first play, the reception of the next two stage productions of Pinter's plays – the revue sketches *Trouble in the Works* and *The Black and White* (in *One to Another*, 15 July 1959) and the plays *The Dumb Waiter* and *The Room* (Hampstead Theatre Club, 21 January 1960, transferred to the Royal Court Theatre 8 March 1960) – reflected a shift in critical perception. The reviewers repeatedly pointed to a certain resemblance to established works or the influence of such works, especially Beckett's.[9] This shift in perception of Pinter's plays was marked by yet another issue, that of his 'puzzling' dramatic style. Perceived previously as the major flaw of *The Birthday Party*, it now became attributed to his originality.[10] The reviews following the production of *The Caretaker* (27 April 1960) addressed the issue of Pinter's 'puzzling' style in accordance with this altered perspective. The enigmatic style was now presented as this drama's main source of attraction.[11] Pinter was praised for his unique ability to 'create a world of his own, an entirely personal world, and he compels a desire in his public to penetrate it': 'effortlessly he produces atmosphere at once puzzling, dramatic, and charged with fascination'.[12] This second phase saw the beginning of the reviewers' marketing of Pinter to the public, presenting him as offering a unique and enigmatic theatrical style.[13] What contributed to this gradual acceptance of his drama were the influences that the reviewers alleged they had traced in his plays to accepted theatrical models.[14]

The process of critical acceptance entails two oppositional tendencies: a presentation of the recognisable and an introduction of the original. Contradictory in nature, the two tendencies become reconciled during the phases of a playwright's acceptance. Pinter's drama, having become affiliated with established theatrical models, thus became part of a historical sequence. Yet his theatrical language has been presented by the reviewers as decodable only up to a certain point. While seen as a chapter in the theatrical tradition, at the same time his enigmatic image seems to have been preserved by the reviewers in order to secure their presentation of his innovation.

The reviews of *The Caretaker* described the play as 'an unmistakable hit'.[15] A few reviewers even went as far as presenting Pinter's dramatic work as a source of pride and a major contribution to the development of British drama,[16] an ironic reversal of their initial rejection of the local talent. Many compared Pinter to Beckett and Ionesco, apparently suggesting that Pinter could be regarded as a British representative of the European avant-garde. This comparison might have contributed to Martin Esslin's decision to promote Pinter from the margins to the centre in the updated third edition of his book, *The Theatre of the Absurd* (1980), presenting him as a major Absurd playwright. Esslin's promotion, in turn, contributed to Pinter's later establishment as a British absurdist.

Thus, the inexplicable quality of Pinter's dramas, used by the critics to justify their initial rejection, served subsequently as their means for marketing his work to the public, and eventually became his trademark. In line with their policy of arousing curiosity about Pinter's plays, the reviewers, apparently encouraged by the dramatist's own conduct,[17] presented Pinter himself as an enigmatic figure.

Indeed, the dramatist employed a very intricate approach when speaking of his own work, simultaneously collaborating with and manipulating his addressees. One of the earliest press exposures – a talk delivered by the playwright at the Seventh National Student Drama Festival (Bristol, 1962), printed in the *Sunday Times* (4 March 1962) exemplifies this approach. Pinter did not supply explanations;[18] rather, he presented the inexplicable quality of his works as rooted in his ideology and perception of life. Furthermore, he expressed his view of language, proposing to alter the norms by which language spoken on stage is judged. He called attention to the central role of dialogue in his plays, while providing, implicitly, an alternative to the epithet 'puzzling': namely, the term 'ambiguous', which suggests a more positive evaluation of the dialogue. He thus manipulated his addressees towards valuing the language spoken in his plays for its ambiguous quality, rather than perceiving it as deviant, and hence puzzling. Pinter's implicit proposal to change the contract between audience and playwright can be seen as an active step designed to influence and shape the reception of his own plays.

The influence of Pinter's self-description on subsequent reviews is apparent in the critical responses to the production of *The Lover* and *The Dwarfs* (18 September 1963). The reviews are loaded with the critics' cumulative impressions of Pinter's previous plays on the one hand, and the dramatist's own views, as displayed in *The Sunday Times*, on the other.[19] The shift that marks these reviews is reflected in the dominance of the issue of dialogue, which seems to have occupied most reviewers, presumably partially as a result of Pinter's particular attention to this subject when speaking of his own work.

It is significant that during the transitional period (especially 1959–61) new plays by Pinter were broadcast both on television and radio. Perceiving these years as constituting the turn in his career in Britain takes into account the favourable critical reception of his work outside Britain (in the United States, for example), for Pinter's international acclaim seems to have contributed to his critical acceptance in Britain. Moreover, the international and British prizes awarded to Pinter's work during the years of the second phase reflect the growing recognition of his unique contribution as a dramatist and screenwriter.[20]

The reviews of the revival of *The Birthday Party* (18 June 1964), six years after its first London production, can be seen to mark the third phase of Pinter's critical reception. The reviews demonstrated the critics' general approval of the play, their reduced need to compare it to accepted theatrical models, and their particular praise of Pinter's 'gift for dialogue'.[21] The reviewers were now ready to recognise Pinter's plays as an original contribution to British drama. This is further confirmed by their choice of the 'package of attributes', which served as a marketing strategy. At this point Pinter's drama was presented to the public under the label 'Pinteresque'.[22] This label, which exemplifies the strategy of name-giving, can be perceived as the final version of the epithet 'puzzling', attached previously to Pinter's dramatic work. Its use marks Pinter's acceptance, in reflecting the reviewers' assumption that from now on Pinter's plays could be marketed under a 'Pinter' label, detached from the association with Beckett. This label seems to have functioned as a substitute for clarification of the 'incoherent' elements, thereby familiarising Pinter's unique style, the unfamiliarity of which had led to his initial rejection.[23]

The reviews of Pinter's next play, *The Homecoming* (3 June 1965), indicate the completion of the process of the dramatist's admission into the theatrical canon. Although the critical reactions to the play were not wholly favourable, and the majority of the reviewers expressed reservations, they nonetheless recognised and acknowledged Pinter's dramatic talent.[24] The general tendency reflected a borrowing from the critical repertoire of previous reviews. The reviewers either chose to treat, in various combinations, the different 'Pinteresque' aspects of the play,[25] or made explicit references to the familiarity of those aspects and/or attributes that had been mentioned and commented on in earlier reviews.[26]

The critics' choice to exploit the existing critical repertoire, rather than adding innovations, or altering their previous attitudes, indicates that their repertoire regarding this playwright was – for the time being – complete. By this point a critical consensus had emerged on the following issues: first, Pinter's association or affiliation with specific dramatic figures (especially Beckett); second, Pinter's place in the context of British drama and the European dramatic tradition; and third, the characteristics of his dramatic and directing style, which had been given a specific label (Pinteresque). By this stage a well-defined 'Pinter' construct had come into being, based on the augmented critical repertoire. Now stored for future use, this critical construct had evolved from the initial package of attributes allotted to Pinter in the early perceptions of his plays, in the phases leading up to his acceptance. The construct comprised attributes that were either stamped explicitly or associated implicitly with the label 'Pinteresque'. The reviewers' frequent use of this label reflected their implicit agreement regarding the distinctive attributes of his dramatic work.[27] Moreover, this construct implied the reviewers' recognition of the new dramatic norms that had come to be associated with Pinter's work. The term 'Pinteresque' thus functioned not only as shorthand for certain agreed-upon dramatic attributes, but also as a signifier of new dramatic norms, which both drew on and expanded the existing repertoire of theatrical modes. Although Pinter's work was still being perceived as enigmatic, its presentation was now descriptive in nature rather than suggesting 'abnormality'. Subsequently, Pinter's style was presented as a dramatic paradigm, serving the reviewers during their reception process of new playwrights.[28]

The reviewers' active involvement with a playwright's career, however, does not terminate once the latter is admitted into the theatrical canon. In the later stages of such a career the reviewers seek to ensure the dramatist's position in the theatrical canon, thereby reconfirming and reinforcing their own authority within the theatrical field. The reviewers, reacting to the new plays, will tend to affirm the now established playwright's image as previously constructed. The playwright thus seems to acquire a critical existence that belongs to the critics who had created his or her construct.

In light of the above, any established playwright who goes on to write a play apparently incompatible with his/her previous works, seems to challenge the constructed image and consequently the particular critical criteria by which he or she had been judged.[29] Pinter's mid-career play *A Kind of Alaska* exemplifies this case.[30]

A Kind of Alaska, produced in London in 1982,[31] surprised the critics. The play depicts a woman, Deborah, who had fallen victim to the sleeping sickness (encephalitis lethargica). She is awakened twenty-nine years later by a drug (L-Dopa) injected by the doctor who has taken care of her all these years, and is now married to her sister. The play centres on Deborah's awakening. Pinter acknowledges a specific literary source (Oliver Sacks's *Awakenings*, 1973),[32] thereby supplying a context within which one can, or should, grasp the unusual situation depicted.

In light of the medical condition, that is, a woman who has been asleep throughout the years of her maturation, neither the dialogue nor the characters' motivation appears enigmatic, but rather evokes the audience's understanding and sympathy. Although Deborah's awakening into a different world and her realisation of her own physical transformation elicit questions relating to forms of adjustment and human interactions in general, the particular situation depicted in the play appears coherent rather than puzzling. In *A Kind of Alaska*, therefore, Pinter, having executed an unexpected move, seems to challenge the image that had been attached to his dramatic work by the critics during the process of his establishment. In this play, I would suggest, Pinter ventured to free himself from the confinement of the reviewers' construct.

The reviewers, it appears, endorsed the playwright's unexpected move. Most reviews were highly favourable. The critics' puzzled attitude towards Pinter's poetics, which had come to dictate their marketing strategy throughout the process of his acceptance, seemed to vanish utterly when they encountered *A Kind of Alaska*. It is as though, to their great relief, 'Pinter-land' had finally ceased to be obscure.[33] Following this production Pinter was presented as an engaged playwright whose play offers human concern; and no longer a playwright who portrays 'an entirely personal world'.[34] The majority of the reviewers referred to the literary source of the play, Sacks's highly popular book (based on medical phenomena) that had aroused a wide public interest.[35] Wardle, for instance, claimed that Pinter's new play 'shows him breaking into new ground. Most unusually for this author, the play comes with an explanatory programme note citing a literary source.'[36] Or as Morley commented: 'instead of harking back to past triumphs', *A Kind of Alaska* suggests 'that Pinter is in fact now moving forward into some altogether new direction. In the first place, and extremely unusually for him, the play is derived from a book, and a book of medical fact.'[37]

Although the reviewers' attitude to Pinter's 'deviant' play reflected a critical eagerness to draw attention to the new and different image of the enigmatic playwright, it did not relate specifically to the theatrical components on which the new image was based. Caught by surprise by the nature of the play, the reviewers were at a loss: the previous Pinter construct was not compatible with the playwright's new work, yet they did not have a ready-made alternative. The reviewers thus embraced, simultaneously, a critical mode that welcomed the abandonment of enigma while striving, in light of the play's seemingly anomalous nature, also to devise an emergency mode that would not endanger their authority with respect to the playwright's image. Consequently, they chose to highlight the reference to the literary source (Sacks) as the play's major 'anomalous' feature, suppressing, or rather avoiding, a direct consideration of the other, more radically different dramatic attributes.

Striking evidence for this claim can be found in the reviewers' selective treatment of the literary source. None, excluding Nightingale,[38] mentioned Sacks's particular case history of Rose R.,[39] which is most probably the one on which the play is based. None of the reviews, including Nightingale's, related to Pinter's specific choice to base his play on this particular case history rather than on another (Sacks's book consists of several cases, of both men and women). Moreover, the reviewers, while repeatedly acknowledging the literary source, neither mentioned nor discussed Pinter's changes to the source data. These changes are quite significant: unlike Deborah (the awakened woman in the play) who was sixteen years old when she fell victim to sleeping sickness, Rose was twenty-one years old. Whereas Deborah's awakening occurs after twenty-nine years when she is forty-five years old, Rose's awakening occurred after forty-three years when she was sixty-four. Furthermore, recalling the passive conduct of the princess in 'The Sleeping Beauty' fairy tale, Deborah's attempt to confront the implications of her situation, in Pinter's play, suggests an independent and autonomous female figure, which corresponds to a more contemporary view of women. Relating to Pinter's particular decision to base his play on Rose's case, as well as to his fictional or differing 'data', would have required from the reviewers a consideration of new issues (such as the possible influence of a feminist approach) that were 'foreign' to the established critical repertoire concerning Pinter's plays.[40]

The policy of promotion adopted by the reviewers in the case of *Alaska* can thus be perceived as a defence tactic. Avoiding any direct treatment of the play's novelty, the reviewers employed modified applications of the two major strategies of comparison and forecasting. Comparing *Alaska* to Pinter's previous works, however, the reviewers related primarily to the absence of the familiar Pinteresque attributes. The use of this strategy served simultaneously as a retrospective affirmation of earlier critical assertions, and as a confirmation of the reviewers' continuing role as the authoritative force in determining the playwright's image. The reviewers' modification of the strategy of forecasting marked the new play by the established playwright as a turning point, thereby shifting dominance from the particularities of the play in question to the broader implications concerning future changes in the playwright's poetics.[41] To discern and proclaim a change in an established playwright's poetics can be viewed as assisting the reviewers to further enhance their marketing of that playwright, and so to reinforce his canonical position.

The reviewers' reaction to the play's revival, in 1985,[42] further attests to the selective nature of their criticism.[43] From the reviews of the two productions, it appears that the reviewers – rather than extending their critical repertoire – adjusted the existing repertoire to meet their (then) current needs. Since their discourse was restricted to the existing repertoire, the critical means available to them were in fact incongruous with the emergent requirement: a direct critical consideration of the playwright's unpredicted poetic move. Consequently, the reviewers seem to have devised a form of modification that served to disguise their critical repertoire's restricted nature, while simultaneously ensuring their own authority. In other words, the reviewers – rather than opening up and enlarging their repertoire, or freeing the 'rebellious' playwright, as suggested by Almansi and Henderson[44] – actually reclaimed his unpredictable move as further corroboration of their own powers in the field.

Following *A Kind of Alaska*, Pinter, seemingly adhering to the reviewers' prophecy, moved 'forward into some altogether new direction'.[45] His revue sketch *Precisely* (18 December 1983) and especially his play *One for the Road* (13 March 1984), were regarded as his 'self-proclaimed début as a political writer'.[46] Scholarly studies published through the 1990s suggested that Pinter's development as a playwright consists of two major and distinct phases: his early and mid-career phase (1958–82), and his later 'political' phase (1983–91).[47] Martin Esslin, a proponent of this view, refers to this distinction, claiming:

> Whereas all his previous work was enigmatic, multilayered, relying on pauses, silences, and a subtext of far greater importance than what was actually being said, these later pieces operate unambiguously on the surface, even relying on voice-overs to make characters' thoughts crystal clear and proclaiming a message of blinding simplicity, a message which is a call to political action.[48]

With regard to Pinter's later drama, the critical view, represented by Esslin's claim, seems to correspond with the playwright's own statements, such as those expressed in his interviews with Mel Gussow and with Nicholas Hern,[49] in which he acknowledges a change of objective towards a more explicit politics of commitment.[50] Esslin's comment exemplifies the critical perception as to the major difference between the two phases of Pinter's writing with respect to the nature of the represented domain and to the degree of explicitness. Whereas the early/mid-career phase is seen as representing the private–personal domain and is distinguished by its mode of inexplicitness (labelled at the time 'Pinteresque'), the later phase is held to represent the public–political domain, and is marked by an explicit and direct dramatic mode.

Pinter's play *Ashes to Ashes*, directed by the playwright and produced in London in 1996,[51] challenged reviewers and scholars alike. In *Ashes to Ashes* a man, Devlin, interrogates a woman, Rebecca, about her former love affair. Devlin and Rebecca are apparently living together, and Rebecca supplies the information concerning her relationship with a former lover quite voluntarily. If Pinter's play *A Kind of Alaska* had surprised the reviewers, but was eventually endorsed by them, *Ashes to Ashes* left them bewildered and dissatisfied. Although critical puzzlement had generally been a routine reaction to Pinter's early and mid-career plays, in this particular case the critical response can be seen to have derived from juxtaposition of the two apparently incompatible 'modes' on which the play is constituted.

The verbal interaction in this play consists of two contradictory discursive modes. Throughout most of the play, each of the two figures seems to adhere to a different code of conversation: one conversational pattern, represented by Rebecca, echoes the earlier 'Pinter', while the other, represented by Devlin, portrays the later 'Pinter' through the direct, explicit style that has come to be associated with his overtly political plays. The kind of verbal interaction emerging from these apparently contradictory tendencies thus creates a unique discursive exchange, as illustrated in the following:

DEVLIN: You understand why I'm asking you these questions. Don't you?
            Put yourself in my place. I'm compelled to ask you questions.
            There are so many things I don't know. I know nothing ...
            about any of this. Nothing. I'm in the dark. I need light. Or do
            you think my questions are illegitimate?
                                Pause
REBECCA: What questions?
                                Pause
DEVLIN: Look. It would mean a great deal to me if you could define him
            more clearly.
REBECCA: Define him? What do you mean, define him?[52]

The two different conversational modes are played one against the other, producing a dialogue that is not compatible with either mode, yet alludes to the co-existence of both.

Furthermore, in this play Pinter deploys readily identifiable, horrifyingly familiar references to the conduct of the Nazis. These references are presented as fragmented images constituting Rebecca's memories associated with her former lover. Collective memory ostensibly associated with a vast public domain is thus crossed with an individual woman's personal memoirs.

Unable to dismiss the personal context, the reviewers had difficulty in ascribing to the play a political theme, yet in view of the specific political associations it evokes, they also found it difficult to perceive the play merely as the dissection of a couple's relationship. Hence, they turned their own difficulty in associating the play with either of the two perceived phases of Pinter's writing into its major flaw.

'It's About Nothing – and Everything', read the title of Casey's review. 'Real or false? Collective memory or more disconnected fantasy? … Only my friend Michael Billington will have the bother of supplying explanations to add to the footnotes of his Pinter biography. For that is all this play adds up to', wrote Tinker; and Spencer commented: 'Ashes to Ashes often comes across as a pale imitation of his [Pinter's] own earlier – and better – work … the suspicion grows that this time the emperor really might not be wearing any clothes.'[53]

I would argue that Ashes to Ashes conjoins (but does not resolve) two very different critical images of the playwright in a single play. Consisting of two incompatible 'Pinter' modes, Ashes to Ashes can thus be perceived as a 'metaplay', that is, as a play in which Pinter seeks to incorporate and thus simultaneously converse with all the surrounding modes of critical discourse.

Ashes to Ashes manifests the playwright's poetic response to the critical distinction between his two writing modes. It activates the perceived early and later modes simultaneously, and hence can be said to delineate a sort of riddling dramatic map for his entire dramatic oeuvre. Challenging the 'clear-cut' distinction, Ashes to Ashes is confusing. It does not deal distinctly with either the public or the private domain, and, in encompassing both, turns out to belong to neither. Moreover, it is not fully compatible with Pinter's explicit or inexplicit dramatic modes; it corresponds to both and thus to neither in particular. In Ashes to Ashes Pinter seems to blur the boundaries that had led in the first place to the critical dichotomy between the two modes of his dramatic writings. Consequently, the play acknowledges the boundaries, while resisting their imposition and complying with neither. Although it bears traces of his later, political drama, this play reflects the playwright's acknowledged shift between represented domains and between levels of explicitness. Moreover, it is punctuated by the juxtaposition of various voices that echo different plays from Pinter's dramatic repertoire. The play's riddling map, which consists of incompatible modes on the one hand, generates counter 'traces' on the other.[54]

Perceiving this play as comprising two incompatible 'Pinter' modes enables one to observe the way in which it converses with the critical discourse. Indeed, it is this dialogue, emerging from the dialectical structure of Ashes to Ashes, that I view as Pinter's most effective, albeit elusive, response in his combat against critical constraints.[55]

NOTES

1. See Yael Zarhy-Levo, 'The Theatre Critic as a Cultural Agent: Esslin, Marowitz and Tynan', *Poetics*, 21 (1993), 525–43, and *The Theatrical Critic as Cultural Agent: Constructing Pinter, Orton and Stoppard as Absurdist Playwrights* (New York: Peter Lang, 2001).

2. See detailed discussion of major critical strategies in Zarhy-Levo, *Constructing Pinter*, chapter 5.

3. Discussing the agents' representation of the social world, Pierre Bourdieu, 'The Social Space and the Genesis of Groups', *Theory and Society*, 14, 6 (1985), 723–44, analyses the strategies employed by the agents. He draws a link between the element of uncertainty, which derives from a degree of indeterminacy that is always included in the objects of the social world, and 'the cognitive "filling in" strategies that produce the meaning of the objects of the social world by going beyond the directly visible attributes by reference to the future or the past'. In political struggles, too, Bourdieu claims, references to the past and the future are employed as strategic means. The past is reconstructed in accordance with the needs of the present, and the future 'with creative forecasting, is endlessly invoked, to determine, delimit and define the always open meaning of the present' (p. 728).

4. Pierre Bourdieu, 'Mais qui a créé les créateurs?', *Questions de Sociologie* (Paris: Éditions de Minuit, 1980), pp. 207–21, asserts that:

> Words – the names of schools or groups, proper names – are so important only because they make things. These distinctive signs produce existence in a world in which the only way to be is to be different, to 'make one's name', either personally or as a group. The names of schools or groups ... are pseudo-concepts, practical classifying tools which create resemblance and differences by naming them; they are produced in the struggle for recognition by the artists themselves or their accredited critics and function as emblems which distinguish galleries, groups and artists and therefore the products they make or sell.
>
> (p. 289)

Examining various forms of political power, Bourdieu ('Social Space', p. 729) refers to the power to name, claiming that 'one of the elementary forms of political power, in many archaic societies, consisted in the quasi-magical power to name and to make exist by virtue of naming'.

5. *The Birthday Party* was performed successfully on a tour of the provinces that preceded the first London production of the play. One should note, however, that none of the reviews following the London production of the play refers to the successful run of the play outside London. The possible explanations for the negative reactions of the London critics, as opposed to the favourable critical reaction out of London, are discussed by Randall Stevenson, 'Harold Pinter – Innovator?', in *Harold Pinter: You Never Heard Such Silence*, ed. Alan Bold (London: Vision Press, 1984), pp. 29–60, p. 55.

6. See, for example, Shulman, 19 May 1958, in the *Evening Standard*; *The Times* (anonymous), 20 May 1958; and Trewin, 31 May 1958, in *The Illustrated London News*.

7. See, for example, Darlington, 20 May 1958, *Daily Telegraph*: 'it turned out to be one of those plays in which an author wallows in symbols and revels in obscurity', and in *The Times*, 20 May 1958: 'Mr Harold Pinter's effects are neither comic nor

terrifying: they are never more than puzzling and after a little while we tend to give up the puzzle in despair.'

8. Harold Hobson, 25 May 1958, in *The Sunday Times*. Note also the favourable critical views of the first London production of *The Birthday Party* that were published several months later in *Encore* magazine, in particular Irving Wardle's article, titled 'Comedy of Menace', published in the September–October 1958 issue of *Encore*, 28–33.

9. See, for example, the review in *The Times* (16 November 1959), reacting to the revue sketches (*One to Another*): 'The evident interest in loneliness, difficulties of communication, and waiting for something to happen seemed to suggest a certain resemblance to Beckett.' In the reviews of *The Dumb Waiter*, see, for example, Walker, 9 March 1960, in the *Evening Star*, who refers to the characters in the play: 'You might, in fact, describe them as waiting upon Godot', or Gibbs, 9 March 1960, in the *Daily Telegraph*: '*The Dumb Waiter*... recalled parts of *Waiting for Godot*, not so much because it consisted of a dialogue, between two men who, like Beckett's tramps, were large and small, but because the themes were also similar.'

10. The 'baffling mixture' (see Wilson, 20 May 1958, in the *Daily Mail*) is perceived anew as a 'unique blend' and as 'a special brand', highly recommended (*Observer*, 24 January 1960). In reviews of the production of Pinter's first play reviewers said things such as 'Mr Harold Pinter's effects are neither comic nor terrifying: they are never more than puzzling' (see *The Times*, 20 May 1958). By contrast, only two years later Pinter is said to have an 'extraordinary gift for comic dialogue, and an ability to keep an audience at once puzzled and intent' (*Daily Telegraph*, 22 January 1960).

11. Austin E. Quigley, *The Pinter Problem* (Princeton, NJ: Princeton University Press, 1975), dealing with the critical reactions to Pinter's work, points to the transformation that occurred in the critics' attitude, claiming: 'rather than being rejected because of that irksome obscurity, however, the plays are now frequently held to be successful because of that same element' (p. 11). Quigley's argument, however, differs from that presented here, because his intention is 'to account for the use of the inexplicit' in Pinter's work, rather than accounting for criticism's dynamics.

12. Muller, 30 April 1960 in the *Daily Mail*. See also Gibbs (28 April 1960, in the *Daily Telegraph*), who claims: 'Mr Pinter is to be admired for having mastered so thoroughly the precarious art of mystifying an audience and entrancing them at the same time.'

13. See Herman T. Schroll, *Harold Pinter: A Study of His Reputation (1958–1969)* (Metuchen, NJ: Scarecrow Press, 1971), who perceives the first production of *The Caretaker* (April 1960), as the one that 'probably marked the opening phase of the Pinter fashion' (p. 18).

14. See for example Rossely (27 April 1960, in the *Guardian*) and Tynan (5 June 1960, in the *Observer*), who claims: 'The piece is full of those familiar overtones that seem to be inseparable from much of avant-garde drama.'

15. See Rossely, 27 April 1960, in the *Guardian*.

16. See for example Muller, 30 April 1960, in the *Daily Mail*: 'this is a play and a production which no one, who is concerned with the advance of the British drama, can afford to miss. This is theatre.'

17. Throughout the early years of his career as a dramatist the playwright himself seemed to contribute to the 'enigmatic' image attributed to him. See for example

the unsigned note enclosed in the programme brochure of the production of *The Room* and *The Dumb Waiter*, at the Royal Court, 1960; several interviews (see especially the conversation with Richard Findlater (*Twentieth Century*, February 1961), the interviews on the BBC with John Sherwood (BBC European Service, 3 March 1960) and with Kenneth Tynan in the series 'People Today' (28 October 1960), and the later interview with Laurence M. Bensky, ('The Art of the Theatre III: Harold Pinter: An Interview', *The Paris Review*, 10, fall 1966)); and Pinter's famous reply (28 November 1967, in the *Daily Mail*) to the woman who asked him to explain his play *The Birthday Party*. The woman's letter and Pinter's reply are quoted in the lead-in paragraph of a later interview that Stephen Moss conducted with Pinter (4 September 1999, in the *Guardian*).

18. Pinter's unique mode of explanation is manifested in his letter to Peter Wood, director of the first production of *The Birthday Party*: see Harold Pinter (1958), 'On *The Birthday Party* 1', in *Various Voices: Prose, Poetry, Politics* (London: Faber, 1998), pp. 8–11.

19. The impact of the playwright's pronounced views is manifested in two ways. The first one is the reviewers' direct borrowing of Pinter's own 'vocabulary', in order to describe, or argue over, the meaning of his new plays. The second is the decision by other reviewers to describe the plays, or the style of direction, in words such as 'pinterisms', or 'pinteresquely' (see especially Darlington, 19 September 1963, in the *Daily Telegraph*).

20. The prizes awarded to Pinter include the following: *The Caretaker* received the *Evening Standard* Drama Award for the Best Play of 1960; on 1 July 1963, the film version of *The Caretaker* won one of the Silver Bears at the Berlin Film Festival; on 30 September 1963 the Joan Kemp-Welch production of *The Lover* won the Prix Italia for Television Drama at Naples; on 23 November 1963 the script and leading performances in *The Lover* received awards from the Guild of British Television Producers and Directors; on 2 March 1964 Pinter won the British Screenwriters' Guild award for his screenplay of *The Servant*.

21. See for example *The Times* (anonymous), 19 June 1964, and Darlington, 19 June 1964, in the *Daily Telegraph*.

22. See, for example, Levin, 19 June 1964, in the *Daily Mail*.

23. Schroll, *Harold Pinter*, p. 77, note 13, presents the critics' usage of the label 'Pinteresque' as an outcome of their inability to find a suitable label for the playwright's works. Although Schroll acknowledges that the use of this label occurred at the stage when Pinter was already accepted by the critical community, he disregards the connection between the use of this particular label and the playwright's critical acceptance. Furthermore, Schroll perceives the label as an obstruction to the playwright's career, rather than as a critical strategy that served this playwright's promotion.

24. See for example Levin, 4 June 1965, in the *Daily Mail*: 'by the end the conclusion grows that the home to which Mr Pinter has come is only the house which he left at the end of *The Caretaker*. And a playwright must always be moving on.' And also Shulman, 4 June 1965, in the *Evening Standard*: '*The Homecoming* undoubtedly works... But the nagging doubt remains that this is not drama but a confidence trick.'

25. See for example Shorter, 4 June 1965, in the *Daily Telegraph* and also Levin, 4 June 1965, in the *Daily Mail*. One interesting example is Hobson's review,

6 June 1965, in the *Sunday Times*, in which he deals with the ambiguity in the play, turning it around to prove 'that Mr Pinter tricks his audience into believing that he is writing a play about the homecoming of a son'. Hobson's claim, concerning Pinter's hidden intentions, appears in his early review of *The Birthday Party* (1958). In both reviews Hobson praises Pinter's dramatic talent, presenting the unfavourable critical reactions to the plays as reflecting the reviewers' shortcomings, rather than Pinter's.

26. For example see *The Times* (4 June 1965): 'Several familiar Pinter motives are involved in this', or, 'At this stage in the play Pinter shows all his old cunning in twisting clichés and formal phrases into unexpected freshness.' See also Trewin, 19 June 1965, in *The Illustrated London News*.

27. See especially Hope-Wallace, 19 September 1963, in the *Guardian*, and Shulman, 19 September 1963, in the *Evening Standard*, and the *Daily Telegraph* (19 September 1963).

28. This claim is corroborated by the reviews of the first production of Joe Orton's play *Entertaining Mr. Sloane* (1964), in which the reviewers pointed out 'Pinteresque' aspects in Orton's drama.

29. Although there may be cases when the playwright is unaware, or only partially aware, of the possible implications of writing a play that is incompatible with his dramatic construct, Pinter's responses in various interviews appear to reflect such awareness. See especially the interview with Harry Thompson for *New Theatre Magazine*, 2.2, 1961, reprinted in *Pinter in the Theatre*, ed. Ian Smith (London: Nick Hern Books, 2005), pp. 43–9.

30. Pinter's earlier play *Betrayal*, performed at the National Theatre on 15 November 1978, can be seen as this playwright's first 'deviant' dramatic work. On the critics' optional modes of operation in the case of a deviant play, and their particular responses to *Betrayal*, see Zarhy-Levo, *The Making of Theatrical Reputations: Studies from the Modern London Theatre* (Iowa City: University of Iowa Press, 2008), pp. 176–80.

31. The play was directed by Peter Hall in a triple bill with *Family Voices* and *Victoria Station* at the National Theatre, Cottesloe, on 14 October 1982.

32. Oliver Sacks, *Awakenings* (London: Harper, 1973).

33. See Barber's comment (16 October 1982 in the *Daily Telegraph*): 'He was never less obscure than here, or more profoundly eloquent about the fragile joy of being alive.'

34. See Muller, 30 April 1960, in the *Daily Mail*.

35. The majority of the reviews include in their account of Pinter's *A Kind of Alaska* some mention of Oliver Sacks's book and the medical phenomena on which his case histories are based (see *Country Life*, 25 November 1982; Shulman, 15 October 1982, in the *Standard*; Cushman, 17 October 1982, in the *Observer*; Barber, 16 October 1982, in the *Daily Telegraph*; Coveney, 15 October 1982, in the *Financial Times*).

36. 15 October 1982, in *The Times*.

37. 27 October 1982, in *Punch*.

38. *New Statesman*, 22 October 1982.

39. See Sacks, *Awakenings*, pp. 74–87 (note 32).

40. See for example an alternative critical treatment of this same play in studies such as Katherine H. Burkman, *The Arrival of Godot* (London: Associated University

Presses, 1986), and 'Deborah's Homecoming in *A Kind of Alaska*: An Afterword', in *Pinter at Sixty*, ed. Katherine H. Burkman and John L. Kundert-Gibbs (Bloomington: Indiana University Press, 1993), pp. 193–9; Moonyoung C. Ham, 'Portrait of Deborah: *A Kind of Alaska*', in *Pinter at Sixty*, pp. 185–92; and Ann C. Hall, '*A Kind of Alaska*': *Women in the Plays of O'Neill, Pinter and Shepard* (Carbondale: Southern Illinois University Press, 1993), pp. 82–90. These four academic studies revolve around the centrality of the female figure, Deborah, and perceive Pinter's main interest in the play as lying in the process undergone by Deborah, through which she comes to recognise herself as a grown woman. For an in-depth discussion of these studies' treatment of the play as compared with the reviewers' responses, see Zarhy-Levo, 'Critical Modes and the Rebellious Playwright: Pinter's *Alaska* and Stoppard's *Arcadia*', *Journal of Dramatic Theory and Criticism*, 16, 1 (2001), 81–99.

41. The strategy of forecasting (as used by most reviewers when approaching *Alaska* as reflecting a major change in Pinter's poetics) is not employed in the cautious review appearing in *Country Life* (anonymous, 30 March 1985), which seems to solve the 'problem' of the 'anomalous' nature of *Alaska* by presenting the current Pinter enigma in other terms. This review suggests, 'on the face of it, this compassionate play has little in common with Pinter's previous work. It has never been easy to isolate the plays in which Pinter seems to be striking out in new directions from those in which he simply offers variations on familiar themes and patterns.'

42. Directed by Kenneth Ives in a triple bill, *Other Places*, this time with *One for the Road* and *Victoria Station*.

43. See especially Billington's review of the 1985 production, entitled 'A New Map of Pinterland' (8 March 1985, in the *Arts Guardian*) and Wardle's review (8 March 1985, in *The Times*).

44. See Guido Almansi and Simon Henderson, *Harold Pinter* (London and New York: Methuen, 1983), p. 101.

45. See Morley, 27 October 1982, in *Punch*.

46. See Wardle, 8 March 1985, in *The Times*.

47. Pinter's overtly political plays comprise: *Precisely*, 18 December 1983; *One for the Road*, 13 March 1984; *Mountain Language*, 20 October 1988; *The New World Order*, 19 July 1991; *Party Time*, 31 October 1991. Note that the first productions of these plays were directed by the playwright himself.

48. See Martin Esslin, 'Harold Pinter's Theatre of Cruelty', in *Pinter at Sixty*, ed. Burkman and Kundert-Gibbs, pp. 27–36 (p. 27). On Pinter's 'shift' to political drama see also the extensive discussion by Susan H. Merritt, *Pinter in Play* (Durham, NC: Duke University Press, 1990), pp. 171–86.

49. See Mel Gussow, *Conversations with Pinter* (London: Nick Hern Books, 1994), pp. 65–93; and Nicholas Hern, 'A Play and its Politics', Introduction to Harold Pinter's *One for the Road* (London: Methuen, 1994), pp. 7–23.

50. Pinter's play *One for the Road* is acknowledged by the playwright himself as a move towards the explicit: 'The facts that *One for the Road* refers to are facts that I wish the audience to know about, to recognise. Whereas I didn't have the same objective at all in the early days' (Harold Pinter in interview with Nicholas Hern, *One for the Road*, p. 11, note 49).

51. The play was first staged by the Royal Court Theatre at the Ambassadors Theatre, on 12 September 1996.

52. Pinter, *Ashes to Ashes* (London: Faber, 1996), p. 12.
53. Casey, 18 September 1996, in the *Daily Telegraph*; Tinker, 20 September 1996, in the *Daily Mail*; Spencer, 20 September 1996, in the *Daily Telegraph*.
54. For an in-depth discussion of this play see Yael Zarhy-Levo, 'The Riddling Map of Harold Pinter's *Ashes to Ashes*', *Journal of Theatre and Drama*, 4 (1998), 133–46. See also Michael Billington, *The Life and Work of Harold Pinter* (London: Faber, 1996), pp. 375–83, who concludes his discussion of the play by claiming: 'It is, at one and the same time, one of his most profoundly personal plays and one of his most deeply political' (p. 383).
55. On Pinter's 'combat' against critical constraints through the different stages of his career see Zarhy-Levo, *The Making of Theatrical Reputations*, chapter 4.

16

HARRY DERBYSHIRE

Pinter as celebrity

Harold Pinter's artistic achievements and political activities have made him a celebrity and, like other processes of enlargement or amplification, fame can distort that to which it draws attention. As early as 1971, Pinter was making distinctions between his own perception of himself and his public image:

> I must admit I tend to get quite exhausted about being this Harold Pinter fellow … He's not me. He's someone else's creation. Quite often when people meet me and they shake me warmly by the hand and say they're pleased to meet me, I have very mixed feelings – because I'm not quite sure who it is they think they're meeting.[1]

It is likely that Pinter was referring at that time to an idea of who he was drawn from the plays he had written and what had been written about them, what Robert Cushman has described as 'this thing in the public consciousness - this cryptic, aloof, uncommunicative thing called "Pinter"'.[2] More recently, Pinter's political interventions and the reactions they have garnered have called another version of himself into being, 'the Angry Playwright', in Michael Billington's words, 'who made good knocking copy for journalists'.[3] Public perception of Pinter as an individual is shaped by others as much as it is by the man himself, and the associations brought to the public mind by the word 'Pinter' lie further still from his control. This chapter explores Pinter as he is perceived, for better or for worse.

Through the media, the opinions of the famous are sought and disseminated on all kinds of matters, as notable figures are quizzed about their likes and dislikes across a range of fields. We learn from questionnaires published in the *Guardian*, for example, that Pinter is the living person whom novelist Tim Lott most admires, 'not', Lott is quick to point out, 'for his politics but because he's England's only surviving literary genius'.[4] Radio presenter and fellow novelist Libby Purves, however, does not share Lott's view. Asked to 'tell us a secret', she replies that 'Harold Pinter is not actually as good as everyone says he is.'[5] These randomly harvested opinions introduce some of the themes that will be discussed in this chapter: how far a distinction should be drawn between Pinter's art and his politics; the extent to which he is a credit to his country; a suspicion that the respect he is accorded reflects some kind of conspiracy on the part of the elite. It is also worth noting that in itself the publication of these opinions is indicative of the licence that celebrities receive to voice their views on subjects that may or may not lie within their area of expertise.

When considered within the specialist arenas of theatre, literature and culture Pinter has for many years been treated with the greatest respect, but when he has gained the attention of commentators outside these spheres, he has sometimes been given a rough ride. The years since this consideration of Pinter as a celebrity was first published have seen some significant developments in terms of the way the playwright is perceived and discussed in the media and the press. In 2001, Pinter was still dealing with the fallout from his truculent protests during the Thatcher years, and was regularly subjected to mockery from various quarters. Three crucial events have since intervened: Pinter has contended with a succession of serious illnesses; he has won the Nobel Prize for Literature; and the ongoing conflict in Iraq and other international developments have made his views on perceived US imperialism seem much less outspoken than they once did. Each of these, in different ways, has made it harder for commentators of all stripes to present Pinter as anything but an eminent figure, not to be derided but to be genuinely celebrated.

Here, Pinter's celebrity is explored from three angles: the playwright's use of his fame as a means of promoting political causes; impressions of Pinter as they have been created in the British press; and citations of the dramatist in popular culture. In each case the intention is to shed light on the ways in which Pinter's literary eminence and his status as a well-known personality have interacted with each other and, more broadly, the relationship between the high culture which his art represents and the wider culture into which his renown periodically propels him.

Playwright and citizen

In his early career, Pinter rarely exposed himself to public scrutiny, preferring to let his work stand apart from perceptions of its author. In the 1980s, however, he became eager to enter into public discussion of political issues. As he told Mel Gussow in 1988:

> I understand your interest in me as a playwright. But I'm more interested in myself as a citizen. We still say we live in free countries, but we damn well better be able to speak freely. And it's our responsibility to say precisely what we think.[6]

Pinter's conception of citizenship appears to derive from the Aristotelian definition of the citizen as possessed of a moral obligation to participate in public debate, a formulation which originally applied to an elite privileged by birth and property. Pinter's fame makes the Greek ideal particularly appropriate: 'celebrity status confers on the person a certain discursive power … in society', as P. David Marshall has written, 'the celebrity is a voice above others, a voice that is channelled into the media systems as being legitimately significant'.[7] When Pinter 'speak[s] freely', he is able to do so from a position of privilege, but his status as a respected artist complicates the reception of his political interventions even as it guarantees them a hearing.

When it was announced in 2005 that Pinter had been awarded the Nobel Prize for Literature, there was no consensus as to how far the playwright's political activities had influenced the committee's decision. Pinter himself 'suspected they must have taken my political activities into consideration since my political engagement is very much woven into my work',[8] and indeed that is what is implied by the presentation speech.[9] However, when the BBC reported the news online and readers were invited to submit their responses, there was a considerable divergence of views. Raymond Rudaizky commented that 'Pinter deserves this prize not only for his writing but his campaigning', but Brian F. Beatty disagreed, saying that 'Pinter deserves the prize, despite his political views, not because of them.' Peter Bolt wrote that 'Though undoubtedly a worthy recipient … he would not have been awarded it had he approved of the invasion of Iraq', while Chris of Milwaukee believed that the award was given on the basis of Pinter's 'hatred of the United States rather than on his merits as a writer. If his merits were the basis then he could have won the award years ago.'[10] These contradictory readings of the situation suggest that Pinter's art and his politics have indeed come to be inextricably intertwined, with the result that reactions to the latter colour assessment of the former and vice versa.

Perhaps what has complicated the situation above all other factors is the range of different modes in which Pinter has expressed his political views. He has voiced them when speaking in public, whether in his speech of acceptance to the Nobel committee or appearing in person before literary or theatrical audiences;[11] he has put them in writing in articles for and letters to newspapers and other publications on issues of the day, whether he is the sole signatory or one of many;[12] he has put his points on television, usually to interviewers but on at least one occasion directly to camera in a programme of his own scripting.[13] Pinter has also expressed his political concerns through artistic means, not only in plays such as *One for the Road* and *Mountain Language*, but in *Voices*, a piece for radio with music by James Clarke broadcast in 2005, and a series of poems, many of which have appeared in the national press. It is a testament to the strength of Pinter's convictions that he should use every means at his disposal to put his point of view across; however, whether he is using his fame as a playwright to gain a platform from which to speak or whether he is framing political points in the language of drama and poetry, the position adopted is not a straightforward one.

One instance of Pinter's status as playwright and citizen affecting the way in which his statements are received occurred in February 1998, when he wrote an article in the *Guardian* criticising the then Prime Minister Tony Blair. Following a series of damning indictments relating to Blair's co-operation with US foreign policy, the letter ironically concludes, 'Oh, by the way, meant to mention, forgot to tell you, we were all chuffed to the bollocks when Labour won the election.'[14] The *Guardian* printed four letters responding to Pinter's, two in support of his stance on Iraq and two to comment on his use of the phrase 'chuffed to the bollocks'.[15] Similarly, in a 1999 letter to the *Guardian* condemning Nato's 1999 bombing of Serbia, Pinter again ventured beyond the conventional language of politics to make his point:

> US foreign policy can be defined as follows: 'Kiss my arse or I'll kick your head in' … Blair is the one who kisses Clinton's arse fervently and dreams that he is Mrs Thatcher. The level of intelligence employed in the whole enterprise is pathetic if not infantile.[16]

The vehemence of Pinter's tone was widely seen to undermine whatever virtue lay in his position and, once more, responses focused on literary style. The letter was described the following day as 'histrionic' by one respondent, and as a collection of 'hysterical and scatological rantings' by another.[17] In a subsequent issue, Nick Simpson of Cheadle was the only correspondent to attempt a detailed rebuttal,[18] and later still a fellow celebrity, the musician Larry Adler, wrote to point out that 'ass', rather than 'arse', is the standard American term.[19]

If Pinter's literary style can be seen to have eclipsed his intended point in these letters to the editor, the same may certainly be said of his political poetry. Pinter first used violent imagery and obscene language to comment poetically on a political state of affairs in his 1991 poem 'American Football – A Reflection on the Gulf War', and has stated that he believes the poem was refused publication in various periodicals because the editors were 'frightened … I was astonished by their lack of guts'. The fact that the *New York Review of Books* declined to publish his poem 'Democracy' in 2003, he believes, is a further indication of reluctance to publish dissenting opinion, though he adds that 'I don't think any piece of rubbish I write necessarily warrants publication.'[20] This is a thorny question: are we dealing here with editors' prerogative to turn down work they deem to be of insufficient quality, or which uses offensive language, or is Pinter right to see timidity and conformism behind these decisions? The subsequent critical reception of Pinter's political poetry offers contradictory evidence. When

War, Pinter's slim volume of poems opposing the invasion of Iraq, was published in 2003, it was received with derision in some quarters yet was also substantially responsible for winning him the Wilfred Owen award for poetry in 2004. Were political objections behind the apparently literary criticisms made, for instance, by the poet Don Paterson, who said in a speech that 'writ[ing] a big sweary outburst about how crap the war in Iraq is' is something that 'anyone can do'?[21] In what way was critic Mark Kermode influenced by his own feelings about Iraq when he described the poetry of *War* as 'infantile facile waffle of the highest order ... so bad it actually does the anti-Bush camp harm'?[22] Is it illegitimate if political considerations influenced Michael Grayer, chairman of the Wilfred Owen association, when he described the same poems as 'hard-hitting and uncompromising, written with lucidity, clarity and economy'?[23]

Pinter's commitment to the causes he espouses is undoubtedly considerable, and there are grounds for seeing his 'long march leftwards', as Paul Foot does, as an 'exhilarating progress',[24] or, in Irving Wardle's words, 'a heartening story'.[25] Certainly he was not always the political firebrand he is now. In 1966, it was Pinter's view that, 'I don't think I've got any kind of social function that's of any value, and politically there's no question of my getting involved.'[26] By 1985, acknowledging that this long-held policy had changed, he nonetheless retained some of his old wariness:

> But at the same time ... it's a bit difficult to take an objective view of myself ...
> You have to look very carefully at your motives if you become a public figure.
> The danger is that you become an exhibitionist, self-important, pompous.[27]

It was this danger, which 'politicians fall into ... all the time', which had previously held him back, the risk, as his interviewer Nick Hern put it, of 'dealing in the same coin as the demagogues whose power you're questioning in the first place'. Pinter agreed this was 'the great trap'.[28] This view remains unchanged, the playwright stressing in 2003 that, 'I really do not make wild and unsupported assertions. I research very carefully.'[29] Not all of Pinter's statements, however, appear to have been as carefully measured as this claim suggests. He has asserted, for instance, that 'human life and human death ... mean nothing to Blair';[30] of the United States he has said that 'there is only one comparison: Nazi Germany';[31] he has even described a proposed housing development near his home as 'an aberration, an environmental disaster'.[32] It may well be that no public figure, however determined, can always avoid 'the great trap'.

Pinter in the press

One consequence of Pinter's outspoken political interventions since the mid-1980s has been to make him a public figure in a fuller sense than was previously the case. People in the public eye cannot help but have a public image, and one which is not entirely theirs to control. That image is inevitably a simplification: in the 1960s and 70s, for instance, Robert Cushman's 'cryptic, aloof, uncommunicative' Pinter was the version most commonly presented. The playwright was known for the 'Pinter pause' and 'the weasel under the cocktail cabinet', 'the master of the sinister silence' as *Channel 4 News* had it in 2005.[33] Since the 1980s, however, a second Pinter has been conjured up for the British public by its newspapers. This Pinter is an intemperate political agitator in an apparently ceaseless state of rage, a caricature created through the exaggeration and distortion of certain aspects of the dramatist's personality. As Ronald Knowles wrote in 1992, accounts of Pinter at that time were frequently 'disingenuous and dishonest', characterised by 'the calculated use of small detail to represent the playwright in a facetious light'.[34] The effect has been both to mock Pinter as an individual and to encourage the dismissal of his political views, and only in recent years has this tendency begun to wane.

It is largely through anecdotes that this caricatured Pinter has been given substance, and the easiest way to see the process in action is to compare different versions of the same anecdote. In 1996, Michael Coveney related the following story:

> [Pinter] once mobilised the entire upper echelons of the west London constabulary in search of a car that he believed had been stolen from a theatre car park; hours later, the vehicle was discovered directly outside the front door. He had simply forgotten where he had left it.[35]

Coveney's account is not the first telling of this tale; the incident is originally described in Simon Gray's book *An Unnatural Pursuit*. Gray's account differs significantly, however: in this version Pinter realises his error after alerting the car-park attendant but before the police have been informed of the imagined theft.[36] Coveney's description of the 'entire upper echelons of the west London constabulary' searching for 'hours' is an invention intended to increase the story's comedic impact.

As the dramatist has discovered, good stories may take on a life of their own, whether or not they are accurately told. A feature called 'King of Comedy' appeared in Robert Yates's *Observer* diary in 1998, describing Pinter lobbying to have London's Comedy Theatre renamed in his honour. According to Yates, 'though the cricket-loving playwright would never be so immodest as to admit it, he would, we learn, like nothing better than the ultimate thespian honour: a West End theatre named in his memory'. Pinter's alleged vanity, however, is punctured when it is suggested by fellow playwright Tom Stoppard that it might be easier to secure his wish if he instead change his name to Harold Comedy.[37] As a humorous story, it is well constructed, but as a factual account it is unconvincing, particularly given the existence of the Pinter Studio Theatre in Mile End. The dramatist was quick to refute it:

> It's totally without foundation. Sure, I had five plays put on there since 1990 and Bill Kenwright made a joke and said, 'Why don't they call it the Pinter Theatre?' But now I find myself landed with this extraordinary reputation.[38]

The story, it seems, bears little resemblance to the real events upon which it is based, but that has not prevented its repetition in a 2006 *Observer* column by Michael Coveney and even in the leader of *The Times* on the occasion of Pinter's receiving the Nobel Prize.[39]

There is one anecdote which, above all, has appeared repeatedly, and the variations between its tellings are indeed telling of how the character of a public figure can be constructed in the press. The story began life when Pinter, himself highly amused, related it to Mel Gussow, who then recorded the tale in the introduction to his *Conversations with Pinter*. Gussow writes:

> Because [Pinter] is eager to know how people he trusts feel about his work, he circulates his manuscripts among a select group. When he wrote his three line ode to the cricket star, Len Hutton ('I saw Len Hutton in his prime / Another time / Another time'), he sent a copy to Simon Gray, then called to ask if he had received it. 'Yes', said Gray, 'but I haven't finished reading it yet.'[40]

Until Gray's death in 2008, the two playwrights were longstanding friends; if his witticism mocks Pinter at all, it does so gently. The story, however, has since been retold in such a way as to throw a different light on events. Michael Coveney (again) places the anecdote in a passage describing 'the hard … task of saying something flattering to the author's face' after the première of Pinter's 1996 play *Ashes to Ashes*. This context gives the tale a twist:

> A few years ago, [Pinter] wrote a poem about cricket which ran, in its entirety: 'I saw Len Hutton in his prime; another time, another time.' The gem was circulated to friends. After a few weeks, a furious Pinter had not heard from best chum Simon Gray, the playwright. He rang Gray. 'Have you got my poem?' 'Er, yes, Harold.' 'Well, what do you think?' 'I haven't finished reading it yet.'[41]

Coveney's implication is clear: the 'furious' Pinter is demanding the praise he believes to be his due, and Gray is anxiously attempting to avoid giving the negative evaluation the poem obviously merits. This version of events has also been related in the columns of Simon Hoggart, Frank Keating and others,[42] but Tim Adams presents his readers with a retelling of the story which is different again:

even the smartest serial bluffer can be caught out. Harold Pinter, I'm told, recently put down his latest thoughts on East Timor in the form of a succinct two-line poem and circulated it among his fellow-travellers. A couple of weeks later he happened to be speaking to one of these friends on the phone. 'What did you make of my poem?' he inquired. 'Actually, Harold', said the friend, without a second thought, 'I'm only halfway through.'[43]

Pinter's no doubt explosive response is left to the reader's imagination. This ever-shifting anecdote can be seen as a practical example of Volosinov's notion that a 'text or a practice or an event is not the issuing source of meaning, but a site where the articulation of meaning – variable meaning(s) – can take place'.[44] Gray's comment, presented first as a self-conscious witticism and next as an inventive evasion, now becomes an out-and-out gaffe, betraying ignorance rather than disapproval. Adams's account abandons every concrete detail of the original story except Pinter's involvement, but brings in fictitious, though plausible, detail, such as the reference to East Timor. These are as much different narratives as they are different accounts, varying to suit the journalistic occasion.

Evaluation of pieces of this kind will clearly differ according to whether they are judged as factual accounts or as entertaining narratives, but what is problematic is that they are generally presented as both. It is the question of accuracy on which Pinter focused when refuting the 'King of Comedy' story:

> There's an illness in the press in this country. To quote a stupid little tale like that, without any attempt to confirm that there was any truth in it whatsoever, is only too common. They feel they can say what they like just for the hell of it.[45]

John Walsh, Pinter's interviewer on that occasion, replies, 'Actually … it's more to do with the journalistic habit of hoarding up apocryphal stories like squirrels storing acorns', a comment which softens the dramatist's accusation but does not refute it. The difference is that Pinter believes a story which appears in a newspaper, even one presented as comment or gossip, ought to be true, or at least ought not to be known to be false, while Walsh seems more to take the view that the pages of a newspaper must be filled somehow. It is hard to say what proportion of readers take these stories with the pinch of salt that Walsh feels to be requisite.

However seriously the reader is expected to take them, it is largely through anecdotes such as these that Pinter has been made an unwilling part of what Billington describes as 'a "celebrity" world, largely created by the British press, in which everyone is assigned a one-dimensional role'.[46] Pinter himself commented on this phenomenon in a 1999 interview:

> To a great extent my public image is controlled by the press. That's the Harold Pinter they choose to create. I'm perfectly prepared to admit that there have been

> times in the past when I have exploded, sometimes justifiably, sometimes stupidly. But most of these incidents are at least ten years ago. I don't do that kind of thing any more – or very rarely anyway...[47]

Here Pinter acknowledges that he has, at times, given way to the anger with which he has so often been associated, without accepting that he is in the perpetual state of fury many journalists would have us believe. He also, by mentioning that most such incidents took place 'at least ten years ago', alludes indirectly to the circumstances in which the press onslaught began, the politically polarised climate of the last years of the Thatcher administration. Hostile press coverage of the June 20th group of writers, convened by Pinter to discuss issues of the day, prompted the playwright to respond in a way which was not conciliatory. 'We have a precise agenda', he notoriously said, 'and we are going to meet again and again until they break the windows and drag us out.'[48] Elsewhere, Pinter declared his 'absolute contempt'[49] for those who had attacked the group and, asked in 1990 if he had a message for the *Evening Standard*'s 'Londoner's Diary', replied, 'Tell it to go fuck itself and you go with it.'[50]

'Never reply to a critic', wrote Peter Nichols, 'it's feeding the hand that bites you',[51] and Pinter's retaliations in the late eighties and early nineties seem to have functioned as the green light for more than a decade of journalistic mockery and misrepresentation. The playwright's own belief was that this was 'a calculated act, though who is doing the calculating I can't say',[52] though this might appear somewhat paranoid from an outside perspective. Even if we take the view, however, that this was a tendency rather than a conspiracy, we might still note that it was at the moment that Pinter began to rehearse dissenting political views in public that elements in the British press began to undermine his credibility by presenting him as intemperate and irrational. There are many reasons why Pinter has been presented in this way, some to do with the entertainment value that it affords and some to do with the words and actions of the playwright himself, but among them there is a manifestly political agenda which we should not entirely ignore.

This is not to say, however, that the tendency to mock Pinter has been exclusively located in any particular sector of the press, despite Paul Vallely's suggestion that the June 20th group was 'mocked mercilessly' by 'the Tory press',[53] and Susannah Clapp's reference to 'the cross Harold Pinter of the tabloids'.[54] Ridiculing Pinter in print is a pastime that has been widely enjoyed, by its practitioners if not by their readers. Now, as the Thatcher years recede ever further into the past, it seems that the cessation of hostilities to which I looked forward in the first version of this chapter has at last arrived, though traces of past conflicts remain. On landmark occasions such as Pinter's birthday or his award of the Nobel Prize, most commentators have found it in themselves to celebrate his achievements, though the headlines under which they do so might yet cause their subject to groan: 'Angry old man'; 'Still angry after all these years'; 'The angry genius'; even 'a grump to cherish'.[55]

Pinter in popular culture

Given the marginalised position of serious theatre in contemporary society, references to Pinter in popular culture tend to occur unexpectedly. One popular context in which Pinter's name makes sporadic appearances is the quiz show. On *Fifteen to One* in 1996, William G. Stewart asked, '*Ashes to Ashes* is the first play in three years by which leading British playwright?'.[56] In 2000 Anne Robinson asked contestants on *The Weakest Link* what Pinter's nationality was.[57] On *University Challenge* in 2001, Jeremy Paxman asked which writer coined the phrase 'the weasel under the cocktail cabinet'.[58] Pinter has been brought into play at least three times on *Who Wants to be a Millionaire?*: host Chris Tarrant has asked for the author of *A Man for all Seasons*, giving Pinter as one of four possible answers; he has asked for the author of *The Caretaker*; and he has asked for the author of *The Dumb Waiter*.[59]

Lest it be thought that these references betoken a nation of Pinter experts, it should be mentioned that the answers given are not always correct. Both Stewart and Paxman were met with the response, 'Alan Ayckbourn?', while all three of the contestants faced with a question about Pinter on *Who Wants to be a Millionaire?* opted to phone a friend. Pinter's name has been further bandied about in the form of incorrect guesses on *University Challenge* in response to the questions 'Who in 1997 became the first playwright to be knighted since Sir Noël Coward?' and '*The Waters of Babylon* was the first play by which British playwright?'[60] The relatively sober nature of these quiz shows and the stage of the contest at which these questions were asked (generally at a point when the level of difficulty has significantly increased) suggests that familiarity with Pinter's career is impressive rather than expected: in other words, that he belongs to the realm of specialist knowledge.

In the 1990s, Pinter was twice referred to in the *New Musical Express*, a weekly music magazine aimed at teenage readers. One critic describes a concert as 'more literary than musical, more Pinter than Pulp',[61] so that Pinter, representing an art form which readers are expected to find arid next to pop music, suffers in comparison to a well-regarded group. Rather more direct, the second reference occurs in a May 1999 opinion column in which David Stubbs discusses the Nato bombing of Serbia, declaring that 'anti-war protests from far-left figures like Tony Benn and the idiot Harold Pinter ring hollow'.[62] Pinter's use of the argot of the street in his letter to the *Guardian* had clearly not persuaded Stubbs, and, though his stance may not have reflected *NME* readers' views, it might well have influenced them. Two references to Pinter in the lyrics of 1990s popular music are similarly disrespectful. The Pet Shop Boys' 1996 track 'Up Against It' describes 'such a cold winter / With scenes as slow as Pinter',[63] while in 1994 the Manic Street Preachers reached number 16 in the UK single charts with a song about 'the regurgitation of 20th Century culture'[64] whose narrator declares that he has 'spat out Plath and Pinter'.[65] More flattering, perhaps, is the fact that Nick Cave's first band The Birthday Party was named in tribute to Pinter's 1958 play, the intense and often discordant nature of their music making this a fitting point of reference.[66]

The British tabloid press mention high-culture figures such as Pinter rarely and with ambivalence. The *Sun*, listing his 1997 television appearance on *Face to Face*, describes him as 'the famous playwright',[67] indicating a level of fame which is not self-evident to its readers. The *Daily Mirror*, courting a relatively upmarket readership, is more informative; here Pinter is 'the author of enigmatic classics like *The Birthday Party*' and readers are warned, prophetically as it turned out, to 'expect plenty of pregnant pauses'.[68] Particularly revealing is the way in which the tabloids reported Pinter's award of the Nobel Prize. The *Mirror* has Melvyn Bragg contributing a page-long appreciation on p. 6, but trails it on p. 2 with the story that *Sky News* presenter Ginny Buckley had blundered by announcing Pinter's death before correcting herself.[69] The *Star* also carries the news of Buckley's mistake, but mentions the prize itself only in passing.[70] The *Sun* makes no mention of either event; its readers are clearly not expected to be interested in such things.

References to Pinter in works of fiction often function as cultural signposts. In Neil Simon's *California Suite*, the high-art credentials of an actress are established by her complaint that, 'eight years with the National Theatre, two Pinter plays ... and I finally get [an Oscar nomination] for a nauseating little comedy'.[71] The distinction between Pinter and 'nauseating ... comedy' is clear, but, because Simon is an author, and his audience presumably admirers, of light comedies, the compliment is double-edged. Similarly, in Stephen Sondheim's *Company*, 'a matinée, a Pinter play'[72] is cited as a suitable outing for New York's fashionable classes, showing Pinter to be valued while casting doubt upon the criteria of the valuers. A reference in Alan Bleasdale's 1995 drama series *Jake's Progress* functions in a comparable way; here a pretentious playwright, watching a rehearsal of one of his works, exclaims, 'What happened to the pause? That pause there is my *homage* to

Pinter!'[73] A more positive reference was made in the American teen-soap *Dawson's Creek*, the lead character Dawson attempting to break through a friend's evasive commonplaces by saying: 'So there's this playwright. Pinter. Harold. You say one thing, you mean another. What do you make of that?'[74] Dawson's status as a sympathetic character makes this an encouragement, however small, for the show's target audience to investigate Pinter's work further.

In comedy, Pinter generally stands for forbidding high art, as when, in *The Fall and Rise of Reginald Perrin*, the Sunshine Desserts Strolling Players are said to have found 'last year's Harold Pinter ... a bit heavy', prompting them to follow it with 'a musical, based on puddings ... called The Dessert Song'.[75] Victoria Wood has twice referred to Pinter, firstly in a 1985 sketch concerning an amateur theatre group rehearsing Shakespeare in which one cast member is told, 'You see, this is our marvellous bard, Barbara, you cannot paraphrase. It's not like Pinter where you can more or less say what you like as long as you leave enough gaps.'[76] The dramatist is also referred to in Wood's 1998 TV series *Dinnerladies*, one character bizarrely reporting an edition of the day-time discussion show *Kilroy* devoted to '"Impotence: The New Celibacy", with celebrity guests Miriam Stoppard and Harold Pinter'.[77] These examples variously present Pinter and his work as bleak, incomprehensible and comically out of place in the context of popular culture.

Michael Billington has suggested that Pinter's plays 'have reached out far beyond the hermetic world of drama addicts to become part of the general culture'[78] but, if this is so, there is scant evidence of it. The necessarily random sample here surveyed suggests that references to Pinter in popular culture are rarer than his literary and dramatic eminence might lead one to expect. This, I would argue, corresponds to the marginalised position of high culture in general (a position that I note without approval and notwithstanding the – in my view – unrealistic postmodernist notion of a culture without hierarchy). Moreover, several of the references surveyed draw attention to this very marginalisation, invoking Pinter as a representative of a high, bourgeois and, sometimes, avant-garde culture to which the reader or viewer is expected to relate in one way or another. Sometimes a familiarity with this culture is expected or encouraged, as in the quiz shows or *Dawson's Creek*, and some-times the reader or viewer is invited to join the commentator in rejecting it, as in the *NME*. Most commonly, however, there is an ambivalent mixture of the two, indicating a feeling of unease towards a perceived exclusivity. It may be that Pinter is particularly well placed to epitomise this high culture because his work, often inscrutable and ambiguous, is seen to exemplify how inaccessible a whole stratum of culture seems to those who are excluded from it by class, education and intermediaries such as the *Sun*.

A celebrated dramatist

The fact that Pinter has indeed entered the world of the celebrity is indicated by two sightings of the dramatist reported in the British press, each involving him in an unlikely pairing. In 2000, Pinter's old friend the 'Londoner's Diary' reported:

> Spotted at the Caprice yesterday: Camilla Parker Bowles lunching with her two children. Rather incongruously, just behind them at another table was the brooding figure of Harold Pinter.[79]

More recently, following the first night of a revival of *The Dumb Waiter*, Pinter was photographed for the free evening newspaper the *London Lite* sitting next to former Spice Girl Geri Halliwell, a bemused smile on his face as he clutches a glass of white wine. Anna Davis, author of the accompanying article, remarked, 'it wasn't exactly a meeting of minds'.[80]

In both of these instances, it is the incongruity of the pairing that is remarked upon. There is an acknowledged difference between a celebrity such as Pinter, whose fame is based upon recognised achievement in a serious sphere, and notables such as Parker Bowles and Halliwell whose prominence has been attained by other means, or in less elevated fields. Nonetheless, there he is, among the throng, his presence mentioned and his image presented because he is famous. P. David Marshall, one of a number of critics to have considered what has been called the 'celebrification' of culture in the last fifty years, writes:

> In the public sphere, a cluster of individuals are given greater presence and a wider scope of activity and agency than are those who make up the rest of the population. They are allowed to move on the public stage while the rest of us watch. They are allowed to express themselves quite individually and idiosyncratically while the rest of the members of the population are constructed as demographic aggregates. We tend to call these overtly public individuals celebrities.[81]

Pinter has made use of the increased agency which Marshall describes to promote the political causes and views in which he believes, and many will conclude, like David Hare, that 'he has used his reputation for good'.[82] A position of privilege attained on the basis of achievement in one sphere has been put to determined use in another but, at least while we agree that Pinter's cause is just, we need see no dishonour in this.

Pinter's political engagement and belligerent attitude to criticism exposed him to sustained flack, as acknowledged in his remark that 'any writer who pops his head over the trenches and dares to speak in this country is placed beyond the pale'.[83] That there was a political aspect to the years of ridicule that the playwright had to weather must be acknowledged, but it might also be suggested that presenting Pinter as comically self-important was a defensive response to the intimidating, inaccessible high art that he has been taken to represent. The British are culturally insecure, deriding what they fear they will not understand, and particularly mistrustful of anybody who seems to take him- or herself seriously, either as artist or as citizen. When reference is made to Pinter in popular culture, which is infrequently, this insecurity is often what is most apparent. Whether patriotic support for our Nobel-winning playwright will mitigate this defensiveness remains to be seen, but for now we can at least say that the award of that prize, along with other recent developments, has caused many of Pinter's most scornful detractors to revise their attitudes.

NOTES

1. Quoted in Mel Gussow, *Conversations with Pinter* (London: Nick Hern, 1994), p. 25.
2. Robert Cushman, 'Playing Pinter', *Independent*, 15 September 1996.
3. Michael Billington, *Harold Pinter*, rev. edn of *The Life and Work of Harold Pinter* (1996: London: Faber, 2007), p. 321.
4. Rosanna Greenstreet, 'The Questionnaire: Tim Lott', *Guardian*, 15 July 2000.
5. Rosanna Greenstreet, 'Q and A: Libby Purves', *Guardian*, 3 March 2007, 'Weekend', p. 8.
6. Quoted in Gussow, *Conversations with Pinter*, pp. 71–2.
7. P. David Marshall, *Celebrity and Power: Fame in Contemporary Culture* (Minneapolis: University of Minnesota Press, 1997), p. x.
8. Quoted in Michael Billington, '"They said you've got a call from the Nobel committee. I said, why?"', *Guardian*, 14 October 2005, p. 1.
9. Available at http://nobelprize.org/nobel_prizes/literature/laureates/2005/presentation-speech.html (accessed 28 August 2007).
10. These views and others may be seen in full at http://news.bbc.co.uk/1/hi/entertainment/4338082.stm (accessed 28 August 2007).
11. Pinter's Nobel speech was broadcast on the Freeview channel More4 and appears as an appendix to the revised second edition of Michael Billington's *Harold Pinter*; other examples of public appearances at which he has made political points include appearances in conversation at the National Theatre on 10 June 2003, the Royal Court Theatre on 24 February 2005 and 20 October of the same year, and the Hay-on-Wye literary festival 2006 (see Charlotte Higgins, 'Two-act rant from Sean and Harold', *Guardian*, 26 August 2006, p. 11). His largest public audience was the gathering of marchers against the Iraq war which he addressed in Hyde Park on 15 February 2003.
12. See, for example, 'US should end all illegal detention', a letter to the *Guardian* signed by Pinter and 420 other writers and artists, published 15 March 2006, p. 33; 'A message to Tony Blair: Call for a ceasefire now', a short letter signed by Pinter and forty-one other luminaries which appeared on the cover of the

Independent on 28 July 2006; and 'Darfur: a letter from Europe's leading writers', of whom Pinter was one, in the *Independent*, 24 March 2007, p. 45.

13. Pinter was interviewed, for example, by Kirsty Wark for *Newsnight Review*, BBC Two, 23 June 2006; the programme he scripted was a thirty-minute argument against then-current NATO air strikes in Serbia (*Counterblast*, 'Against the War', BBC Two, 4 May 1999).

14. On its later publication in his collection of writings *Various Voices*, the letter was headed by Pinter 'An open letter to the Prime Minister', but the heading it was given by the newspaper on its initial publication was 'Writer outraged', *Guardian*, 17 February 1998, p. 17.

15. 'A pint (or two or three) of bitter', *Guardian*, 18 February 1998, p. 17; 'Pinteresque war of words', *Guardian*, 19 February 1998, p. 19.

16. 'Artists against the war', *Guardian*, 8 April 1999, p. 21.

17. 'More artists waging war', *Guardian*, 9 April 1999, p. 21.

18. 'Yet more artists against the war', *Guardian*, 10 April 1999, p. 32.

19. 'Larry Adler kicks Pinter's ass', *Guardian*, 17 April 1999, p. 21.

20. Pinter discusses the publication history of both poems in Fiona Maddocks, 'Pinter's war against Bush', *Evening Standard*, 5 June 2003, p. 43.

21. Reported in Charlotte Higgins, 'Pinter's poetry? Anyone can do it', *Guardian*, 30 October 2004, p. 1.

22. Speaking on *Newsnight Review*, BBC Two, 13 June 2003. The text of the discussion is available at http://news.bbc.co.uk/1/hi/programmes/newsnight/review/2994364.stm (accessed 29 August 2007).

23. Quoted in John Erzad, 'Pinter awarded Wilfred Owen prize for poetry opposing Iraq conflict', *Guardian*, 4 August 2004, p. 9.

24. Paul Foot, 'A polemicist who loves cricket. Now that's what I call radical', *Observer*, 8 November 1998, 'Review', p. 15.

25. Irving Wardle, 'The Master and the Muse', *Independent on Sunday*, 20 October 1991, 'Sunday Review', p. 18.

26. Pinter, quoted in Kay Dick (ed.), *Writers at Work: The Paris Review Interviews* (Harmondsworth: Penguin, 1972), p. 307.

27. Pinter, 'A Play and its Politics', in *One for the Road*, rev. edn with introduction and photographs (London: Methuen, 1985), p. 19.

28. *Ibid.*, pp. 19–20.

29. Quoted in Maddocks, 'Pinter's war against Bush', p. 43.

30. 'Pinter accuses Blair of "oil access" war', *New Camden Journal*, 1 July 1999, p. 8.

31. Quoted in Angelique Chrisafis and Imogen Tilden, 'Pinter blasts "Nazi America" and "deluded idiot" Blair', *Guardian*, 11 June 2003, p. 9.

32. Quoted in Jay Rayner, 'Pinter of discontent', *Observer*, 16 May 1999, p. 27.

33. *Channel 4 News*, 13 October 2005, 7.00 pm.

34. Ronald Knowles, 'From London: Harold Pinter 1992', in *The Pinter Review: Annual Essays 1992* (Tampa: University of Tampa Press, 1992), p. 92.

35. Michael Coveney, 'Harold Pinter, playwright and player: dramatic persona', *Observer*, 29 September 1996, 'Review', p. 20.

36. Simon Gray, *An Unnatural Pursuit* (London: Faber, 1984), pp. 137–9.

37. Robert Yates, 'Diary', *Observer*, 15 November 1998, 'Review', p. 4.

38. Quoted in John Walsh, 'That nice Mr Pinter', *Independent*, 8 February 1999, 'Review', p. 1.

39. See Michael Coveney, 'That's a West End name-drop too far, Cameron', *Observer*, 2 July 2006, 'Review', p. 11 and 'Pause for Thought', *The Times*, 14 October 2005, p. 23.
40. Gussow, *Conversations with Pinter*, p. 13.
41. Coveney, 'Harold Pinter, playwright and player: dramatic persona', p. 20.
42. Frank Keating, 'Undercover listening on Radio 4', *Guardian*, 16 April 1998, p. 28; Simon Hoggart, 'Diary', *Guardian*, 27 March 1999, 'Saturday Review', p. 12. The story appears again in an unattributed story, 'The abusive playwright', in *The Week*, 1 April 2000, p. 8.
43. Tim Adams, 'Comment: So who ... whisper it ... hasn't actually seen *E.R.?*', *Observer*, 28 February 1999, p. 27.
44. As explicated by John Storey (ed.), *Cultural Theory and Popular Culture: A Reader*, 2nd edn (Athens: University of Georgia Press, 1998), p. xiv.
45. Quoted by Walsh, 'That nice Mr Pinter', p. 1.
46. Billington, *Harold Pinter*, p. 321.
47. Quoted in Stephen Moss, 'Under the volcano', *Guardian*, 4 September 1999, 'Review', p. 6.
48. Quoted in Billington, *Harold Pinter*, p. 309.
49. Quoted in Gussow, *Conversations with Pinter*, p. 77.
50. Quoted in Billington, *Harold Pinter*, p. 321.
51. Peter Nichols, *A Piece of my Mind* (London: Methuen, 1987), p. 32.
52. Quoted in Moss, 'Under the volcano', p. 6.
53. Paul Vallely, 'A new Pinter play, So what?', *Independent*, 18 September 1996, 'Review', p. 14.
54. Susannah Clapp, *Observer*, 17 May 1998, 'Review', p. 13.
55. See Michael Billington, 'Angry old man', *Guardian*, 14 October 2000, 'Saturday Review', p. 5; Steve Grant, 'Still angry after all these years', *Independent on Sunday*, 19 November 2000, p. 26; Christopher Hudson, 'The angry genius', *Daily Mail*, 14 October 2005, p. 29; and an unattributed article called 'Harold Pinter: a grump to cherish', in *The Week*, 22 October 2005, p. 21.
56. *Fifteen to One*, Channel 4, 6 November 1996.
57. *The Weakest Link*, BBC Two, 25 October 2000.
58. *University Challenge*, BBC Two, 21 January 2001.
59. *Who Wants to be a Millionaire?*, ITV1, 4 April 2000, 19 October 2000, and 6 November 2004 respectively.
60. *University Challenge*, BBC Two, 22 October 1997 and 10 February 2003 respectively. Alan Ayckbourn (again) and John Arden were the correct answers; Pinter was offered a knighthood in the 1990s, but turned it down.
61. April Long, 'Live Reviews', *New Musical Express*, 7 March 1998, p. 38.
62. David Stubbs, 'Banging on about ... Not enough protest songs', *New Musical Express*, 1 May 1999, p. 13.
63. Neil Tennant and Chris Lowe, 'Up Against It', on *Bilingual* (Parlophone, 1996). The song's title is lifted from Joe Orton.
64. Nicky Wire, *Melody Maker*, 27 August 1994, p. 5.
65. Nicky Wire and Richey James, 'Faster', on *The Holy Bible* (Epic, 1994).
66. See Louise Gray, 'Nick Cave – being a musician with a passionate and shocking talent', *New Internationalist*, March 2000, available at http://findarticles.com/p/articles/mi_moJQP/is_321/ai_30301683 (accessed 29 August 2007).

67. *Sun*, 21 January 1997, 'Sun TV', p. 2.
68. *Daily Mirror*, 21 January 1997, 'Mirror TV Plus', p. 1.
69. See Melvyn Bragg, 'Nobel art of Harold Pinter', *Daily Mirror*, 14 October 2005, p. 6, and the unattributed news item 'Curtain comes down on Pinter' on p. 2 of the same edition.
70. 'TV dead wrong', *Daily Star*, 14 October 2005, p. 23.
71. Neil Simon, *California Suite, The Collected Plays of Neil Simon*, vol. II (New York: Plume, 1986), p. 596.
72. Stephen Sondheim, 'Ladies who Lunch', in *Company* (London: Valando, 1970), p. 41.
73. Alan Bleasdale, *Jake's Progress*, Channel 4, 16 November 1995.
74. *Dawson's Creek*, Channel 4, 31 March 1999.
75. David Nobbs, *The Fall and Rise of Reginald Perrin*, series 1, episode 3, repeated BBC Two, 1 February 2000, originally shown 1976.
76. Victoria Wood, *Up to You, Porky* (London: Methuen, 1985), p. 91.
77. Quoted in Adam Sweeting, 'Last night's TV', *Guardian*, 27 November 1998, 'G2', p. 50.
78. Billington, *Harold Pinter*, p. 1.
79. 'Londoner's Diary', *Evening Standard*, 19 July 2000, p. 12.
80. Anna Davis, 'Fancy a Pinter, Geri?', *London Lite*, 9 February 2006, p. 7. 'It is not known what the 34-year-old ex-Spice Girl thought of Pinter's absurdist comedy', Davis continues, before contrasting the rave reviews the play received with the withering reception accorded to the 1997 film *Spice World*.
81. Marshall, *Celebrity and Power*, p. ix.
82. David Hare, 'In Pinter you find expressed the great struggle of the 20th century – between primitive rage on the one hand and liberal generosity on the other', *Guardian*, 14 October 2005, 'G2', p. 8.
83. Quoted in Steve Grant, 'Pinter: my plays, my polemics, my pad', *Independent*, 20 September 1993, 'Living', p. 3.

17

MIREIA ARAGAY

Pinter, politics and postmodernism (2)

Because 'reality' is quite a strong firm word we tend to think, or to hope, that the state to which it refers is equally firm, settled and unequivocal. It doesn't seem to be ... Language, under these conditions, is a highly ambiguous business.[1]

Do the structures of language and the structures of reality (by which I mean what actually *happens*) move along parallel lines? Does reality essentially remain outside language, separate, obdurate, alien, not susceptible to description? Is an accurate and vital correspondence between what *is* and our perception of it impossible? Or is it that we are obliged to use language only in order to obscure and distort reality – to distort what *is*, to distort what *happens* – because we fear it? We are encouraged to be cowards. We can't face the dead. But we must face the dead because they die in our name.[2]

Since the mid-1980s, the appearance of the full-length plays *One for the Road* (1984), *Mountain Language* (1988), *Party Time* (1991) and *Ashes to Ashes* (1996), as well as the sketches *Precisely* (1983) and *The New World Order* (1991), has led critics of Pinter's work to speculate as to whether they embody a fresh departure by which the playwright's *oeuvre* has become openly, ostensibly political as opposed to his earlier, more metaphorical explorations of power games,[3] or whether, on the contrary, it has been political through and through from the very start.[4] Each position is grounded on a different conception of the 'political', a discrepancy that may be clarified in the light of the ongoing controversy regarding the vexed question of postmodernism's political import. Indeed, the two epigraphs at the head of this chapter, taken from Pinter's non-dramatic writings, highlight a preoccupation central both to the playwright's work and to the debate about postmodernism: how language, and hence individuals, are bound up with reality, and whether it is possible to speak of reality at all or only of 'versions' of it. In an attempt to discriminate between two distinct treatments of that overriding preoccupation within Pinter's work, this chapter looks at *The Homecoming* (1965) and *Ashes to Ashes* (1996) through the lens of postmodernist culture, its contributions and its discontents.

Both champions of postmodernist culture and its most severe detractors have been led by the complex, heterogeneous nature of the phenomenon to acknowledge its double-edged ethico-political character, as potentially both enriching and revitalising, and utterly disabling.[5] On the one hand, the postmodernist emphasis on language-as-discourse, as the site where power relations are both produced and reproduced, has subversive political implications that range from the problematisation of the liberal-humanist, autonomous, transcendental, coherent subject to the contesting of any direct, stable anchorage of language in reality. This has ultimately resulted in a thorough reconceptualisation of the field of the political, a simultaneous enlarging, deepening and revitalising of the meaning and scope of both 'power' and 'politics'. Thus, the binary opposition between the 'private' and 'public' domains has been deconstructed – both, postmodernism claims, are political, wholly permeated by power relations. So has the distinction between language and reality – the postmodernist view of language as always already discursive, never a transparent, objective window onto reality, problematises the very concept of 'truth' and lays bare the fact that access to reality (past and present) is not unmediated but inflected through discourse and hence through power relations. It is precisely such a view of language that is captured in the first epigraph to this chapter. In Pinter's postmodernist argument as exemplified in this extract, dating from the early 1960s, and in his plays up to the mid-1980s, neither reality nor subjectivity are understood as stable, transcendental signifieds which language unproblematically refers to or expresses. This was, in part, first noted by Austin Quigley in *The Pinter Problem* (1975), a veritable turning point in the abundant criticism on the role of language in Pinter's plays.[6] Quigley argues that the difficulties critics and audiences experienced in grasping Pinter's use of language were due to their reliance on a (normally unacknowledged) theory of language as a referential tool. He rejects that view, and claims instead that language is pre-eminently used by characters in Pinter's plays as an instrument to negotiate relationships of power – this is what he calls the 'interrelational' function of language.[7] Although Quigley never uses the term 'postmodernism' in *The Pinter Problem*, his analysis of the role of language in Pinter describes precisely the postmodernist problematisation of the relationship between language on the one hand and reality on the other.

   In a more recent reconsideration of the role of language in Pinter's dramatic work, *Harold Pinter and the Language of Cultural Power* (1993), Marc Silverstein extends Quigley's argument so as to claim that the prominence of the interrelational function in Pinter's plays should not be analysed in isolation but historicised, that is, the constant negotiation of power relations amongst characters should be firmly inserted in the context of the dominant cultural/symbolic order the plays inhabit. By invoking concepts derived from Louis Althusser, Michel Foucault, Luce Irigaray, Jacques Lacan and other contemporary, postmodernist theorists of language, power and subjectivity, Silverstein claims that Pinter's preoccupations, articulated through a radical rejection not only of a referential but also of an expressive theory of language, have always been thoroughly political – that is, his dramatic practice may be read as an ongoing investigation into whether there is a space for the subject outside the dominant order.[8] Even though, like Quigley, Silverstein never uses the term 'postmodernism', his argument that there is no fundamental discontinuity within Pinter's *oeuvre*, since all his plays address political questions, clearly partakes of the postmodernist reconceptualisation of the field of the political. However, by focusing on *The Homecoming* and *Ashes to Ashes*, the claim is made in this chapter that a significant shift seems to have taken place since the mid-1980s as regards Pinter's view of the relationship between language, reality and subjectivity. While the earlier works display a postmodernist politics, the later ones both expose and seek to transcend its limitations. Taken as a whole Pinter's dramatic output may be described as one which, having made an immense contribution to postmodernism's deepening and enlarging of the field of the political, has eventually, since the mid-1980s, come out on the other side with plays which are informed by postmodernism yet at the same time increasingly denounce and renounce its potentially quietist conception of language and subjectivity.[9]

The Homecoming is representative of the earlier phase of Pinter's playwriting career in its postmodernist 'micropolitical'[10] concern with the patriarchal family as the site where gender and sexual relations are both produced and reproduced. Through Ruth, the play explores the crucial question as to whether it is possible to resist the power relations within the family imposed by the dominant patriarchal order, whether there is an 'outside' to them at all. And it does so by means of a use of language which foregrounds its discursive, non-referential nature, as well as by presenting the patriarchal family as a cultural construct rather than a 'natural', pre-given unit. In all of these respects *The Homecoming*, like the rest of Pinter's dramatic work up to the mid-1980s, may be described as political in postmodernist terms.

While, as Quigley amply demonstrates,[11] the instability of the all-male family headed by Max becomes evident right from the very beginning of the play, it is Ruth – Max's daughter-in-law and the only female character in the play apart from Max's dead wife Jessie and the various women Lenny mentions – who most effectively challenges the patriarchal family structure. She does so by repeatedly insisting on the discursive, non-referential nature of language, which constructs men as subjects and women as objects of speech and of exchange within a male homosocial circuit.[12] Both Ruth's challenge and the issue of male homosociality may best be understood in the light of the cultural climate of post-war Britain, dominated, as Jane Lewis and Alan Sinfield among others have claimed, by an ideology of domesticity and a culture of femininity, presented as the cornerstones of social reconstruction in a wide variety of cultural products.[13] Sexually, the images of the potent, virile male and the responsive, passive female were increasingly promoted.[14] According to Sinfield, such persistent ideological work sought to conceal uncertainty and contradiction.[15] His and other analyses point to forces that bear witness to the unstable state of the family and sexual and gender roles in the post-war period. The war had legitimised the idea of the working mother and the post-war boom, as Michelene Wandor has also argued, continued to encourage women to take employment outside the home.[16] The war had disrupted marriages and conventional family life in other ways too: the divorce rate rose dramatically following the war, while the increasing limitation of family size, together with the post-war Welfare State legislation, contributed to disturbing the ideology of domesticity, the culture of femininity, virile masculinity and the male breadwinner function.[17] The family, sexuality and gender relations, in short, were by no means untroubled.

Class tensions intersected with the above. The recurrent presence of what Sinfield calls the 'revisiting fable' in post-war literature bear witness to a contemporary conflict within working-class culture: that between the impulse to 'better' oneself, and the suspicion that those who do so may be 'getting above' themselves. The critical moment, claims Sinfield, is the return, by means of which the revisitor seeks personal ratification. It is then that class anxiety comes to the surface, and it is therefore not surprising to find such complex moments frequently represented in post-war literature.[18] Although *The Homecoming* is not among Sinfield's examples, it fits the pattern in an almost emblematic manner. The play maps class anxiety on to the themes of the traffic-in-women and male homosocial desire, so that class 'betterment' is paid for by the upwardly mobile male, Teddy, a university professor of philosophy in the States in search of ratification as a young patriarch from his father Max, with the transfer of his wife, Ruth, to his all-male working-class London family. The female character, then, becomes the conduit through which class resentment between the male characters is mitigated.

Yet, obviously, all is not entirely well with such an account of the action of *The Homecoming*. Its neatness is disturbed, above all, by Ruth. From her very first appearance, it becomes obvious that she will resist the role of passive conduit of the highly-strung cross-currents within her husband's homosocial family circuit. Above all, she repeatedly undercuts the dominant cultural order by exposing the constructed, discursive nature of language and hence the arbitrariness of the gender roles inscribed in it and the entire patriarchal family structure. On arrival, she immediately begins to labour towards an active subject position by refusing to follow Teddy's instructions to stay in the house and go to bed and by securing for herself the key to the house and leaving him without.[19] She is clearly intent on providing herself with access to her husband's all-male family on her own terms. Similarly, she destabilises the growing patriarchal alliance between Max and Teddy, based on jointly constructing her as the supportive mother and wife, by stating 'I was ... different ... when I met Teddy ... first'.[20] That she succeeds in stirring the men's anxiety becomes evident in Teddy's peremptory reply, 'No you weren't. You were the same', and Max's dismissive 'Who cares?'.[21] And she subverts Teddy's idyllic description of their life in America, 'It's a great life, at the University ... you know ... it's a very good life. We've got a lovely house ... we've got all ... we've got everything we want. It's a very stimulating environment',[22] through her unambiguous assertion of sterility, 'It's all rock. And sand. It stretches ... so far ... everywhere you look. And there's lots of insects there.'[23] But, above all, her response to one of the two stories of violence inflicted on women Lenny tells her, in an attempt to neutralise her capacity to disturb the (precarious) balance of the family circle, typifies her potential subversiveness. It is a story about a diseased prostitute who made Lenny 'a certain proposal' and whom he battered almost to death.[24] By asking one single question, 'How did you know she was diseased?',[25] Ruth forces Lenny to admit the constructedness of the whole story and, by implication, the discursive, non-referential nature of language and the arbitrariness of the gender roles and power relations built in and through it: Lenny's lame reply, 'I decided she was',[26] clearly amounts to that much.

However, both the potentiality and the limitations of Ruth's subversive role become most obvious if compared with that of Jessie, Max's dead wife. Jessie is no more than an offstage, inarticulate figure, made to play the role of the 'recipient' female as Max verbally constructs and reconstructs her along the patriarchal mother/whore dichotomy, to suit the shifting requirements of his struggle to reclaim the dominant position within the current all-male family arrangement. Max's boast about his business success with a 'top-class group of butchers with continental connections'[27] is propped up by his construction of Jessie as the stay-at-home, supportive wife – 'That woman was the backbone to this family', he claims, 'I was making my way in the world, but I left a woman at home with a will of iron, a heart of gold and a mind'.[28] Yet, as with Lenny, by means of one single question, 'What happened to the group of butchers?',[29] Ruth again manages to bring to the surface the arbitrariness of the gender roles encoded in language – following her enquiry, Max reconstructs Jessie as 'a slutbitch of a wife'.[30] However, while Max's incongruous juxtapositions do reveal the constructedness of the mother/whore dualism, they are far from allowing Jessie to escape representation within the dominant patriarchal symbolic order, that is, to inhabit a position outside that order.[31] Rather, they bear witness to the exchange-of-women paradigm, with the female figure being quite literally unable, because dead, to disrupt the male homosocial traffic. In contrast, Ruth can and does attempt to resist that dominant order and its attempts to fix and categorise her, most famously perhaps in the play's crucial 'contract' scene.

The factual outcome of the contract scene is well known – Ruth agrees to stay on with her husband's London family, earning her keep as a prostitute, while Teddy goes back to the States and to their three children on his own. It is the significance of this which has proved controversial. Some critics have insisted that Ruth wields power at the end of the play; at last, they claim, she finds an alternative, autonomous subject position outside the male homosocial circuit through an open treatment of prostitution in economic terms which disrupts Lenny's, Teddy's and Max's euphemistic formulations and lays bare the economic and sexual exploitation, the traffic-in-women, that lies at the basis of the patriarchal family structure.[32] And yet, what kind of power does she wield? Is she not ultimately entrapped in precisely the same disabling dualism – the same dominant cultural paradigm – as Jessie? In rejecting the 'mother' pole of the patriarchal dichotomy, is she not simply driven towards the other extreme? In short, she *both* subversively demonstrates the constructedness of the dominant sexual and gender relations and of the language which inscribes those relations *and* she is bounded by the patriarchal symbolic order, thus remaining an object in the men's homosocial traffic, 'inside' rather than 'outside'.

Silverstein's reading of *The Homecoming* emphasises the latter interpretation, as does his overall assessment of Pinter's dramatic work. Throughout *Harold Pinter and the Language of Cultural Power*, he claims that Pinter's conceptualisation of power tends to reify it disturbingly as a totalising essence which invariably resists, suppresses and/or appropriates any form of resistance.[33] This is what Sinfield objects to as the 'entrapment model', according to which any form of resistance to power ultimately works to reinforce it, since the subject, radically enmeshed with language and power structures, can never find a position 'outside' them from which to carry out the task of critical reflection.[34] It is a Foucauldian, postmodernist approach, one which (subversively) lays bare the constructedness of existing power structures and the discursive nature of language, yet stops short of exploring any effectively transformative, oppositional practice, thus laying itself open to the charge of political quietism.[35] It is precisely the equivocal and, in his view, pernicious ethico-political nature of postmodernism which Terry Eagleton is concerned with exposing in *The Illusions of Postmodernism* (1996), a recent reworking of arguments originally put forward in the mid-1980s.[36] According to Eagleton, the postmodernist positing of the discoherent, isolated subject forecloses the possibility of any truly productive, transformative kind of action, while the enshrining of discursivity implies that neither reality nor discourses about reality nor the subject itself can be submitted to any sig-nificant critical discussion – they are all discursively constituted and there is, consequently, no 'outside'. On the basis of this, the possibility of resistance is effectively denied. The challenge embodied by Ruth in *The Homecoming* is of this postmodernist kind – a point that may be extended to Pinter's plays up to the mid-1980s, which makes them such compelling demonstrations of both the strengths and the shortcomings of the postmodernist conceptualisation of the political.

However, the charge of political quietism, of an inability to imagine an 'outside', becomes far less tenable when made against Pinter's 'openly pol-itical' plays, especially the longer *One for the Road, Mountain Language, Party Time* and *Ashes to Ashes*.[37] While they do not dismiss the postmoder-nist encompassing of the whole range of 'micropolitical' power relations existing across the social network, these later plays broaden their focus to include an understanding of politics as the world of state power, torture, repression and violence. Indeed, these plays vividly demonstrate the absolute interdependence of the 'private' and the 'public'. Together with this, there seems to have occurred a re-examination on the playwright's part of the relationship between language, reality and subjectivity leading to statements such as the second epigraph to this chapter which question the postmodernist emphasis on discursivity, reinstate categories such as truth, value and knowl-edge as legitimate, and draw a line between discourse and reality.[38] Not surprisingly, terms such as 'reality', 'facts' or 'truth' and their distortion in language are recurrent motifs in the pieces included in Section iv, 'Politics', of the volume *Various Voices: Prose, Poetry, Politics 1948–1998*, where Pinter focuses his attention primarily on US foreign policy in Latin America.[39] In the 'openly political' plays Pinter has written since the mid-1980s, we are left in no doubt as to what reality is – the reality of political oppression, torture and violence – or where truth and value lie – with the tortured and the oppressed. And crucially, there transpires in these plays, most prominently in *Ashes to Ashes*, a concern with articulating a social, shared sense of subjectivity, arguably the necessary condition for the emergence of a truly transformative kind of agency that will bypass the individualism underlying both the liberal humanist and the postmodernist subjects.[40] The undermining of the post-modernist devaluation of human agency leads to the claim that history is the result of human actions and, therefore, it brings up the crucial question of responsibility. As Pinter has pointed out, Mrs Thatcher's claim that 'There is no such thing as society' encapsulates the all-too-common view that 'we have no obligation or responsibility to anyone else other than ourselves'.[41] It is such an attitude, one fostered by postmodernist culture, that *Ashes to Ashes* forcefully denounces.

Ashes to Ashes does not renounce the postmodernist insight that absolute 'truths' may lead to oppressive political practices. In the play, Devlin's dogmatism and his pursuit of 'facts' and 'truth' are linked to his psychological and physical brutality. In a revealing mirror effect, he eventually, near the end of the play, 'becomes' Rebecca's torturer, apparently attempting to suffocate her, via both his obsessive interrogation of her in pursuit of the 'truth' about the man who supposedly tried to strangle her and his appeal to God as the ultimate guarantor of absolute certainties. It is Rebecca's defiant claim that God is sinking into a quicksand which prompts Devlin's reply:

> That's what I would call a truly disgusting perception. ... Be careful how you talk about God. He's the only God we have. If you let him go he won't come back. ... You know what it'll be like, such a vacuum? It'll be like England playing Brazil at Wembley and not a soul in the stadium. ... The game of the century. Absolute silence. Not a soul watching. ... No score for extra time after extra time after extra time, no score for time everlasting, for time without end. Absence. Stalemate. Paralysis. A world without a winner.[42]

At the same time, however, *Ashes to Ashes* poignantly asks, where do we go from here? Once absolute 'truths' have been dismantled, are we left with a truly transformative, liberating play of differences? Or rather does such a paradoxical phenomenon as an absolute relativism merely make it possible for men such as Devlin to posit the alarming doctrine that 'It's the man who ducks his head and moves on through no matter what wind or weather who gets there in the end. A man with guts and application. *Pause.* A man who doesn't give a shit. A man with a rigid sense of duty. *Pause.* There's no contradiction between those last two statements. Believe me'?[43]

Ashes to Ashes also problematises the postmodernist view of language and reality as radically discursive. In the play, Rebecca seems to move from a denial of reality – 'I don't have a baby', 'I don't know of any baby', 'I don't know of any baby', she replies to the woman who asks her what happened to 'her' baby, the baby 'she' gave up to the soldiers as 'she' was being deported[44] – through embodying the claim that reality is distorted in language because of fear, to a full-blown rejection of the postmodernist understanding of language, subjectivity and history. The distortion of reality in language is a recurrent motif in the play. It becomes obvious in Rebecca's account of the man who apparently tried to strangle her, which misrepresents him in turn as her lover, as a tourist guide, as someone who adored her and never tried to kill her. Their visit to a forced-labour camp becomes a tour through a factory where the workers took their caps off and smiled as Rebecca walked down the aisles.[45] As in *Old Times*, the past seems infinitely malleable. However, unlike in *Old Times* – a play informed, like *The Homecoming*, by a postmodernist sensibility – reality does not diminish to a vanishing point in *Ashes to Ashes*. Rather, the reality of repression, torture and violence gradually emerges through Rebecca's words as she recounts that part of her lover's job consisted in tearing babies away from their mothers[46] and that (other) so-called 'guides' were responsible for ushering people into the sea to drown.[47] Crucially, it is Devlin's questioning of Rebecca's authority to speak about such atrocities – 'Now let me ask you this. What authority do you think you yourself possess which would give you the right to discuss such an atrocity?'[48] – which prompts her to articulate both a social, shared sense of subjectivity and a view of history as the undeniable result of human agency.

Rebecca begins by admitting that she lacks the authority of direct experience – 'I have no such authority. Nothing has ever happened to me. Nothing has ever happened to any of my friends. I have never suffered. Nor have my friends.'[49] Yet, as Pinter has suggested, that is precisely the point of the play.[50] Not having actually experienced any atrocities herself, Rebecca ultimately comes to embody the claim that that is no excuse for opting out of the harsh reality of human suffering, or indeed for disclaiming responsibility. A sense of a shared subjectivity in pain emerges in her remark about the police siren, 'It just hit me so hard. You see … as the siren faded away in my ears I knew it was becoming louder and louder for somebody else',[51] while the view that history, particularly the history of political oppression and violence, is not random but the result of human agency comes through in her description of mental elephantiasis as the condition by which

> when you spill an ounce of gravy, for example, it immediately expands and becomes a vast sea of gravy. … It's terrible. But it's all your own fault. You brought it upon yourself. You are not the *victim* of it, you are the *cause* of it. Because it was you who spilt the gravy in the first place, it was you who handed over the bundle.[52]

Rebecca's refusal to evade responsibility is anticipated elsewhere in Pinter's 'openly political' plays. In *Party Time*, the split between the party hosted by Gavin in his elegant apartment, where the guests discuss the sophisticated 'club' to which most of them belong, and the unspecified kind of political disturbance and repression going on outside is a powerful metaphor for our deeply divided world. As Dusty insists on asking what has happened to her brother Jimmy outside in the streets, her husband Terry, like Devlin in *Ashes to Ashes*, seeks to set limits to what she, or indeed anyone, is allowed to speak about: 'I thought I had said that we don't discuss this question of what has happened to Jimmy, that it's not up for discussion, that it's not on anyone's agenda.' 'It's on my agenda', replies Dusty[53] – a reply which is paralleled, at the start of *Mountain Language*, by the Young Woman's protective attitude towards the Elderly Woman whose hand has been bitten by one of the guards' dogs.[54] But of the three women, it is Rebecca who ultimately comes to embody the claim that it is only by extending ourselves beyond ourselves, only by truly taking on the implications of a shared, social sense of subjectivity, that any kind of effective resistance may be envisaged.

Rebecca's final story[55] is a gripping *tour de force* which simultaneously rehearses the human capacity for generously constructing a shared sense of subjectivity and, hence, for taking responsibility for the suffering of others – Rebecca imaginatively 'becomes' the woman whose baby was torn away by the soldiers, in a move which reverses Devlin's 'becoming' her torturer and enables her to resist his violent attempt to silence her, i.e. turns her into a potentially transformative agent of history – and also, paradoxically, the human capacity for resigning that responsibility, for allowing babies to be brutally torn away from mothers, for 'handing over the bundle'. And just as in connection with the police siren Rebecca had said, 'I hate it *echoing* away' [my italics],[56] in the play's final moments Rebecca's successful resistance, her refusal to submit to Devlin's attempted violence against her, is shown to be dependent on her capacity to inhabit a shared sense of subjectivity. This is manifested in the echo which repeats each of her lines, powerfully suggesting that through Rebecca there speak all those who have been or continue to be victimised.[57] At the same time, the triple denial of reality which closes the play – 'I don't have a baby', 'I don't know of any baby', 'I don't know of any baby'[58] – is itself a biblical echo; in the context of Western culture, the archetypal denial of the reality of human-inflicted suffering and therefore inclusive of all similar dismissals. As such, it stands as a potent reminder that it is only by reversing that denial, by rescuing language's capacity to speak about reality, that a shared sense of subjectivity and responsibility can begin to emerge and enable resistance.

'Let's start again.'[59] Devlin's attempt to bring Rebecca back to 'normality' significantly comes right after her account of a visit to the cinema to see a comedy which everyone in the audience found funny except for her and a man sitting near her: 'He was absolutely still throughout the whole film. He never moved, he was rigid, *like a body with rigor mortis*, he never laughed once, he just sat *like a corpse*. I moved far away from him, I moved as far away from him as I possibly could' [my italics].[60] 'But', Pinter and the play ultimately claim, 'we must face the dead because they die in our name'; 'the dead', Pinter has argued elsewhere, 'are still looking at us, steadily, waiting for us to acknowledge our part in their murder'.[61] We cannot really 'start again' or 'move away' as if nothing had ever happened; as human beings it is our ethical duty to take responsibility for history, for the reality of the suffering endured by other human beings. Devlin's repeated attempts to insulate his and

Rebecca's 'private' existence from the horrors of the 'public' sphere – 'Let's talk about more intimate things, let's talk about something more personal, about something within your own immediate experience',[62] he tells her in response to her account of how her 'lover' used to tear babies from the arms of their mothers – are undermined both by Rebecca's resistance and by the play's demonstration of Devlin's own fixation with violence and power. At the end of the play, when he 'becomes' Rebecca's torturer, the inextricable bond between 'private' brutality, 'public' violence and utter insensitivity to the suffering of others is visually exposed. As in postmodernism, then, the 'private' and the 'public' are seen to form one complex whole; unlike in postmodernism, this leads to the positing of a shared sense of subjectivity as the necessary grounds for resistance.

No doubt this is the conviction informing Pinter's increasingly prominent political commitment over the last two decades, which has fundamentally taken the shape of a tenacious denunciation of violations of human rights wherever they may happen.[63] As Rebecca finds in *Ashes to Ashes*, Pinter's authority to take such a stand has been frequently questioned. Surely it is symptomatic of a profoundly diseased culture when someone's refusal to 'hand over the bundle' is dismissed offhandedly as mere posturing. Possibly, however, there is nothing unpremeditated about such dismissals at all, given the fact that the assertion of the need for a shared sense of subjectivity and the recognition of human responsibility for history challenge the complacent political quietism – and the cowardice? – that hostility is intended to camouflage. The cost of turning a deaf ear to Pinter's courageous interrogation of the pitfalls of our postmodernist political culture may be far too high to pay.

NOTES

I am grateful to Jacqueline Hurtley, Ana Moya and Pilar Zozaya, who read an early version of this chapter and provided helpful insights. Needless to say, all remaining inadequacies are my own responsibility.

1. Harold Pinter, 'Writing for the Theatre', *Plays One* (London: Methuen, 1986 (1976)), pp. 12–13. 'Writing for the Theatre' was the speech made by Pinter at the National Student Drama Festival in Bristol in 1962.

2. Harold Pinter, 'Oh, Superman', broadcast for *Opinion*, Channel 4, 31 May 1990, repr. in *Various Voices: Prose, Poetry, Politics 1948–1998* (London: Faber, 1998), p. 182.

3. This is, to name but one example, Martin Esslin's argument in 'Harold Pinter's Theatre of Cruelty', in *Pinter at Sixty*, ed. Katherine H. Burkman and John L. Kundert-Gibbs (Bloomington and Indianapolis: Indiana University Press, 1993), pp. 27–36.

4. The view held by Marc Silverstein in his re-examination of the much-discussed question of the role of language in Pinter's dramatic work, *Harold Pinter and the Language of Cultural Power* (London and Toronto: Associated University Presses, 1993).

5. See, for instance, Linda Hutcheon's celebration of postmodernism in *A Poetics of Postmodernism: History, Theory, Fiction* (New York and London: Routledge, 1988) and Terry Eagleton's almost undiluted condemnation in *The Illusions of Postmodernism* (Oxford: Blackwell, 1996).

6. Quigley devotes the first two chapters in *The Pinter Problem* (Princeton: Princeton University Press, 1975) to surveying the Pinter criticism focusing on the role of language in the plays. See, too, chapter 1 in this volume.

7. *Ibid.*, p. 54.

8. Silverstein, *Harold Pinter*, pp. 19–25.

9. *Moonlight* (London: Faber, 1993) stands on its own in a fascinating in-between territory. As Katherine H. Burkman has shown, it echoes the concerns present in Pinter's plays up to the mid-1980s ('Echo[es] in *Moonlight*', *The Pinter Review: Annual Essays* (1994), 54–60), yet it is also, as Francis Gillen has claimed, 'more direct and openly emotional', 'more deeply felt' than any of the early plays, possibly as a result of Pinter's having written the 'openly political' *One for the Road, Mountain Language* and *Party Time* ('*Moonlight* in New York', *The Pinter Review: Annual Essays* (1995–6), 183).

10. Steven Connor, *Postmodernist Culture: An Introduction to Theories of the Contemporary* (Oxford: Blackwell, 1989), pp. 224–5.

11. Quigley, *The Pinter Problem*, pp. 178–89.

12. For a reinterpretation of Claude Lévi-Strauss's exchange-of-women anthropological paradigm, see Gayle Rubin, 'The Traffic in Women: Notes on the "Political Economy" of Sex', in *Toward an Anthropology of Women*, ed. Rayna Reiter (New York: Monthly Review Press, 1975), pp. 157–210. Eve K. Sedgwick's concept of male homosocial desire enlarges the scope of Rubin's model; see her *Between Men: English Literature and Male Homosocial Desire* (New York: Columbia University Press, 1985). See my 'Exploring Gender Roles in the 1960s: Ann Jellicoe's *The Knack* and Harold Pinter's *The Homecoming*', *Atlantis*, 16, 1–2 (1994), 5–19, for a fuller exploration of the relevance of Sedgwick's model to Pinter's play.

13. Jane Lewis, 'From Equality to Liberation: Contextualizing the Emergence of the Women's Liberation Movement', in *Cultural Revolution?: The Challenge of the Arts in the 1960s*, ed. Bart Moore-Gilbert and John Seed (London: Routledge, 1992), pp. 96–117; Alan Sinfield, *Literature, Politics and Culture in Postwar Britain* (Oxford: Blackwell, 1989), p. 205. In *Harold Pinter*, Silverstein's historicising project paradoxically fails to inscribe Pinter's plays firmly in their historical contexts.

14. Michelene Wandor, *Look Back in Gender: Sexuality and the Family in Post-War British Drama* (London: Methuen, 1987), p. 4.

15. Sinfield, *Literature, Politics and Culture*, pp. 204–5.

16. *Ibid.*, p. 206; Wandor, *Look Back in Gender*, p. 3.

17. Arthur Marwick, *British Society since 1945* (Harmondsworth: Penguin, 1990 (1982)), pp. 45–60.

18. Sinfield, *Literature, Politics and Culture*, pp. 266–7.

19. Harold Pinter, *The Homecoming, Plays Three* (London: Methuen, 1978), pp. 38–40.

20. *Ibid.*, p. 66.

21. *Ibid.*

22. *Ibid.*
23. *Ibid.*, p. 69.
24. *Ibid.*, p. 46–7.
25. *Ibid.*, p. 47.
26. *Ibid.*
27. *Ibid.*, p. 62.
28. *Ibid.*
29. *Ibid.*, p. 63.
30. *Ibid.*
31. This is Deborah A. Sarbin's claim in '"I Decided She Was": Representation of Women in *The Homecoming*', *The Pinter Review: Annual Essays* (1989), 34–42.
32. See, among others, Martin Esslin, *Pinter: The Playwright* (London: Methuen, 1982), p. 159; Kristin Morrison, *Canters and Chronicles: The Use of Narrative in the Plays of Samuel Beckett and Harold Pinter* (Chicago and London: University of Chicago Press, 1983), p. 190; and the feminist account of the play by Anita R. Osherow, 'Mother and Whore: The Role of Woman in *The Homecoming*', *Modern Drama*, 17, 4 (1974), 423–32.
33. See also 'Keeping the Other in Its Place: Language and Difference in *The Room* and *The Birthday Party*', *The Pinter Review: Annual Essays* (1992–3), 1–10, where Silverstein describes Pinter's conception of cultural power as 'dystopian', since it invariably succeeds in resisting resistance (p. 8).
34. Alan Sinfield, *Faultlines: Cultural Materialism and the Politics of Dissident Reading* (Oxford: Clarendon, 1992), p. 39; Sinfield is discussing New Historicism at this point.
35. Connor voices a similar reservation concerning postmodernism – i.e. claiming that everything is political may amount to saying that nothing is really effectively political, transformative or oppositional (*Postmodernist Culture*, pp. 226–7).
36. Eagleton, *Illusions*; see also his 'Capitalism, Modernism and Postmodernism', *New Left Review*, 152 (1985), 60–73.
37. Silverstein, *Harold Pinter*, pp. 141–60.
38. As does Eagleton in *Illusions*, pp. 18 and 72–3.
39. Pinter, *Various Voices*, pp. 167–202.
40. Eagleton, *Illusions*, pp. 91–2; Sinfield, *Faultlines*, p. 37.
41. Mireia Aragay, 'Writing, Politics and *Ashes to Ashes*: An Interview with Harold Pinter', *Various Voices*, p. 67.
42. Harold Pinter, *Ashes to Ashes* (London: Faber, 1996), pp. 39–41.
43. *Ibid.*, p. 47.
44. *Ibid.*, pp. 83–4.
45. The factory, like other Holocaust-inspired images in *Ashes to Ashes*, may well have been suggested to Pinter by his reading of Gitta Sereny's *Albert Speer: His Battle with Truth* (New York: Alfred A. Knopf, 1995), a biography of Hitler's favourite architect and Minister of Armaments and Munitions. See Michael Billington, *The Life and Work of Harold Pinter* (London: Faber, 1996), pp. 374–5, and Katherine H. Burkman, 'Harold Pinter's *Ashes to Ashes*: Rebecca and Devlin as Albert Speer', *The Pinter Review: Annual Essays* (1997–8), 86–96.
46. *Ashes to Ashes*, p. 27.
47. *Ibid.*, pp. 47–9.

48. *Ibid.*, p. 41.
49. *Ibid.*
50. Aragay, 'Writing, Politics and *Ashes to Ashes*', p. 64.
51. *Ashes to Ashes*, p. 29.
52. *Ibid.*, p. 51.
53. Harold Pinter, *Party Time, Plays Four* (London, Faber, 1996), pp. 440–1.
54. Harold Pinter, *Mountain Language, Plays Four*, pp. 399–402.
55. *Ashes to Ashes*, pp. 71–85.
56. *Ibid.*, p. 31.
57. In this connection, see Silverstein's discussion in '"Talking about Some Kind of Atrocity": *Ashes to Ashes* in Barcelona', *The Pinter Review: Annual Essays* (1997–8), p. 84.
58. *Ashes to Ashes*, pp. 83–4.
59. *Ibid.*, p. 67.
60. *Ibid.*, p. 65.
61. Harold Pinter, 'It Never Happened', the *Guardian*, 4 December 1996, repr. in *Various Voices*, p. 234.
62. *Ashes to Ashes*, pp. 41–3.
63. For a detailed survey of Pinter's political activities over the 1980s, see Ronald Knowles's 'Harold Pinter: Citizen', *The Pinter Review: Annual Essays* (1989), 24–33. See also his yearly reports on Pinter's activities published in *The Pinter Review: Annual Essays* since 1990.

18

STEVE WATERS

The Pinter paradigm: Pinter's influence on contemporary playwriting

Ian Rickson's revelatory revival of *The Hothouse* at the Lyttelton Theatre in London's National Theatre in 2007 came in a year that confirmed the centrality of Pinter's work to the British stage, following on from equally notable new productions of *Old Times* (directed by Peter Hall) and *Betrayal* (directed by Roger Michell). These shows also confirmed a new generation of actors taking on the mantle of staging Pinter's work, Finbar Lynch and Paul Ritter in *The Hothouse* reviving their double-act in Lindsay Posner's production of *The Birthday Party* in 2005 and the triad of Sam West, Toby Stephens and Dervla Kirwan in *Betrayal*, the male leads scions of acting dynasties, dressed up in the clothes of their parents' generation to confer a contemporary chic on the play's mordant exploration of sexuality and memory.

These three productions, amongst others, serve to confirm Pinter's status as the dominant British writer of the post-war era. His ubiquity on stage is matched by his undeniable yet rarely articulated impact on the wave of new British playwriting emerging from the early 1990s through to the present. Pinter's writerly ethic, his commitment to voice rather than narrative, his shunning of the epic or the ideological and his profound scepticism concerning gender relations seem perfectly pitched for the contemporary stage. Watching *The Hothouse* it was striking how the conventional notion of the 'Pinteresque' as a preoccupation with silence, the unsaid and the incommunicable was displaced by a new version of the Pinter aesthetic powered by a plenitude of language and quixotic wit. Where Jimmy Porter's rantings in John Osborne's *Look Back in Anger* (1956), Beatie Bryant's eulogies in Wesker's *Roots* (1959) or the passionate polemics of Howard Brenton seem increasingly historical, Pinter's savage cackle, ruthlessly mapped demotic and dazzling non-sequiturs speak to a generation steeped in the surreal, amoral world of contemporary television comedy from *Seinfeld* to *Green Wing*. What must have felt chillingly disengaged and strange in 1960 now feels familiar, fresh and morally undeceived. As David Hare has noted, Pinter has outstripped his mentor Samuel Beckett in pertinence; whilst the social surfaces of his plays are becoming ever more redolent of the past, the deep structures of his sensibility speak to us with increasing urgency.

It was not always so. When Pinter first emerged into the public gaze in the 1960s he was striking for his singularity. With the exception of Joe Orton, few playwrights emulated or corresponded to his uniquely threatening oeuvre. In addition, his success was notably fostered outside the Royal Court Theatre which had established itself as the natural home of new plays. Pinter's vision unfolded in the pitiless and unmodish context of the West End or, even more curiously, the Royal Shakespeare Company at the Aldwych. In fact, it is possible to read plays such as *The Birthday Party* or *The Homecoming* as offering a coded critique of much of the social realism that emerged from the Royal Court. Stanley, languishing in his pyjamas all day, is an anti-type of Jimmy Porter, forced to succumb to a much more alarming exterior world than Porter's paper tigers of English mediocrity and well-bred women, in the form of Goldberg and McCann. *The Homecoming* also brilliantly inverts the default class play of the era, staging the agonised return of *embourgeoises* children to their working-class origins; in Pinter's hands Teddy, who might be Beatie Bryant in Wesker's *Roots* or Nigel Barton in Dennis Potter's television play *Stand Up, Nigel Barton* (1965), is, however, as Peter Hall suggests, simply 'the biggest bastard in a house full of bastards'.[1] Pinter's most analogous contemporary at this point, Edward Bond, likewise repudiated the default mode of social realism; yet Bond's turn to Brechtian dramaturgy paved the way for the pre-eminence of the Socialist dramatists of the 1970s. In contrast Pinter's dark laughter and profound pessimism won him few favours amongst either the new realists or the New Left.

This deficit of influence continued into the 1970s. Notable here is Pinter's resistance to the work of Howard Brenton, revealingly documented in *Peter Hall's Diaries*.[2] This was more than a matter of taste, as Brenton himself had fingered Pinter as part of the scenery of a bourgeois stage; and the dramatist of the day who later would emulate Pinter's conception of dialogue as destiny, Caryl Churchill, was then linked to a set of explicit social agendas that Pinter disavowed. While the Leftist dramatists used national stages to excavate history, Pinter chose to tunnel deeper into the façades of middle-class life with his Proustian trilogy *Old Times*, *No Man's Land* and *Betrayal*. Michael Billington's landmark critical review of the latter in 1978, denouncing the play as 'high-class soap opera',[3] revealed just how far from the party Pinter was when in some respects he was at the height of his powers. Even his directorial outings confirmed his turning away from the Leftist paradigm, with his championing of the plays of Simon Gray.

The paradox of Pinter's prominence *and* lack of influence on the dramaturgy of the day is intriguing, and becomes even more so when we consider the

15 Dervla Kirwan and Sam West in *Betrayal*, Donmar Warehouse, 2007

ubiquity of his influence in the theatre of the 1990s. Probably the clearest conduit for the Pinter ethic is the work of David Mamet who, from the late 1970s onwards, sends out clear signals of affinity to Pinter, most overtly in his dedication of *Glengarry Glen Ross* (1983) to him. The kinship between the two writers is striking; both work within a classical, almost Aristotelian conception of play form, Mamet obsessively so; for both, the immediate event embodied in dialogue is where their genius fixes, eschewing complex back story or epic form; both fashion hermetic and often masculine worlds. There is certainly a direct genealogy extending from *The Caretaker* to *American Buffalo* (1975), both plays focusing on marginal characters sealed off from the wider world in detritus-strewn environments. The critical wit with which this underclass is rendered, the Darwinian quality of their struggles and the absence of any historical recourse to mediate their stasis underlines this shared sensibility. Yet what makes both Pinter and Mamet so influential on the re-florescence of playwriting in the 1990s is their 'writerly' values. Neither dramatist validates their work by reference to social realities beyond the text, nor are they borne up by theatrical experiment or formal innovation; and, perhaps most importantly, they do not promulgate any overt political ethic. As T. S. Eliot once said of Henry James, both dramatists '(have) mind(s) so fine no idea could violate (them)'.[4]

Yet implicit in this shared stance is a frank refusal of the ideologies of liberation that informed the dominant theatrical paradigms of the seventies, and slowly petered out in the bleaker world of the eighties. It is no coincidence that the defining salvo against this progressive dramaturgy and the loosely articulated values of 'political correctness' that flowed from it was Mamet's *Oleanna* (1992), whose début in British theatre was directed by Pinter. An implicit misogyny informs and finds representation in both writers' work, with women forming a threat to their closed male universes. This is most evident in *The Homecoming*, in the predicament of Deeley in *Old Times* or Robert in *Betrayal*, and is mirrored by the absent yet structuring women in *American Buffalo* and *Glengarry Glen Ross* and compounded in *Edmond* (1982). Such unblinking images of sexuality as a struggle between competing confusions pave the way for the unaligned post-feminist ferocity of the so-called 'in-yer-face' writers.[5]

Ironically, just as Pinter's influence was becoming endemic, he commenced a revisionist account of his work which aligned it to the Left theatre he had previously disavowed. Yet the plays following *One for the Road* (1984), with their increasingly explicit engagement with raw, coercive power and fragmented, almost epic dramaturgy (most apparent in *Mountain Language* (1988)), nevertheless also find their counterpart in the work of Sarah Kane, Mark Ravenhill and even Caryl Churchill.

So who then are Pinter's legitimate children? Where is his influence most apparent and what does it reveal about this turn away from committed theatre in the 1990s? Is his legacy simply discernible in stylistic tics or do his acolytes deepen the possibilities he has opened up? And which strands of his work open up creative territories and which prove to be dead ends?

Firstly, it is necessary to note the convergence of Pinter with a theatrical universe that once excluded him, that of the Royal Court. This indeed coincides with the period under discussion, beginning with a production at the Theatre Upstairs in 1991 of his short play *The New World Order*, continuing with the aforementioned staging of *Oleanna*, consolidated with the début there of *Ashes to Ashes* in 1996, directed by Pinter and confirmed with Katie Mitchell's revival of *Ashes to Ashes* with *Mountain Language* in 2000. *Ashes to Ashes*, with its elliptical, chilly account of sex and sadism, could be seen as a response to the landmark opening at the Royal Court the previous year of Sarah Kane's *Blasted* (1995), in itself responding to the gender end-game mapped out by fellow two-hander *Oleanna*. Pinter had been a notable defender of Kane's excoriated work, as had Bond and indeed Churchill, appropriately enough given that homages to their plays pepper the text of *Blasted*.[6] *Ashes to Ashes* in some respects offers a more benign version of the mutual evasions and desire for male appropriation so cunningly mapped in

Old Times. The play takes that debate further through its allusions to more systematic modes of oppression than those exacted in the private sphere, such as the hauntingly re-played gestures of the Holocaust invoked by Rebecca, babies torn from 'the hands of their screaming mothers',[7] in the incongruous bucolic setting. This allusive strategy echoes *Blasted*'s movement from Ian and Cate's violent intimacy to a wider field of political atrocity. In this respect Kane's vision clearly owes much to the explorations into the poetics of cruelty adumbrated by Pinter in *Party Time, One for the Road* and *The New World Order*. In this mutual allusive interchange, what is apparent is both Pinter's and Kane's predilection for the political to be embedded in micro-gestures and primary relationships, their refusal to accept abstract rationalisations of power and their stripping away of euphemism; in these respects Pinter offers a dramatic paradigm for representing the neo-liberal universe of the nineties that Kane captures so dazzlingly in *Blasted*. With Katie Mitchell's pairing of *Ashes to Ashes* and *Mountain Language* in 2000, Pinter's long exile from the *soi-disant* home of radical theatre was entirely revoked. Mitchell's championing of his work cross-fertilised with her engagement with another emergent playwright, Martin Crimp, thereby establishing another filament of influence between Pinter and the contemporary stage.

Put simply, there are three modes of the Pinter paradigm that work their way into the bloodstream of the new writing of the 1990s. The first is rooted in Pinter as comic, the documenter of the improvised confusions of masculine dialogue, of selves lost in language, pitted in unending competition. This strand of the Pinteresque, inflected by Mamet, is most evident in the plays of Jez Butterworth (*Mojo* (1995), *The Winterling* (2006)), Patrick Marber (*Dealer's Choice* (1995), *Closer* (1997)), Joe Penhall (*Some Voices* (1994), *Blue/Orange* (2000)) and David Eldridge (*Serving it Up* (1997)). Pinter in this mode is the patron of the so-called 'new laddism' that stormed the stage in the mid-nineties, embodied in sharply crafted, linguistically exuberant, predominantly urban plays chiefly concerned with male groups.

The second strand of the Pinter paradigm stems from his incarnation as a 'modernist' dramatist, attuned to European theatre and in the tradition of Kafka and Beckett. Here the key plays are *The Birthday Party, No Man's Land, The Hothouse* and *Old Times*, all elliptical, cool and attuned to the small-print of cruelty. This is Pinter as minimalist, the comedy very dark, the dialogue prone to surreality and poetic swerves. This tributary of Pinter feeds the work of Mark Ravenhill (*Shopping and Fucking* (1996), *The Cut* (2006)) and most especially Martin Crimp (*No One Sees the Video* (1991), *The Treatment* (1993), *The Country* (2000)).

The third variant derives from Pinter's explicitly political work (*One for the Road, Mountain Language, Party Time*) and finds particular echoes in the early work of Sarah Kane (*Blasted*, *Cleansed*) and in the late, reduced, meticulous plays of Caryl Churchill (particularly *This is a Chair* (1999), *Far Away* (2000) and *Drunk Enough to Say I love You* (2006)).

Common to all three modes is the way in which Pinter's linguistic concerns, structural ploys and deeply sceptical philosophy seem newly available to contemporary writers. Evidently all of Pinter's avatars plough their own personal furrows. Nevertheless their very different plays display the hallmark of Pinter's influence in a manner that cannot be discerned in dramatic writing from the previous decades of his long career. Unsurprisingly this flourishing of the Pinter aesthetic in writing has coincided with a period in which revivals of his work are rarely absent from the stage. Each production establishes fresh-minted links between a new generation of directors (David Leveaux, Roger Michell, Sam Mendes, Katie Mitchell, Ian Rickson) and actors (Lindsay Duncan, Indira Varma, Lia Williams, Douglas Hodge, Greg Hicks, Sam West) who have together redefined the Pinter aesthetic for the modern stage.

Firstly, then, Pinter's comic idiom. If there is an aesthetic implicit in his work, it is most clearly evident in the rich dialogic possibilities he released for the stage, framing a new set of rhythms and thereby fostering a relish for textuality in and of itself. Pinter's work can be seen in a tradition of wit and verbal dexterity within British theatre with roots in the work of Noel Coward or the music hall. This tradition has little in common with the puritanical poetics of writers such as Edward Bond or the shrill expressionist rhetoric of a Brenton or Barker. So whilst Pinter is notorious for his suspicion of language, he is also remarkable for his celebration of language's inherent performativity. Indeed his plays frequently release language altogether from the burden of exposition or sociology central to the naturalist tradition. This wildly irresponsible notion of dialogue behaving badly is the source of his ambivalent comedy, which revels in the unnavigability of the demotic.

This poetics of everyday speech suffuses the plays of Butterworth, Marber, Penhall and Eldridge. *Mojo*, Butterworth's début, which in its filmed version (1997) featured a Pinter cameo, is located in a 1950s Soho inhabited by professional criminals and improvisatory chancers who, with their profane, joyously inarticulate idiom could be on leave from *The Dumb Waiter*. Patrick Marber's *Dealer's Choice* is similiarly populated by amiable Pinter émigrés, prisoners of their sociolect, strung up over intricacies of terminology and unexpressed feeling. Elsewhere Joe Penhall's *Some Voices* extends Aston's bathetic, involuted idiom from *The Caretaker* to offer an examination of mental illness as a malfunction in expressivity. Finally, David Eldridge's razor-sharp début *Serving it Up*, with its portrait of damaged East End masculinity mixed with Oedipal conflict, surely draws its shocking comic strength from *The Homecoming*. What all these plays share with their Pinterian antecedents is their use of inarticulacy as a source of dramatic energy, thereby shaping exuberant rather than depressing tales of the city, a London fuelled by words that enact lives in free-fall. With their characters' confused essayings into expression, these plays serve up unfettered, anarchic voices, and release energies rarely evident in the dutiful social realism they displace.

Yet Pinter the modernist goes deeper into the implications of language unmoored from its referential burden. Here words are weapons, sources of evasion, mechanisms of repression, and the horror of a world built by words, creating and abolishing reality with impunity, links Pinter to his early reading of Kafka, Joyce and Beckett rather than to an anodyne English comic tradition. In this mode Pinter is a postmodernist *avant-la-lettre* and not a cheerful one at that. Partially, this is his 'Absurdist' ancestry, drawing upon the terrifying linguistic autonomy apparent in Ionesco's *Les Chaises* (1951) or *La Cantatrice chauve* (1950). Mick's troubling monologue in *The Caretaker*, Lenny's excursions into logical positivism in *The Homecoming*, the infamous interrogation of Stanley in *The Birthday Party* or the circular accounts of the film 'Odd Man Out' in *Old Times* conjure up an arbitrary universe where reality evades definition and naked power is screened in language games.

These insights inform the plays of Sarah Kane, Mark Ravenhill and Martin Crimp. Kane exerts a radical reduction on her own language, almost to resist such dissolutions. However, increasingly her plays succumb to the affliction of unlimited textuality where utterance proves treacherous. Tinker's amiable idiom in *Cleansed*, belied by his systematic cruelties, is symptomatic of the tendency throughout Kane's work for the language of desire to be violently contradicted in the sphere of the body. In Ravenhill's plays, particularly *Shopping and Fucking* and *The Cut*, language is so commodified by the jargon of capitalism or political expediency that expression itself becomes hollow verbiage barely masking brutal exploitation. In *Shopping and Fucking*, for instance, the failed patriarchs of Brian and Mark speak in the same bad faith as Kane's 'bad' fathers Tinker and Ian, and all four can be linked back to such nihilist functionaries as Roote in *The Hothouse* or Nicholas in *One for the Road*.

Crimp, the most overt inheritor of the Pinter idiolect, moves rather like Pinter did himself, from the darkly comic linguistics of his early plays to an increasingly bleak account of language as the source and symptom of human isolation and mutual oppression. In early work such as *No One Sees the Video* this affinity is revealed within a quasi-naturalist frame, the silences given a sociological source, whether in the language of estate agents or market research, subjected by Crimp to pastiche or estrangement. Yet in Crimp's later plays from *The Treatment* through to *Attempts on Her Life* and *The Country*, explicable social sources for the sickening accretion of language are less evident. The removal of specifying markers for character and the refusal in *Attempts on Her Life* even to disclose the setting itself take Pinter's project into a more comprehensive *mise-en-abyme*. However, even in his bleakest work Crimp honours the comic quality of these worlds built in language; irony remains the key-note, as it does in mid-period Pinter.

To really establish the workings out of Pinter's aesthetic in contemporary writing, we need to look more closely at plays that echo or rework his motifs, and in the process evaluate the impact of his work on contemporary writers. One of the most striking examples of affinity across the years can be discerned between *The Hothouse* and Sarah Kane's *Cleansed*. The former, anomalous in Pinter's canon given its retrospective emergence in 1980 at the Hampstead Theatre in London, offers a uniquely nightmarish panorama of welfare-state repression, unplaced in history yet unmistakably fusing images of totalitarianism with English geniality, epitomised in the fumbling governance of Roote or Lush's hilarious audit of this elusive institution's calendar:

> The autumn art exhibition, the monthly concert of orchestral music in the bandroom, the half-yearly debate on a selected topic held traditionally in the men's changing room ...[8]

This is a world that anticipates Foucault in its fusion of hospital with torture chamber, prison with clinic, a vision first adumbrated in Pinter's work in the ferocious double-act of Goldberg and McCann and revisited in Aston's experiences in *The Caretaker*. Yet with its unseen patients and elusive action, its uncertain position between farce, satire and dystopia, *The Hothouse* eludes classification. *Cleansed* is more graphic in its depiction of society as an institution imposing its norms through mutilations and medical experiment. Instead of the self-pitying isolated Roote we have the cool insinuating Tinker, whose tenure is equally predatory and dispassionate. Roote, who never leaves his office, foreshadows Tinker's masturbatory position at the heart of the panopticon. Similiarly the staff in both plays disavow the horrors they preside over as actions to which they acquiesced, evident in Roote's reaction to Gibbs's revelation that Patient 6459 was raped: 'If a member of the staff decides that for the good of a female patient some degree of copulation is necessary then two birds are killed with one stone.'[9] Kane's asylum without portfolio in *Cleansed* is a disorientating fusion of the familiar and the unfamiliar, with the spaces of a university now improvised *loci* of violation, chillingly multi-purpose with healing and wounding, tending and raping in horrible proximity. The key difference between the plays, which accounts for the bleakly comic tone of Pinter's play as opposed to the solemnity of Kane's, is that *Cleansed* focuses on victims who in *The Hothouse* remain unseen, embodied only in sound. The most striking echo lies in the fate of the two newcomers, Pinter's Lamb and Kane's Grace, their names suggesting their shared biblical, sacrificial functions. The horrific yet self-willed torture of Lamb, through offstage voices and onstage electrodes, accompanied by an unseen act of voyeuristic sex between Gibbs and Cutts, is mirrored in Kane's image of Grace assaulted by unseen forces. Pinter's prescient vision is confirmed by Kane's distressing account of 'soft' and hard power in lockstep, the intermingling of what Augusto Boal calls 'the cop in the head'[10] with more visible forms of coercion. Both plays depict society as a prison without walls, where the zone of oppositional agency is hopelessly attenuated. For Kane a kind of inner, even spiritual resistance remains, evident in her transcendental stage imagery, but Pinter's culminating unseen revolt and massacre feels less a liberation and more the workings-through of the sinister vision of Gibbs, and thus a curtain-raiser for further repression.

Another telling intertextual affiliation is evident in Martin Crimp's *The Country*, which offers a sustained homage to *Old Times*. Crimp has disavowed the notion of his play as a conscious act of revisionism, but the fact that he directed a rehearsed reading of *Old Times* shortly before Katie Mitchell's production of his play at the Royal Court does suggest Pinter's work played a part in the genesis of *The Country*. If one were to identify the contemporary dramatist most steeped in the Pinter idiom it would have to be Crimp, our most 'continental' writer, thoroughly *au fait* with the modernist tradition that underpins his forebear's critique of social realism. However, his relationship moves far beyond emulation and Crimp's work offers a canny critique of Pinter's gender politics, whilst echoing his predecessor's sexual pessimism and frank exploration of misogyny. *Old Times* is in this respect Pinter's most revealing and candid work; Deeley's struggle over the autonomy of his wife's past and his ultimate submission to her almost unfathomable power through the ritualised 'slaying' of the interloper Anna are re-fashioned as a three-way conflict between Crimp's Corinne, her hapless spouse Richard, and Rebecca, an American found on the road in the middle of the night and brought, like some latter-day Helen of Troy, into the fastness of the couple's rural retreat. The milieux of both plays are strikingly similar and in both instances epitomise the wife's predicament. Kate is evidently as alone as Corinne in her exile from London ('Sometimes I walk to the sea. There aren't many people. It's a long beach.');[11] Corinne's unresolved deliberations, satirised by Rebecca, echo this sense of unwilled retreat:

– He showed me the house – this house – and that convinced me.
– He convinced you. He convinced you to come.

– Yes.
– He convinced you that this was good.
– It is good. It is good. I didn't need / to be convinced.
– The land. The stream. The beautiful house.
– Yes. The beautiful house. Why not?[12]

The shared isolation casts all offstage events into profound doubt. In Crimp's play the circumstances of Rebecca's 'abduction', the mysterious incursions of Richard's colleague Morris and the unexplained final disappearance of Rebecca re-work Pinter's unresolved mysteries, such as the ontological status of Anna, her implied metaphorical or actual murder, and Deeley's role as shadowy interloper into a past of female self-sufficiency. Yet the differing emphases of the two plays' sexual politics is equally revealing. *Old Times* is in some respects a riposte to and a retreat from the menace of feminism, whereas *The Country* examines the fall-out of post-feminism. Pinter's women, in narrating their shared past, evoke an idyllic pre-lapsarian world without men, whereas Crimp's are locked into a conflict over proprietory rights to a man, unmitigated by female solidarity. Kate's almost Buddhist serenity, forming a still point around which Deeley and Anna spar, is replaced by the edgy, unchannelled energy of Corinne in a world devoid of pastoral stillness. Both plays end in a type of sacrifice, as only by repelling the invasive threat of Anna or Rebecca can pastoral completion be achieved. Yet their final images suggest further indeterminacy, Deeley 'slumped', Kate impassive and Anna still present, Corinne and Richard caught between kisses, harried by the ever-ringing telephone.

The final strand of influence, Pinter as political dramatist, is perhaps the most problematic. Pinter's sequence of plays following the paradigmatic *One for the Road* in 1984 relentlessly engage with torture and unlimited power, linking sexual humiliation and male dominance, linguistic and physical abuse, grafting distant oppression onto familiar and domestic settings. These works undoubtedly informed the work of the so-called 'in-yer-face' dramatists, and most spectacularly the defining text of that 'movement', Sarah Kane's *Blasted*. Pinter's vignettes of political abuse forge a chamber theatre of cruelty which disdains to analyse the oppressions it documents. Arising from Pinter's sincere swerve to overt citizen activism, his work for PEN and *Amnesty International*, these plays, whilst provoked by American-sanctioned abuses in the 1980s, eerily foreshadow the more explicit and shocking actions of the US after 9/11 with its deployment of 'extraordinary rendition' or the extra-legal enclave of Guantanamo. Equally they anticipate the new-minted savageries of the 1990s as failed states from Yugoslavia to Rwanda presided over the revival of genocide as a political tool. *Mountain*

Language suggests atrocities in Bosnia or Chechnya as much as actions in East Turkey and, as Caryl Churchill's aptly titled *Far Away* implies, the spread of such techniques of racist violence throughout the planet during the 1990s and the subsequent 'War on Terror' have formed a world-system of fear and complicity.

Yet one might also argue that for all Pinter's theatrical acuity, the predominance of his aesthetic as the model for the latter-day political work of Churchill, Kane and even Ravenhill is one of his more contestable legacies. Implicit in these chamber pieces, which have largely unfolded on studio stages to small audiences, is a curiously passive notion of political theatre, more concerned with enacting the impotence of the stage or the liberal imagination itself, than with spurring audiences to resist an increasingly barbarous world. The entire absence of alternative agency in these works, where opposition is rendered as the endurance of endless sadism, yielding, at best, a poetics of pain and mortification, makes them less provocations than images of despair.

This problematic paradigm is most striking when we look at the late works of Caryl Churchill, who after all, in plays from *Light Shining in Buckinghamshire* through to *Serious Money*, managed to combine political analysis and theatricality with an unparalleled power. Yet Churchill's late, Pinteresque works such as *Far Away* or *This is a Chair* eschew such specific encounters for increasingly minimalist images of complicity. *This is a Chair* offers a constant questioning of the relationship between history and experience in curt private actions set against Brechtian captions, evoking larger struggles and thereby deepening the bathos of Pinter's *The New World Order* where a grand Francis Fukuyama-like strapline plays off against the banal chatter of torturers. *Far Away* takes the process further, elegantly spinning its allegory of generalised and ubiquitous oppression into an all-consuming myth. This is apparent in the progress of the play; the first scene brilliantly dramatises a parable of innocence and experience as Joan is tutored into political quietism by her sinister aunt, Harper: 'You're part of a bigger movement now to make things better. You can be proud of that.'[13] However, this idea is extended into an increasingly whimsical scenario, exceeding Pinter in its surrealism, where millinery serves as an image of embellishing totalitarian rule. Churchill's target here is much vaguer; the Orwellian structures her allegory offers, echoing the milieu of Pinter's besieged celebrants in *Party Time*, do not extend beyond the self-defining terms of her exquisite fable, and are thus unable to connect with the pressing realities beyond the theatre.

The link with Pinter's unflinching assault on American power is most explicit in Churchill's most recent political work *Drunk Enough to Say I Love You*, which offers an image of the Anglo-American 'special relationship' as a kind of homoerotic clinch. Yet as with Pinter's *The New World Order*, the dramaturgy does not permit progression beyond the confines of a sketch. Here the barely individuated double-act of Sam and Jack rehearses a litany of geopolitical terror as the small-talk of a mutual, yet unequal *folie à deux*. Yet the influence of Pinter's theatre of political banality is again apparent in the way Churchill overlays the contents of agitation propaganda on top of a static image eschewing narrative, and by extension forecloses analysis. The result is a curiously closed off, even passive form of theatre; as in Pinter's political poetry, confrontation is all, but the refusal to elucidate (which by no means implies that the object of critique might be validated) precludes the sort of debate implicit in the promise of political theatre. The result is a hyper-aestheticised political cartoon, neither funny enough to be satire nor precise enough to enrage. With characteristic candour, Pinter himself acknowledged this possible by-product of his political work whilst discussing *One for the Road* with Nick Hern:

> You're looking at the man who actually walked out of Peter Brook's *US* at the RSC, saying 'Who the hell do you think you're talking to?' ... 'Do you think I'm a child?' I said to myself, raging out, at the interval. And exactly, I always find agit-prop insulting and objectionable. And now, of course I am doing exactly the same thing.[14]

This is not to suggest that Pinter's aesthetic may not generate a powerfully precise political theatre. The opening of *Far Away* or the bold imagery of *Blasted* are palpable in their impact. Yet a more fruitful development of the Pinter aesthetic for political purposes is evident in the plays of Joe Penhall, and in particular *Blue/Orange*, where Pinter's notion of dialogue as masked aggression and his scepticism as to whether language might bridge the gap between self and other is re-invented in the play's brilliant dissection of professional rivalry intersecting with the corrosive fault-lines of multiculturalism. Yet as in all Pinter's great plays, this struggle takes place now, in London, and grows out of a closely observed agony, the fate of a patient.

It is a testimony, however, to the richness and profundity of Pinter's work that the finest dramatists of our time from Churchill to Crimp pay such open homage to his *oeuvre*. In an era when the theatre of spectacle or the director's ascendancy threatened to displace the play altogether from the stage, Pinter's example has granted courage to playwrights to hone and focus their craft. Equally when a culture of development or generic schematism has wrested plays out of the hands of their authors and into the clutches of script editors or producers, Pinter's steely defence of the autonomous role of the playwright truly empowers the generations of writers that follow him. Most movingly of all, the sheer durability of both the man and his work offers a notion of theatre writing that resists the short term, excavating the larger gestures of contemporary life rather than chasing after the topical and modish. If, as W. H. Auden suggests in his poem 'In Memoriam W. B. Yeats', that great poet in his death '(became) his admirers', Pinter's astonishing achievement has been to effect this act of transubstantiation whilst still very much alive.

NOTES

1. Peter Hall, quoted in an interview with Catherine Itzin and Simon Trussler, *Theatre Quarterly*, 16 (1974), in *Pinter in the Theatre*, ed. Ian Smith (London: Nick Hern Books, 2005), p. 136.
2. For example, Hall notes: 'A memorandum against Howard Brenton's *Romans in Britain* is in from Harold. It is about as strong as it could be.' *Peter Hall's Diaries*, (London: Hamish Hamilton, 1983), p. 412.
3. Quoted in Michael Billington, *The Life and Work of Harold Pinter* (London: Faber, 1996), p. 258.
4. 'From *Henry James*', in *Selected Prose of T. S. Eliot*, ed. Frank Kermode (London: Faber, 1975), p. 151.
5. See Aleks Sierz, *In-Yer-Face Theatre* (London: Faber, 2000), p. 4; Sierz offers up this confusing term for what he discerns as an experiential and confrontational dimension common to the plays of Mark Ravenhill, Sarah Kane, Anthony Neilson and others. He offers a variety of definitions: 'any drama that takes the audience by the scruff of the neck and shakes it until it gets the message ... a theatre of sensation ... employs shock tactics ... questioning moral norms ... it is experiential not speculative'.
6. *Ibid.*, p. 97; Sierz cites Pinter's comment that Kane was 'facing something actual and true and ugly and painful'.
7. Harold Pinter, *Ashes to Ashes*, *Harold Pinter: Plays Four* (London: Faber, 1998), p. 419.
8. Harold Pinter, *The Hothouse* (London: Faber, 2007), p. 45.
9. *Ibid.*, p. 33.
10. See Frances Babbage, *Augusto Boal* (London: Routledge, 2004), p. 23.
11. Harold Pinter, *Old Times*, *Harold Pinter: Plays Three* (London: Faber, 1997), p. 258.
12. Martin Crimp, *The Country* (London: Faber, 2000), p. 37.
13. Caryl Churchill, *Far Away* (London: Nick Hern Books, 2000), p. 14.
14. Harold Pinter, *One for the Road* (London: Methuen, 1985), p. 18.

19

JOHN FOWLES

Afterword: Harold Pinter and cricket

I have very slightly kept in touch with Harold over these last years, those in which all his work has of course been much discussed. His treatment of one of my own books (*The French Lieutenant's Woman*) at least gave me an excellent reason to admire him, as I hope I made clear in a little essay about my feelings called *The Filming of the French Lieutenant's Woman* in 1981. This was published in a collection of such essays that I did recently. Only two summers ago I went near here in Dorset to have lunch with both the director of the film, Karel Reisz, and Harold and their respective wives. It was a pleasant occasion and once again brought very close to me what I regard as a kind of secret gate-key to all his work. That is his very intense and evident love of cricket. It is one fixation I share with him and is what I would like to devote most of this little chapter to. Meeting and re-meeting him somehow burrows deep into a part of me I now in general claim to keep forgotten. I should perhaps mention here that I was a captain of the game at my public school, Bedford, played for my college at Oxford (New College) and indeed was once to reach the heights of a county trial (for Essex). Unfortunately I don't dream at all any more. (Unfortunately, because I always used to find dreaming a very fertile source of imagery.) I don't know if cricket is in any way responsible for the mature playwright Pinter. I rather suspect that, as with me, he prefers to keep the odd ethos and imagery of the game deeply obliterated in the past. I used when younger to have some ability at bowling leg-cutters at medium pace. I had no great skill with the bat, but in making the ball suddenly and unexpectedly – at best, subtly – deviate in direction I could claim some ability. I wrote about all this some years ago, comparing cricket to baseball in the American magazine *Sports Illustrated*, and again in a book *Quick Singles* published in 1968 by J. M. Dent. I am proud not of my ability to 'cut' a bowled delivery (I did in my last year at school manage to dismiss six old Test cricketers, which gained me a sort of schoolboy and very local fame) but very soon afterwards, when I was living in Devon, I had to face a hurdle that most cricketers will know. I realised cricket was taking up altogether too large a part of my life. In effect it was slowly stifling me. I didn't come to some sudden decision and give up any interest or hope in the game. I simply sort of let myself slide sideways out of it. But as I learned only recently with the World Cup played here in England, to forget it totally was impossible, my bowling muscles would never have allowed that, nor did the rare occasions when I saw Harold again.

My sort of bowling required a certain run-up and also a series of variations of the throwing body that are very deeply ingrained in my physical memory. This is very probably what attaches me closest to the game: my preparations for bowling, my stance as I bowled and a constant planning of what particular variation I should try to deliver. In other words, a fairly deep thought of how the mind of the opposing batsman was working; whether he could be deceived and how he could be tricked.

Perhaps this is the crux of it; in short, learning how to fool. I am sure the very early training at that has influenced both Harold and myself. Such a frequently experienced dilemma must have its effect and that is perhaps the best way to understand either of us. We are trying to trick our way through an elementary predicament of all young people. All audiences are for us batsmen to be dismissed and essentially to be left gasping. This is why both of us are counted difficult to understand. I also, like him, happen to be very much on the left politically. Indeed I think the world would be a far happier place if our political views were more widely held. There are no doubt certain similarities with other games – perhaps all games – and whatever it is in Harold's past that first led him to this very English invention is undoubtedly what needs to be explored and commented on by those who favour his dramatic work. In some way I hope one day to read a play by Harold himself that admits this correspondence and the essential displays of it in his drama. Meanwhile I shall treasure the cricketing echoes, however remote, in all he creates.

BIBLIOGRAPHY

WORKS BY PINTER

Plays

Harold Pinter: Plays One (Introduction: 'Writing for the Theatre'; *The Birthday Party*; *The Room*; *The Dumb Waiter*; *A Slight Ache*; *The Hothouse*; *A Night Out*; *The Black and White* (monologue); *The Examination* (short story) (1991; London: Faber, 1996).

Harold Pinter: Plays Two (Introduction: 'Writing for Myself'; *The Caretaker*; *The Dwarfs*; *The Collection*; *The Lover*; *Night School*; Revue Sketches: *Trouble in the Works*; *The Black and White*; *Request Stop*; *Last to Go*; *Special Offer* (1991; London: Faber, 1996).

Harold Pinter: Plays Three (Introduction: speech by Pinter on being awarded the 1970 German Shakespeare Prize; *The Homecoming*; *Tea Party*; *The Basement*; *Landscape*; *Silence*; *Night*; *That's Your Trouble*; *That's All*; *Applicant*; *Interview*; *Dialogue for Three*; *Tea Party* (short story); *Old Times*; *No Man's Land*) (1991; expanded edn London: Faber, 1997).

Harold Pinter: Plays Four (Introduction: speech by Pinter on receiving the David Cohen Literature Prize, 1995; *Betrayal*; *Monologue*; *Family Voices*; *A Kind of Alaska*; *Victoria Station*; *Precisely*; *One for the Road*; *Mountain Language*; *The New World Order*; *Party Time*; *Moonlight*; *Ashes to Ashes*) (1993; expanded edn London: Faber, 1998).

'Celebration' and 'The Room' (London: Faber, 2000).

One for the Road (Methuen: London, 1984) (contains a discussion between Pinter and Nick Hern on the play and its politics).

Remembrance of Things Past (adapted for the stage from the original screenplay, by Pinter and Di Trevis) (London: Faber, 2000).

Screenplays

The Proust Screenplay: À la Recherche du temps perdu (London: Methuen, 1977).

The Servant and Other Screenplays (The Pumpkin Eater, The Quiller Memorandum, Accident, The Go-Between) (London: Faber, 1991).

The French Lieutenant's Woman and Other Screenplays (The Last Tycoon, Langrishe, Go Down) (London: Faber, 1991).

The Heat of the Day (London: Faber, 1989).
The Comfort of Strangers and Other Screenplays (Reunion, Victory, Turtle Diary) (London: Faber, 1990).
The Trial (London: Faber, 1993).

Other writing

The Dwarfs (London: Faber, 1990).
Collected Poems and Prose (London: Faber, 1991).
Ten Early Poems (Greville Press pamphlets, 1992).
Various Voices: Prose, Poetry, Politics 1948–1998 (London: Faber, 1998); revised as *Various Voices: Prose, Poetry, Politics 1948–2005* (London: Faber, 2005).

WORKS ON PINTER

Gale, Steven H., *Harold Pinter: An Annotated Bibliography* (Boston: G. K. Hall, 1978).
Page, Malcolm, *File on Pinter* (London: Methuen, 1993).

Interviews

Gussow, Mel (ed.), *Conversations with Pinter* (London: Nick Hern Books, 1994).
For a comprehensive list of interviews with Pinter, see Mark Batty, *About Pinter: The Playwright and the Work* (London: Faber, 2001), pp. 234–9.

Secondary sources

Almansi, Guido and Henderson, Simon, *Harold Pinter* (London: Methuen, 1983).
Anderson, Michael, *'Anger' and Detachment: A Study of Arden, Osborne, and Pinter* (London: Pitman, 1976).
Armstrong, Raymond, *Kafka and Pinter: Shadow-Boxing: the Struggle Between Father and Son* (Basingstoke: Macmillan, 1999).
Baker, William and Tabachnick, Stephen Ely, *Harold Pinter* (Edinburgh: Oliver and Boyd, 1973).
Batty, Mark, *Writers and their Work: Harold Pinter* (Tavistock: Northcote House, 2001).
  About Pinter: The Playwright and the Work (London: Faber, 2005).
Billington, Michael, *The Life and Work of Harold Pinter* (London: Faber, 1996); rev. edn published as *Harold Pinter* (London: Faber, 2007).
Bold, Alan (ed.), *Harold Pinter: You Never Heard Such Silence* (London: Vision Press, 1984; Totowa, NJ: Barnes and Noble, 1985).
Burkman, Katherine H., *The Dramatic World of Harold Pinter: Its Basis in Ritual* (Columbus, OH: University of Ohio Press, 1971).
Burkman, Katherine H. and Kundert-Gibbs, John L. (eds.), *Pinter at Sixty* (Bloomington and Indianapolis: Indiana University Press, 1993).
Cave, Richard Allen, *New British Drama in Performance on the London Stage: 1970–1985* (Gerrards Cross: Colin Smythe, 1987).
Diamond, Elin, *Pinter's Comic Play* (Lewisburg, PA: Bucknell University Press, 1985).

Dukore, Bernard F., *Where the Laughter Stops: Pinter's Tragi-Comedy* (Columbia, MO: University of Missouri Press, 1976). *Harold Pinter* (London: Macmillan, 1982; revised edition, 1988).

Elsom, John (ed.), *Post-War British Theatre Criticism* (London: Routledge & Kegan Paul, 1981).

Esslin, Martin, *The Theatre of the Absurd*, Revised edn (New York: Doubleday/ Anchor, 1969).

   Pinter the Playwright (London: Methuen, 1982) (revised, originally published as *The Peopled Wound*, 1970).

Gabbard, Lucina Paquet, *The Dream Structure of Pinter's Plays: A Psychoanalytic Approach* (Cranbury, NJ, and London: Associated University Presses, 1976).

Gale, Steven H., *Butter's Going Up: A Critical Analysis of Harold Pinter's Work* (Durham, NC: Duke University Press, 1977).

   Harold Pinter: Critical Approaches (London: Asssociated University Presses, 1986).

   Sharp Cut: Harold Pinter's Screenplays and the Artistic Process (Lexington, KY: University Press of Kentucky, 2003).

Gale, Steven H. (ed.), *Critical Essays on Harold Pinter* (Boston: G. K. Hall, 1990).

Ganz, Arthur (ed.), *Harold Pinter: A Collection of Critical Essays* (Englewood Cliffs, NJ: Prentice-Hall, 1972).

Goodwin, John (ed.), *Peter Hall's Diaries* (London: Hamish Hamilton, 1983).

Gordon, Lois, *Stratagems to Uncover Nakedness: The Dramas of Harold Pinter* (Columbia, Missouri, 1969).

Gordon, Lois (ed.), *Harold Pinter: A Casebook* (New York and London: Garland Publishing, 1990; 2nd edition, New York and London: Routledge, 2001).

Grimes, Charles, *Harold Pinter's Politics: A Silence Beyond Echo* (Teaneck: Fairleigh Dickinson Press, 2005).

Hall, Ann C., *'A Kind of Alaska': Women in the Plays of O'Neill, Pinter and Shepard* (Carbondale, IL: Southern Illinois University Press, 1993).

Hall, Peter, *Exposed by the Mask* (London: Oberon, 2000).

   Making an Exhibition of Myself (London: Sinclair-Stevenson, 1993).

Hayman, Ronald, *Harold Pinter* (London: Heinemann, revised edition, 1980).

Hinchcliffe, Arnold P., *Harold Pinter* (New York: Twayne, 1975).

Hollis, James H., *Harold Pinter: The Poetics of Silence* (Carbondale, IL: Southern Illinois University Press, 1970).

Innes, Christopher, *Modern British Drama, 1890–1990* (Cambridge: Cambridge University Press, 1992).

Kennedy, Andrew, *Six Dramatists in Search of a Language* (Cambridge: Cambridge University Press, 1975).

Klein, Joanne, *Making Pictures: The Pinter Screenplays* (Columbus: Ohio State University Press, 1985).

Knowles, Ronald, *Understanding Harold Pinter* (Columbia, SC: University of Southern Carolina Press, 1995).

Lahr, John, *A Casebook on Harold Pinter's 'The Homecoming'* (New York: Grove Press, 1971).

Marowitz, Charles, Milne, Tom, and Hale, Owen (eds.), *The Encore Reader* (London: Methuen, 1965).

Merritt, Susan H., *Pinter in Play: Critical Strategies and the Plays of Harold Pinter* (Durham, NC: Duke University Press, 1990).

Morrison, Kristin, *Canters and Chronicles: The Use of Narrative in the Plays of Samuel Beckett and Harold Pinter* (Chicago and London: University of Chicago Press, 1983).

Peacock, D. Keith, *Harold Pinter and the New British Theatre* (Westport: Greenwood Press, 1997).

Prentice, Penelope, *The Pinter Ethic: The Erotic Aesthetic* (New York and London: Garland, 1994).

Regal, Martin S., *Harold Pinter: A Question of Timing* (Basingstoke: Macmillan, 1995).

Renton, Linda, *Pinter and the Object of Desire: An Approach through the Screenplays* (Oxford: Legenda, 2002).

Quigley, Austin E., *The Pinter Problem* (Princeton, NJ: Princeton University Press, 1975).

Sakellaridou, Elizabeth, *Pinter's Female Portraits: A Study of Female Characters in the Plays of Harold Pinter* (Basingstoke: Macmillan, 1988).

Schroll, Herman T., *Harold Pinter: A Study of His Reputation (1958–69) and a Checklist* (Metuchen, NJ: Scarecrow Press, 1971).

Scott, Michael (ed.), *Harold Pinter: 'The Birthday Party', 'The Caretaker' and 'The Homecoming': a Casebook* (Basingstoke: Macmillan, 1986).

Silverstein, Marc, *Harold Pinter and the Language of Cultural Power* (London: Associated University Presses, 1993).

Smith, Ian (ed.), *Pinter in the Theatre* (London: Nick Hern Books, 2005).

Strunk, Volker, *Harold Pinter: Towards a Poetics of his Plays* (New York: P. Lang, 1989).

Sykes, Arlene, *Harold Pinter* (New York: Humanities Press, 1970).

Thompson, David T., *Pinter: The Player's Playwright* (Basingstoke: Macmillan, 1985).

Trussler, Simon, *The Plays of Harold Pinter: An Assessment* (London: Gollancz, 1973).

Worth, Katharine, *Revolutions in Modern English Drama* (London: G. Bell and Sons, 1972).

Zarhy-Levo, Yael, *The Theatrical Critic as Cultural Agent: Constructing Pinter, Orton and Stoppard as Absurdist Playwrights* (London: Peter Lang, 2001).

The Making of Theatrical Reputations: Studies from the Modern London Theatre (Iowa City: University of Iowa Press, 2008).

PERIODICALS

Reference to articles in periodicals will be found in the notes to individual chapters.

Modern Drama, 17 (December 1974) (Harold Pinter issue).

Francis Gillen and Steven H. Gale (eds.), *The Pinter Review* (Tampa, FL: University of Tampa Press) (This is an invaluable annual record and commentary on Pinter studies.)

Note: the Pinter Archive is housed in the British Library.

MAIN INDEX

WORKS INDEX

Cambridge Companions To ...

AUTHORS

CAMBRIDGE COMPANIONS TO TOPICS